WALKER PERCY

WALKER PERCY

BOOKS OF REVELATIONS

GARY M. CIUBA

THE UNIVERSITY OF GEORGIA PRESS

ATHENS & LONDON

© 1991 by the
University of
Georgia Press
Athens, Georgia
30602

All rights reserved
Designed by
Richard Hendel
Set in Ehrhardt
The paper in this
book meets the
guidelines for
permanence and
durability of
the Committee
on Production
Guidelines for
Book Longevity
of the Council
on Library
Resources.

Printed in the
United States
of America
95   94   93   92   91
5   4   3   2   1

Library of Congress Cataloging in Publication Data

Ciuba, Gary M.
   Walker Percy : books of revelations / Gary M. Ciuba.
      p.   cm.
Includes bibliographical references (p.   ) and index.
ISBN 0-8203-1355-6 (alk. paper)
   1. Percy, Walker, 1916–   —Criticism and interpretation.
2. Apocalyptic literature—History and criticism.   I. Title.
PS3566.E6912Z58   1991
813'.54—dc20   90-23278
                    CIP

British Library Cataloging in Publication Data available

To Anne Ciuba

and Raymond and Mark Ciuba

In memory of Walter Ciuba

CONTENTS

ACKNOWLEDGMENTS

I am glad to thank many people who are a part of this book. Patrick Samway, S.J., gave me early encouragement in studying Percy's fiction; Philip Sicker and Gerard Reedy, S.J., read first drafts of my work. Grants from the National Endowment for the Humanities and from Kent State University enabled me to study the Walker Percy Papers and the Shelby Foote Papers at the University of North Carolina at Chapel Hill, where the staff of the Southern Historical Collection graciously helped me with every request. I owe special gratitude to Mrs. Walker Percy, who allowed me to quote passages from "The Gramercy Winner," and to Shelby Foote, for permission to quote from his letters to Walker Percy.

I thank the editors of *American Literature*, the *Flannery O'Connor Bulletin*, the *Mississippi Quarterly*, *Notes on Contemporary Literature*, *Notes on Mississippi Writers*, and *Thought* for permission to reprint parts of this book that first appeared, in different forms, in their journals. I appreciate the personal and professional support liberally given by my colleagues at Kent State University as well as by John Desmond, Anna Marie Graf, Joan Nourse, and, in a very special way, Julie Pielech Suchodolski. I am particularly indebted to John Edward Hardy, who read the manuscript for the University of Georgia Press; his acumen and zeal enabled me to see its pages as if for the first time.

Two people have helped to hand me along in this project from beginning to end. Richard Giannone generously advised, challenged, enlightened, and inspired. And Patricia Rogan showed me how gifts are signs of givers and then showed me again and again.

Finally, I am most grateful for those to whom this book is dedicated. They are a continuous revelation.

WALKER PERCY

NOVELS TO MAKE ALL THINGS NEW

I   Walker Percy ends the mocking question-and-answer session with himself published in 1977 by describing a painting over his fireplace that was done by his friend Lyn Hill. He lets his last words appropriately tell of last things. The composite portrait of Percy and his fictional apocalyptists depicts a wryly smiling and gently abstracted figure who resembles the novelist as well as many of his ironic seers. The gentleman stands before another painting, a picture within a picture that shows "a bombed-out place, a place after the end of the world, a no man's island of blasted trees and barbed wire."[1] Dominating the blackened landscape is an elongated tree cleft at the center and forking again at its base, halves hugged together by loops of spiky string. Yet as Percy meditates on the wasted land, he notices promises of renewal. The dead tree seems as if it is being transformed into an imprisoned figure, perhaps a woman or, quite possibly, the trunks of lovers writhing in an embrace, and the thorny wire is actually a brier that blossoms into a rose. Out of this black world a window opens onto the sky and sea of a new heaven and earth.

The painting frames Percy's apocalyptic vision. His searchers begin their spiritual journeys when they are startled to see the ends of their own old worlds in the smallest of signs. As they wander amid the last days of their lives, these pilgrims increasingly view their present plight as intimating the day of doom for all of America. They often try to escape their personal eschatons or save the nation from certain disaster, but their misguided quests usually herald further and unexpected catastrophe. Although such ruins provide the physical and psychic landscape of Percy's fiction, he does not write what John May terms the "apocalypse of despair" often characteristic of modern American fiction.[2] Rather, Percy looks beyond such sadly antic endings to the beginnings of renewal. Only when his apocalyptists confront the wreckage of their lives do they gain the impetus for discovering the love amid the ruins portrayed in Lyn Hill's painting. Percy's fiction retells the ancient story of biblical apocalypse in which judgment and destruction culminate in re-creation. Especially influenced by the Apocalypse of John, his novels are books of revelations and, however tentative and inchoate, renovations.

The apocalyptic literature of the Old and New Testaments makes a vision of the end the beginning of vision.[3] The I is the eye, a privileged and private witness to divine mysteries. In its most radical sense, *apokalypsis* causes an unveiling that transforms ordinary sight into sacred insight so that the visionary sees somewhat as God does. At the beginning of Revelation, John has been banished to the small island of Patmos because of his Christian testimony, but on Sunday, the day of the week most completely taken into God's time, he is caught up in ecstasy and immediately ordered to write everything that he witnesses. His everyday vision, restricted still further by confinement, suddenly opens onto a spectacular glimpse of the glory of the invisible God. Yet even as John beholds the liturgy of the eternal Sabbath, he weeps because no one in heaven is fit to open the book sealed with seven seals. Finally, the Lamb of God, who is worthy because he was slain, reveals to John the eschatological mysteries that define his life as much as the life of the world.

Isolated and exiled, John on Patmos lives out the situation that Percy has made paradigmatic for all those lost in the cosmos. In the title essay of *The Message in the Bottle*, Percy borrows Marcel's image of the castaway and envisions humanity as a homesick island dweller walking by the shore. The shipwrecked survivor without any memory of the past yearns for a less splendid but no less significant revelation than John's sight of the coming Lord. Having suffered some forgotten catastrophe at his genesis, Percy's searcher looks for the paper set to sea in glass and hopes that he will at last find the good news of "where he came from and who he is and what he must do" (*MB* 149). Cast into the world and never at home in heart, Percy's nameless castaway lives out a primordial estrangement from the very ground of his being, the land with which he feels intimately but obscurely connected. The beachcomber may discover knowledge about his surroundings or news of events directly pertinent to his life, but the most sophisticated arts and sciences are always as self-confined as their creator. The islander can never really be satisfied with such information because it does not tell him of his original home that is elsewhere. He hopes that the longing for self-definition may be met by the initiative of the first and final source of identity—the mysterious and true country beyond the sea. Only through such tidings from *outre-mer* is the seeker discovered to himself and granted a recovery of his essential being in the world. Although at the end of "The Message in the Bottle" Percy suggests that the news heard "by the grace of God" is ultimately the gospel (*MB* 149), neither in the parable-essay nor in his novels does revelation bring any direct and immediate awareness of the Divinity. It grants no gnostic salvation and does not even preclude virtual damnation, as *Lancelot* demonstrates. Rather, the apocalypse is the precondition for seeing anything at all.

Percy's spiritual expatriates need such revelation because they suffer from the particular doom of the twentieth century. Like John and the stranger in "The Message in the Bottle," they dwell apart from the land of their true selves. Because they live in absentia, Percy's exiles frequently compensate for their displacement by becoming that most provincial of islanders, the egotist. "What is the nature of the catastrophe of the self?" Percy asks in *Lost in the Cosmos*, and he wonders whether it might not be "a turning from the concelebration of the world to a solitary absorption with self" (*LC* 109). Before recovering the ability to see, Percy's solipsists either react as organisms in an environment, as collections of needs to be satisfied, or they remove themselves from the world to become seraphic intelligences. Often his castaways embody both extremes without ever reconciling the dichotomy. These antipodal creatures, lost in the routines of making money and making love, at the same time suffer from Percy's "loss of the creature," so that severed from creation, they inhabit no place and abide by no time (*MB* 46–63). They lose objects in their categories, and people in their functions; they know the person as a thing, and the thing as an abstraction.

Since Percy's lost selves live as if they were completely of the cosmos or above the cosmos, they do not really see. They never perform an act of attention to the thing at hand, like the unmindful commuter described in "The Man on the Train." Traveling through but not in the world, he is separated from the physical universe, other people, even his own flesh, as he speeds on a journey defined by its end. But after the shock of suffering a heart attack during his travels, suddenly the alienated passenger may examine his hand "as if he had never seen it before. He is astounded by its complexity, its functional beauty. He turns it this way and that" (*MB* 109). Unlike the nauseated Roquentin, he enjoys an "immediate encounter with being" that compels him to notice the pleasing intrigue of existence (*MB* 52). At the beginning of their quests, Percy's apocalyptists likewise experience what he calls "a kind of natural revelation . . . a revelation of being" (*MB* 109). From the sickly William Grey in "The Gramercy Winner," who sees from "the dead center of things" while in a hospice (GW 17), to the returning Dr. Tom More, who sees a sign of the thanatos syndrome, sight causes the world to come back to Percy's seers as they come back to themselves. The initial good news of this self-discovery brings Percy's castaways both judgment and grace. His displaced people recognize that they have fallen away from what they should be and that they have fallen into themselves, but they find some memento of a bond, the amazing and seemingly accidental message in a bottle, that mysteriously joins them with the homeland of what they truly are and at last must be.

This coming to consciousness does not cause the romantic primal fall into self-consciousness; nor does it deliver Percy's seers into the "vision-ary universe—of infinite subjectivity" that Nathan Scott repudiates in the apocalypses of postmodern romanticism.[4] Although such self-collapse later does endanger Percy's visionaries, revelation at first frees his blind outcasts from their solitary self-absorption so that they are no longer objectified or abstracted but are aware of themselves and attentive to the world. They now enjoy what Eric Voegelin calls the "reflective tension in existence" by which humanity finds it is "a part of being, capable of experiencing itself as such."[5] Eyes open and fixed on what is in front of them, they see and therefore exist; or rather, what they see is that they exist. They now view themselves as selves who are viewers. Their apocalypses lack the grandeur of the visions in Revelation, for John's hierophany becomes a much more per-sonal form of epiphany. After years of obliviousness when they traveled away from themselves, Percy's seers recall that they live now and here as people in predicaments. Although John's revelation manifestly comes from God, the Percyan apocalypse is "natural" by his own description; yet this existential self-recovery is the prelude to any act of faith. Once Percy's apocalyptists are troubled, their easy accommodations challenged, and their egotistical immersions unsettled, they are quickened by an almost Augustinian restless-ness of heart. Despite their penchant for familiar ways of knowing and loving, these seekers can no longer return to a homogeneous world of being either identical social organisms or complete universes unto themselves. Instead, they must look beyond their insularity to what is increasingly heterogeneous and finally to what is divinely Other. Citing the influence Hopkins's sacra-mental vision of the world had on him, Percy speculates that "if your gaze is sufficiently fresh and if you could see it sufficiently clearly," nature might be seen as "an act of existence, a gratuitous act of existence which was evidence of God's existence."[6] The gift that did not have to be points the naturalist in Percy to the astounding Giver that lets it be. The end of becoming aware of presence may be glimpsing the divine presence, the home, the Fatherland that allows the castaway to reconcile being both of the world and above the world.

This vision at the beginning of the novel announces that the old world of Percy's apocalyptists is coming to an end. In the first chapter of Revelation, John's exile changes to ecstasy as he escapes confinement to behold the court of heaven. Vision determines the cosmos for an apocalyptist so that a new way of seeing amounts to a new world. The world in apocalypse is not so much a physical universe or historical age but rather what Walter Wink calls a "meaning grid . . . the field of determinants which dominates an entire age, culture or civilization . . . some configurational summary of being."⁷ Composed of all the unquestioned assumptions about reality, the world is the accustomed manner of looking or, for the unseeing seers at the beginning of Percy's novels, the way of not looking. The end of the world is really the end of a worldview. Revelation itself brings catastrophe for Percy's visionaries because it causes the collapse of this old world where nothing is ever noticed. The Percyan apocalypse is intrinsically eschatological, for the very act of unveiling exposes the ruins amid which the seers live and reveals new possibilities of vision.⁸

If revelation opens the eyes of apocalyptists, then what they traditionally see is the end of time when the world is judged, destroyed, and finally renewed. They read the last pages of an ultimate book. In *The Sense of an Ending* Frank Kermode proposes that through fiction we "project ourselves— a small, humble elect, perhaps—past the End, so as to see the structure whole, a thing we cannot do from our spot of time in the middle."⁹ Since the ends of stories delight readers because they bring the rare comprehension of retrospective vision, apocalypse is the consummate fiction. It allows an anxious audience living in medias res to glimpse the close of the universal narrative, when the eschaton turns into the inauguration of a new age. Indeed, apocalypse had its literary and spiritual origins in the most radical form of the desperation and hope that Kermode imagines as motivating all readers of fiction—in the longings of a beleaguered community to discover symbolic sense in what seemed so senseless to its time-bound observers. Amid national crises these books of revelations gave the people of Israel a way of interpreting the daily texts of their lives that promised a salvific conclusion to their stories. Beginning as a child of prophecy, apocalypse emerged after the fall of Jerusalem in 587 B.C., for such books as Daniel, Zechariah, Joel,

Enoch, 4 Esdras, and 2 Baruch offered a visionary response to the threats against Israel's identity. When Israel was no longer able to find fulfillment as a nation in the historical present, its people under Hellenistic and Roman rule looked to their consummation in the kingdom of God's future. Christian seers came to share a similar hope amid contemporary disorder. From 200 B.C. to A.D. 200, apocalyptic literature understood the course of history by viewing it backward from the perspective of the end of all history.

Like prophecy, apocalypse sees time as significant because of God's revelation. The Deity is known not primarily in the cycles of nature but in human events that move toward the achievement of a divine purpose. Percy has commented on such biblical teleology in discussing Will Barrett's "post-Christian shakiness about historic time," a disorientation that affects all of Percy's unstable wanderers in the twentieth century. Alluding to *The New Science of Politics*, he notes that Voegelin "contrasts the unhistoric cyclical time of the Greeks and Orientals with the historic linear time of Israel—historical time began when Israel emerged." [10] And Israel emerged, as the title of the first volume in Voegelin's *Order and History* makes clear, through the call of a graced disclosure of being. In *Israel and Revelation* Voegelin understands divine revelation as heightening the kind of natural revelation that illuminates the lives of Percy's seers. If humanity understands through its own self-reflection that it participates in being, sacred revelation may be regarded as causing a "leap upward in being" through which participants reorient themselves to the true source of all order. Both prophets and apocalyptists give witness from such a new direction. They lack the temporal confusion of Percy's dazed modernists because these messengers and seers acknowledge what Voegelin considers the central revelation of Israel: the order of history "reveals the ordering will of God." [11] Yet although these two ways of viewing time often overlap, apocalypse grows out of a shift in prophetic eschatology that places greater emphasis on transcendence rather than on immanence, on the fate of individuals and the cosmos rather than on the destiny of the nation, and on cataclysm rather than on continuity. [12] Since classical apocalypse is so pessimistic toward the whole of history, it believes that everyday time must come to an end through God's decisive advent. The era that was and is will be no more.

Apocalypse emphasizes neither God's saving actions in the past nor human cooperation in living out divine laws to create a messianic era, but rather God's future salvific deeds. Prophecy does not regard the world or time as itself sinister but recognizes evil in human hearts and in the heathen empires that threaten the nation of Israel. Apocalypse, however, creates what Voegelin describes as "an ideal type of evil" based on imaginatively intensifying the wickedness of contemporary life.[13] A view of history as being in a state of irreversible degeneration envisions God's enemies not so much as transgressors of the law or as unholy foreign lands but as cosmic powers that have usurped dominion of the world. Because prophecy does not view evil as necessarily so triumphant, it finds hope in calling the people of God back to the covenant. According to Voegelin, the biblical prophets reminded Israel that not just its origin but also "its continued existence depended on its continued response to Yahweh's revelation." Offering warnings and promises rather than predictions, these divine spokesmen told the nation not only of the punishment for turning away from God but also of the salvation for changing its heart.[14] They typically imagined the future as following naturally from the alterable direction of the present. Although apocalypse maintains that each individual must finally choose to be a part of the new era, it foresees the course of history as ultimately ended by inevitable heavenly intervention. The hour is late, much too late, to avert disaster by returning to God; the faithful must only wait and persevere. Since prophecy does not look to a closed future, it conceives of a new beginning for Israel within history and the world as human time assumes a sacred dimension. However, apocalypse looks beyond the end of secular time to a radically discontinuous mode of temporality, when salvation extends to all the righteous and the entire cosmos is renewed. Traditional apocalypse is thus dualistic, deterministic, and transhistorical. It condemns the sinful time, expects a divinely ordained end, and hopes for an epoch to come outside the time of this world.

Voegelin has criticized this "metastatic denial of the order of mundane existence" that he sees beginning in prophecy, culminating in the apocalyptic desire to annihilate the cosmos, and again threatening the modern age in the politics of gnosticism. Since revelation should inspire "a leap upward in being," not a "leap out of existence," he distrusts all dreams to circumvent the daily world.[15] And some readers of Percy have been disturbed because they view him as advocating this same otherworldliness.[16] But Percy's apocalypticism rejects a totally transcendent eschatology by continually affirming that salvation is found not out of time but in and through it. His books of revelations combine the virtues of classical apocalypse—its defiant hope amid hopelessness, its emphasis on personal choice, its disbelief in humanity's proud schemes for its own deliverance—with the older prophetic conviction that the daily world is the sphere of God's activity, and human response is the way of participating in the coming kingdom of God. In drawing inspiration from both biblical traditions, Percy's fiction does not propose a new religious synthesis but simply follows the New Testament tradition of reinterpreting apocalyptic judgment, catastrophe, and re-creation by its faith in the person of Jesus.[17] Christian Scripture views its central figure as incarnating the salvation traditionally located at the end of the world and giving a proleptic glimpse of what is already moving toward its consummation. Hence, D. S. Russell explains that the kingdom of God announced by Jesus in the synoptic Gospels "will not come as the end product of long epochs of history" when time is annihilated; rather, it breaks into history and grows in the lives of believers.[18] And the Fourth Gospel, to which Father John bears witness in *Lancelot*, likewise affirms that the believer in Christ has already undergone eschatological judgment and passed from death to life (John 5:24–27; 6:47; 11:25–27). The New Testament does not abolish the time-to-come as the time of salvation to which classical apocalypse looks, but it regards that sacred future as actively at work in the time of this world.

The Revelation of John ends the New Testament by celebrating how this conclusion in Christ has transfigured the meaning of the present. From its opening doxology, which glorifies the Jesus risen from the dead who "has made us a royal nation of priests in the service of his God and Father" (Rev. 1:5), Apocalypse joins the Gospels in testifying to the historicity and humanity of the God whose kingdom has begun anew and now. Jacques Ellul even contends that the very center of the book contains a visionary depiction of the death and resurrection (Rev. 11) as well as the Incarnation (Rev. 12) of Jesus.[19] The One worthy to unroll the scroll of history is the slain Lamb, the very God who entered history by assuming the mortality of the flesh (Rev. 5:9, 12), and he now receives honor precisely because he abandoned honor. The heady triumphal imagery often overpowers the memory of such sacrifice, but amid the glory is the God who reigns because he forsook all the trappings of godliness to which Percy's Lancelot and many misinterpreters of Revelation aspire. The divine acceptance of subjection to death has created the priestly kingdom commended in the opening benediction.

Since the New Testament proclaims that the new eon has dawned already in the kingship of Christ, the traditional two ages of apocalypse—Before and After—represent not simply successive times for the world but also the result of a believer's commitment to the burgeoning kingdom of God. Following the Pauline tradition that the Christian "is a new creature: old things are passed away; behold all things are become new" (2 Cor. 5:17), Augustine read his own spiritual autobiography in the pages of the last book of the New Testament. Armageddon was "translated into psychomachia" as the saint's own clashing wills reflected the conflict between the forces of Christ and of his enemies.[20] Percy likewise reimagines the Book of Revelation on its most intimate terms, while also recognizing that each version of ending and beginning is not just a mythic repetition but also part of a cosmic narrative unfolding in history. The Apocalypse of John is the story of all of Percy's stories. Each novel explores ever-varying reverberations of this fundamental pattern in its image of time and in its fictional artistry. Living under a God who has come and is coming, Percy's seers wander fitfully toward a discovery of the divine presence that has entered into the world, dwells in each day, and will consummate history. This dynamism makes Percy's fiction more earthly and open-ended than traditional apocalyptic literature, which tends to juxtapose a hopeless present against an antithetical and atemporal future. Precisely because he understands Christianity as "a unique Person-Event-Thing in time," his novels recount the revelations that may disturb an ordinary Wednesday afternoon and announce the eschaton with just a single glance (*MB* 141). Although such widespread catastrophes as social chaos and nuclear destruction constantly loom in Percy's writing, he traces the public threats back to a spiritual disaster. And so he focuses on the imperative choices that his seers must make as they confront a continual series of endings while always living before the ultimate end of the world.

I I   The apocalyptist delivers judgment on the age because his new vision discloses the error of its choices. The Book of Revelation begins with a series of seven letters from the Son of Man that criticize and commend the churches of Asia Minor. "John uses the most offensive language he can to delineate his spiritual enemies," G. B. Caird writes, because he recognizes how they try to escape such designation.[21] In such later images as the beasts and the Whore of Babylon, the apocalyptist diagnoses the ills of the idolatrous time with uncompromising clarity, names what otherwise seems unnameable, so that evil may be seen as evil. And in depicting the attendants of the Lamb of God, John uses the most exalted language because he wants to celebrate those who have borne the divine word in life and through death as the universal chorus of the kingdom of God (Rev. 7; 14:1–5). Through such contrasts John unveils the crisis, the radical choice between life and death, that is the timeless meaning of all temporality for the readers that he so clearly imagines as sharing in the life of his book (Rev. 1:3; 22:7). Revela-

9

tion unfolds a theological commentary on all tenses because it discloses the "last things," the final direction toward which history has been moving up to the crucial moment of decision in the life of the reader.

Although Percy warns against "the seduction of crepe-hanging for its own sake" (MB 104), his fiction also recognizes the last judgment continually at hand. The loose structure of novels devoted to wayfaring allows his seers to meet on their progress a whole company of angelic scientists, beguiling ladies, stoical gentlemen, miserable romantics, and fatuous utopians who form a collective portrait of the doomed century. Because his wanderers see from the odd angle of vision, Percy uses William Grey's homesickness, Binx's irony, Will Barrett's youthful innocence and more mature lunacy, Tom's research, and Lancelot's tirades to reveal the radical failures of the age. Yet if these seers indict the time, each with varying degrees of insight and intensity, they exemplify its most grievous wrongs as well. Percy regards it as the task of the eschatological novelist to warn against danger and to pronounce "anathemas upon the most permissive of societies, which in fact permits him everything" (MB 110), but his apocalyptists can never simply be reduced to the role of spokespersons for their disaffected author because Percy perceives the blindness of his own visionaries. In the moment of revelation his seers find their old lives exposed by the new recognition of their freedom to act and responsibility to choose. Although these seekers try to discover how consciousness fulfills itself in love and how love makes possible faith, they often turn their attentive self-awareness into selfishness. Percy's novels condemn his prophets precisely to the extent that they try to surpass the role of John and the great company of heaven in Revelation: refusing to be witnesses, they proudly pursue gnostic speculations and messianic pretensions. These deluded apocalyptists still need further revelation in order to see themselves and other Percyan wayfarers more clearly.

Just as John imagines a thousand-year reign between the destruction of the old order and the beginning of the new, Percy sees his flawed prophets, always in a state of progress and often literally on the road, searching during a similar time of transition. Their initial recovery of themselves enables them to begin the long journey of coming fully into consciousness that lasts the entire novel. Since these wayfarers live in hope and promise rather than in conclusion, at a beginning after the end, they have only the most tentative sense of how to act and what to do. Revelation does not so much confer a fixed and final identity upon Percy's seers as return to them authority over their own incomplete lives. They discover that they are like the castaway of "The

Message in the Bottle" who is "not in the world as a swallow is in the world, as an organism which is what it is, never more or less. Our islander may choose his mode of being" (*MB* 142). Percy's fictional islanders seek hints and clues that may guide them in their choices. Their coming to consciousness makes them aware of the possible significance of what they once overlooked. If the classical apocalyptist views "all mundane occurrences as signs of God's presence,"[22] Percy's counterparts behold the semiotic universe pictured in his linguistic essays. Although this world of meaning points less directly to God than does the biblical cosmos, it abounds with telling connections between the apparently disconnected—memories, chance meetings, portents in nature, the curious behavior of people observed on the search. The task of Percy's apocalyptists is to decipher the significance of these signs not so much for the end of the world but for the mystery of their own eschatological identities.

Percy's visionaries receive guidance in their semiotic quests through news bearers who testify to the ultimate meaning of these signs. In Apocalypse, the vocation embraced by Jesus, John, and the martyrs is the life and death of a witness. The One to come is "the faithful witness"; the apocalyptist was confined to Patmos "for the word of God, and for the testimony of Jesus Christ," and he beholds the multitude who defeated Satan "by the blood of the Lamb, and by the word of their testimony" (Rev. 1:5, 9; 12:11). Jacques Ellul explains that witnesses in Greek and Roman jurisprudence point to that which is completely outside the situation while themselves being within it. Given authority by their testimony, they intervene as onlookers in the course of events and introduce the unexpected, unknown words that challenge the already established understanding of history. The witness in Revelation "speaks in this world while pointing to the Wholly Other and prays to the Wholly Other while pointing to this world and bearing it with him."[23] Percy's fictional messengers perform exactly this function of telling what they have seen or heard and of taking up the incarnate world to God. All bear the truth in the aftermath of catastrophe: the despair and disrepute of Scanlon, the illnesses of Lonnie and Samantha, the dilapidated academy where Val Vaught teaches, the spiritual crisis of Father John, the collapse of Fathers Weatherbee and Smith into old age's inertia. Yet precisely because these witnesses show such wisdom and charity while often struggling with their own flaws, they can act as mentors to those Percyan castaways who are typically abstracted from or absorbed in the cosmos. Knowing creation through a love at the end of the world, these evangelists embody the tidings from across the sea, which alone can make sense of the islander's predicament in "The Message in the Bottle." Their news offers the promise of the new creation. Just as the herald in Percy's essay cries, "Come! I know the way out!" when the building is on fire (*MB* 138), his fictional messengers offer direction to apocalyptists astray amid the ruins.

Whereas Percy's wanderers come to consciousness at the beginning of the novel through a natural revelation, the guides they meet live in response to the Christian revelation. Since they have been generally freed from the extremes of self-division, these apostles represent a unity of being grounded in a communion with others and with God. They try to bring those who have come to themselves as castaways to a second coming through love and to faith. The news that these witnesses bear is the kind called good, the gospel. Although Lonnie in *The Moviegoer* quotes the language of the catechism, and Val in *The Last Gentleman* charges Will to attend to Jamie's baptism, the faith of Percy's apostles is never simply a matter of orthodox belief and practice. Rather, the message is the Word that has been taken into their lives, the lives that have been renewed in love. The news comes not in an abstract set of propositions but through the reception of and living of the Logos in personalities. It is incarnational rather than noetic, always happening in the voice of the messenger, ever ready to encounter the listener who is prepared to receive it.

Since Percy's messengers signify this good news in their very being, the union of the sacred word with their own flesh causes their speech to gain new authority. "In the beginning was Alpha and the end is Omega," Percy writes at the beginning of "The Delta Factor" (and then repeats this profession of faith at the end of his essay), "but somewhere between occurred Delta," his name for the point at which humanity came to consciousness through language (*MB* 3). As Percy's speakers and listeners live between the ultimate letters of all time, they affirm in every dialogue the existence of the self as namer and the intrinsic value of the hearer, both of whom are joined in the communion of giving and receiving words. But the disastrous fall into self-absorption often causes language to fail, so that the sign is separated from the signified, the namer from the listener. This schism produces such infernal confidence men as Art Immelmann in *Love in the Ruins* and Lawyer Barrett in *The Second Coming*, and that enemy of the Word whose diatribes create a world unto himself, Lancelot Andrewes Lamar. Percy appropriately locates his world of the delta factor between the boundaries of an apocalyptic alphabet, for its first and last letters name what is for him the source and end of all language. In the opening and closing chapters of Revelation, the Lord identifies himself as "Alpha and Omega, the beginning and the ending" (Rev. 1:8; 22:12); between these extremes all of John's visions celebrate the potency of divine speech. The word of God comes to the prophet at the start, dictates the seven letters, inspires the three cycles of disasters, and continually bids John to write what he has seen, the faithful and true words that it is anathema to alter.

The Apocalypse of John is a supreme demonstration of Percy's belief that language is revelatory. The word of God names what it signifies and accomplishes what it names, unites the divine speaker and human listener in the profoundest intimacy, and invites all future readers to become fellow participants in the visions of its words. Percy's messengers at point delta gain new power for their own discourse by joining it to the word of the Alpha and Omega, the Author who creates by speech in Genesis and renews that creation by speech in Apocalypse. Scanlon's secret directions, Lonnie's and Samantha's poignant words from the heart, Val's unmannerly imperatives, Father John's purified monosyllables, as well as Father Weatherbee's and Father Smith's impassioned eloquence, return language to the service of the Logos. If words define the way by which the characters of a novelist-linguist look at the world, Percy's news bearers renew sight by recovering the primordial force of speech. They become visionaries of and through the word who turn language into the semiotics of the new creation.

III   Percy's seers gain this renewed order only after apocalyptic catastrophe. Judgment traditionally leads to disaster in apocalypse, for the corruption of the age must be destroyed. In Revelation, the breaking of the seven seals, the sounding of the seven trumpets, and the pouring of the seven bowls initiate successive cycles of calamities until it almost seems that the process of coming to an end threatens to usurp the end itself. Visions of war, famine, plagues, martyrdom, and heavenly convulsions are followed by the sight of hail, fire, pollution, darkness, and demonic beasts. Although these woes might seem to point to God's absence from history or his triumphant cruelty, they actually reveal his saving role in the course of events. Jacques Ellul explains that every approach of God toward creation implies a judgment on the world that clings to its separation, its enslavement to all that opposes heaven.[24] The violence of the divine coming helps to free humanity from such thralldom. Having threatened five of the seven churches in the opening letters, the figure like the Son of Man declares, "As many as I love, I rebuke and chasten" (Rev. 3:19). After the sixth trumpet the survivors of the plagues still continue to worship demons and idols, and after the seventh blast the twenty-four elders celebrate that God "shouldest destroy them which destroy the earth" (Rev. 11:18). The catastrophes serve as the very sign for the negation of negation. But if they correct and purify as the prelude to a new world, they are a divine privilege alone, not a validation for millennial campaigns. John makes clear that the end arrives not through human means, historical forces, or evolutionary progress; indeed, the believer does not even know the hour of its coming. Since it happens only in God's own time, apocalypse rebukes the messianic ambitions of so many of Percy's arrogant seers by teaching the most radical form of dependency. Yet if humans can only wait for the end and never cause it by themselves, their own end is not predestined, and their moral responsibility is not diminished. They must choose to lose or to live for the future by deciding between membership in the old decaying world or in the new cosmos coming into being.

Percy's fiction recognizes the potential blessings, limitations, and perversions of apocalyptic disaster.[25] In *The Message in the Bottle* Percy suggests that traditional scientific investigations need to be supplemented by such studies as "How Bad Is Bad News?" and "Catastrophe as Catalyst in the Ontology of Joy" (*MB* 29). Perhaps such mock treatises would answer his question, "Why is the good life which men have achieved in the twentieth century so bad that only news of world catastrophes, assassinations, plane crashes, mass murders, can divert one from the sadness of ordinary mornings?" (*MB* 7). Although such fondness for destruction is a gruesome commentary on modern deadness and indifference, Percy's apocalyptists welcome doom because they hope that it will end the old, intolerable order. Catastrophe disturbs the round of everyday events that isolates Percy's scientists and sensualists from their own experiences and suddenly transforms what is everyday into what is only today. Americans remember the precise moment and place in which they heard the news of John F. Kennedy's assassination, Percy explains, because "the scene and the circumstances of hearing such news become invested with a certain significance and density which they do not ordinarily possess" (*LC* 57). Cataclysm provides a revealing foil for consciousness. The bad news, near riots, accidents, storms, snipers, wars, and revolutions enjoyed by Percy's seers renew the moment by disclosing what has been present all the time but has simply gone unseen until the threat of Ground Zero. Poising all against annihilation, such menace frees time and space from simply being dimensions of perception, restores self and others in wonder and delight because their very existence has been endangered. Each of Percy's apocalyptists is that archetypal commuter whose heart attack on the New York Central turns a possible coup de grace into a graced stroke of good fortune. The disaster performs the apocalyptic task of unveiling by breaking down the "absolute partitioning of reality" that screens the disheartened traveler from the city, his fellow commuters, even his own body. At the station on Fordham Road where he is taken off the train, the lucky victim sees his hand for the first time (*MB* 87).

Although Percy's jaded seekers often need the shock of the last day so that they might live as if it were the first, many of these despairing Southerners pervert an eschatological passion into a purely egotistical end. They seek a stoical, aesthetic, or suicidal apocalypse rather than undergoing a more profound transformation. Percy detects in the South's stoic inheritance "a grim sort of pleasure to be taken in the very deterioration of society, the crashing of the world about one's ears." [26] Such forbidding classicists as Aunt Emily, Lawyer Barrett, and Lancelot see the ruins but not, like biblical apocalyptists, beyond them to true renewal. Since social collapse confirms the stoics' "original choice of the wintry kingdom of self," Percy's twentieth-century Romans become as self-obsessed as the age, isolated in the sanctuary of their own inner integrity.[27] While such tight-lipped and transcendent naysayers cast a cold eye on the end, Percy's last romantics turn apocalypse into an aphrodisiac. Binx and Kate on the train to Chicago, Will and Kitty in Central Park, as well as Tom and his ladies in the Howard Johnson's, hope to achieve love in the ruins, but the result is usually frustrated sex in a strange place. The most desperate of Percy's deluded visionaries convert this love at the end into a love of their own end. Both William Rodney Allen and Ted Spivey recognize how the longings of Percy's apocalyptists may actually conceal a glorified death wish.[28] Kate Cutrer flirts with danger to feel more alive, Sutter Vaught courts suicide, and Ed Barrett actually kills himself because of his passion for doom. Although in the upside-down world of Percy's novels the worst of times are frequently the best, his self-destructive seekers cannot look beyond despair to discover the joy of abandoning their misplaced hopes. The genuine Percyan apocalypse leads not to thanatos but to a new life in the flesh and spirit.

The catastrophe that finally overwhelms Percy's apocalyptists is unexpected and unwanted. It does not bring the saving thrill of toppled cities and emptied streets but instead devastates his characters' most interior lives and intimate preserves. If Percy's seers are ever to behold their own new heaven and earth, they can neither savor the decline of Western civilization nor romanticize the ruins. They cannot even remain content to enjoy the momentary shocks to consciousness caused by storms and snipers because such disasters never sufficiently transform creatures of sensation so that they can live amid the dullness of their everyday world. The bad news of natural catastrophes, stoic pessimism, or lovely fatalism is never bad enough. The doom is never really internalized as an impetus to renewal but enjoyed only as a perverse change in the environment, and so it never heralds the genuinely good news: a more profound change of heart.

In "Notes for a Novel about the End of the World," Percy declares that the eschatological novelist "must reckon not merely like H. G. Wells with changes in the environment but also with changes in man's consciousness which may be quite as radical. Will this consciousness be more or less religious?" (*MB* 114). Immediately before World War I, Wells's *The World Set Free* (1914) envisioned the destruction of the earth's major cities by atomic bombs. Such novels as Nevil Shute's *On the Beach* (1957) and Pat Frank's *Alas, Babylon* (1959), published while Percy was writing *The Moviegoer*, follow the Wellsian tradition of portraying the end of the world as a purely external transformation. The same nuclear catastrophe looms in the background of Percy's fiction. In *The Moviegoer* Binx fears that the bomb will not fall on his deadened world; and in *The Second Coming* Will notices a cloud that resembles the atomic vapors over Hiroshima. Indeed, Percy has speculated that it is difficult for a novelist not to write eschatological fiction when "the only reason we are not all dead at this very moment is that the Soviets, for whatever reason, did not choose to press the button thirty minutes ago."[29] *Love in the Ruins* acknowledges what Percy's comment in an interview overlooks: the United States can easily annihilate itself. Percy comes closest to creating the traditional finale of apocalyptic fiction in this futuristic satire of an America only days away from destruction, but the novel follows its predecessors in the genre only to depart from them at the very moment of catastrophe: America is spared its day of doom.

Percy does not depict the expected natural disaster in this novel whose science fiction conventions virtually require it because the apocalypses that interest him most cause a religious change in consciousness rather than a Wellsian change in the environment. Terrence Rafferty charges that Percy's eschatological imagination condemns his novels to futile repetition, for each keeps announcing the end while its successor implies that Judgment Day has not yet dawned but is certainly coming.[30] But such a dismissal results from a too-literal reading of Percy's apocalypses. The last day *does* happen for Percy—not in the cosmos but in daily life, where deeds measure time and ages may begin or end with a single action. Despite the alarm that Percy's fiction registers about America at large, each of his novels shows how the world ends for only a few individuals, yet the entire history of the City of Man depends on such personal choices to live in the City of God. "Everyone knows about the awesome new weapons," Percy admits, before he describes the true source of catastrophe in his apocalyptic fiction. "But what is less apparent is a comparable realignment of energies within the human psyche." That spiritual conversion is the very subject of Percy's fiction. "The psychical forces presently released in the postmodern consciousness open unlimited possibilities for both destruction and liberation, for an absolute loneliness or a rediscovery of community and reconciliation" (*MB* 112).

Percy's fiction turns catastrophe into a crisis of consciousness that challenges his visionaries when they have exhausted all of their strategies to create a supposedly new world. His novels look beyond physical ruins like the wrecked cityscape of New Orleans in *The Moviegoer*, Jamie's deathbed in *The Last Gentleman*, or the smoking golf course in *Love in the Ruins* to the less apparent destruction that they dramatize. As Percy explains, "When the novelist writes of a man 'coming to himself' through some such catalyst as catastrophe or ordeal, he may be offering obscure testimony to a gross disorder of consciousness and to the need of recovering oneself as neither angel nor organism but as a wayfaring creature somewhere between" (*MB* 113). The end occurs in the unseen and inmost world of each seer's consciousness as the erring wanderer discovers the fulfillment of the initial moment of revelation, a second coming to selfhood. Although Percy's prophets begin to recover their personal sovereignty at the start of the novel, by its climax they have repeatedly used their freedom to become exemplars of the ruined age. Disaster exposes the failure of their dubious attempts at newness, so that the seers may finally come upon what in fact they feared and desired most: an encounter with another, and possibly with God. After learning how to live at the end, Percy's apocalyptists need to discover how to live without the end—on those ordinary Wednesday mornings or at that intermediate afternoon hour of four o'clock when the glorious Second Coming seems as if it will never come. At the end of the novels they are challenged to live out their long days and weeks by achieving "a rediscovery of communion and reconciliation" in a new life that Percy understands as radically religious.

I V   Although apocalypse denounces the current order, it culminates in a resplendent affirmation of the age to come. Negation and renewal are not simply contrasting but complementary revelations, for the destruction of the perverted cosmic order lifts the final veil and makes possible a world wonderfully sacred. In Revelation the whorish city of Babylon is replaced by the holy city of Jerusalem, the beasts by the Lamb, the plagues by the life-giving water and tree. The commonplace is taken up into the very life of God, whose glory pervades the universe. All the nations stream into Jerusalem in a community of the sanctified, but the city needs no temple, for God is the temple, his radiant presence making unnecessary the sun and moon. The Lord who created the world does not merely herald a glorified continuation of the old era but now re-creates it.

Amos Wilder misses this phase of "miraculous renovation" in contemporary apocalyptic literature and charges that "the catastrophic imagination alone is therefore not genuinely apocalyptic." [31] Despairing visionaries like Sutter Vaught and Lawyer Barrett keep their eyes on the approaching doom, but Percy agrees with Wilder that the end is not in fact the end. What begins in revelation and climaxes in ruins finds its consummation in renewal, however uncertain and undefined it may appear in Percy's novels. This lack of resolution seems contrary to the very nature of literary apocalypses, for as Lois Parkinson Zamora observes, such fictions "address the very nature of finality—historical and narrative—more explicitly and emphatically than most plotted narratives." [32] But the incompleteness of Percy's novels conveys a wayfarer's truth. Precisely because he writes about humanity as wanderers, his fictional eschatons require openendedness, closing without concluding. Characters still living in the midst can only come to ends that are relative, irresolute, and suggestive. Percy's often-criticized last pages are not muddled resolutions to the dichotomies that he has been exploring in the novel. Rather, their persistent ambiguity dramatizes the lives of travelers who have come to a certain end in a pilgrimage that itself is a continual coming. Looking to an ongoing end or a final beginning, the last pages of Percy's novels consider last things in hope. John's final vision of a world filled with God's glory may seem more decisive than Percy's signs of a time to come, but Apocalypse actually ends with the promise, not the attainment, of re-creation. Douglas Robinson might be describing Percy's novels as well when he writes that the Book of Revelation shows "a semiotic of completion that contains within itself the telling trace of incompletion."[33] The Lord affirms that he is coming soon, while the Spirit and the Bride cry, "Come!" John repeats the prayer, the call of *Marana tha* used in early Christian liturgy that testifies to the immense gap between desire and fulfillment. Chapter 21 hopes that the renovation may be imminent, but like Percy's fiction, the epilogue recognizes that it is definitely not yet here (Rev. 22:6–21).

The cry to "come!" that echoes throughout the final verses of Apocalypse is the summary word of Percy's fiction. Beginning with a coming to consciousness, his seers wander toward discovering glimpses of the Second Coming, the title of Percy's fifth published novel. "Come back" is the fourfold summons that ends the concluding space odyssey in *Lost in the Cosmos*. Its last pages recount a science fiction version of the homelessness portrayed in "The Message in the Bottle" as a new community assembled after the earth's near destruction receives signals from a higher form of consciousness. The extraterrestrial's questions ask about the significant comings in Percy's fiction: "Do you know who you are? . . . Do you know how to love? Are you loved?" (*LC* 262). Percy's castaways come to themselves when they learn who they are, and they learn how to love when they come to another.

The alien's questions to those lost in the cosmos are really one, for Percy regards consciousness as "knowing with" rather than as a solitary "knowing of" (*MB* 274). Since it is communal and concelebratory, his seekers only know who they are when they know how to love. John Edward Hardy properly cautions that their eschatological yearnings may express a desire for "relief from the wearisome responsibilities of everyday faith and judgment—above all, perhaps, from the tedium and indignities of human love,"[34] but the Percyan apocalypse actually returns his lovers to these very ruins. All of his seers fear genuine love. They try to escape its labors by living in some heartless age of their own envisioning, or they seek to replace its receptive vulnerability with such substitutes as aestheticized eroticism, old-fashioned romance, self-absorption, and suicide. They finally discover that all of these ways lead to disaster rather than to the communion that brings personal awareness to fulfillment. Amid such absolute failure, when all the barriers to shared consciousness have been reduced to nothing, the seer meets another person, a fellow survivor at the end of the world. Percy claims that no writer could make credible love at first sight on the 5:30 P.M. commuter train to Hackensack. "But if the Bomb is going to vaporize New Jersey any minute and the boy knows how to get the girl to Delaware in time," then romance may be possible in such a scenario for a Hollywood melodrama.[35] Fascinated by mysteries and thrillers, Percy stages just such moments of intimate discovery and tender self-giving between his archetypal travelers at the ends of his novels—except that his saving meetings are not confined to the simple boy-girl pairings of old-time movies. Not just those who end up as husband and wife but also William Grey and Scanlon, Will Barrett and Sutter, perhaps even Lancelot and Father John, come closer to learning that, in different ways, their doom is love.

If Percy's novels begin with an ending, they end with a beginning. The newly discovered communion amounts to a change in consciousness so that the cosmos is seen anew in its perpetual freshness. Since time and place, people and things, now exist in the light of such ultimate concerns as love and faith, John's vision of a new heaven and earth becomes in Percy a new way of looking at and living in the world.[36] This renovation differs from the romantic apocalypse of Blake or Wordsworth because it depends not on imaginative perception but on the bonds formed with other people, the consciousness that finds its greatest receptivity to the world in sharing it with another.[37] Such a personal apocalypse lacks the communal and cosmic dimensions of the new order in Revelation. Yet if this new heaven and earth only extends to a few lives, Percy's visionaries never escape from history into transcendence or simply retreat into a solipsism for two like the lovers in Donne who frequently create their own uncharted sphere. The end of the world returns Percy's seers at the end to the world where they begin the work of renewal. Having moved from the privacy of initial revelation to the intimacy of love in the ruins, Percy's apocalyptists discover that this coming to another leads to a new bond with the community in time: Binx's deepened sense of brotherhood, Val's and Father John's proclamation of the Word, Tom's and Will's ministry to the sick in body and spirit. Like Paul, who urged the Thessalonians not to give up their daily labors because they looked to the Second Coming, Percy insists that his wayfarers work at, not for, the end (2 Thess. 3:6–15).

These human bonds mediate the divine ending.[38] The discovery of love with a fellow searcher forms the very basis of the religious faith achieved by Percy's searchers. In *The Message in the Bottle* Percy uses the "word 'religious' in its root sense as signifying a radical *bond*, as the writer sees it, which connects man with reality—or the failure of such a bond—and so confers meaning to his life—or the absence of meaning" (*MB* 102–3). Because Percy is so aware of the rift between immanence and transcendence, he conceives of religion through the radical image of connection. The root of the word indicates that it is the ultimate ligature in his writings. Indeed, the entire course of Percy's wanderers is religious, for it begins when they rediscover their bondedness to their own lives in the world, proceeds to show how his seers form bonds with others, and implies at the end the possibility of being mysteriously bound to God.

Although Percy's typically male seekers seem more open to discovering their life in God, the women they have loved are never clearly shown to have come as far in their wayfaring. Sometimes they are not even present at the close. When Allison Sutter disappears from the final pages of "The Gramercy Winner," she almost sets the pattern for Kitty, Anna, and Lucy to be absent at the conclusion of Percy's later apocalypses. Even when such women of faith as Kate, Ellen, and Allie are depicted as still living amid the ruins of these final scenes, they never achieve a religious understanding that receives the same affirmation in the novel as the spiritual vision of Binx, Tom, and Will. Although both *The Moviegoer* and *The Second Coming* end by looking to such apocalyptic hopes as the general resurrection and the Parousia, Kate and Allie do not directly participate in these glory-filled moments in Percy's fiction. Ellen is a lapsed Presbyterian in *Love in the Ruins* and then a spirited Pentecostal in *The Thanatos Syndrome*, but her dualistic faith tends to perpetuate the disjunctions that Tom has learned to oppose in both novels. Indeed, Percy's searchers usually find it more compatible to talk about the progress of their souls with other men—with Scanlon, Lonnie, Father Smith, Father John, and Father Weatherbee. Only Val Vaught in *The Last Gentleman* and Samantha More in *Love in the Ruins* seem as spiritually discerning as these male evangelists; but the steely nun and the sickly daughter are not the kind of women with whom Percy's apocalyptists seek romantic love in the ruins.

When Percy's restless and rootless everyman discovers religious bonds, the seeker celebrates these essential connections in a Christian context. Although Percy detects "the massive failure of Christendom itself" in the Western world (*MB* 111), he looks to the possibility of the faith, not the discouraging example of the faithful, because its reconciliation of apparent opposites seems to bridge the schism that he often traces back to Cartesian dualism. The sacramental vision of Christianity affirms a bond between thing and spirit, while the Incarnation unites Word of God and human flesh as if it were the consummate sign in Percy's semiotic universe. Since language establishes a bond between speaker and listener, for Percy the Word that connects divinity and humanity is the Logos incarnate.

Percy's faith honors the same phenomena as his fiction. "Since novels deal with people and people live in time and get into predicaments," he explains, "it is probably an advantage to subscribe to a world view which is incarnational, historical, and predicamental, rather than, say, Buddhism, which tends to devalue individual persons, things, and happenings" (*MB* 111). Through signs, people, and situations, Percy's visionaries discover the Deity who despises none of the elements of fiction, who as Speaker and Word has been a part of the story told since the beginning. Those castaways restored to the world by discovering their bonds may at last see their lives according to their most meaningful connection. They may hear God at work through words, sense him in a situation, glimpse his holy being in a person. At such revelatory moments the seers come to the God who has been coming to them.

Percy's vision is the eschatology of a walker. His wayfarers do not so much get to God at last as come to him all along, finding by indirect routes the holiness at the heart of their lives. They journey toward the divine end that has already begun, the sacred future that grows in and out of the present. Percy's wanderers live in the dawning kingdom of God that Frank Kermode recognizes as conferring eschatological significance not simply on the last days but on "the whole of history, and the progress of the individual life . . . as a benefaction from the End, now immanent."[39] This eschaton is not just imminent; it breaks into the world to encounter Percy's apocalyptists amid their everydayness. However, if the God of Percy's fiction draws near to his characters from the end of time, he is yet still coming. The deliberate irresolution of Percy's novels, in which love is so often imperfect and faith seems so unfinished, rejects any completely realized eschatology. His novels always intimate that there is more to come and often express this incompleteness by looking to some future consummation. But since this end is ultimately unspeakable, his novels have more to say about the hope and love that must begin in the present when the castaway hears the word.

V   Percy disavows any apostolic mission for his own writings and confesses that his art is often as bad as his news. He claims for the eschatological novelist only a "certain prescience," the odd angle of vision known by the wounded soldier, who can see the battle better than those still shooting (*MB* 101). Or he likens his books to the seismographs on each side of the San Andreas fault that record the hidden tremors and fissures in an apparently ordinary time.[40] Percy's view of his own work is modest, but it is also a strategy to reassure readers wary of proselytizing, for he is an apocalyptist in spite of himself. Just as the end of Apocalypse looks beyond its writer to those seers yet to come, for whom reading his words means reviewing his visions, the last pages of Percy's fiction may mark the true beginnings of his books in the lives of his readers. If they bring any final revelation, it comes from what Percy understands as a process of recollection. Stressing the cognitive task of art in the Thomist tradition, the novelist has said that his fiction seeks to make his audience recognize what it already knows.[41] Percy's apocalypses try to recall readers to themselves so that like his newly aware seers, they eye the world and wonder about their curious placement in it. Yet if Percy hopes that his readers may discover the ultimate bonds that he understands as religious, he realizes that his audience may be more like Binx Bolling, who only has to hear the name of God for a curtain to come down in his head. The novelist knows that he simply needs to "say one word about salvation or redemption and the jig is up."[42] His deepest faith almost seems unspeakable because the "old words of grace are worn smooth as poker chips" in an age when the traditional signs of the Spirit have been devalued by scientists and consumers (*MB* 116). Seeking to proclaim the bad and good news, the eschatological novelist finds that his message is no longer new but as numbly familiar as any commercial on television.

Percy's fiction tries to destroy his age's dullness to words and deadness to the Word by relying on the traditional aesthetics of Apocalypse so that all might be made new. Since John records not the ordinary sights of one restricted by an island's geography or by the knowledge of first-century history, but vision throughout space and into time, he eschews literal reports and factual descriptions. Instead, he uses bewildering images, abrupt tonal contrasts, rapid dissolves, and an apparent absence of logic to disclose the theological mysteries at work in a world where all teleology seems absent. Despite its reputation for being enigmatic and obscure, John's writing actually unveils rather than conceals by showing what Northrop Frye sees as "the inner form of everything that is happening now" to a world that prefers to keep its eye on the more obvious screen of history.[43] Apocalypse seems so very strange because it does not allow the truth to be hidden at all from readers whose purview is normally limited by that small and commonplace pile of rocks called Patmos. In presenting God's perspective, its symbolic language and dreamlike narration recklessly dare to show earthbound readers too much. But the apocalyptic writer believes that truth can only be revealed by extreme methods that avoid the worn-out words of everyday sight for the bolder language of the visionary imagination. Hence, John favors verbal, physical, emotional and poetic violence—the vehement denunciations in the opening letters, successive panoramas of destruction, ecstatic voice, and surreal imagery—because only such calculated daring can disclose the eternal realities at the heart of history.

In "Notes for a Novel about the End of the World," Percy explains that a novelist counters the failure of language and of Christendom by calling on "every ounce of cunning, craft, and guile he can muster from the darker regions of his soul" (*MB* 118). Often Percy's linguistic artifice gives back to readers a share in creation through making its presence lyrically palpable, conferring upon it the force and density, sound and visibility, that justify descriptions of the novelist as a sensualist and poet.[44] He repeatedly salutes moments of such plenitude that the world wells up in his writing—not just in the Hopkinsian visions of fish and fowl but also in more prosaic epiphanies: enduring seats in a movie theater, mechanical harvesters browsing along cotton rows, the mottled altarpiece of a bar, a castle of a stove, a glittery snowfield of a computer projection. By paying tribute to the cosmos that many of Percy's characters have lost, his novels save the common from being merely commonplace and reveal the world to readers by its first light. When Percy's art is drawn from even "darker regions of his soul," he relies on what might exaggerate, distort, and confound in the effort to illuminate. Since conventional signs no longer claim the attention of readers, a writer may make the "fictional use of violence, shock, comedy, insult, the bizarre . . . the everyday tools of his trade." Percy adopts O'Connor's rationale for her spiritual cartoons as his own: those who are nearly blind require large and startling figures (*MB* 118). Percy's early fiction demonstrates an increasingly radical use of such disorientation and reorientation, until these drastic techniques reach a climax in the ferocity of *Lancelot*, are redefined in the celebration of *The Second Coming*, and then are reexplored in the satirical melodrama of *The Thanatos Syndrome*.

Some of Percy's readers view the novelist's growing extremism as the cause of his own near ruin. Harold Bloom summarizes their complaints when he laments Percy's shift from rueful spiritual comedies to prophetic indictments,[45] and Percy himself indirectly recognizes the potential problems of his artistry in "Notes for a Novel about the End of the World." Whereas British novels often seem carefully circumscribed, Percy claims that American fiction typically errs through "pretension, grandiosity, formlessness, Dionysian excess, and a kind of metaphysical omnivorousness. American novels tend to be about everything. Moreover, at the end, everything is disposed of, God, man, and the world" (*MB* 103–4). Revelations of the end have marked American literature from its very origins. Because the apocalyptic vision encompasses such ultimate concerns in such a radical style, it can only intensify what Percy regards as the already gargantuan proportions of the native tradition. Percy works to counter this egotistical enormity through strategies that subvert the possible excesses of writing about the end of the world: his attention to little, easily overlooked, details; his ironic view of his own apocalyptists; his creation of news bearers who prefer not to preach and who gain credibility because of their own involvement in frailty and failure; his passion for endings that do not end but return his seers to "God, man, and the world" rather than disposing of the essential triangle in his art. When Percy does not control this immense universe in its last days, the focus can become diffuse, the action unwieldy, the chronology confused, and the characterization undeveloped.[46] Yet despite these dangers, Percy's apocalypticism has inspired his writing with its vigorous imagination. It has challenged him to reconceive such genres as the comedy of manners, picaresque narrative, utopian fantasy, mystery, romance, and thriller by discovering in all of these forms a common story about revelation, ruin, and renewal. This ancient pattern of judgment and promise has given the incisiveness to his humor, the immediacy to his language, and the elusiveness to his last pages that make readers ponder the same questions asked by his sly likeness in Lyn Hill's painting: *"True, this is a strange world I'm in, but what about the world you're in? Have you noticed it lately? Are we onto something, you and I? Probably not."*[47]

Percy's apocalypses seek to make his readers be "onto something" by following the practice suggested in the last lines of "Notes for a Novel about the End of the World": perhaps "it is only through the conjuring up of catastrophe, the destruction of all Exxon signs, and the sprouting of vines in the church pews, that the novelist can make vicarious use of catastrophe in order that he and his reader may come to themselves" (*MB* 118). These books of revelations hope that the end of the world envisioned by the apocalyptic novelist will be reexperienced in art so that readers who only seem to live amid the latter days may at last reverse their loss, recover creation, and ponder the mystery of a possible bond with the Creator. Only then will the novel live up to the promise of renewal revealed in its name.

2

FROM AUTOBIOGRAPHY TO APOCALYPSE

"THE GRAMERCY WINNER"

I   During interviews in the 1960s, Dr. Walker Percy so often answered the question about how he became a novelist that the story of his life assumed the familiarity of a southern literary legend. When he gives the most revealing account of this conversion in a 1966 essay titled "From Facts to Fiction," he intimates the enduring fiction behind the facts that he has been narrating for years. His autobiographical sketch tells the story of his own apocalypse. After he was graduated from Columbia University's College of Physicians and Surgeons in 1941, he worked as a pathologist at Bellevue Hospital in New York, where his duties included conducting autopsies on more than one hundred patients who had died from tuberculosis. "Then came the cataclysm," Percy recalls, "brought to pass appropriately enough by one of these elegant agents of disease, the same scarlet tubercle bacillus I used to see lying crisscrossed like Chinese characters in the sputum and lymphoid tissue of the patients at Bellevue. Now I was one of them."[1] Perhaps because he did not take sufficient sanitary precautions while performing the autopsies, Percy contracted the tuberculosis that confined him for two years to Trudeau Sanatorium in Saranac Lake, New York. And although he tried to return to medicine by teaching pathology at Columbia in 1944, a relapse forced another rest cure at Gaylord Farms in Connecticut.

"What was the effect of the cataclysm," Percy wonders in "From Facts to Fiction," "the interruption of my chosen career and the two years of physical inactivity which followed?" The disaster was revelatory, for Percy came to himself by witnessing the collapse of his entire old way of seeing the cosmos. "Did my eyes deceive me or was there not a huge gap in the scientific view of the world . . . an oversight which everyone pretended not to notice or maybe didn't want to notice?" His major in chemistry at the University of North Carolina and his studies at Columbia, where professors taught the mechanism of disease, had trained Percy to see the diversity and random-ness of life as a series of exquisitely ordered variations on increasingly fewer generalizations. Since truth might be discovered by the purest induction, Percy specialized in pathology, the most depersonalized of medical careers for an already disembodied practitioner. Postmortems removed him "farthest from the arts and crafts of the bedside manner" so that every patient became a dead specimen.[2] The doctor who claimed that he spent his four years at Columbia attending movies in Washington Heights found that the micro-scope, test tube, and colorimeter enabled him to watch "the beautiful theater of disease" as a fascinated but disengaged spectator. Science was a "religion for me," he told Robert Coles, but contracting tuberculosis revealed to Percy the inadequacy of such faith in exalted abstraction.[3]

Lewis Lawson suggests that the stricken physician suffered the trial that he later described in "Notes for a Novel about the End of the World" and in so much of his fiction:[4] "When the novelist writes of a man 'coming to him-self' through some such catalyst as catastrophe or ordeal, he may be offering obscure testimony to a gross disorder of consciousness and to the need of recovering oneself as neither angel nor organism but as a wayfaring creature somewhere between" (MB 113). The future linguist learned in this private apocalypse that his identity was his first name. He was not simply another organism known by science and limited by death; nor was he the angelic doctor who could contemplate disease yet not identify with diseased people. Rather, while reading Dostoyevski, Sartre, Camus, Jaspers, Marcel, and Hei-degger on a search into his own personal mystery, Percy discovered that he had been left out of his own earlier medical research. His own life was the great gap overlooked by science, which accounted for everything except the human predicament, "what it means to be a man living in the world who must die."[5] The doctor-patient came to consciousness by discovering that he was himself a walker on a journey whose end in death forced him to reclaim his life.

Percy chose to explore these matters of life and death as a writer rather than as a pathologist. He admits in an interview that his tuberculosis was relatively mild and he could have resumed his profession, but the illness gave him an honorable opportunity to leave the practice of medicine. Despite his delighted wonder at science, he might have become a physician only out of propriety. Percy had no desire to follow the other traditional vocations—law, the army, and religion—for the scion of a reputable southern family that produced planters, lawyers, statesmen, and soldiers. And he suspected that a career in medicine might please William Alexander Percy, who adopted Walker and his two brothers after his father's suicide in 1929 and his mother's death in a car accident more than two years later.[6] His father's cousin raised the adolescent Percy in a gentlemanly home and educated him in stoic ethics and romantic literature, although Uncle Will's poetry and melancholy memoirs (*Lanterns on the Levee*) clearly foresaw the last days of the classical ideals that he bequeathed his foster son. Indeed, the title work of *Enzio's Kingdom and Other Poems* (1924) was an apocalyptic elegy for Will Percy's own father.[7] Just as Enzio confronted the defeat of his sire, Frederick II, the eschatological emperor of medieval legend, so Will mourned Senator LeRoy's inevitable failure in defending gentility against the immorality of the rising mob. LeRoy Percy was one of those stalwart planters who carried a lantern on the levee to keep vigil during flood scares, bearing a halo of light before a tide of darkness. Yet in his family history, subtitled *Recollections of a Planter's Son*, Will Percy saw those fires gradually being extinguished. Published a year before his own death, the remembrances of William Alexander Percy were a nostalgic celebration and a gracious demonstration of southern stoicism. In his last years Will Percy nobly and eloquently chronicled the last days of a cultural ideal with the heroic bleakness that Walker Percy would respect but finally reject in his own fiction and essays. When the foster son wrote an introduction to the memoirs of "the most extraordinary man I have ever known," he acknowledged that "the overall pessimism of *Lanterns on the Levee*, its gloomy assessment of the spiritual health of Western civilization, is hard to fault these days," yet he warned against "a certain seductiveness which always attends the heralding of apocalypse." More hopeful and less certain than his prescient kinsman, Percy claimed that "what is upon us is not a twilight of the gods but a very real race between the powers of light and darkness."[8]

If Percy inherited part of his apocalyptic vision from the combination of Roman despair and romantic sadness in the gentlemanly tradition, he found urgent confirmation for his views in the seemingly exhausted temporality of the modern world. "What does a man do when he finds himself living after an age has ended and he can no longer understand himself because the theories of man of the former age no longer work and the theories of the new age are not yet known?" Percy wonders in *The Message in the Bottle* (7). The South restated the question of the contemporary everyman with special force. As Lois Parkinson Zamora has shown, writers of twentieth-century southern fiction, like their counterparts in Latin America, have often looked imaginatively to the apocalypse because they shared a common anxiety about their cultural history. Since these artists have felt disconnected from the aristocratic past, disappointed with a materialistic and rootless present, and distrustful toward a future of utopian progressivism, many of them believed "that contemporary culture has reached a crisis point—an end point—when the old forms are no longer sufficient and new forms are struggling to establish themselves."[9] Percy knew this particular dilemma of the South in his own life, for he discovered that neither the grave heritage of an outdated order nor the promise of scientific modernism could sustain him. Uncle Will died in January 1942 shortly before Walker Percy's own diagnosis of tuberculosis gave him "a respectable excuse" to leave medicine.[10]

Percy never ceased to admire the beauty of his first career, which continued to inform his novels through the doctor's watchful eye for precise and lovely details. Nor did he ever simplistically dismiss the southern traditions of his family, the admirable but insufficient legacy from the uncle to whom he dedicated *The Moviegoer*. But Percy found that the novel in its radical meaning provided the salutary way to a more comprehensive vision. Just as he recommended in answering his earlier question about what to do in an eschatological era, he decided to "start afresh as if he were newly come into a new world," look at the birds and beasts, and "notice what is different about man" (*MB* 7). Percy began to find himself anew. Writing fiction helped the pathologist to analyze the illness of the twentieth century, to notice the sublime as well as the sick in humanity, and perhaps even to begin healing his own malaise. Ted Spivey regards the former physician as having been transformed by his diagnostic tales into the archetypal medicine man, the shaman.[11] Percy attempted to portray in his novels what medicine never considered and what his own disaster had revealed—the peculiar situation of one's being in the world and under God. Both the stoicism and scientism in which the beginning writer had been schooled, as Ralph Wood explains, left "no room for the self-revealing God transcendently to create, redeem, or judge."[12] But in discovering a new vocation as both a Christian and a novelist, Percy rejected such closure in order to explore the openness of human existence to its divine source and end. "From Facts to Fiction" does not record the other significant details of Percy's life that prepared the doctor to become a writer. After spending several years wondering in the North, he spent just over another year wandering in New Mexico, whose desert sites for nuclear tests later entered his writings as the ominous landscape of the apocalypse. Percy finally returned to the South, married Mary Bernice Townsend in 1946, and converted to Catholicism in 1947. They lived in Sewanee and then

29

New Orleans, but finally settled on the northern side of Lake Pontchartrain in Covington, Louisiana, around 1950. These facts make Percy resemble many of his fictional seekers. Their common story tells of a possible coming by way of catastrophe to oneself, to another, and to God.

After "Symbol as Need," his first essay since some college journalism, was printed in Fordham University's *Thought* (1954), Percy published articles on language, psychiatry, and southern culture throughout the 1950s. He also continued to work on the fiction first attempted in the preceding decade. Percy has dismissed his apprentice writings indebted to Wolfe and Mann as bad novels that were fortunately never published.[13] When Phinizy Percy visited his brother at Sewanee in 1947, he managed to read only about fifty of the eleven hundred pages in *The Charterhouse*.[14] The novel's country-club setting represented the center of the secular New South for a writer whose earliest memory focused on living across from a golf course. Percy claimed to have destroyed his first novel after several publishers rejected the book, Allen Tate faulted its lack of action, and Caroline Gordon sent him thirty pages of single-spaced criticism and advice.[15] When Percy began another attempt at fiction, he must have sensed what Robert Coles wrote over twenty years later: his own life was "the stuff of a novel," a story out of *The Magic Mountain*.[16] "What a sneaky trick Mann played on you," Shelby Foote later teased his longtime friend, "wrote your *magnum opus* just as you were approaching puberty." [17] But unlike Hans Castorp, William Grey in "The Gramercy Winner" escapes the spell of his sanatorium only through a religious conversion shortly before he dies. Although clearly not yet the work of a journeyman, this unpublished novel shows how from the very beginning of his career Percy's art explored the revelation that might destroy and renew his searcher's world. "The Gramercy Winner" is a fictionalized version of the facts leading to the apocalypse that Percy recounts in "From Facts to Fiction."

| | William Grey, the novel's loser and winner, looks back to Percy himself as well as ahead to Binx Bolling and Will Barrett. William comes from an established family, like Percy's, which is so wealthy that it has lost all interest in money. The Greys may reside in Gramercy Park, but William's sensitivity to the overture of gesture and response makes him by the novel's geography of manners more southern than anyone else from his home in the elite enclave of Manhattan. Like Percy, William suffers from a slight case of tuberculosis, which has confined him to a fairly renowned sanatorium in upstate New York during World War II. During his convales-

cence he keeps thinking about the fighting abroad, just as did Percy, whose brothers had joined the air force and the navy. Since the Lodge proper is so crowded, William stays at Mrs. McLeod's boardinghouse, spending much of his time alone and occasionally listening to the radio as if repeating the solitary pursuits of Percy, who roomed at Mrs. Ledbetter's while waiting for admission to Trudeau.[18] When Percy finally moved there, he lived with two doctors, much as William Grey shares a cottage with Dr. Van Norden that is frequently visited by his rival, Dr. Scanlon. Percy had only a minimal lesion; and Van Norden claims that if William had never had an X ray as part of a military physical, the would-be marine would probably never have known that he needed treatment. Although William, a twenty-year-old Princeton sophomore, is six years younger than the Dr. Percy who became a tuberculosis patient, Van Norden's example persuades his patient to follow Percy's own career and become a doctor.

Despite his parents' objections William has chosen to take treatment at the Lodge because of its reputation for a "philosophic" approach to tuberculosis (GW 9). Dr. Ambrose appropriately prescribes "a philosophic attitude toward life" for William while he is recovering (GW 5). William never reads the existential philosophy or fiction that Percy made part of his own cure while at Saranac Lake, for he seems to prefer scientific texts and mystery stories. If the Book of Revelation may be regarded as "a forerunner of modern existential narrative" because it sounds the "quintessential cri de coeur of the underground man,"[19] then Percy read his way back to the source of his vision and art. William Grey has less intellectual passion, yet, like Walker Percy, he comes to view his disease as a mysterious cataclysm that reveals the inability of science to explain how to exist in the world. Both the Southerner who came north and the Northerner who shares a distinctly southern sensibility take the first steps toward ending their spiritual displacement when they discover their identities as religious wayfarers. For the only time in his surviving fiction, Percy made the end of the novel the end of his seeker's life, as if only in death could he reimagine his less dire conversion, that second coming which all of Percy's religious searchers must live out in prosaic worlds far removed from transcendent enchantments.

"The Gramercy Winner" traces William Grey's long search for a last home as he recovers from tuberculosis in three hospices. Each is a temporary way station for a Percyan wanderer. In an attic room at Mrs. McLeod's he spends six months silent and still on his bed, staring at the ceiling in an even more extreme version of Binx's favorite posture. But he is drawn out of himself by the arrival of Laverne Sutter, the first of three characters in the novel who will later converge in Sutter Vaught in *The Last Gentleman*. The temperamental lieutenant and his ambivalent wife, Allison, quickly adopt William for their own purposes, and their marriage turns into an ambiguous triangle of affection and antagonism. Together, the trio enjoys almost idyllic times listening to baseball games or playing cards, but the camaraderie is subtly strained by the growing fondness between William and Allison as well as by Sutter's latent resentment at his apparent betrayal. The jealous husband seems almost cheerful when William moves to another cottage because the Gramercy Winner hopes that it will win him an earlier place at the Lodge.

At Mrs. Zabel's William becomes the focal point of another rivalry. The medical disputes between the physicians Van Norden and Scanlon, both recovering from tuberculosis, reflect a deeper philosophical conflict about the limits of reason and the possibility of revelation. William learns from Van Norden, a lewd mentor much like Sutter Vaught, not only to love romantic music and scientific inquiry but also to make a scientific inquiry out of romance. Van Norden's teachings help to corrupt William's friendship with Allison, who now works at the Lodge and plans to leave Sutter. Like Will Barrett in *The Last Gentleman*, William feels a courteous regard for Allison that increasingly conflicts with his sexual passion. When the pair go on an island picnic, William shows that he has indeed become Van Norden's student by asserting how much he wants to know her. On the following weekend he receives another opportunity to study the flesh: an invitation from Van Norden to attend a postmortem. After William discovers that the corpse is Sutter's, he can feel nothing, only the confused restlessness of a seeker who has no home. He finally persuades Allison to make love out of this nothingness, but he feels no love for her, only self-satisfaction that he at last knows the flesh. When William's tuberculosis unexpectedly spreads infection throughout his entire body, the depressed and alcoholic Scanlon gives up his bed in the Doctor's Lodge and ministers to William in his last days. Like Sutter Vaught, he denies knowing any private revelations, yet the two friends spend hours in mysterious, often joyous conversation. Scanlon baptizes William before he dies on August 3, 1943, the day on which the marines begin the invasion of Vella Lavella.

In "The Gramercy Winner" patients in the sanatorium and soldiers overseas share the same struggle and the same disease. Throughout the novel Percy uses the war as a global counterpoint to William's tuberculosis because both signify a more profound catastrophe. At the beginning William lies in bed, regularly listening to news bulletins about the fighting, while the Germans start their advance on Russia. When he first ventures outside the sanatorium, which his mother compares to a POW camp, he feels like a soldier on leave. Mrs. Floyce Sutter includes her son Laverne, who actually dies of Addison's disease, as a battle casualty when she mourns losing two boys to the war. At the end William joins the list of such victims, for his dehydrated body and hardened face remind Scanlon of a marine's after a long tour of combat. Although he never shared Scanlon's fellowship with William, Van Norden uses a similar image when he consoles the Greys that their son died like a gallant soldier. Disease as much as the war threatens to doom the body politic. The doctors are only recovering patients, and the widows who run the rest homes had husbands who died from tuberculosis. An X ray reveals that even Allison may have the same disease, humorously illustrated in a book sent by William's sister. It shows the connection between worldwide and personal disaster by depicting the bacillus as Huber the Tuber, an enemy invader who roams the cells of the lung with a bomb in its hand. In a sick world tuberculosis is only the war within the body.

Although Percy sets William Grey's private apocalypse in a sanatorium against the backdrop of world catastrophe, his castaway fights not war or disease but the pervasive death-in-life that results from spiritual homesickness. He suffers from the same "fatal weakness" as the deluded Nazi armies attacking Russia: "Somewhere a terrible mistake had been made. Each new success, every added mile of the advance, brought them, the flower of German youth, not closer to victory but farther away from home" (GW 1). Where they are defines who they are. Like the land won by the army in its steady progress, medical victories cannot restore exiles to the place from which they started. "The Gramercy Winner" follows William Grey as he approaches his own end as a sickened wayfarer and learns that health and home depend on the orientation of the heart. The "real enemy" that unmindful soldiers and convalescents must overcome is a dulling and deadly abstraction, "a dryness, not hatefulness, but a withering of souls, a drawing away from one another beyond reach or call and into a greyness, a neutrality whose particular horror was the forgetfulness that there had ever been anything else" (GW 211). In Percy's earliest surviving novel, tuberculosis is an incipient stage of what Tom More, himself preoccupied with German slaughter, would discover in Percy's last novel as the thanatos syndrome.

If the disaster of tuberculosis has saved William Grey from the disaster of war, it has brought him to the same curious place that Binx Bolling reaches

33

in *The Moviegoer* when he lies flat under the chindolea bush in Korea or on his bed in Gentilly. Lying motionless in his room at the beginning of the novel, William has arrived at "the dead center of things from where he might look out" (GW 17). In her critique of illness as metaphor, Susan Sontag observes that tuberculosis was often seen as "a way of affirming the value of being more conscious, more complex psychologically."[20] Although the diagnosis hardly means doom for William, the threat of nonbeing drives home to this castaway the peculiar predicament of his own immediate existence. Before his illness Grey faded into the neutrality of his name. "If there was anything remarkable about his past life," the narrator speculates, "it was that absolutely nothing had happened to him" (GW 10). William was not so much an individual as a type for a whole generation of the wealthy and well educated, all having "the same open-faced clear-eyed expression" and keeping into manhood "something of the child, something of the pleasing yet unformed look of a child" (GW 2). The same face blurred into no face as Grey was generalized out of existence, yet he considered such facelessness a sign of good taste. The Gramercy Winner was the consummate spectator, not out of laziness or inability but from a "prescience that excelling, winning, would be almost as gross a lapse as failing" (GW 3). Since he never stood forth in victory or defeat, he paled into amiable banality. Remembered by his classmates as "Nice guy, good man, ace gent" and loved by his parents and servants, William lived by his manners as if he were a study for the equally prepossessing Will Barrett (GW 4). But whereas the last gentleman's empty life before his coming to consciousness is convincingly embodied in several narrative flashbacks, Percy does not use any such revealing anecdotes to dramatize William Grey's lack of identity. Will Barrett may suffer from amnesia, but William Grey has nothing even to forget. The Gramercy Winner has such tangential being that he does not even exist in the beginning novelist's own imagination of nonexistence.

The diagnosis of tuberculosis calls William back to himself like a harbinger of some more distant and final judgment. Since even this minimal form of the disease singles him out of his class, he recognizes that at last something has happened in his eventless life and gladly leaves behind the sad old actualities of his undifferentiated existence for the new possibilities that open before him. William senses that his future draws near with both threats and promises. In the sanatorium William joins the company of mortals, those who live daily against the background of approaching death. Each patient is a temporary winner, reprieved between examinations "until at last one's capital is spent and one is no longer living on past glory but in fear of the judgement to come" (GW 39). Yet William does not so much dread this end as deliver himself to the mechanism of fortune. He is as resigned to the predestined outcome of medical exams as he is submissive to his corresponding destiny in a grander apocalyptic drama:

X-rays were too important to worry about, too big and therefore removed from his responsibility. He might as well worry about the end of the world. It was absurd to think as some did that the verdict could be changed during these last days by taking especial care of oneself. Rather he was certain that he was caught up in the machinery of a much larger judgement, that the wheels had already begun to turn and it was too late now to effect what was being inexorably threshed out for him. (GW 86)

Since his prognosis is as ineluctable as the day of doom, the patient can only yield to the final reckoning. But this impending sentence brings with it a singular blessing. After twenty years of stasis, William intuits that he is moving obscurely toward some terminus even if he does not feel in control of the fateful engine. His awareness of the death sentence has given him back his entire life before its end, so that he now spends each day in quickened attention to what it means to be William Grey. The vigilant castaway searches for news by constantly listening to the war bulletins on the radio and to the reports on the often-declining health of fellow patients; he looks inquiringly at everyone. Like Hans Castorp in *The Magic Mountain* who expects some cataclysm to "snatch life beyond the 'dead point' and put an end to the 'small potatoes' in one terrible Last Day,"[21] William anticipates a climax that once would have seemed unthinkable in his undistinguished past. He waits for some event to happen, some person to come, that will decisively transform his life: "It was almost as if he were expecting something and was assured of its coming, some great good thing the merest thought of which was enough to render everything else trivial and absurd" (GW 6). Having never won or lost, the passive onlooker from Manhattan begins a journey toward becoming the victor of the title, an identity he only discovers at the very heart of loss. But before that apocalypse he seeks the "trivial and absurd" knowledge that will yield immediate and self-gratifying triumphs. Like the German advances, this deadly pursuit of abstracted ways of knowing and loving only takes the wanderer from Gramercy Park farther from the only home that can define him.

Although William lacks the vehemence of Percy's later prophetic critics, his coming to consciousness makes him recognize that other people seem barely alive. He is most like Will Barrett, through whose gentle and innocent eyes Percy exposes a lost world. The Greys understand their son's illness only as incomprehensible loss. "So great a catastrophe" was his confinement to his parents, "so luckily beyond their grasping it, that they had gratefully refused even to try" (GW 59). His mother cannot understand why he rejected a more comfortable sanatorium in favor of an ascetic cell with the odor of disinfectant. She mounts a campaign to win him back into her social orbit by talking of old friends at nearby Lake Placid and the tempting haven of a more likeable place to recover. William's father "wanted to be liked and he wanted to win," but his well-liked son has no desire to win at his father's games, whether amassing the family fortune or playing a round of table tennis (GW 61). Neither of the Greys understands that William has chosen this sanatorium precisely because it offers a bare place for the beginning of a new world. Here he can live decisively and escape from the parents he loves but who have no greater awareness of their own particular lives than do the supposedly healthy people he sees while riding with Allison to the Lodge. He notices how disagreeable or vacant everyone outside the sanatorium seems and promises himself that he will never forget the fierce intensity of living known by the doomed.

William rejects this grayish life where the sick are lost to themselves and in the world. He knows that he "had died to one life and meant to come alive in another. Already he was awakening to a strange new world" (GW 64). Having regained his own lifetime by virtue of his illness, he seeks to find out how to live in this unfamiliar country. The conventions that he both followed and set in the past—the rolling Princetonian walk, the fashionable mismatch of clothes—simply do not apply, because now he lives not as the paragon of his class but as a unique individual before the boundary of his death. He begins by cultivating a scientific version of the spectatorship that has long characterized his life. Since mortality invades his body, he decides to live as little as possible in the flesh by not moving from his bed for six months, speaking hardly at all, and never even wincing when he receives his pneumothorax injections. This shell-shocked detachment partly results from being stunned into consciousness. It allows him to consider the oddity of his own life: as millions work in New York or fight in the war, he lies still and reflects, a self at last aware of being a self. But this withdrawal becomes dangerous because William seems determined to retreat from close observation into complete abstraction.

36

William is not interested in such "non-essentials" as language and literature, the very means of exploring and expressing the human dilemma for a linguist-novelist (GW 6). Instead, he tries to locate the very heart of twentieth-century reality by reading *Subatomic Particles* because he imagines that the book's authors investigate not things but ideas, "mystical quantities" never seen but developed in hypothesis to account for slight miscalculations in scientific formulas (GW 24). William aspires to join their visionary company while he stays on his own magic mountain. He resents the planned visit of his parents because they seem to look over his shoulder as he performs "the most delicate of experiments" (GW 39). He hopes that someday he might discover the grand unifying theory that has eluded all researchers. Physics offers William an escape from the personal and physiological by a kind of ultimate science that transforms the most elementary matter into the pure pursuit of the mind. However, the would-be scientist does not even do much of his planned reading in the field. Despite all of his yearning for transcendent knowledge, he finds himself continually attracted to the curious world much closer at hand as he listens to the vireos in the maple below his window or questions a practical nurse about her date last night at the movies. Although he tries to reduce his life to a mere detail in a larger pattern, "always he was brought back to the oddity of his predicament," especially by Laverne and Allison Sutter (GW 10).

| | | The Sutters prevent William from escaping himself by drawing him into joyous and frustrating existence in the world. Bursting into the life of this solitary watcher and waiter, they come to him suddenly, by surprise, as if *they* were the mysterious event that he long expected, and unhesitatingly offer him a share in their lives. Unlike William, who enjoys the spareness of his room, Lieutenant Sutter arrives at Mrs. McLeod's equipped like "a small army" with six suitcases, golf clubs, and skis (GW 23). This dashing and outgoing wayfarer, very much here and at home in the world, invites the silent William into the closeness of conversation. At their first meeting Sutter talks away the time, telling of his life on army bases and his dealings with doctors as if William were already familiar with them. The Northerner notices in Sutter and his wife something he regards as characteristic of the South: "an aggressive intimacy, a disarming lack of reserve, an easy affection and yet not unambiguous" that completely overcomes his affable politeness by the force of its irresistible cordiality (GW 49). William comes to feel that he has never known anyone as well as he knows Sutter.

37

Allison explains that since her husband usually spends a great deal of his energy in disliking people, he has few friends, yet he depends on people more than anyone else she knows. William serves as his ally, and Sutter is William's necessary bond with the world.

Even when the garrulous lieutenant is not present, William feels more alive. He enjoys the freedom of getting out of his high iron cot, which he now sees clearly not just as a bed but also as the past that he has left behind. He stares at the unfamiliar bathroom, cheaply furnished but light and clean, and walks again in the world, although a little weak-legged. When William tumbles outside Sutter's room, falling at the feet of Allison, with whom he later falls in love, he establishes "a kind of humorous intimacy far beyond the power of introduction" (GW 44). The pratfall obviates weeks of preliminary formalities by putting them on the easy footing of immediate friendship. The three form a family, going for drives, exchanging visits in rooms, listening to the World Series on the radio. The Gramercy Winner has won a temporary home. William's friendship with the Sutters saves him from his impersonal withdrawal into the mystical realm of ideas and brings him the more completely human communion always necessary for Percy's seekers to come fully to themselves. Their hospital camaraderie has the same brave splendor as the Cardinals' victory in four straight games after losing the first game of the World Series to the Yankees. Yet the news of this seemingly impossible triumph was relayed as "a kind of götterdammerung. There was a feeling that Fall of valedictory: that the war would last a long time and no matter how it came out, things would not be quite the same again." Like the Cardinals, the would-be marine, the aviation lieutenant, and the officer's wife achieve a personal victory in "the twilight of a time" (GW 116), for their friendship is always a precarious and uncertain truce enjoyed amid the omens of war. When Laverne and Allison are late in returning from a drive, William foresees that they "had a fatal attraction for disaster, these two. They were the sort to whom things happened" (GW 52). Disaster always looms to jeopardize the trio's domestic intimacy because of the twin complications of living in the world of the body: death and desire.

Unlike William's apparently minor case of tuberculosis, Sutter's possibly fatal Addison's disease threatens their friendship from the first meeting. Sutter fills William with "horrible fascination" as he sits with his feet propped on the bed frame and makes William's scalp prickle with every jolt that he sends through the metal supports (GW 32). That tingle becomes the standard reaction of all of Percy's apocalyptists before the shock of the last day. Much like Peeperkorn in *The Magic Mountain,* Sutter is so compelling because his vital figure embodies the agony of the personal eschaton that William has glimpsed in his own life. As his friend spiels into the night, William notices that despite his hollowed and feverish eyes, the dying soldier gives no sign of stopping but only of talking himself into dementia. His endless words enable him to avoid his imminent doom through living in the only two tenses when winning is possible for him: the past when he hunted for ducks, and the future when he makes impossible plans to raise bird dogs in South Carolina. Sutter still sees himself as he appeared in a photo taken a few years ago, the noble and magnificent soldier, although William thinks that this frail and scholarly looking patient seems less like a lieutenant than anyone else he has known. To preserve this heroic image Sutter adopts the swaggery of tunic pajamas and foulard dressing gown as he lives out this last battle. The manic and melancholy officer disturbs William's comfortable equipoise by preventing him from subsiding into quiescent watchfulness. Sutter's anxious defiance of his own mortality furthers the process by which catastrophe keeps coming closer to home for the Gramercy Winner throughout the novel, until William feels that he too, like Sutter, is under the sentence of death.

Although the two patients share the fraternity of the sick, William also joins Allison as a more detached witness to the lieutenant's doom. Friend and wife each listen with silent exasperation while he repeats already familiar tales. Sutter's illness makes them feel like "the loving parents of an attentive but retarded son, a graceful perennial child whom they loved especially for its very weakness" (GW 88). William becomes virtually all that Sutter and Allison, who have become increasingly estranged, have in common. But the multiple roles of foster brother, surrogate father, and spouse involve William in emotional entanglements that are the inevitable burden of living in the human world rather than in the transcendent sphere to which he once aspired.

The complexities of the Gramercy Winner's double allegiances are played out in his nightly game of hearts with Sutter and Allison. The three pass cards in a ritual of apparent friendship, but Sutter senses an implicit betrayal dealt in his hand. Frustrated by his own illness, which has left him impotent, he grows angry when Allison hands him unlucky cards, and he cannot accept losing the game, especially when he is left with the death-dealing queen of spades. Since the mutual bonds of this triangle limit the expression of their passions, they love and hate indirectly. Sutter never openly vents his rancor at the affection between his comrade and his wife but converts his enmity into criticism of the scotch that William brings for his birthday or into the epithets aimed at a nurse who looks at him askance. Likewise, Allison can only signify her detachment from Sutter through her vacant looks and cordial overtures to William. She resents William's closeness to her husband as much as Sutter envies his friend's intimacy with his wife. When William and Sutter delight in the World Series and in their anticipated escape from Mrs. McLeod's, Allison, the excluded player, reminds them that the baseball championship is only a game. The scoffing of a bad sport expresses her own sense of loss in the ongoing game of hearts that she plays with the Gramercy Winner.

Like her dying husband, Allison both implicates the would-be scientist in the world and heralds his doom. When she drives William to the Lodge for his X ray, he leaves the sanatorium for the first time and rediscovers a lost cosmos as he flies through light and air, feeling as if he has returned "home again, back in the good green land, with all the merit and freedom and happiness of the soldier come home" (GW 107). William idealizes his benefactress as a southern version of Dostoyevski's Sonia. Her visits to Sutter and her ability to convince William's own parents that his life is less gloomy than it seems make Allison resemble "the good little woman in the Russian novels who goes off to Siberia with her man and becomes the sainted little sister to all the poor exiles" (GW 72). William considers it "the surest sign of her noble southern origins" that in the middle of the night she can bring him a stack of mysteries with naked women on their covers and yet never seem improper (GW 52).

Although Allison seems a saintly gentlewoman, Percy's version of Clavdia Chauchat can be as mysterious and provocative as any of the vamps from William's new pile of detective fiction. As Allison leaves his room, William notices how the light falls down her dress. And an embittered Sutter reveals that his wife's own taste in mysteries favors not puzzling whodunits but the more hard-boiled crime stories in which "every other chapter some beautiful babe either gets beat up or laid" (GW 81). Shortly before William leaves for Mrs. Zabel's, he overhears these apparently cordial Southerners during a vicious argument in which they seem "metamorphosed into ravening animals" (GW 119). Sutter charges that his wife is known for picking up in her convertible any second lieutenant she sees standing on a corner. William, who earlier had been told by Allison to dismiss his taxi and accept a ride to the hospital from her, lies paralyzed, "the really incredulous witness of what can take place between man and wife," the passionate intimacy of their hatred

(GW 119). William discovers in Sutter's death and in Allison's ambiguous femininity the consequences of living in the body: mortality and carnality. He had wanted to withdraw to a high and inhuman point where all the complexities of the universe could be resolved by a single scientific principle. However, William's first home offers him neither an orbit beyond this world nor even the communion of perfect friendship. Instead, the Sutters introduce him to the burden of incarnate existence, the whole finite and yearning world of personalities that William had once hoped to escape.

I V   When William has a chance to move to Mrs. Zabel's in part 2, he seems to have left behind his part in this triangle with its entangled alliances, envious affections, and inevitable violations. The seedy luxury of this new hospice offers a more gratifying image of being at home in the world after the exile of his sparsely furnished attic at Mrs. McLeod's. William joins the other patients for dinner rather than eating in his room and begins to take walks as part of his exercise treatment. But the wayfarer discovers that all of the exigencies of the flesh are only intensified at Mrs. Zabel's. William confronts again the same imperatives of eros and thanatos as he is drawn into the jesting rivalry between Van Norden and Scanlon, physicians whose disagreements echo the debates between Settembrini and Naphta in *The Magic Mountain*. Having been baffled by desire and death, William learns from Van Norden the desire that leads to death, and only discovers at his own end the saving love that Scanlon brings amid the ruins.

William immediately dislikes Scanlon because the surgeon will not allow him to escape his doom. When William dismisses his illness as only a minimal lesion, Scanlon correctly reminds him that he suffers from tuberculosis like the rest of the patients. Scanlon insists that William confront the extent of his illnesses, both physical and spiritual, but the mocking and materialistic Van Norden charges his opponent with actually believing that the wages of sin are disease. He caricatures Scanlon as a medieval doctor of physic who believes in humors and demons. Although Scanlon howls with laughter, he recognizes that the sanatorium is a community of those ill in body and soul. Scanlon encourages William to leave as soon as he can because "it's a symbiotic society in an advanced state of decay. It's an organism healthy and suntanned without and all corruption and caseation within. There is a Faustian pact between man and bacillus and each lives feeding on the other. There is a breakdown and liquefaction of all strata and structure. It's all purulence and fornication and whoredom" (GW 146). Scanlon sounds as if he were warning Hans Castorp against the International Sanatorium Berghof rather than warning William Grey against this American *Kurhaus*, for Percy's rest home never acquires the dissolute and demonic air of Mann's Alpine retreat. In a novel that hardly even tries to imitate the panorama of *The Magic Mountain*, the decay is more personal than communal. William is led into this supposedly sick and sinful world through his friendship with Van Norden. He discovers with his mentor the same kind of friendship that he knew with Sutter, "an intimacy peculiar to men, generated by a common adversity and a common endeavor. They were comrades" (GW 140).

Van Norden schools William in the most disembodied ways of knowing and loving. In the name of science he deadens all flesh even before the post-mortem by reducing the human being to nothing more than a system of organs that follow certain predictable laws. Every person becomes a body, similar and anonymous; each body becomes a corpse for Van Norden's analysis, and the corpse becomes the means to arrive at incorporeal truth. Scanlon warns William that Van Norden wants to be seen as "the Selfless Man, the Dedicated Man, the humble worker"; however, the scientist is actually not interested in helping individuals as individuals but simply in discovering the same Grand Theory that William sought when he began studying at Mrs. McLeod's (GW 160). Scanlon jokes that the pathologist would not know how to treat a breathing body. He has no understanding of the human complexities that William has begun to discover, only a passion for pure science and an even greater obsession with his own self as the supreme mind.

Scanlon attends to the person that Van Norden and sometimes even his pupil overlook. When William studies his X rays, he marvels at this "figure of perfect beauty and perfect meaning" (GW 190). Seduced by the abstraction that makes his chest cavity look like an intricate, translucent underwater creature, William is reassured by the loveliness of his physiology that indeed he is like all other people. He does not realize that in adopting Van Norden's aloof intellectuality he has disappeared into the similarities of human anatomy. What William needs to discover is not how he resembles everyone else, but what it means to be uniquely himself. Van Norden conjectures that if William had never undergone the marine physical, the undetected disease would probably never have drastically affected the course of his life. He tries to deny the very illness that has made William examine how he is set apart as William Grey, yet Scanlon protests, "But you see, he did have the x-ray and he's here and that makes the difference" (GW 192). X rays, Susan Sontag writes, enable the tuberculosis patient "to become transparent to oneself." [22]

Scanlon wants William to see into himself by confronting the predicament that is his alone. He faults Van Norden for viewing his patient as a case and overlooking William as a person: "Here's the mystery right under your nose, man! not Willy's lung but Willy himself. How about it, Willy, what's on your mind?" (GW 194).

Scanlon's objections voice what occasionally has been on Willy's mind. When he views not just his lung but himself, William senses the blindness of Van Norden's scientific absolutism. Since William brings the manners of a gentleman to the study of medicine, he is shocked by the professional irreverence of Van Norden and company. These cavalier physicians fail to respect science as sacred. "His very life, he felt obscurely, depended upon the orderly and august procession of judgement, which took place, must take place, in some inner sanctuary of Science. He would as soon these doctors conduct their business behind closed doors. He felt himself delivered over to a gang of boys" (GW 187). William honors physicians as priests in the mystery religion of science, but their scorn profanes some of the necessary mystique that guarantees his life. Although William's medical piety may indicate that he is even more abstracted than the sophomoric doctors, it fosters a healthy outrage at being personally abandoned by science. Its ministers do not really care about his existence and are particularly heedless toward the catastrophe that William anticipates. "How could they be so irresponsible in the face of his imminent doom," he wonders, "—for doom it might be for all they knew." William realizes that he is different from such learned fools, for despite their acquaintance with disease and death, they do not labor under his eschatological awareness. They laugh rather than see the end, but "what he felt with the utmost clarity was the absolute conviction of disaster" (GW 188).

Despite Van Norden's transcendent vision, his cult of objectivity actually conceals only a more passionate form of subjectivity. His apparent neutrality fosters not a selfless detachment from the world but a perverse selfishness expressed in his rage at professional enemies and his clinical treatment of women. William recognizes that supposedly impersonal science is still conducted by personalities as he views the increasingly hostile disputes between Van Norden and Scanlon. He is shocked at the salvos that his mentor fires off in editorial replies to the letters of fellow scientists, for "he had supposed venom and vituperation were excluded from the Temple of Science" (GW 224). The young purist had imagined that the religion of medicine did not allow loyalties and prejudices, but Van Norden's polemical warfare reveals his egotistical involvement in the world that he pretends to transcend.

Women gratify this same scientific conceit by providing carnal knowledge for the pathologist who lives in his head. Van Norden casually tells William of his affairs with a Russian princess who was also his patient and offers to introduce his protegé to her sister. He delivers discourses on the immense variety of female sexual responses and on the superiority of continental attitudes toward the flesh. His lust for science finds its consummation in a virtual science of lust. Because William's own romantic experiences are limited to an awkward kiss, he is embarrassed at Van Norden's sermons and prefers to hear the doctor recount the story of some beguiling diagnosis. By vicariously living in this world of medical abstraction, William can ignore the consequences of such ruthless scientific detachment as his mentor preaches. Accused by Scanlon of organolatry and necrophilia, Van Norden devitalizes women by depersonalizing their flesh, for he can only know and love what is dead.

William learns to embody this fatal view of sexuality. He brags of imaginary liaisons and even suggests that his own illness may have been caused by practicing undefined perversions in a New Jersey brothel. The boasts of the sexual innocent reveal how he has been tainted by the moral illness against which Scanlon warned him. William is sick because he only understands the person as a body that leads to the mind's theories and as a mind that theorizes about the body. Van Norden's intellect makes desire converge with death by reducing both to their physiology—the ecstasy of the autopsy or of anonymous intercourse. Scanlon suggested this fatal intimacy when, like Dr. Krokowski in *The Magic Mountain*, he once proposed an erotic theory of tuberculosis in which the disease impregnates the body of the welcoming Beloved with the sperm of bacilli. Van Norden ridicules his enemy for a typically mystical analysis of the disease, and Scanlon laughs at the recollection, but his outrageous etiology explains a persistent cause of doom in all of Percy's fiction. Van Norden makes sexuality itself corrupt and contagious by reducing it to the union of flesh but not of persons. William is nearly lost as one of the casualties of this deadly syndrome.

Van Norden's teachings prove fertile by infecting William's fondness for Allison. Even before he left Mrs. McLeod's, Allison told him that after years of unhappiness she finally planned to divorce Sutter. However, since she still works to pay her husband's hospital bills and even performs unpaid social work on the weekends, William often feels that he must behave chastely and chivalrously toward this lady from the South. Allison seems to seek an intimacy beyond mere good manners. When the couple walk outside the roadhouse where they have gone with friends for a wartime steak dinner, Allison wishes for the selfsame continuity gained through the perduring knowledge of love: "Everything is so—like nothing now. I wish you could look at me and say, Allison, do you remember the time we— Allison, you were wrong that time—Billy, I feel like I was so many people. I wish I knew one person who knew me all my life and could tell me what I was—!" (GW 218). Allison longs for a different kind of knowledge than the carnality pursued by William's mentor. Such love integrates and affirms identity without exploiting it, admitting to a need for others rather than triumphing in proud isolation. After William tries to cool his desire by breathing the cold air and washing his face in the snow, Van Norden's drunken pupil seeks to wrestle a kiss out of Allison despite her protesting thrusts and blows. Since William has come to understand winning as sexual conquest, the wanderer from Gramercy Park overlooks how much Allison may actually be like himself. She admits to a homesickness that cannot be healed by simply returning to the South, for home is the spiritual city that Percy's lost seekers start from and to which they must return. Allison feels the same restlessness of soul that William only barely understands in himself.

This pair of exiles comes close to discovering each other as fellow castaways from "The Message in the Bottle" when they set out for an island picnic, but William's scientism prevents the retreat from becoming a place of healing for two who seek home. As they explore the mountain, away from the rest of the picnickers, Allison grieves because William does not recognize that he exists complete in her love: he "did not dream that she saw him whole or that he was whole, who imagined instead that he was legion and showed her whichever mysterious self he pleased—the Billy of the cave, of desire, of pilgrimage" (GW 250). Allison, who longed for someone who knew her throughout her entire life, offers William the affirmation of his own wholeness, but he sees himself as a bedeviled collection of roles. Suffering from chronic abstraction, the would-be scientist plays the Billy of desire by arguing that nothing is as important as sexual knowledge. "It's the knowing and the not knowing. . . . If I don't know that I don't know anything" (GW 252). Such experimentation makes Allison secondary and impersonal. "It could be you. It probably is you," he assures her. "But that is all later" (GW 253). Allison rebukes his sad self-obsession: "it's all in you, Billy. I'm left out. I have nothing to do with it. . . . Oh, Billy, you've got it all wrong. What have they done to you?" (GW 253). Allison's diagnosis of William's illness recognizes that she herself is excluded from his eroticism just as William was overlooked by Van Norden's X ray. Billy's sexuality, confined to his head, reduces her to an object of inquiry for his private intellectual pleasure.

William's scientific devaluation of his life is nearly a terminal condition. When the Sutters finally complete his initiation into the facts of death and life, he feels how the lust for knowledge brings disaster to the world of the body by emptying the flesh of all significance. The funeral home where William goes to view a postmortem at Van Norden's invitation minimizes death. The nondescript building easily blends into the other residences, so that the town's mortality rate becomes just another ordinary statistic like the amount of rainfall. Absorbed into the norm, death never stands out as the unique crisis that may bring a life into focus. William watches an autopsy conducted there with the same depersonalized abstraction. Van Norden skillfully slices out triangular cross-sections of organs and hoses away the merest trace of blood that might indicate they came from a once-living body. He is jubilant because the stark physicality of the cadaver makes possible the consummate deductions of his mind. Percy does not at first reveal that the body is Sutter's because such identity has no significance to Van Norden. His intellect reduces William's one-time ally to just another corpse.

Van Norden views the autopsy as another medical lesson for William and asks his pupil to describe precisely what he sees. Reality extends just as far below the surface as the pathologist's eye can observe, but Van Norden understands the immanent world only to the extent that it conforms to a transcendent model. The body exists to confirm his theories. Although William answers Van Norden's questions with clinical precision, he is aware of what cannot be seen: the corpse's face, obscured by a flap of skin cut from the chest and curling around the neck. Van Norden imagines that his probing can fathom Sutter's inward nature. Since he does not have permission to make any incision in the head, he extracts the medulla through the throat so that he can prove his scientific contention. The sight returns William from his physiological understanding of the body, coolly expounded in anatomy texts, to the actuality of bone, organs, and blood. He sees that Van Norden's abstraction eviscerates humanity until the body is left in shambles, "a hopeless enigma, almost a blank space in the room" (GW 262). William realizes that although Van Norden pronounces a medical last judgment on the body, science cannot draw any conclusions about the person, for the dead man has taken his innermost secrets with him. His name, the very word for his self, is unknown. Van Norden's ignorance exemplifies Percy's argument in *Diagnosing the Modern Malaise* that the scientist "cannot utter a single word about an individual thing or creature insofar as it is an individual but only insofar as it resembles other individuals."[23] The doctor understands why an organism has died, yet he has overlooked the more elusive mystery of an individual's identity. William strains to see, hoping to discover the final revelation that he has long sought (GW 264). But when William finally examines the corpse's head and sees death in all its personal and bare-faced horror, he can feel nothing. Van Norden's pathological vision makes the living as moribund as the dead.

William's indifference compels him to examine what difference his friend made. As if trying to search for the Sutter whom no one even glimpsed at the postmortem, William revisits his old home at Mrs. McLeod's, but the returning stranger discovers there a similar lack of difference. He overhears Mrs. Capp joking with a young man in his former room just as she used to jest with William, and he finds Sutter's room empty of his many possessions, swabbed with disinfectant to eliminate every trace of his very presence. What disturbs William is that he can so easily return, for Sutter's death has apparently left no decisive mark. Nothing shows that he has died, and no one seems to notice the difference: "*Dear Lord, what has become of Sutter? The waters have closed over his head without a ripple*" (GW 287). William, however, is baffled by a fundamental lack, the loss of Sutter as Sutter, who cannot be defined by an autopsy or by his anonymous room.

Sutter's death makes William begin to realize that the knowledge he has sought is actually not the knowledge he needs. Van Norden's teaching leaves William only with the vacancy of being unable to feel for or understand the person of Sutter. However, William cannot see beyond these negations. Rather than using such blankness as the means to discover who Sutter is in the face of who he is not, he comes to hate in Sutter "this miserable inertia" (GW 286). The patient who never left Mrs. McLeod's thereby brought upon himself the insignificance of his own death. William reasons that since Sutter never did anything different, his life and death could make no difference. He deserves his own nothingness. Sutter's death brings William close to confronting the irreducible mystery of existence, but when rage and frustration prevent him from going further, he resorts to the dehumanizing objectivity that he has learned from Van Norden. Having seen the dead body of Sutter, William embraces the death-in-life of abstracted intercourse. This erotic

47

strain of tuberculosis kills both lover and beloved by making them nothing more than pure, probing intelligence and yielding object for scientific exploration.

If Van Norden's penetrating eye reduced Sutter's death to insignificance in the scientist's pursuit of knowledge, William now seeks insignificant sex as a means of knowing Sutter's wife. Always somewhat detached from her husband's anguish, Allison seems rather unaffected by his death, as if for her too it had made little difference. William makes love with her out of despair at such insignificance, but his impersonal passion hollows carnality as much as Van Norden's professional egotism has exhausted mortality. When William insists that he wants Allison on her back, just after she has been tracing the channel down his own spine, she asks if he ever thought of her as human. Although Allison has often behaved with sometimes confusing wantonness, she seems to understand sexuality as personally rather than abstractly embodied. But when William finally affirms that he loves her, she orders, "Get up and lock the door" (GW 296). If her bossy compliance is unconvincing, Percy ignores the unresolved contradictions of her character to show how William's reduction of love to a science of sex causes his doom. After spending several days with him, Allison seems to have fulfilled her role as temptress and abruptly disappears from the novel, except for William's later glimpse of her as she sits with Van Norden in the summerhouse. He recognizes their similar attraction to disaster: "they both like big sad things. Van Norden likes to talk about the end of the world, of civilization and all that stuff—you know. And Allison likes to talk about a Way of Life and how it ended with The War. They both like lost wars" (GW 319). Their marriage, mentioned in the epilogue, is a match between historical pessimists. Drawn to such doom-haunted men as Sutter and Van Norden, Allison becomes the classic woman from her mystery novels, William's femme fatale.

V   None of William's doctors can explain the sudden deterioration in his condition. Their objectivity prevents them from realizing that the patient, who is actually glad to have become a puzzling case study, is dying because of his passionate abstraction. His failing health proves Scanlon's erotic etiology of tuberculosis: the perversion of love may breed death. William has become so completely Van Norden's pupil that he assigns his sexual initiation the ultimacy of apocalypse and deludes himself that the "one event, perhaps, that he had awaited all his life took place. He changed. The secret he had sought, he had found out. He knew" (GW 301). William imagines that the consummation of the flesh has brought him the climactic revelation that his mind long sought, but his very conception of this end reveals its inadequacy. "In knowing her he might turn his back on her," he concludes. "It was precisely the knowing of her that made him free of her" (GW 302). William turns carnal knowledge into the means to scientific transcendence so that sexual intercourse simply becomes the ultimate form of research. Genuine revelation never dispels mystery for Percy's seekers; rather, it makes them aware of the mystery around them and compels them to search even further. William's newly acquired knowledge simply puts a summary end to his quest: "where before she was mystery and he half insane with the not knowing, now she was woman and he was man and he was quiet with the knowing" (GW 302). William settles for a smug and self-exhausting discovery of sexual roles rather than the ever-gradual disclosure of personal identity.

Having tried to live as a scientist of the body, William is recalled to his flesh by his own mortality. Disease and death were always foreign to him. William contracted only a minor case of tuberculosis, and even when confined to bed once with pleurisy, he took pleasure in the sweet safety of his illness. Since the malady never really threatened him but was just severe enough to heighten his singular appreciation of the world, he enjoyed the peculiar well-being of the infirm who know they will recover. He further protected himself by remaining aloof from the news of the war's casualties, Lieutenant Sutter and his longtime friend George Boetjeman. But at the end he can neither savor the catastrophe with delight nor set it at a distance, for it comes home to his own flesh. The Gramercy Winner wins by losing. The dark night of the body brings him near to fatal despair until he hears the good news amid the ruins.

William's illness marks the departure point for his final journey home. When he wakes in part 3, he has been moved to Scanlon's cottage through the hospitality of the doctor who surrenders his own place to an always displaced person. The stop is only another way station, however, for William still yearns to travel, perhaps to Quebec or Arizona, to any place that can chart his own spiritual restlessness. In the past he waited; now the wanderer felt that he "was going. Fatefully the wheels had begun to turn and he was on his way—to what he could not say" (GW 302). Hearing a train even in his sleep, William cannot remain stationary in his newly gained knowledge of the flesh. His own approaching death seems to drive him beyond such self-satisfaction to become one of Percy's archetypal men on the train. Disaster is the vehicle for his salvation, as it is for the commuter in "The Man on the

Train" who sees his hand for the first time only after he has a heart attack on the New York Central. William finally sees the wreckage of his life and then sees the home beyond it.

Only Scanlon recognizes both the physical and metaphysical origins of William's virulence. Ill at ease with the old mountains, the consumptives, Van Norden, and even William himself, the physician speaks frankly out of his own suffering from the malaise. Its symptoms—his reputed alcoholism and disreputable behavior—have already made Scanlon a professional disgrace like the later Sutter Vaught. Although all he wants is to leave the sanatorium and open a service station on Route 66, he provides a more necessary service simply by being the most comprehensive of scientists. Scanlon understands science in "its current and narrow sense of the isolation of secondary causes in natural phenomena" as well as in what Percy calls "its original and broad sense of discovering and knowing." [24] He alone diagnoses the typhoid-like miliary that has scattered the tubercular bacilli like seeds throughout William's body. But he also detects the faulty gnosis that is always deadly for Percy's apocalyptists, glimpses the potential grace of William's catastrophe, and nurses him into new life. Scanlon holds William in the last stages of his disease, reassuring him, giving him drugs that bring a new burst of euphoria. He visits William in the grayness before dawn, when more than at any other time all the physicians' remedies seem ineffective, and he helps William to face the sickness that no medicine can possibly relieve: the sad hollowness plaguing all his life.

Suffering from nausea, William finally brings up the empty reduction of his existence in a weary profession of nihilism. The young man who once knew Sutter as a fellow subject asks Scanlon what he was thinking when he realized that the object of the autopsy was Sutter. Scanlon charitably replies that he wondered how William must have felt, but William admits that he could think of nothing, and that his blankness finally revealed the goal of his search: "The one thing I have been absolutely sure of all my life is that one day I was going to *know* something. There has not been a second of my life when I was not aware of 'it'—and there have been many times when I was on the very verge of knowing. Sometimes I felt that I already did know and that all I had to do was just look and see" (GW 328). At the postmortem William discovered what Lancelot Lamar would later see at the end of his quest, "The secret is that there is nothing" (GW 328). He explains that as in the story about the emperor's new clothes, most people are afraid to point out this essential and obvious vacancy, and so they create false explanations

for why a soldier is killed or someone dies of tuberculosis. "The materialist has a version, the vitalist has a version, Van Norden has a version, you
have your version. And the one thing that never occurred to anybody is that
there is no version. *There is nothing*" (GW 329). Looking at the naked body of
Sutter, William has seen beyond the bare flesh by uncovering a more radical
barrenness.

William's nihilism is the evacuation of all in which he had previously placed
his faith. His desire to know has led him beyond even Van Norden, whose
knowledge of the corpse seems just another disguise that disintegrates before William's more searching exposure of the void. He can know no body
and no thing because of the essential nothingness. Having made this confession, William again feels that he has finally won the secret long sought and
delights in "a solid sense of profit. His fortune was made," as if to win is to
see the underlying loss that all seek to conceal (GW 326). Yet the Gramercy
Winner does not seem content even with the feverish despair that such an
annihilating vision incorporates. William's sight of nothingness is actually
the beginning of hope because it clears away all the illusions so that he may at
last be open to genuine revelation. Hence, he keeps asking Scanlon what his
friend knows but is not telling him. William does not inquire about medical
knowledge but about that fundamental enlightenment which makes Scanlon
seem to sit like a Buddha beside his bed, staring at nothing. Like Fathers
Smith, John, and Weatherbee, Scanlon is one of Percy's failed messengers
who bear the word only at the last hour. Far from being proselytizers, they
often prefer silence, partly because of their own weakness, but also because of
their awareness that Percy's intellectual seekers can so easily hear revelation
as simply more information. Scanlon keeps denying that he has any special
knowledge. What he knows is not a truth to be told, a sublime version of Van
Norden's scientific intelligence, but news that must be lived through dying.

In the end William's sufferings enable him to heed the message at first
hand. Unlike the other detached physicians, Scanlon enters into his friend's
agony, so that when dawn finally comes, the sleeping William seems the
healthy one and the doctor mortally ill. Scanlon points the way for William's
journey by asking the castaway about his religion. After William replies that
his family is Unitarian on both sides, the wanderer from Gramercy Park hears
in the question a spiritual direction. He cries that he is homesick and has
been so all his life. William's search for knowledge has unknowingly been a
misguided quest for the good news from the first and true home across the
sea. His bonds with Sutter, Allison, Van Norden, and Scanlon have been at-

tempts to assuage the loneliness of exile, a separation from the source of his being that appears at its most devastating in his vision of total loss, the nothingness of any knowledge. Having named this bereavement, William Grey seeks a favor for the first time in his life: he asks Scanlon not to leave him.

Disaster drives William to rediscover his original communion with the companion of his youth, George Boetjeman. William has sought to recover this foremost bond in all of his friendships, even with Allison, who strides like a long-legged boy when she wears William's clothes during the island picnic and shows "a quick boy's response, the gift of understanding and the gift of silence" (GW 230). The Gramercy Winner first shared with George the comedy of losing. When the two would play checkers in prep school, it "was funny to beat George and even funnier to get beat. It was really very funny, the very act of losing—when George decoyed him and jumped four or five kings" (GW 239). As they howled with explosions of laughter, defeat was transformed into hysterical rejoicing because it lost its ultimacy by being absorbed into a more lasting fellowship. William had wandered so far away from this primal connection that when he learned of George's death by a battlefield sniper, he felt nothing, just as he did at Sutter's autopsy. He waited, expecting it to portend some future event. But the news also made no difference, for the very ability to feel loss had itself been lost in the anesthesia of William's abstraction.

As William lies dying, the memory of George keeps coming back to the young man who always expected some mysteriously significant advent. William especially recalls the day when he and George were returning on a train from Christmas vacation in Aiken. After he awakens from this dream memory in Scanlon's room, William feels "an agreeable sense of profit, as from a successful transaction of the night before" (GW 310). The new place of confinement, a trim metal-and-glass ship of a room, becomes one more stage in the journey begun years ago in his friendship with George. His haunting recollection of a fellow traveler preserves a spiritual truth that is especially healthy because the "particular horror" of the malaise is "the forgetfulness that there had ever been anything else" (GW 211). After that memorable Christmas vacation, the fifteen year olds planned to spend the day together before going to their homes. Since they had time before the movies opened, William suggested that they walk down to the Battery to catch the elevated and ride uptown. George did not really want to go, "but he went anyway because he was very fond of William and because he didn't want to be left alone" (GW 331). As they walked through the vaulted waiting room of Penn Station, George passed first through the concourse and into the city, and now, after a lifetime of looking and being lost, William follows him.

William's enigmatic memory of this holiday in New York with George Boetjeman becomes a proleptic image of the communion amid all wayfarers, living and dead, that William achieves as he sets out for his final destination. Although Van Norden later consoles the Greys that their son died like a gallant soldier with a song on his lips, William's victory transcends such stoicism. Rather, he travels beyond his personal doom to arrive at renewal and restoration. When William awakens in these last days, he is so elated that he inspires friends and family to talk among themselves and even smile. The joy of Percy's wanderer comes from his new sense of spiritual direction as he follows a friend. As William dies, he calls often for Scanlon, who plays the role of news bearer at last. They talk in low voices "as if he were imparting information, data, of great value and usefulness, William interrupting once in a while to put a short sharp question. It was as if one were going somewhere and the other were giving him instructions for the journey" (GW 336). Scanlon's whispered advice enables William to join George in a sacramental progress through death. No one can fathom their secret meetings punctuated by laughter, the humor amid defeat that William once shared with his boyhood friend. And the night supervisor is scandalized when she sees Scanlon sneaking into William's room with a glass of water to baptize him shortly before he slips into an irreversible coma. Since the words of grace are always disgraceful when judged by the manners of Van Norden's scientific society, Scanlon later resigns, and after disappearing for a while takes a job as a resident physician in a small Catholic sanatorium. He has oriented a lost seeker to the divine way at the end, yet those who overhear these sessions simply react to the gospel as if it were more of the knowledge that William has been seeking. Percy does not even record exactly what Scanlon tells his friend, for revelation only speaks to a listener otherwise in jeopardy of losing self and soul. Although William dies of a meningeal infection on August 3, 1943, the pilgrim from Gramercy Park journeys beyond the terminus of death. He wins home thanks to God's grand mercy.

Percy seems a little baffled when he tries to explain in "From Facts to Fiction" how he wrote "two bad novels and then a third which is a great deal better." He can only account for the progress as a kind of aesthetic apocalypse, relying on images of ruin and renovation that he would repeat over the next two decades to describe his process of writing. Failure and discouragement regularly follow all of one's most diligent efforts: "Then there comes a paradoxical moment of collapse-and-renewal in which one somehow breaks with the past and starts afresh. All past efforts are thrown into the wastebasket, all advice forgotten. The slate is wiped clean. It is almost as if the discouragement were necessary, that one has first to encounter despair before one is entitled to hope. Then a time comes when one takes a pencil and paper and begins. Begins, really for the first time."[25]

"The Gramercy Winner" does not mark such a beginning in Percy's fiction because William remains for most of the novel curiously disembodied, watching and waiting but not wandering. The novel comes closest to re-creating Percy's own self-discovery in the ruins—"what it means to be a man living in the world who must die"—when it portrays losing or winning.[26] "The Gramercy Winner" transforms this existential insight into such scenes as Sutter's autopsy or the beginning of William's spiritual homecoming, yet it never conveys the reality of "living in the world" by giving William a personal or family past and by making the sanatorium into a genuinely credible, rather than merely symbolic, setting. When Percy returns in *The Last Gentleman* to the story of a young man's gnostic quest in the company of his ambivalent lady and fornicating mentor, he makes his searcher live in a fictional time and place even if his engineer tries to live outside them. Will Barrett bears a grievous legacy as he travels from New York to Ithaca, Mississippi, and finally to Santa Fe, but William Grey, a more muted and undefined Northerner, never really seems to live until the last pages.

Unlike Percy's later, more irresolute apocalypses, "The Gramercy Winner" ends with a strong sense of closure finalized by William's death and by the epilogue that tells the fates of the novel's principal characters, yet the progress to that end never becomes as vividly realized as the end itself. In this early book of revelation, Percy saw the eschaton more clearly than he depicted daily existence in history. After "The Gramercy Winner," however, he discovered the kind of renewal that made the very act of writing itself the apocalyptic adventure that he records in "From Facts to Fiction." Percy recalls that in writing *The Moviegoer* he abandoned the traditional concepts of plot and character because they reflected "a view of reality which has been called into question. Rather would I begin with a *man* who finds himself in a *world*, a very concrete man who is located in a very concrete place and time. Such a man might be represented as *coming to himself*."[27] The doctor

54

faced precisely that apocalypse in the catastrophe of his illness and tried to re-present it in "The Gramercy Winner." But in *The Moviegoer* Percy finally came to himself as a novelist by discovering not just the end of the world but the world itself, standing out more concretely in its hour and locale at the end. Here Percy began, really for the first time.

LAST PICTURE SHOW

THE MOVIEGOER

I   Binx Bolling, the moviegoer of Percy's first published novel, never mentions having seen Stanley Kramer's apocalyptic *On the Beach* (1959). Five years later, Stanley Kubrick's *Dr. Strangelove: Or How I Learned to Stop Worrying and Love the Bomb* would have delighted his "death house" sense of humor toward an age that fears "not that the bomb will fall but that the bomb will not fall" (*M* 193, 228).[1] But at the end of *The Moviegoer* (1961) Binx views a disquieting scene true to the spirit of both of these end-of-the-world films. The sky is yellow and smoky; New Orleans's Elysian Fields "glistens like a vat of sulphur," and the playground where Binx is accustomed to sit while planning what movie to see that evening "looks as if it alone had survived the end of the world." Amid the ruins of the city and his own life, Binx comes to a revelation: "Is it possible that—For a long time I have secretly hoped for the end of the world and believed with Kate and my aunt and Sam Yerger and many other people that only after the end could the few who survive creep out of their holes and discover themselves to be themselves and live as merrily as children among the viny ruins. Is it possible that—it is not too late?" (*M* 231). Kubrick's zany countdown to Armageddon and Kramer's more sobering melodrama about the aftermath of a nuclear catastrophe showed an anxious nation of moviegoers their possible doom in the cold war. The film of Percy's moviegoer plays to a more private audience. New Orleans still stands, neither renovated to live gloriously up to its name nor even reduced to ruins, for the wreckage is only a self-projection. The scenery beheld by Binx's inner eye makes visible his own unseen catastrophe and suddenly brings into focus the moviegoer's apocalyptic drama. Binx now realizes what he has been trying to evade throughout the novel: the end of the world is both what he most feared and, almost unknowingly, most desired.

Binx sees coming attractions of this last picture show from the beginning of the novel. As he dresses for work a week before the end, the stockbroker views his possessions for a startling first time on an ordinary Wednesday morning and glimpses an apocalyptic vision in the radical sense of which Percy is so fond. The revelation unveils what has been actually hidden by being so apparently and excessively obvious.

> But this morning when I got up, I dressed as usual and began as usual to put my belongings into my pockets: wallet, notebook (for writing down occasional thoughts), pencil, keys, handkerchief, pocket slide rule (for calculating percentage returns on principal). They looked both unfamiliar and at the same time full of clues. I stood in the center of the room and gazed at the little pile, sighting through a hole made by thumb and forefinger. What was unfamiliar about them was that I could see them. They might have belonged to someone else. A man can look at this little pile on his bureau for thirty years and never once see it. It is as invisible as his own hand. Once I saw it, however, the search became possible. (*M* 11)

If the images in the Book of Revelation dissolve into each other in an almost cinematic flow,[2] Binx's vision begins when the moviegoer spies through his makeshift camera lens the signs of his personal apocalypse.

Binx's revelation at once exposes his old way of seeing and initiates a new form of perception. The shift in perspective causes the loss of one world and the attainment of another. Since whatever is seen on the screen determines reality, a moviegoer's cosmos depends primarily on vision. Hence, even such a trivial moment as sighting his belongings for the first time means that Binx has regained an unfamiliar universe. Once sitting obliviously in the dark, the moviegoer now beholds the projector's pale blue beam that lights up his world. Binx's new watchfulness appropriately begins with the most ordinary objects possible. Because the items normally stuffed into his pockets neither merit any description nor deserve any attention, they perfectly typify Binx's theatrically nondescript exile in Gentilly. For the past four years Binx has pretended not to exist by dedicating himself to an almost manic cultivation of unconsciousness. He chose the most standardized life possible and made himself disappear into an all-encompassing abstraction—as commonplace and uncompelling as car keys, as familiar and heedless as a wallet. "I am a model tenant and a model citizen and take pleasure in doing all that is expected of me," the supernumerary drones about his very minor part on the American scene (*M* 6). The first-person pronoun degenerates into a series of impersonal generalizations, for Binx was actually a blank, a no one living nowhere at no particular time.

Binx has hardly ever existed at all because of his inertia, his vicarious life in the movies, and his routine work where he meets his equally routine loves. He has surrendered his identity to his diploma, GI discharge, and stock certificates, while he takes pleasure in receiving "a neat styrene card with one's name on it certifying, so to speak, one's right to exist" (*M* 7). John Bickerson ("Binx") Bolling can rightfully claim neither the patrician title to his life nor his own jaunty soubriquet. He has become so anonymous and invisible that he needs official validation for what Percy regards as the very symbol of one's being. Perhaps most disastrously, Binx has tried to secure himself against catastrophe, the very means of renewal in apocalypse. Into his drab olive strongbox, sturdy against theft and double-walled against fire, he has deposited all the papers that preserve his own dubious existence. Binx's compulsive care for his shadowy status quo proves that he needs catastrophe above all else.

Binx's new vision foreshadows that approaching disaster. "But things have suddenly changed," he notices. "My peaceful existence in Gentilly has been complicated" (*M* 10). Seeing his personal effects as if they really were personal jolts him out of his drowsy unawareness about his own life. On Wednesday morning, the most middling day of the week, the most everyday items dispel the everydayness that has made Binx feel as if he has lost both the cosmos and the microcosm. He comes to consciousness, which for Percy is never pure but always a consciousness *of* something (*MB* 272). In recovering his belongings as belongings, he recovers his identity as Binx Bolling. His possessions are not props, Gentilly is not a setting in a studio, and he is not just a Hollywood "extra." Rather, he is extra—that extraordinary and extravagant self that is always perplexingly left over because it can never be completely reduced to a role.

Binx comes to himself by becoming conscious of how he is both alienated from and involved in the world around him. When he perceives the contents of his pocket as foreign, he discovers himself as other, detached from his surroundings, standing over and above his belongings. Percy's stockbroker is amazed to behold the opposite of the greedy self-dispossession described in *Lost in the Cosmos* when consumers devour their goods until their novelty and uniqueness are lost in the black hole of the self (*LC* 21–25). Binx sees not absorption but differentiation. Lost in his everyday world so that there was virtually no difference between himself and his wallet full of credit cards, identity cards, and library cards, he now views the wallet as wallet. Keys become not the means for taking a seductive spin to the Gulf Coast but car keys anew. The slide rule, no longer calculating his passion for making money, is restored to being a slide rule at last. Once Binx recognizes the space between himself and the discrete boundaries of his too-common property, the everyday once again becomes available and valuable to him. His new sense of detachment is thus balanced by a renewed awareness of his bonds with the cosmos, a nexus made concrete by the mysterious pile of objects that are at once familiar but "at the same time full of clues." If he examines his belongings with the impartial gaze of a detective inspecting a dead man's possessions, he also scrutinizes them with the fascination of one searching for a solution. These signs of his existence now on Wednesday morning and here in New Orleans tease him with meaning and implicate him in the very world from which he is set apart. Since Percy believes that the "end of the age came when it dawned on man that he could not understand himself by the spirit of the age, which was informed by the spirit of abstraction" (*MB* 26), Binx has awakened on Wednesday morning to a new era.

Binx's apocalypse at the beginning of the novel is actually his second coming. He claims that his search first began not on Wednesday morning but years before while he lay bleeding in a ditch in Korea: "I came to myself under a chindolea bush. . . . Six inches from my nose a dung beetle was scratching around under the leaves. As I watched, there awoke in me an immense curiosity. I was onto something" (*M* 10–11).[3] Since catastrophe intensifies notice of what is least catastrophic, Binx perceived the ordinary cosmos in the negligible dung beetle. He felt the kind of revelation that comes not by personal force but by having the world forced into his face with the surprise of its gratuitous existence. "Perhaps there was a time when everydayness was not too strong and one could break its grip by brute strength," he speculates. "Now nothing breaks it—but disaster" (*M* 145). In becoming aware of the insect, Binx discovered his own consciousness; after the war, however, he lost the urgency to explore his life under the threat of death until the sleeper finally rose from his living death on Wednesday morning. Although no obvious disaster explodes the everydayness of a peaceful morning that begins as every Wednesday might, the Korean veteran wakes that morning with the taste of war in his mouth and discovers that except in body he has been metamorphosed into the dung beetle that he sighted in Korea. He is one typical dweller in what he later scorns as the age of excrement. This vision is equally catastrophic because it returns Binx to his wartime search for how to live at the end of his world.

Although Binx does not record his Wednesday morning apocalypse in the earliest pages of *The Moviegoer*, his presentiment of doom looms over the formal beginning of the novel. The opening triptych of scenes shifts from present-tense narration to memory in a series of quick cuts that lack any apparent connections, but this cinematic montage actually dramatizes the moviegoer's awareness of how his life is beginning to end. In the first scene Binx tells of receiving an invitation from his aunt to Wednesday lunch: "It will be extremely grave, either a piece of bad news about her stepdaughter Kate or else a serious talk about me, about the future and what I ought to do" (*M* 3). Binx does not yet realize that his future and his cousin's fate are intertwined, but from the very beginning of the novel he senses the ominous significance of this visit. Binx's reaction to this portentous message is characteristically mixed. He considers a serious talk with his formidable aunt "enough to scare the wits out of anyone," yet he does not find "the prospect altogether unpleasant" (*M* 3). John the Divine knows the moviegoer's same blend of displeasure and delight when he eats the scroll in Revelation that tastes sweet but is sour to his stomach (Rev. 10:8–11), a paradoxical response that Percy calls "the authentic oxymoronic flavor of pleasurable catastrophe" in his review of the eschatological science fiction novel *A Canticle for Leibowitz*.[4] Emily's melodramatic gravity promises too many thrills to be completely unappealing for such a confirmed moviegoer; however, as long as Binx reacts merely with an enjoyable tremor, he will never get beyond the emotional self-indulgence of a satiated boulevardier to the more drastic response of changing his heart.

Emily's fateful invitation reminds Binx of another message of doom, also announced by his aunt, more than twenty years earlier. Even as a child Binx was attuned to disaster. "Something extraordinary had happened all right," he remembers. Behind the hospital where the blowers and incinerators seemed to exude the odor of carnality, his aunt told him, "I've got bad news for you, son. . . . Scotty is dead" (*M* 4). Binx responded to this report of the end with typical ambivalence, taking pleasure in his aunt's leisurely conversation yet feeling an anxious surge of adrenaline. But the bad news was not merely a stimulus to an aesthetic or physical response. Binx began to come to himself amid the wreckage when he realized that his aunt's advice to act like a soldier simply asked too little of him. Binx's memory actually foresees his future. At the end of the novel he will repeat the same discovery about Emily's military code and recover the merriment of childhood amid the catastrophe of another brother's death.

In the third of the opening scenes the moviegoer recalls a film in which an accident causes a man to lose not only his memory but also his entire old and deservedly forgotten world. Since Binx feels as foreign as a castaway, he can sympathize with the stranger's dilemma when the film character finds himself in an unknown city: "It was supposed to be a tragedy, his losing all this, and he seemed to suffer a great deal" (*M* 4). Percy's exile in New Orleans does not overlook the more salutary dimensions of the catastrophe, however, for the amnesiac has been freed to discover a new world in his life on a houseboat with the local librarian. Hollywood has filmed Binx's own fantasies of romance amid the ruins, but he can neither forget the past nor discover a future of love with any of his very similar secretaries. In Percy's fragmented but finely edited opening sequence, Binx glimpses both his aunt's ethical fatalism and the screen world's sentimentalized apocalypse that he must finally reject as too simplistic a way to live out his revelation.

Emily Bolling shares her nephew's sense of an ending but lacks any intimation of a search that might lead beyond the ruins. As the heir of the southern stoic tradition, she views her age with eloquent pessimism, yet her grandly rhetorical set pieces on the decline of the West do not lessen in any way her dedication to a soldier's heroism. In the midst of the gloom Emily stands as implacably as did Marcus Aurelius. As Binx and his aunt walk along the promenade on Wednesday afternoon, she pronounces her own credo—a Roman matron's version of "This I Believe," the Edward R. Murrow program that Binx regularly enjoys on radio: "The world I know has come crashing down around my ears. The things we hold dear are reviled and spat upon. . . . It's an interesting age you will live in—though I can't say I'm sorry to miss it. But it should be quite a sight, the going under of the evening land. That's us all right. And I can tell you, my young friend, it is evening. It is very late" (*M* 54).

Emily sees signs of the imminent end all around her, from the obscenity shouted on Prytania Street to her own unstable family—the sorrowful Kate and seemingly dissolute Binx—who lack her dedication to a high moral purpose. But she has the apocalyptist's ability to understand this apparent disorder. Despite its surreal images and scenes of destruction, apocalypse is not at all illogical, for it seeks meaning in and behind the apparent confusion. As Emily prophesies the coming collapse, Binx realizes that "for her too the fabric is dissolving, but for her even the dissolving makes sense. She understands the chaos to come" (*M* 54). Emily views the coming catastrophe as the inevitable consequence of society's forsaking the ideals dear to her conservative tradition, and in the face of such disaster she knows exactly how to act. She simply reasserts the warrior's discipline to the very end. "A man must live by his lights and do what little he can and do it as best he can. In this world goodness is destined to be defeated. But a man must go down fighting" (*M* 54). Consistently described by Binx in martial images, she resolves like a soldier to go down fighting for adherence to inner integrity as the inevitably futile means of illuminating her twilit world.

Emily's stoic apocalypse gains a certain grandeur because she seems so alone in her stalwart battle. At lunch on Wednesday she asks for defenders against the barbarians at the inner gate and chides Kate's fiancé as well as Binx for their fecklessness. Jules Cutrer, her husband, is completely ignorant of any siege on his eternal city. Although the apocalyptist must reject the present order in favor of a completely new way of existence, Binx's contented uncle would keep his secular city just as he loves it, full of cavalier charm and shrewd business deals. Untroubled by the anxiety that drives Binx to seek a new world, Jules finds "the world he lives in, the City of Man, is so pleasant that the City of God must hold little in store for him" (*M* 31). This former Mardi Gras king prefers to reign in New Orleans rather than in the New Jerusalem. So great is his faith in this agreeable and easygoing earthly paradise that Jules believes nothing can really go wrong in his household. He even absorbs the catastrophe of Kate's breakdown into the ordinary course of events as if it were only "the sort of normal mishap which befalls sensitive girls" (*M* 34). Since Jules cannot understand any need for judgment or re-creation, he never imagines the cataclysm that his wife foresees with such unflinching eyes.

Although Emily shares the Book of Revelation's despair for the current, corrupt age, her vision is not genuinely apocalyptic. Judged by the biblical tradition, Binx's aunt is at once too pessimistic and not pessimistic enough. This mournful prophetess lacks any openness to the future; she sees only an end—certain defeat at the triumph of hoi polloi—but no new beginning. Yet Emily finally compromises the hopelessness of her stoic apocalypse by a romanticization as deluded as Hollywood's, for she actually places too much hope in her ethical humanism. Although she disapproves of her nephew's own idle moviegoing, Emily herself produces a film in her own mind that idealizes her household to make her private acting company fit into her high-minded scenario. "She transfigures everyone," according to Binx, casting each member in a noble role of her own devising (*M* 49). Mercer acts the part of devoted family retainer, Jules and Sam Yerger are latter-day Catos, and Binx, himself wounded in Korea, fights as his aunt's legionnaire. Playing the starring role, Emily arms herself with the sword of her letter opener and valiantly tries to keep the mediocre rabble from storming the gates of her Garden District home.

Emily's consummate illusion is her vision of "the new messiah, the scientist-philosopher-mystic who is to come striding through the ruins with the *Gita* in one hand and a Geiger counter in the other" (*M* 181–82). This apocalyptic deliverer of a broken world would heal the deep rifts in the post-Cartesian age that Binx frequently recognizes when he contrasts scientific humanism and romanticism, businessmen and dreamers. Although Revelation looks to a triumphant return of the Lord who lived so completely in time that he died, Emily and her circle hope for a reconciler out of Whitman's "Passage to India," who seems more of a fantastic caricature than the actual embodiment of a messiah. Bearing Western gadgetry and Eastern scripture, this triple-titled deliverer carries such obvious and contradictory emblems that he strides through the ruins with the same flipness that Binx notices in all of the Bollings' talk. In spite of her clear-eyed look at doom, Emily does not see at all. Her nephew reveals that the faithful Mercer is actually a profiteer, while Jules and Sam are not as patrician as Emily imagines. The soldierly Binx spends the whole week in rejecting the lofty advice from Marcus Aurelius that his aunt sends him the day after their interview. And the tragic Emily suffers from a fondness for melancholy histrionics that is exceeded only by the canniness with which she lives in the century of the common man.

Emily invites Binx to her home on Wednesday so that he can play his part in her screenplay for the end. As they stroll on the gallery during one of the storms that always seem to threaten in the novel, Emily offers him one script for the apocalypse: he will abandon his wayward lifestyle, enter medical school in the fall, and, living once again on her estate, serve as confidant to the troubled Kate. Binx senses that Emily's plans mean the doom of his moderate hedonism as soon as his neck begins "to prickle with a dreadful-but-not-unpleasant eschatological prickling" (*M* 50). The paresthesia warns him that the career change and move from Gentilly signify a more profound transformation. The moviegoer must accept his aunt's code of the Old South. But ever since Binx wondered as an eight year old about the narrow limits of Emily's military ethic, dignity and devotion, fortitude and rectitude, as well as aristocratic superiority and noblesse oblige have seemed such minimal ideals. Emily gives Binx's response to her scheme a heightened sense of finality by asking him to return in one week with a decision. Although Emily's imperial mien and patronage may persuade her nephew to accept her version of the end, Binx's rediscovery of the search that morning leads him to a different eschaton.

I I   Percy makes Binx's apocalyptic quest seem even more urgent by causing signs of the approaching end to hover over each day of his search. On the first day Binx sees an ashen sky over Gentilly and the swamps still burning at Chef Menteur. Awakening the next morning from a dreamy flashback to the war, the veteran smells the familiar fear of 1951 and later remembers a *Reader's Digest* human interest story about a subway breakdown, one of Percy's favorite images in his essays for catastrophe. After squalls menace and lightning flickers as he drives Sharon home on Friday, the storm finally descends early Saturday morning when Emily calls him to report that Kate is missing. That night, Binx notices that the Smiths' fishing camp blazes like the *Titanic*, and the next morning he is disturbed by still another ominous dream. When Binx's trip to Chicago is "cut abruptly short by the catastrophe Monday night" (*M* 201), he returns to New Orleans the next evening, where he sees the ruins of Mardi Gras—confetti and glitter turned to pulp by the chilling rain. On Ash Wednesday he sits in the playground amid the wreckage of his world. In such a coolly reticent novel as *The Moviegoer*, Binx's portents create an aura of impending catastrophe throughout the week so that like the disastrous opening of the seven seals, the sounding of the seven trumpets, or the pouring of the seven vials in Revelation, these seven days mark a progress toward catastrophe (Rev. 6–11, 16).

This disaster threatens in its most public form as the result of the age's murderous technology. The moviegoer watches a television drama about an anguished physicist who walks in the desert while enjoying soul searching about the morality of his research. Binx speaks to Mercer about unilateral disarmament and warns a customer who is "not in the best position to take advantage of the dawning age of missiles" (*M* 106). The anxious broker is so troubled by vague terrors that he never awakens completely refreshed because he fears, " 'Suppose you should go to sleep and it should happen. What then?' What is this that is going to happen? Clearly nothing" (*M* 84).[5] As an actor, Binx can never overlook the possibility of a grand scene, even if it is the last, but until he starts acting in and for his own life, the dreamer's days and nights will be filled with illusory climaxes and disappointing nonaction.

The balance between such apocalyptic awareness and more mundane drama typifies the equipoise that makes the fictional center of *The Moviegoer* hold its world in place. Percy locates the novel between the unspecified, dreaded "it" and the daily, predictable "nothing," between a world in which public and private disaster seems imminent and a world in which all disaster seems impossible. *The Moviegoer* takes one self-proclaimed "average" citizen in the glad days of the Eisenhower era and subtly brings to bear on him the pressures of the last week of his old life as well as the uneasiness of a nation over its own destruction. The tensions between the eschaton and everydayness, despair and unawareness, the disquieting search and Binx's satisfying life in Gentilly reinforce each other without seeming calculated and without ever canceling each other out. The novel never compromises its sense of spiritual crisis to become a sociological study of the New South, and it never sacrifices its rootedness in the specialties of Louisiana to cultivate a purely supernatural vision. Instead, *The Moviegoer* sets what is most commonplace next to what is potentially catastrophic so that the world of the novel is finally filled with awe.

Percy's white-collar organization man of the latter 1950s lives at a critical hour, the mid-century point of incipient apocalypticism that Nathan Scott traces to the decade's growing awareness of dehumanization and depersonalization, recorded in such works as David Riesman's *The Lonely Crowd* (1950), C. Wright Mills's *White Collar* (1951), and William H. Whyte's *The Organization Man* (1956): "once the malaise by which we are afflicted is conceived to be so ubiquitous as to leave us without any melioristic possibilities, then we begin to enter that late stage of things where there is no bang but only a whimper and a sense of the historical process being at an end."[6] But despite the threat of doom, things in *The Moviegoer* do not fall apart. Indeed, the novel seems the least overtly apocalyptic of Percy's published fiction. It relies on virtually none of the radical techniques cited in "Notes for a Novel about the End of the World," as if its quietly musing tone and understated, economical language were actively restraining the impulse for fictional form to get caught up in the lateness of the day. Binx poses tentative questions, hesitates to answer, and declares that it is really impossible to say. Even when he contemplates his hidden desire for the eschaton, he wonders uncertainly, "Is it possible that—it is not too late?" (*M* 231).

The effect of this hushed diminution is not only to mollify the sense of catastrophe but also to intensify every element of Percy's fiction. Binx's cautious use of words bespeaks a verbal Little Way, but it also hints at the utter enormity of what cannot be said. Because *The Moviegoer* prefers not to announce and attack, it gains the power to intimate, to glimpse the doom on an ordinary day as well as the ordinary day in the face of doom. Such constant indirection and suggestiveness place the center of this meditative novel not in dogma and polemic but in the dramatization of mystery. Since *The Moviegoer* heeds what can as well as what cannot be said, the "nothing" and the "it," Percy's fiction continually discovers revelations through juxtaposing the diurnal round and the penultimate hour in which Binx searches; it thus attends to the souls of people met on the journey, the resonances of language, the spirit of place, the wryness of daily life. The novel is filled with cameo roles—as woebegone as they are humorous—that could be played by the best character actors in the movies of Binx's time. It hears richly specific speech as an expression of how these characters have come to or fallen from themselves. It portrays place with a curiosity and astonishment that indicate how Percy himself is "onto" something deep at the heart of the world he cherishes. And it finds comedy by exposing everyday pursuits as dalliances before the necessary doom. Kate defines the novel's penchant for the last laugh when she accuses Binx, "all your gaiety and good spirits have the same death house quality" (*M* 193), a perverse joie de vivre like a prisoner's registering to vote when he is condemned to die. Binx's irony toward all of the novel's players, and the novel's own searching irony toward its leading man, result from realizing that they all act before the end as if the end were not there. "What is this that is going to happen?" *The Moviegoer* keeps asking, and then it keeps answering its own question, "Clearly nothing"—no nuclear devastation, no decline and fall of the South, nothing but what Binx discovers at the playground on Ash Wednesday, the stark clarity of repeated revelations.

Because of his revelation on Wednesday morning, Binx sees how the cast of characters in *The Moviegoer* suffers from the same loss of self and the world that has emptied his own life. New Orleans seems more a cemetery than a city. "For some time now the impression has been growing upon me that everyone is dead," Binx eerily announces. "It happens when I speak to people. In the middle of a sentence it will come over me: yes, beyond a doubt this is death" (*M* 99). Percy fills the novel with a large number of such living dead so that the world seems to need a general resurrection. On his search Binx continually meets these bit players just long enough to record the image of their anxiety, for he is as much movie camera as moviegoer. But if he seems to be the last person after an apocalyptic plague, he judges the lifeless souls around him with considerable tolerance. His sympathy is appropriate because he is guilty of everything that he condemns in the other dramatis personae. He can be as sad and obsessed with money as Mr. Sartalamaccia or Harold Graebner, as materialistic as Eddie Lovell or the blade salesman on the Scenicruiser, as self-satisfied with the comfortable Little Way as Nell Lovell. He can be as fond of stylization as Walter Wade or Sam Yerger, as abstracted as Harry Stern, as excessively romantic as the dreamy college student on the bus back to New Orleans. Percy's use of so many walk-on performers dramatizes the moribund world more convincingly than did the sketchy sanatorium in "The Gramercy Winner." These dying and dead are all either so detached that they lack any human bonds to the world that would make a search possible or so attached that the things of the world provide a pleasurable haven that makes any search unnecessary. If Binx had not come to himself as a castaway, he would not be able to review any of these supporting players. He would be merely one of them. Since he is acutely aware of their faults and yet still feels for many of his fellow malaisians, his judgments create a melancholy comedy of manners about an age that prefers artificial acting to the authenticity of the search.

Although *The Moviegoer* generally avoids the fierce extremes of Percy's later apocalypses, occasionally the choler that prompted Percy to describe the novel as "mainly an assault" breaks into Binx's meditations.[7] He parodies the creeds of niceness espoused on radio's "This I Believe" by proclaiming his faith in "a good kick in the ass" (*M* 109). At the novel's climax, he denounces the "very century of merde, the great shithouse of scientific humanism" with a periodic sentence that marshalls the blunt and massive power of his bitterness and despair (*M* 228). Binx's verbal onslaught foreshadows the more violent technique of Percy's later fiction, the growing outrage that is virtually announced in the epilogue of *The Moviegoer*. Although Binx's hostility promises that he will not adopt Nell's values even if he lives in one of the shotgun cottages renovated by his cousin, his belligerence disturbs the otherwise reflective tone of the ending. Binx claims that he cannot even deliver edifying discourses because the time is later than Kierkegaard's, "much too late to edify or do much of anything except plant a foot in the right place as the opportunity presents itself—if indeed asskicking is properly distinguished from edification" (*M* 237). His acerbic creed defines the direction of Percy's apocalyptic aesthetics. As the hour becomes later in his fiction, the oblique reserve of *The Moviegoer* develops into the increasingly bolder means of artistic assault.

In this dead and doomed age Binx is an apocalyptist in spite of himself. Although he spends the week trying to flee the end through aesthetic alternatives to and parodies of apocalypse, he also seeks to discover how to live at the end of his world by looking for clues and signs of the future. In Revelation, John beholds what Romano Guardini calls God's "sign-language in all created things," a universe in which every image is part of a divine code that refers to the eschaton.[8] For John as for Binx, revelation means not simply seeing but seeing what it all means. Hence, the first of Percy's detective-heroes is constantly attuned to mystery as the very dimension in which he lives, as if to be on the search is to be intrigued by existence itself.[9] As Binx's first clues in this semiotic cosmos, his possessions point to what he would call being "stuck" in the world (*M* 233). They locate him at a place and an hour, serve as coordinates on the axes of his existence. Throughout the novel he keeps repeating this primal act of perception, for each shock of being, each exclamation at when and where and whom, keeps connecting the moviegoer to the physical universe. Things, places, and moments must be Binx's first clues because they remind the once-anonymous man that he is a someone who is searching somewhere.

Binx's father serves as a sign of how dangerous the quest may be. "Any doings of my father, even his signature, is in the nature of a clue in my search," he explains (*M* 71). On Friday, Binx never gets to see his father's signature on the deed to the swampland that has become his patrimony, although he takes Sharon along on the pretext of having her copy the title. Instead, Dr. Bolling's whole life, not just his signature, becomes a sign of how the search can find a false end in virtual suicide. Binx has almost inherited his irony, anxiety, and despair from his brooding father, but Dr. Bolling turned this perpetual discontent into the cause of his own doom. After joining the RCAF, Binx's restless father sported the uniform of the flight surgeon as the consummate costume and then "got himself killed before his country entered the war. And in Crete. And in the wine dark sea. And by the same Boche. And with a copy of *The Shropshire Lad* in his pocket" (*M* 25). Binx's succession of staccato phrases reduces his father to a caricatured romantic. No disciple of Housman could have wished for an end as fashionably heroic and pathetic as Dr. Bolling's loss of himself in the very stylishness of his martyrdom. As "the grandest coup of all," his death raised genuine spiritual suffering to the gestural perfection that Binx admires in movie stars (*M* 157). Dr. Bolling's fatal performance gave supreme expression to Housman's stoic world-weariness. Binx himself knows the same exhilarating temptation of the

68

gallant stand before doom so favored by the Bollings, for he once wrote his aunt a mannered note in which he marveled at how the time before battle made every second full of intense anticipation. Dr. Bolling becomes a sign of how consciousness can easily collapse into a painful and pretentious self-consciousness that seeks relief from romantic agony in a poetic death. Binx's father lived so completely up to his Rupert Brooke ideal that he died.

The Jews provide Binx with "my first real clue" about how to live daily and faithfully in the world. Since a psychic Geiger counter clicks whenever he passes a Jew, he senses "a clue here, but of what I cannot say." The sign registers his spiritual kinship, for Binx recognizes that "we share the same exile. The fact is, however, I am more Jewish than the Jews I know. They are more at home than I am. I accept my exile" (*M* 88, 89). Although Binx does not understand the significance of the Jews as fully as does Father Smith in *The Thanatos Syndrome*, his awareness of their status as exiles suggests that the Jewish people, wandering through history and often without a home, testify to humanity's mission as wayfarers under God. They embody the condition that Binx discovered on Wednesday morning when he came to himself as a castaway on a strange island. Like the community whose bond with the Deity defined their very existence in the desert, the man whose sole bible is Doughty's *Arabia Deserta* must discover his religious identity in equally arid New Orleans.

The ultimate sign that the fatherless and faithless Binx discovers is his indifference to the kind of signs revealed to the Jewish father in faith: "Abraham saw signs of God and believed. Now the only sign is that all the signs in the world make no difference" (*M* 146). Binx does not include himself among the 98 percent of Americans who believe in God (according to a survey that he has read), but neither does he belong to the 2 percent who are agnostics or atheists. He is unique in his apathy. He does not so much reject the traditional Thomistic proofs of the Creator as he invalidates their purpose. "It no longer avails to start with creatures and prove God," he writes in his notebook, for even "if the proofs were proved and God presented himself, nothing would be changed" (*M* 146). Nor does he imply that it is impossible to know whether God exists, although he often admits to skepticism about other issues in the novel. Binx simply declares that all the signs and proofs do not matter.

Having often overlooked the ordinary world and nonchalantly exchanged one girlfriend for another, Binx shows equal indifference to God. Whereas agnostics and atheists at least take some position toward the unknown or impossible Lord, Binx's position is an active unconcern about taking any positions. The traditional *deus absconditus* becomes the God whom Binx keeps in hiding, since "I have only to hear the word God and a curtain comes down in my head" (*M* 145). Yet unlike those who cannot or do not believe in God, the moviegoer recognizes that signs and proofs may indeed exist. He simply protests that they are completely irrelevant to him. Binx's attempt to disregard the holiest of clues, however, is itself undermined by a perception of divine comedy. "Is this God's ironic revenge?" he asks about his sacred uninterest. "But I am onto him" (*M* 146). Divine vengeance compels the human search. By a circuitous path the wanderer's apathy points him to God, for he ends in a kind of reversed version of the ontological argument. Anselm proved God's existence from the fact that the mind had the idea of God. Binx's reasoning suggests that since the mind is absolutely indifferent to signs and proofs, in fact draws down a curtain at the very mention of God, its unwillingness even to admit Anselm's idea may lead to the equivocal Deity. Binx's recognition of God's trickery finally turns on himself and then turns him toward God. If the only sign is the lack of interest in signs, Binx transforms human carelessness about God into a testimony of the divine presence: the mind can only be indifferent to God because God already exists. The ironic Binx pursues and is pursued by the divine *eiron*.

Binx's indifference ironically guarantees the authenticity of his search. In *Novel Writing in an Apocalyptic Time* the moviegoing Percy notes one sign of hope in *Ordinary People*, a film about a son's reconciliation with his father through a psychiatrist father surrogate: it did not mention God, "the cheapest word of the media, as profaned by radio preachers as by swearing."[10] Binx's apathy keeps God from being reduced to a profane category in a pollster's survey or to the climax of a theologian's syllogism. Proofs of God's existence speak out of abstract induction, as if God were a law of physics, rather than to the unique predicament of the searcher. Such demonstrations may comfort and confirm the faithful, but they do not convert the seeker like Binx. Instead, the vacuum created by the very insignificance of such signs may open a receptive space for a more graced encounter. "What do you seek—God? you ask with a smile," Binx seems to overhear the reader's question (*M* 13). The moviegoer is "onto" a surprising Lord by the most indirect route of his own indifference.

Although Binx looks for signs that might clarify the meaning of his initial revelation, he also tries to evade the apocalypse that he erratically approaches. Since it demands too great a renovation in his life, Binx spends his last seven days much as he has wasted every other day of his everyday life. He practices a series of schemes and strategies to soothe his restlessness and stimulate his exquisite sensibilities. All of Binx's favorite activities—going to the movies, making money, enjoying aesthetic interludes, romancing his secretary—thrill him with the calculus of a too-deliberate delight; and all of these sublime and self-serving moments offer only diversions from and finally perversions of the last day. Going to the movies defines Percy's title character as a technician of perfect pleasure more dramatically than any of Binx's other ingenious distractions. There is nothing casual about his pursuit of this vocation. Being a moviegoer does not mean attending a screening at the local cinema; it involves performing an entire ritual of going to the movies—deciding what film to see, traveling to distant and desolate theaters, talking to the staff. The films that Binx finally sees reinforce his tendency to turn self into style. Percy's apocalyptic moviegoer mentions none of the science fiction films so popular in the 1950s about alien invasions or nuclear catastrophes, the doomsday unreeled to the delighted eyes of a film buff like Susan Sontag. Although she is disturbed by the way these movies neutralize an audience's horror at their fearsome panoramas, Sontag takes pleasure in their frequent scenes of tumbled skyscrapers and exploding planets.[11] Binx attends movies religiously not for the thrill of their spectacle but for the highly satisfying example of their actors.

Percy's cineaste beholds on the screen his version of the splendid ideals glimpsed in Apocalypse. Viewing the final heavenly visions of Revelation as supreme types, Northrop Frye terms "apocalyptic" those images in literature that express "the categories of reality in the form of human desire."[12] Hollywood unveils for Binx a similarly heightened form of what he wants to be and how he wants to act. If the malaise has hollowed out the cast of *The Moviegoer* so that their lives seem as insubstantial as film celluloid, Binx judges the performers on-screen as more vivid and vital than the spectral world outside the theater. Movies are paradisal picture shows that project selves who completely are what they should be. As Percy explains in *The Message in the Bottle*, film stars possess "a ritual and gestural perfection" because every movement on-screen is flawlessly performed. If Destry must shoot the knobs off a saloon sign, he hits all six. Rehearsal and retakes, special effects and editing, eliminate any errors so that the actors become highly crafted archetypes made more glorious by being magnified on the spacious silver screen. Binx delights in Clint Walker's drawled lines in *Fort Dobbs* or John Wayne's sharpshooting in *Stagecoach* because the artifice of film celebrates the virtues of consummate acting. Every act as an act, even in grade B movies, is executed so impeccably that the performers, according to Percy, embody "perfectly realized actuality, the conscious *en soi*, that is to say, the godhead" (*MB* 94).[13]

Sitting in the theater, half alive in the half-light, the moviegoer gazes on images of the resplendent life that he seeks once the movie has ended. As Binx admires a stunning Amazon who sits next to him on the bus, he regrets that they will soon be separated. "In a better world I should be able to speak to her: come, darling, you can see that I love you. . . . If it were a movie, I would have only to wait. The bus would get lost or the city would be bombed and she and I would tend the wounded" (*M* 12–13). At their best, movies provide Binx with a highly romanticized pop culture equivalent of the doom and deliverance portrayed in the Book of Revelation. However, Binx keeps missing this plenitude off-screen because he interprets Hollywood's apocalyptic images so literally that he tries to become them. Throughout *The Moviegoer* he impersonates a variety of stars as if their acting could provide supremely accomplished models for his own very mannered performances in his daily affairs. He assumes a "Gregory Peckish sort of distance" (*M* 68) toward the secretary he secretly desires, imitates the casual charm of the "old Gable" (*M* 95), or speaks with Brando's sly self-satisfaction as he tries to get a date with Joyce. Yet copying such distinctive role-playing reduces the mystery of existence, which Binx has recently discovered, to an impossible exercise in mimickry. By transforming the revelations of art into the artificiality of life, the self-made star avoids the more difficult act of being Binx Bolling.

Binx detects the limited role that film stars can play in heralding renovation when William Holden strolls through the French Quarter on the first day of the moviegoer's search. Holden's somewhat surprising appearance in New Orleans seems like the coming of a moviegoer's messiah. His off-camera acting is ordinary; like all of Percy's wayfarers, he simply walks. But since moviegoers regularly turn performers into the parts they play, the hallowed star seems to have walked off the screen, "shedding light as he goes," radiating an "aura of heightened reality" to a gaggle of tourists, barkeeps, and B-girls whom he startles into consciousness (*M* 16). The luster of Holden's roles makes the onlookers share in Binx's saving discovery earlier that morning: they come to themselves as seers and come back to the world that is amazingly present before their eyes.

Although Holden brings life to a dead world by revealing the possibility of "as plenary an existence" as his own, the salvation is short-lived (*M* 16). After the actor passes by, Binx prays to his screen idol, "Am I mistaken or has a fog of uneasiness, a thin gas of malaise, settled on the street? . . . Ah, William Holden, we already need you again. Already the fabric is wearing thin without you" (*M* 18). The invocation is a moviegoer's maranatha, a cry for the second coming of William Holden. The insidious return of everydayness illustrates how William Holden and his stellar company can at best provide only an image for the fullness of being that is so missing in the novel's cast of characters. Newman, Peck, and Grant inhabit such distinctive screen personae that in an anonymous age they do not need external validation. They certify themselves, living in each instant not routinely but as the moment of all moments. However, they are neither models nor messiahs. Although a glimpse of William Holden in the theatrical flesh may provide a temporary epiphany, such apocalyptic moments, like Binx's earlier awakening in Korea or his more recent revelation that morning, astound but do not sustain. They grant the freedom to act that the recipient must convert into the necessity to search.

Binx evades this search by clinging to his old order, pursuing money and beauty as distractions from his doom. As a broker of stocks and bonds, Binx makes a career out of making a profit. He wants simply to be seen as the capable manager behind the sturdily respectable front of his uncle's firm. "The young man you see inside is clearly the soul of integrity," the Parthenon façade seems to announce; "he asks no more than to be allowed to plan your future" (*M* 72). Binx knows how to turn time into money, but by making his investments the end of his life, the canny trader tries to avoid the real end and thereby rushes toward a future that he could never have completely planned. The catastrophe occurs on an unexpected business trip to Chicago.

Binx is as shrewd and self-defeating in his private life as in his professional responsibilities. Here too he exploits every advantage and plans for his own enjoyable future, but all of his savoir faire creates only caricatures of the apocalypse. Binx uses Kierkegaardian repetitions, like seeing another Western at the theater where fourteen years ago he saw *The Oxbow Incident* or acting in his own remake of a youthful visit to Chicago, to become a connoisseur of lost time. By doubling the present back on the past, Binx negates the intervening years so that the original experience, abstracted from all events, tastes deliciously pristine, as if "without the usual adulteration of events that clog time like peanuts in brittle" (*M* 80). Apocalypse also depends on a return, a coming again of the savior, the city, and the garden. And as Percy recognizes in *The Message in the Bottle*, repetition may provide a refuge from everydayness. But unlike Will Barrett's exploration of the past, Binx's repetition rarely goes beyond an aesthetic adventure to become the existential search that may lead to a recovery of self. Only his memories of his father lead Binx on what Percy calls "the passionate quest in which the incident serves as a thread in the labyrinth to be followed at any cost" (*MB* 95–96). Binx more often dallies with the past rather than zealously pursuing its significance for the new age that is the future. If Binx plans repetitions to enjoy a sweet nostalgia, he hopes that rotations will lead to the "experiencing of the new beyond the expectation of the experiencing of the new" (*M* 144). The jaded wanderer in the world requires such unusual and unfamiliar pleasures as having a car accident while driving with his new secretary or suddenly going to see *Fort Dobbs* with Lonnie and Sharon because the surprise startles him into awareness. Like Kate, who also lives for original moments, Binx distracts himself with rotations rather than living for apocalypse, the climactic coming of what will always be first and fresh that makes Binx's feverish pursuit of the new seem like trifling sensory gratification.

Binx's succession of office girls who are inevitably promoted to the position of girlfriend makes even his sexual rotations predictable. He regularly travels the same cycle from obsession to apathy with women who seem little different from each other. Such rounds of romance turn love into the repetition of emptied passions, and Binx's praise of Sharon's beauty into the poetry of an exhausted aestheticism. Although his laconic voice repeatedly breaks into lyrical strains to hymn her graces, his rapt absorption in Sharon never gets beyond anatomical eroticism. She is less a person than a carnal future for which he happily plans with as much care as he expends on his stocks and bonds. He calculates each increasingly intimate stage—a business trip to the duck club, working overtime on Friday, typing letters on Saturday—so that the week may climax in a weekend trip to the Gulf Coast in a car designed to outrace the malaise. Hardly loving or even knowing her, Binx finds in Sharon not the genuinely new but the everyday office routine of another possible seduction.

Nothing judges Binx's dalliance with Sharon so tellingly as his joy in their car accident. Before the mishap he silently recognizes that his wearied flirtation needs the renewal that only catastrophe can bring. He aestheticizes the apocalypse by seeking the very rotation that Percy describes in *The Message in the Bottle* as "the coming upon the Real Thing among the ruins" (*MB* 99). The crash temporarily relieves the boredom by making Binx and Sharon briefly visible. Normally unseen, just two motorists in an MG, they lose their anonymity and become a real-life movie that is momentarily but voluptuously watched by the passing traffic that now sees them for the first time. Binx imagines that the small-scale disaster has revived their passion and dispelled the malaise. Yet although Sharon tends to his wound and finally calls him "Jack," Binx celebrates only a mock-apocalyptic moment. It modulates but does not deepen their relationship, for Sharon remains the sweet secretary who is very much her own boss. Hoping to find a romantic hideaway with her on the gulf, Binx stops at his mother's fishing camp, but at last all his calculations for the future come to nought. It is not abandoned as he expected but "ablaze like the *Titanic*," bustling with family life (*M* 136). If the comparison casts the aura of the doomed ocean liner over the house by the dock, it also makes luminous the bondedness that an erring son and brother discovers among the Smiths and especially with Lonnie. In this dwelling place of love, not in Binx's lonely office affairs, he finds the promise of the wonderfully new and surprising life that he seeks, the genuine "Real Thing among the ruins."

| | | Although Binx is paralyzed by everydayness even on his weekend in this pastoral retreat, he feels its grip yield enough so that he can record his "starting point for search" (*M* 146). Bayou des Allemands is uncommonly hospitable to such exploration. Binx feels "the mystery of the swamp" press close in the dark on Saturday night (*M* 140), and early on Sunday this strangeness seems to rise from the etherlike water. Although, like his father, Binx does not enjoy fishing, he manages to "fish out a notebook" and scribble his meditation on "God's ironic revenge" as he lies awake in the vapory whiteness of his mother's camp (*M* 146). But when Mrs. Smith later casts her line from the dock into this morning world, she fishes in much less ambiguous waters and for much smaller catch. Mrs. Smith secures herself against searching in the ruins through the modest means of cultivating the ordinary. Binx admires his mother's daily skill and industry, for she has domesticated the movie actor's gestural perfection. Whether preparing bait or cleaning the table after a dinner of crabs, this fisherwoman simply does what she does extremely well. Since Binx himself has become so responsive to the attractiveness of the world before him, he sees in her everyday chores a beautiful dexterity and maternal providence. Binx recognizes, however, that the goal of his mother's good housekeeping is "the canny management of the shocks of life" (*M* 142). These disasters—her first husband's plane crash, Scotty's death, Duval's drowning, Lonnie's fatal illness—could make her come to herself so that she examines a life as common as her name. But she protects herself from the most minimal shock, the least perceptible revela-

tion, by managing catastrophe as deftly as she does her household duties at the fishing camp.

To preserve her customary and colloquial world Mrs. Smith cuts all down to small-scale size with her handy kitchen knife in a "belittlement of everything" (*M* 142). Her wayfaring husband was simply "overwrought" (*M* 153), the dying Lonnie just will not drink his milk, and God is "but one of the devices that come to hand in an outrageous man's world" (*M* 142). Mrs. Smith's reduced life is an emphatically antiapocalyptic one. She favors the ordinary over the unimaginable, the status quo rather than the sudden inbreaking of the new, and familiar ease to catastrophe. Sometimes as would-be herald of re-creation, Binx tries to "shake her loose from her elected career of the commonplace" (*M* 152). He attempts nothing more disconcerting than asking whether his father was a good husband, but in the homely world of Mrs. Smith such prying resounds with unwanted provocation. She remains, however, even and unperturbed lest the slightest act of self-reflection be cataclysmic.

Over the weekend Binx discovers the possibilities of a genuinely apocalyptic existence through the love of Lonnie Smith. Binx's half brother lives in the advent of the eschaton. Confined to a wheelchair and wasted to eighty pounds, he incarnates the ruins that Binx later glimpses in the cityscape of New Orleans. Although Binx often longs to become an Anyone who lives Anywhere, Lonnie dwells at the most specific moment possible—the days before death—and in the one place that is all his own, the breakdown of his own body. He suffers from a malady but not from the malaise. Although his illness might easily have driven him into the arrogance and acrimony of his own suffering, he has turned personal disaster into a way of living ultimately, not unto himself but under God. Hence he would discipline his flesh even further by fasting to atone for the envy that makes him glad about the death of his brother Duval. Percy shows a new creation rising from the old. In a novel in which so many of the living seem dead, the dying Lonnie's faith and love make him so alive that he belongs to an entirely different order of heaven and earth.

Lonnie is one of the merry children among the viny ruins whom the movie-goer hopes to join at the end of the novel. He takes deep pleasure in simply seeing Binx on his surprise visit to the Smiths, watching *Fort Dobbs* from the hood of his half brother's car, or racing down the boardwalk in his wheelchair. This joy makes Lonnie unique in the novel. It sets him apart from the historical pessimism of Emily, the secret anxiety of the bit players, even the manic exhilaration of Kate and the desperately blissful aestheticism of the moviegoer. Occasionally Binx seems filled with his kin's glad spirit. When he finally uses his acting skills for unselfish ends and terrorizes the delighted Lonnie with his impersonation of the fierce Akim Tamiroff, Binx's playfulness shows that he may yet become one of the merry children of catastrophe. Such joy reflects a new way of life whose center is human and divine communion. The Smith household thrives on such unpretentious love. When Binx arrives on Saturday night, mother and children boisterously concelebrate family ties over mounds of scarlet crabs, a feast that looks forward to the next day's Mass. On Sunday Binx suggests that Lonnie concentrate on "a sacrament of the living" rather than on fasting, and before Binx leaves, Lonnie reminds his half brother that he is still offering his communion for him (*M* 164). Lonnie's life embodies the meaning of this sacrament by his unassuming faith in God and his brotherhood with Binx. Those bonds turn the dying youth into one of the firstborn of the age to come.

Binx almost envies Lonnie's radical centering of his life on the Divine. The teenager's wallet full of holy cards, reliance on the virtue of Extreme Unction, and commitment to fasting could easily make him freakish in his religiosity, yet Percy keeps Lonnie from becoming just a holy grotesque. Since Binx views the adolescent with such sincerity, and the rest of the Smith children treat him without any sentimentality, the youth's pieties express his pure ardor for God. Believing that he can offer "his sufferings in reparation for men's indifference to the pierced heart of Jesus Christ," he demonstrates a love so great that it feels for God; it is human zeal responding to divine fervor (*M* 137). In particular he suffers for Binx, who makes such indifference to God the starting point of his search. Earlier Binx felt "a sword in the heart" in a moment of anguished appreciation for Sharon's beauty (*M* 95), and after visiting the hospitalized Lonnie at the end of the novel, Kate cries, "He breaks my *heart!*" (*M* 239). Lonnie's response is neither aesthetic nor pathetic. His heart becomes the place where patience in suffering is transfigured into fiery passion for God.

Lonnie's communion with God finds its natural expression in his intimacy with Binx. Their profound sharing begins to fulfill the promise of Binx's Wednesday morning revelation, for Percy never regards coming to consciousness as complete unless it leads to a coming together in consciousness. His apocalyptists know who they are only when they know along with another. Through both looks and language Binx and Lonnie jointly attend to the world as moviegoers. Again and again their eyes speak their fellowship.

While Lonnie, as avid a film buff as his half brother, watches *Fort Dobbs* at the drive-in, Binx notices that "he looks around at me with the liveliest sense of the secret between us; the secret is that Sharon is not and never will be onto the little touches that we see in the movie and, in the seeing, know that the other sees" (*M* 143). The film provides a focus for the communion of consciousness between Lonnie and Binx. By simply seeing the screen, they share not only the same frame of mind but also an awareness of their camaraderie. The look ratifies this affection between film aficionados and exposes by contrast Binx's loveless affair with the unenlightened Sharon.

Like sound to the picture on the screen, the dialogue between these film buffs perfectly complements their language of looks. Percy's fiction begins from the premise that "words have become as worn as poker chips, they don't mean anything. Particularly religious words: baptism, sin, God. These get worn out, and there's always a problem of rediscovering them."[14] Binx often hears this same devaluation when in the midst of a conversation he feels overtaken by death, but Lonnie gives language new life. His crooned speech keeps his words from being worn-out formulas and makes them entirely his own, as if they were spoken for the first time with singular force and frankness. And because his life is centered on the Logos, his words are renewed not just in sound but in their very essence, pouring forth in love and eliciting the rediscovered language of love in return. "It is like a code tapped through a wall. Sometimes he asks me straight out: do you love me? and it is possible to tap back: yes, I love you" (*M* 162). Lonnie's speech voices Percy's belief that language is fundamentally intersubjective. Whether or not he actually asks Binx about his love, all of his words make a risky adventure into communion that inspires Binx to answer in kind.

Although the starting point of Binx's search is "the strange fact of one's own invincible apathy," Lonnie's fervor toward God and fondness for his half brother draw forth from the moviegoer a bantering religious belief (*M* 146). When Lonnie speaks of his desire to fast during Lent in order to conquer "an habitual disposition" to envy Duval, Binx understands that the penitent uses the "peculiar idiom of the catechism in ordinary speech" and answers by using the correct term: Lonnie should not be "scrupulous." And when Lonnie confesses that he is still happy about his brother's death, Binx retorts, "Why shouldn't you be? He sees God face to face and you don't" (*M* 163). The debate of these brotherly theologians is filled with the irony that Binx always savors. The indifferent seeker plays the role of jesuitical apostle, and the entire disputation is actually a game that Lonnie wants Binx to enjoy winning. Yet these amusing self-contradictions contain a more profoundly comic reversal. Binx is "onto" the God whom Percy's stalkers often discover precisely as they back away from him (*M* 146). Although he replies half in jest about the beatific vision mentioned in Revelation 22:4, at the novel's end he will affirm a more glorious version of Lonnie's apocalyptic destiny: the prospect of the once-crippled youth enjoying the general resurrection on water skis. Binx shifts from playfulness at the middle of the book to celebration at its end partly because of the life of love sensed in this very moment of sport. Since Lonnie does not abstract religion from the rest of his life, he freely uses catechetical language in everyday conversations. Renewing the worn-out words so that they come from the heart, the vital Lonnie eventually inspires Binx's affirmation of life at the end of the world.

Lonnie, who appears in the only chapter in which Kate is not present, leads Binx to his final love. After the youth says good-bye to his brother with still another poignant expression of affection at the end of chapter 3, Binx drives home with Sharon. On the way the wanderer is overtaken by a despair that even the familiar remedy of a hand on his secretary's thigh cannot cure. Lonnie has taught Binx too much. The moviegoer's life of casual seductions provides no remedy for the malaise after the knowing love shared with his half brother. Binx discovers a similar renewal in the midst of doom only with the woman who also lives for the new order brought by catastrophe, Kate Cutrer.

I V   "Have you noticed that only in time of illness or disaster or death are people real?" Kate asks Binx as she describes her strategy for living near the end (*M* 81). The moviegoer's distant cousin and spiritual kin seeks whatever is thrilling, shocking, and violent. She longs for her too-understanding family to stop supporting her so that she might be forced to discover a new life as a stewardess. She remembers how after once slipping and falling into a fireplace she found the pain a respite from the boredom of her neat and ordinary life. After a storm she feels exhilarated. Kate is so stifled by the malaise known to Binx that she courts whatever extraordinary event will jolt her from the numbness of her everyday world.

Kate lives in this apocalyptic anxiety because of a moment of revelation as astonishing as any of Binx's visions. Alluding to his first intimation of the search in Korea, she claims that the accident in which her fiancé was killed "gave me my life. That's my secret, just as the war is your secret" (*M* 58). Both survivors have known a privileged moment of awareness in the midst of catastrophe that brought them to themselves and inevitably brings them to each other. For a time the car accident gave Kate a sense of actuality that seemed heightened only because the past was so unreal and impermanent. She recalls that "people were so kind and helpful and *solid*. Everyone pretended that our lives until that moment had been every bit as real as the moment itself and that the future must be real too, when the truth was that our reality had been purchased only by Lyell's death. In another hour or so we had all faded out again and gone our dim ways" (*M* 81). Lyell earned an hour of more intense life for the spectators at the movie of his death. By shocking them out of their normal apathy, the disaster allowed sympathetic viewers to become involved with the lives of others, and in so doing they gained a sense of the communion best known by Lonnie and Binx. But the audience soon faded out, dissolving like cinematic images into their once again ephemeral lives.

Kate did not so much fade out as stand forth. The repletion of that hour on the very eve of her wedding exposed the dimness of her former life and freed her to begin a search. She left the dead Lyell behind her, boarded a bus to Natchez, and set out on her own, a wayfarer like Binx, with the world spectacularly before her. Although Emily Bolling believed that the accident traumatized her stepdaughter, and placed her under the care of Dr. Mink, the crash actually signified Kate's first step in coming to consciousness. It made her begin to realize the immense openness of her life, which she later rediscovers during the course of the novel in Mink's office. "I sat up and rubbed my eyes and then it dawned on me," she explains to Binx. "But I couldn't believe it. . . . I had discovered that a person does not have to be this or *be* that or be anything, not even oneself. One is free" (*M* 114). Until that moment Kate had allowed her doctor to determine her self as she frantically tried to live up to his psychiatric model of the joyous and creative person. But at last she recognizes with the eye-opening force of revelation her responsibility for creating her own life. As spiritually exalted as any character played by Eva Marie Saint, Kate shares Binx's search for a way to live in a world of freedom, but her immediate collapse into panicky bewilderment dramatizes her inability to sustain this burden alone.

Kate genuinely yearns for some new beginning, yet by herself she can only live out the most reckless and perverse endings. Although she later charges Binx with being cold-blooded, she coolly walked away from her fiancé's death, and she took almost masochistic pleasure in the pain of fire. Her need for such surcharged moments to make her feel alive leads to the possibly dangerous use of alcohol and tranquilizers. Kate carries the freedom to be "not even oneself" to suicidal extremes. Her apocalyptic renewal threatens to become Kierkegaard's aesthetic damnation as she loses herself in the pursuit of exacerbated sensations. Emily and Sam Yerger view her consumption of barbiturates early Sunday morning as an attempted overdose, but Kate considers it a search for salvation. As Sam can be heard reminiscing about Emily's messianic hopes, Kate explains to Binx that she did not want to die, only to turn the impasse of the end into a time of renewed vitality, to "break out, or off, off dead center" (*M* 181). She sought the same thrilling possibility that Graham Greene described in *The Lost Childhood*. As an adolescent, Greene used to spin the chamber of a revolver, place the muzzle to his head, and click the trigger because the odds of one fatal chance in six replaced his former apathy with jubilation at still being alive.[15] The risk of death helps Kate overcome the living death that Binx so often diagnoses in those he meets. Kate protests that suicide actually keeps her from dying, for if there were ever a moment when she could not kill herself, then she most assuredly would. Reveling in her newfound freedom, Kate seems to transform the threat of suicide into the basis of a creative decision: she renews her choice to exist every instant that she lives. But all her attempts at finding a new order are spurious, her euphoria always short-lived. Whether leaving behind the dead Lyell or breaking off dead center, her quest for the genuinely new turns into a perilous search for the merely novel. The Percyan apocalypse requires a much more radical act of self-negation and re-creation that Kate can only frenetically parody.

Kate's apocalyptic yearning climaxes in what Binx fittingly calls the "catastrophe" of their trip to Chicago (*M* 201). When on Sunday evening she suddenly proposes accompanying Binx on his business trip, she makes a definitive bid for a new and dubious life that surprises even her cousin.[16] Kate breaks with the past by not telling Emily of her travels, and she hopes for a tentative future with Binx by planning to visit Modesto or Fresno afterward. The moviegoer begins the journey with the same sense of promise, for he views the train ride as a progress from "the sorry litter of the past" to "the future bright and simple as can be" (*M* 184). If Binx and Kate lived in a Hollywood movie, they might have reason to be so sanguine; they seem as peculiarly predestined for each other as any screen couple kept apart until the closing scene. Each fathoms much of the other's despair and private methods for living amid such desolation. Binx can decipher Kate's coded language, accept her abrupt way of ending phone conversations, and detect the impersonations of his sometimes fellow moviegoer and actress. Kate "understands my moviegoing," Binx explains, "but in her own antic fashion" (*M* 63), and she is familiar with Binx's favorite existential terms such as "certification," "repetition," and "search." Except for Lonnie and Binx, no other characters in the novel share such confidences or are so privy to each other's hurting and often impossibly demanding heart. Their love is a mutual knowing, an intimacy of consciousness that the moviegoer never sees portrayed on-screen.[17] Yet although Binx and Kate know that they should despair of what leads to despair—Sharon and Walter, savoir faire and suicide—they do not know where to place their hope. It is easier for Binx to dismiss Kate's attempts to understand his search as unserious, just as it is easier for Kate to dismiss marriage with Binx as necessarily ridiculous. Since despair has made both into expert scoffers at their own love, Binx and Kate seek merely a mock consummation en route to Chicago. Both actors discover that the collapse of their self-dramatizations provides the way at last to meet each other amid the ruins of their roles.

On the train Kate can only burlesque renewal. When she approaches Binx in a provocative jacket and skirt rather than the proper flouncy dress that she wore earlier at her aunt's, and with her eyes now sparkling with mascara, he recognizes that Kate is celebrating her own Mardi Gras two days before the festival. Enjoying the seasonal dispensation, the former queen of the Neptune Ball this year adopts the mask of a "Frenchy" Tillie the Toiler. This risqué comic-book version of the stylish doll in Russell Westover's newspaper comic strip enjoys "a little set-to with Mac in the stockroom" during an office party (*M* 199). When Binx tries to tell the hoydenish Kate of his love, she simply grabs him, forestalls him ("No love, please. . . . Just don't speak to me of love, bucko"), and invites him to return to her roomette in five minutes (*M* 198). Kate's attempt to lure Binx into her toils travesties the communion that Binx discovered with Lonnie. Whereas they spoke of the love ratified by their looks, Kate virtually pierces Binx with her black, spiky eyes: she wants none of the words and proposes only "a little fling."

Kate's masquerade as the brazen Tillie typifies her delight in the outrageous moments that always make her feel alive. Through this performance she hopes to reenter the world, for her "droning scientific voice" (*M* 44), transcendent detachment, and chilling ability to deliver frank appraisals of people are the signs of a self dangerously removed from the cosmos. Kate has sought escape from this objectivity in every crisis of her life, every shock that might force her to attend to what always seems so unreal, and now at last in her pose as Tillie. She becomes an actress rather than an aloof moviegoer.

But "flesh poor flesh failed us," Binx admits, partly because Kate is only acting out a role rather than acting for her own life. She is not living in her body
but in shameless illusion. Finding her "not really bold, not whorish bold but
theorish bold," Binx detects the studied pretense behind her sexual bravado
(*M* 200). Despite her attempt to escape abstraction, she has actually adopted
the disengagement of the Deans, the marriage therapists who in Binx's fantasy turn their lovemaking into erotic research. Kate cannot live in the world
as Tillie the Toiler, working at sex.

The failure of flesh is as catastrophic for Binx. Percy's lewd caricature reduces Binx's aestheticism to the farcical simplicity of two-dimensional lust,
for the randy Mac is only a cartoon version of Binx in pursuit of his girl-
friends. Kate's proposition to Binx—"Oh you're a big nasty Whipple and
you're only fit for one thing"—exposes his office romances and especially
the present night as adventures in comic-book sex (*M* 199). As Tillie she
parodies his toiling secretaries, dramatizing for Binx what he realized earlier,
"Beauty . . . is a whoredom" (*M* 196). But Kate even surpasses Sharon in
her frankness. By casting Binx in the part of Whipple, who discovers Tillie
and Mac in the stockroom, she unmasks the diffident moviegoer who prefers to think of himself as the dashing seducer. Binx admits as much: "The
truth is I was frightened half to death by her bold . . . carrying on. I reckon
I am used to my blushing little Lindas from Gentilly" (*M* 200). If the whorish Kate who is abstracted from flesh cannot live up to her part as Tillie the
Toiler, neither can the pseudorakish Binx play Don Juan. Both performers
fail to embody their dissolute ideals in their lovemaking because they place
too much emphasis on flesh alone, summoning it "all at once to be all and
everything, end all and be all, the last and only hope" (*M* 200). As Binx and
Kate reach beyond themselves to achieve the most trivial and superficial of
self-projections, they make the act of intercourse so ultimate that it becomes
the eschaton. But flesh by itself cannot sustain the burden of their loveless
impersonations.

The debacle causes a moviegoer's apocalypse. On-screen, failure does not
exist, for every action is efficacious. In exchange for abandoning sovereignty
to the script and the production crew, stars live in a riskless world where what
should happen does happen. Binx wishes that he could have been so successful by imitating Rory Calhoun, who would have simply tucked his beloved
under the covers and slept with magnificent chastity in an adjoining room, or
by copying some hero from a novel who could turn from his contemplation,
merrily bed a beautiful maiden, and then return to his quest for wisdom. But

on the train Percy's apocalyptic moviegoer inevitably fails to act like either of these paragons. He makes the same mistake as do the moviegoers and readers of apocalyptic tales described by Percy in "The Man on the Train": trying to live by their supernal fictions rather than within the mundane constraints of their lives. Although the tense stranger in the Western wipes his brow with a stylized gesture, Percy speculates that if the anxious film buff tries the same movement, he will find that his forehead is dry and he will only bump his nose. Percy writes against a tradition of eschatological romance that relies on the same self-defeating idealism as do the movies. "The young man in a Robert Nathan novel or in a Huxleyan novel of the Days after the Bomb," Percy explains, "may rest assured that if he lies under his bush in Central Park, sooner or later *she* will trip over him" (*MB* 94). In Nathan's *Portrait of Jennie* a deadened artist meets in Central Park the lovely ghost of a young woman who has drowned. Huxley's satires are typically more skeptical than Nathan's sweet, sad fantasies. But in *Ape and Essence*, a vision of an infernal utopia after nuclear devastation, a neurotic botanist discovers the union of spiritual and sensual love that eluded the Savage in Huxley's earlier *Brave New World*. Percy observes that when the deluded reader of such fateful love stories waits under a tree, no fleeing Pier Angeli ever stumbles into his life. If he tries to seek an introduction, his speech and gestures falter, and "having once committed himself to the ritual criterion of his art and falling short of it, he can only be—nothing" (*MB* 95).

The conventions of fiction and film dictate that the liaison between Kate and Binx on the train should be such a romance by chance, an opportunity for both to star in their minds' screenplays as Tillie the Toiler or as a romantic leading man. Their lovemaking is disastrous because, like the misguided readers of Huxley and Nathan or fans of Hollywood celebrities, they try to create "desperately unauthentic art by transposing the perfect aesthetic rotation to the existential" (*MB* 94). And when life does not reproduce art, Percy's woman and man on the train also "can only be—nothing." Kate and Binx discover waste and loss when their efforts to realize the apocalypses of novels or movies fail. Without the communion revealed by the dying Lonnie, Binx and Kate's attempted union in the flesh can only be one more symptom of the malaise.

The debacle on the train is followed by the catastrophe of Chicago. As Binx feared, he is overcome by "the genie-soul of Chicago," a desolate genius loci that makes itself felt in the city's oppressive wind and intrusive empty spaces. The hollow urban soulscape simply magnifies the same "howling void" that

Kate recognizes in Binx (*M* 203, 202). The city is the fitting end of the line for the train ride because it localizes the terminal despair of failed intimacy. Here, as a boy, Binx rejected his father's invitation for absolute camaraderie, and here again he flees from Stanley Kinchen and the friendly fellows at the Hot Stove League while the salon orchestra plays "Getting to Know You." Under the "nakedest loneliest sky in America," Binx's only hope is Kate (*M* 203). Since she is less sensitive to time and space, and more at home in despair, Kate takes charge of Binx in Chicago. She protects him and directs him, much as Binx will do for her at the novel's end, for the catastrophe has freed them to be vulnerable before each other. They can act with mutual tenderness and trust because they no longer have to play any parts. The film buff's glorification of screen idols has been a twentieth-century version of the romantic faith in impossible ideals. Both Binx and Kate, like the suicidal Dr. Bolling and the student on the Scenicruiser who reads *The Charterhouse of Parma*, were guilty of the "miserable trick the romantic plays upon himself: of setting just beyond his reach the very thing he prizes" (*M* 215). All suffered from what de Rougemont detects in Stendhal: "the Fiasco of the Sublime."[18] As connoisseurs of perfect acting and ultimate actions, they lost any appreciation for what was ordinary and incomplete, yet at least humanly embodied. But after Binx and Kate face their mutual inability to live up to their imaginary roles, they are like characters who have stepped off the screen and gradually learn to speak their own lines in their own lives. Kate's care and management inspire the moviegoer with a moment of revelation and re-evaluation similar to his earlier epiphanies: "There I see her plain, see plain for the first time since I lay wounded in a ditch and watched an Oriental finch scratching around in the leaves—a quiet little body she is, a tough little city Celt; no, more of a Rachel really, a dark little Rachel bound home to Brooklyn on the IRT" (*M* 206). Binx discovers the special strength of the frail and anxious Kate. This wayfaring woman, who resembles the mother of the people with whom Binx feels such kinship, may be a possible fellow-traveler on his religious search. But even Kate is not completely safe from the ominous spirit of Chicago. As they walk back to their hotel after a depressingly hopeful movie, Kate turns the mournful wind into words: "Something is going to happen" (*M* 211).

V   The trip to Chicago, doomed from the start, is "cut abruptly short by the catastrophe Monday night" (*M* 201). After having discovered Kate's unexplained absence, Emily summons Binx to New Orleans with a peremptory telephone message. When the disaster finally arrives, it hardly seems to have happened. Although Binx often longs for the Bomb to clear away the ruins caused by everydayness, nothing so spectacular culminates his hapless journey. Instead, the moviegoer simply performs a nonact, a mysterious failure that he is unable to justify. On the phone Binx cannot explain why he did not tell Emily about Kate's trip to Chicago, yet his world has ended with that breach of her code. When Binx stands unrepentant before his aunt on Ash Wednesday, he undergoes Emily's version of the last judgment. She had long been accustomed to fondly mocking him as "the last and sorriest scion of a noble stock" (M 26), but despite the theatricality of this scene, even Binx senses that Emily is not just playing the high-toned southern lady to his disgraced cavalier. Wearing a "quizzical-legal sort of smile" reminiscent of Judge Anse, she delivers a magisterial speech, which interrogates, indicts, and expels Binx from her world on the very day when she had hoped, just a week ago, he would decisively join it (M 220). Emily at last recognizes that Binx has betrayed the tradition that she honors in her grand oration: "At the great moments of life—success, failure, marriage, death—our kind of folks have always possessed a native instinct for behavior, a natural piety or grace, I don't mind calling it" (M 222). This innate sense of propriety provides the basis for her class and the reason for its superiority. As the most civilized of performers, Emily's kind knows unfailingly how to act in all the big scenes. But Binx is no longer acting out the mannerisms of film stars or the manners of Emily's gracious aristocracy. His reckless trip to Chicago shows that he has gone beyond the stylizations of both Hollywood and the South to discover in his intimacy with Kate a more radical form of piety and grace.

Percy uses the voice of the old moral order to announce the arrival of a new and baffling age: "It was the novelty of it that put me off, you see. I do believe that you have discovered something new under the sun" (M 219). Emily contends that the collective experience of Western civilization shows that people in times of crisis react in certain familiar patterns. But the unorthodox Binx has discovered that he "need not after all respond in one of the traditional ways. No. One may simply default. Pass. Do as one pleases, shrug, turn on one's heels and leave. Exit" (M 220). Emily views her nephew's disregard of the customary and accepted response to Kate's near suicide as a sign of radical irresponsibility. Binx will not protect her moral domain from the barbarians at the gates, as she hoped last week, because he belongs to that uncouth horde. Emily judges correctly according to her Roman ethic, for Binx violated a trust by taking the desperate Kate away without telling anyone. However, her censure is based on the laws of a world already dead to her nephew. When Binx allowed Kate suddenly to accompany him and changed his morning flight to an evening train ride to accommodate her, he acted not out of duty or suavity but out of immediate fellow feeling for one likewise at the end.

Binx's judgment before Emily marks both the official end of his membership in her aristocratic circle and the beginning of what he calls "my new status" (*M* 227). Percy conveys the transformation through his characters' use of language. During the long interview with Emily, Binx remains unusually silent. Emily speaks like a rhetorician—questioning, rebuking, pleading—but Binx barely responds at all, resorting to a nod of his head, a spare yes or no, an explanation that he really cannot explain. And when Emily asks whether he was intimate with Kate, he replies, "I suppose so. Though intimate is not quite the word." Although Binx equivocates out of well-bred reticence to explain precisely how flesh failed Emily's stepdaughter and nephew, his ambiguity also alerts his aunt that he no longer speaks purely out of her genteel tradition. Emily hears the breakdown of their common code: "All these years I have been assuming that between us words mean roughly the same thing, that among certain people, gentlefolk I don't mind calling them, there exists a set of meanings held in common" (*M* 222). No longer sharing these select understandings, Emily and Binx even interpret the same word differently. Binx's "intimacy" with Kate resulted not from the sexual intercourse that his aunt understands by her delicate term but from the discovery of each other amid disaster that Emily can hardly comprehend. Binx's rejection of his aunt's words quietly witnesses to his rejection of her values. And Emily finalizes the breach through responding in kind. Throughout the trial her financial ledger has lain open on her desk, until at the end she snaps it shut with a smile "which, more than anything which has gone before, marks an ending" (*M* 226). Signaling the completion of the interview, Emily's smile closes the account book of Binx's disappointing life and disowns any moral kinship with her nephew. "But it is her withholding my name that assigns me my new status," he realizes (*M* 227). The anonymous dismissal indicates that the estranged Binx no longer enjoys his aunt's intimacy.

Having rejected and been rejected by the old regime, Binx sits amid the ruins of his life at the playground that has defined all of the moviegoer's previously amusing diversions. Now he can only wait. "Wait," Lonnie called when Binx last saw him; and Kate's last words were "Wait for me there" (*M* 165, 227). The compulsive wanderer and walker needs to learn Eliot's prayer in "Ash-Wednesday"—"Teach us to sit still"—as he sits on the ocean wave in the schoolyard on the first day of Lent.[19] The person living in apocalyptic times, Walter Schmithals writes, "can only *wait* for the dawning of the new age. God will bring it in."[20] But like later Percyan prophets determined to declare the eschaton at their own convenience, Binx cannot wait for God or Kate. Instead, he concedes defeat, "My search has been abandoned," and resumes playing a familiar game (*M* 228). Despair at the ruins drives him to desire. At the playground Binx calls Sharon, reaches Joyce, and agrees to attend a party on Saturday night. But then he sees Kate and speculates about secretly desiring the end of the world.

Percy's masterly juxtaposition of Kate's coming and Binx's eschatological meditation dramatizes the only terminus for both of these searches. The apocalypse is not an atomic holocaust but a revelation of love. While the city seems to burn behind him, Binx recognizes a deeper kinship with his cousin: "she could be I myself, sooty eyed and nowhere" (*M* 231). Kate too has reached the end. Sitting behind the steering wheel, she even resembles a bomber pilot to the apocalyptist who earlier feared that the Bomb would not fall. Disaster "removes the ennui of ordinary Wednesday afternoons," according to Percy. "If the Bomb is going to fall any minute, all things become possible, even love."[21] The shadow of doom destroys the normal limitations on what can reasonably happen in carefully managed lives so that amid the midweek doldrums Percy's apocalyptists can at the end feel, and fall in love, and perhaps even discover the faith that seemed so impossible a moment ago and a world away. On Wednesday, in the apparent ruins of New Orleans, Binx and Kate meet as survivors of catastrophe and find something in the emptiness that they can affirm. Binx performs the act that Percy considers a virtual celebration of being (*MB* 271). Whereas Emily indicated his new status by not using his name, he affirms his new intimacy with Kate by naming her. "May I bring along my own fiancée," he asks Joyce over the phone, "Kate Cutrer?" (*M* 231).

The new life of Kate and Binx is religious in its radical bondedness. Kate defined a debased version of this communion earlier when the train to Chicago stopped at Jackson. As the moonlit capital glimmered "like the holy city of Zion" (*M* 196), Kate announced that she had at last found a way to live in a city. She thought that earthly citizenship might be possible only if she could find membership in some *civitas dei*. Identifying herself for the first time as a religious person, the spiritual novice told Binx that she sought one to whom she could respond in perfect faith and obedience. Kate's anxiety taught her that a humble sense of dependency is essential to the religious life, but she proposed that the indifferent and independent Binx be her god: "You can do it because you are not religious. God is not religious. You are the unmoved mover. You don't need God or anyone else—no credit to you, unless it is a credit to be the most self-centered person alive. I don't know whether I love you, but I believe in you and I will do what you tell me" (*M* 197). Kate searched for a lord who would authorize her to act by becoming the center of her life, and she appropriately recognized Binx's transcendent egotism. Yet in choosing the moviegoer as her divine mover she reduced belief to mindless idolatry. The would-be disciple sought a caricature of the religious life based on her subservience and Binx's selfishness, but her disastrous lovemaking with Binx exposed the failure of such faith without love.

On the playground Kate seems to envision the same kind of servitude as the basis for their marriage: "But I think I see a way. It seems to me that if we are together a great deal and you tell me the simplest things and not laugh at me—I beg you for pity's own sake never to laugh at me—tell me things like: Kate, it is all right for you to go down to the drugstore, and give me a kiss, then I will believe you. Will you do that?" (*M* 234). But love now transforms the former bondage into bondedness. Kate's solution is "a way" for her, a person intimidated whenever she is not with Binx, not a pattern for others. Moreover, the moviegoer gives not a director's commands but reassurances to a beginning actress. Earlier that afternoon, Kate wanted some cigarettes but was too frightened to go to the drugstore. When she imagines Binx saying that it is all right for her to go, he gives her the possibility rather than grants permission. He also gives her a kiss. For Percy, love by its very nature inspires, affirms, and enables.

The religious love between Binx and Kate achieves a bond so profound that it seems a communion of consciousness. The entire scene in which they discuss the terms of their marriage takes place in Kate's car, which "has become gradually transformed by its owner until it is hers herself in its every nut and bolt" (*M* 232). At the end of his travels, Binx lives in Kate, shares at the most intimate level her very being. Even his language echoes hers in the same constant assent and affirmation that Percy would explore more fully in *The Second Coming*: "You can be sure. . . . I will. . . . Yes. . . . I know that. . . . You might. . . . Yes, I'll do that" (*M* 234). Whereas Binx once thought of opening a service station as a profitable investment, he discovers a life of service to a woman who has made her car her own. Hence the moviegoer can later enter medical school as his aunt desires, but the new profession no longer means that he has adopted Emily's ethical humanism. Rather, he has gone beyond a career to a vocation. He will attend to the driver in the car whose "very grease itself seems not the usual muck but the thrifty amber sap of the slender axle tree," the vital, centering, and lubricious Kate (M 232). Binx signifies the ultimate nature of his bond with Kate by receiving a version of the sacrament at the center of Lonnie's religion. When Kate begins tearing away shreds of skin from her thumb in a typically self-destructive gesture, Binx takes her hand and kisses the blood. Both pledge themselves to communion with each other. Unlike Emily in her Spenglerian pessimism, Binx and Kate commit themselves to a future of hope.

As prophetess of doom, Emily might see the burned-out cityscape of New Orleans behind the playground but not the promise of the ashes that Binx contemplates at the end of the novel. Sitting in the car of his "sooty eyed" love (M 231), he watches a black man come out of church on the first day of Lent, not sure whether or why the ostentatiously middle-class businessman may have received ashes. The rite may simply be a social ritual in old Catholic New Orleans, or it may signify a genuine act of faith in the God who dwells at the corner of Elysian Fields and Bons Enfants. But then Binx considers a third possibility that may be as divinely comprehensive as the allusion to "Pied Beauty" suggests. "Or is he here for both reasons: through some dim dazzling trick of grace, coming for the one and receiving the other as God's own importunate bonus?" (M 235). Binx cannot be certain, but he intimates that the God of ironic vengeance is also the Lord of amazing grace. The possibly token gesture of the businessman's coming up in the world may be converted into a sign of his coming to God. Binx imagines the Divinity who defies human expectations and embraces clear contradictions. If this Lord tantalizes by seeming to disappear behind all theological signs and proofs, he may also dispense the lagniappe of social recognition or spiritual blessing regardless of which of the two is sought.

Percy's novel recognizes the indirect and unknown routes that lead to God in spite of oneself. The way is through the ashes for both the black man who comes to church and for Binx who finds Kate coming to him. Ashes have been a sign of last things from the first day of Binx's search when he noticed that the "swamps are still burning at Chef Menteur and the sky over Gentilly is the color of ashes" (M 12). Whereas the heavens foreshadow the world's ultimate conflagration, the Catholic sacramental marks the believer as doomed by a personal eschaton. Signed with a cindery cross, each recipient on Ash Wednesday hears the traditional prayer that echoes God's judgment in Genesis 3:19 and reminds the children of Adam and Eve that fallen life from its very beginning is bounded by an end: "Remember, man, that you are dust, and unto dust you shall return." But if the ashes stamp this mortality on the penitent's flesh, they also signify the first turn to a new and final life. Although Binx does not formally receive the seal of Lent, he lives out its significance in his conversion at the end of chapter 5. After wandering in the spiritual wasteland of *Arabia Deserta*, he chooses a bleaker desert than his barren pleasures because only it can lead to the renascence anticipated on Ash Wednesday. The day after Mardi Gras celebrates the end of carnal Binx's valedictory "Carnival in Gentilly" (Percy's title for an early sketch of the novel) even while his love for Kate promises a lenten spring emerging from the ashes of his own life in the epilogue.

The use of such a conclusion calls attention to the end as decisively the end. Percy does not allow the emphasis to be overlooked, for the last section begins, "So ended my thirtieth year to heaven, as the poet called it. . . . Reticence, therefore, hardly having a place in a document of this kind, it seems as good a time as any to make an end" (*M* 236–37). The confessions of Binx Bolling close with a self-consciously formal resolution. The epilogue almost seems a nineteenth-century anachronism in a novel that began as disjointedly as *The Moviegoer*. Writing more than a year later, Binx informs the reader in summary fashion about the destinies of many of the characters: his own marriage to Kate and attendance at medical school, the deaths of Jules and Lonnie, Mr. Sartalamaccia's purchase of the duck club, Emily's acceptance of her déclassé nephew. Such a deliberate ending reads like the fictional equivalent of Binx's eschaton, as if he had now put his old life behind him. Percy, however, does not allow this end to be the end. Just after Binx has recorded these fates and announced that it is "as good a time as any to make an end," the proposed end turns into its opposite (*M* 237). If *The Moviegoer* began with omens of the end, it ends with a scene so open-ended that it becomes a new beginning as Percy depicts the bond of love that joins Binx and Kate in their daily struggle.

Percy's end purifies the Hollywood sentimentality from the film about the amnesiac's new life with the librarian that Binx wishfully recalled at the beginning of the novel. Yet it avoids the wailing despair at the end of Nathanael West's more overtly apocalyptic novel about cinematic illusions when a swarm of moviegoers, who love to read about catastrophe, turn from their boredom to wreak devastation. Percy's last pages look beyond the day of the locust by completely re-creating the ideals of traditional screen romance so that his final scene dramatizes a disillusioned moviegoer's uncertain, imperfect, and demanding life of love. Although Kate goes to see Lonnie at Touro Infirmary on the day before he dies, Binx dismisses her visit as "an extravagant womanish sort of whim," what he categorizes in tiresome existential terms as a "doubling" (*M* 238). Despite his condescension, he is partly right about questioning the prudence of his wife's visit, for she leaves the hospital in horror at Lonnie's jaundiced and emaciated body. When Binx explains that his brother has hepatitis, Kate charges her husband with the professional apathy and arrogance of a medical student, and when he later kisses her, she accuses him of being "grisly" (*M* 239). Binx is more sensitive and Kate less capricious than either seems. Kate feels genuine pity for Lonnie and his heartbroken parents, and Binx seems so composed because he shares his brother's joy. As Binx tells his wife, Lonnie whispered that he had at last conquered his habitual disposition and that Kate was a "very good-looking girl" (*M* 239). When Binx kisses her head and repeats Lonnie's compliment as his own, he is not being macabre but as affectionately appreciative as his brother who showed him the necessity of loving in the ruins. Percy never idealizes the trials or ignores the failures of love, yet although Kate and Binx misunderstand the best intentions of each other, they provide mutual support for their difficult journeys. By performing an errand, Kate makes it possible for Binx to spend time with Lonnie and the rest of his brothers and sisters, and Binx makes it possible for Kate to perform a more ardent and arduous form of toil than Tillie ever attempted, a labor of love.

Fearing the possibility of war, Emily wants some of her government bonds retrieved from the office vault so that she can store them at home. Binx does not respond to her anxiety with "the old authentic thrill of the Bomb and the Coming of the Last Days" (*MB* 84), for he already lives beyond the end with Kate. On the train to Chicago Kate accused the unreligious Binx of needing neither God nor anyone, but now as a less self-centered wanderer he asks his wife, "Will you do me a favor?" (*M* 241). Kate "understands him perfectly and depends on him in a very scary way," Percy told Jo Gulledge. "And in the end, I think, he depends on her."[22] Binx tells her exactly where to get off the streetcar, what to do at the office, and how to return. But he does more than just give Kate instructions. Offering her a flower, he promises to share the trip by traveling with her in thought. Twice before she leaves, Kate makes sure that Binx will be thinking of her; the second time she frames the scene: "I'm going to sit next to the window on the Lake side and put the cape jasmine in my lap? . . . And you'll be thinking of me just that way?" (*M* 242). Binx speaks the tender guarantees that make Kate's own journeying possible, but he does not simply turn his wife into a patient. Although Kate seems more desperate than Binx, she too responds in love. Kate twice calls him "sweet," and whereas she once described him as the unmoved mover, she now sets him in motion as well. Their valedictory scene acts out Binx's creed—to listen to people, watch them, "hand them along a ways in their dark journey and be handed along" (*M* 233). Kate's venture on the streetcar enables Binx to join his brothers and sisters in the same community of fellow travelers by taking them on the train at Audubon Park. The end of *The Moviegoer* looks forward to the reciprocal awareness of Kate and Binx. While she is away, Kate will know what Binx knows. She will be on the streetcar, but she will also be the final image in the mind's eye of the moviegoer.

This last scene, however, is only anticipated, for the frightened Kate may very well abandon the trip. Yet the willingness to embark on the very riskiness of love is itself decisive for Percy's wanderers. On this journey Kate is not fleeing the dead center of her life, as when she boarded the bus with short-lived euphoria after Lyell's death. She is traveling through her despair because she and Binx are focused on each other. And if Kate never reaches Mr. Klosterman, there is now no catastrophe, for Binx tells her simply to get off the streetcar and walk home. He does not eliminate the threat of disaster from his wife's world, but his love keeps it from becoming Kate's doom. Although Percy does not resolve the outcome of the novel as definitively as the epilogue first promises, Binx and Kate dare the trials of wayfaring even amid the possible ruins. Having experienced both an end and a new beginning, they know why Percy agrees with Sartre, "*L'enfer c'est autrui*," and then adds, "But so is heaven" (*MB* 285).

At the end of his "thirtieth year to heaven, as the poet called it," Binx's coming to consciousness on Wednesday morning leads to his sharing of consciousness with Kate (*M* 236). While their new life is religious in the communion of love that binds them together, from the beginning Binx has implied that the search may end in a coming not just to self or to another, but to God. Even in the epilogue Binx's natural reticence prevents him from saying whether his new life is held fast by the most religious of all bonds. A "peculiar word this in the first place, *religion*," Binx comments toward the end of the novel; "it is something to be suspicious of" because it is used too glibly in an age that devalues language (*M* 237). Percy renews the meaning of the word by dramatizing the ultimate connections that his moviegoer cannot quite profess. In the final scene with his half brothers and sisters, Binx realizes his image of life after the end of the world—merriment among children in the ruins. On the day before Lonnie's death, Binx comforts the Smith children, yet the mood is celebratory. He delivers a message of love from Lonnie and offers to take them to ride the train; they cry out their affection and ask for kisses. And in the last sentence of the novel, Binx names Thérése and Mathilde, Donice and Clare "my brothers and sisters" (M 242). As Kate walks away in front of him and the children call out behind him, Binx stands in full communion. His joyous acceptance of his family makes his union with Kate part of a larger life in love.

The end of *The Moviegoer* shows how far Percy has come in portraying the way his lovers live under God. Whereas Allison virtually disappeared at the end of "The Gramercy Winner" as William discovered salvation through Scanlon's sacramental care, Kate is integral to the last scene of Percy's first published novel. More troubled than Allison, Kate shows greater spiritual strength because she is willing to search in the face of doom. Yet although Binx's progress to God would be impossible in the novel without Kate, she never exhibits the same degree of religious awareness as does her husband. When Kate asks Binx about the meaning of Lonnie's "habitual disposition," he does not answer. And after Binx rejoices with his siblings in a vision of the apocalypse, Kate compliments Binx on his gentle-heartedness toward them, but, in a novel whose scenes are staged and edited as carefully as those in the best film, she "stands a ways off" from the merriment (M 239). Kate understands the quest amid despair more completely than any of Percy's fictional women until Allie in *The Second Coming*, yet she is never fully taken up in the drama of proclaiming the new life that she has even now tentatively begun.

Like Alyosha at the end of *The Brothers Karamazov*, Binx is questioned about the general resurrection before his final dialogue with Kate.[23] "When Our Lord raises us up on the last day," Donice asks, "will Lonnie still be in a wheelchair or will he be like us?" And when Binx answers that indeed their brother will be like them, Donice interprets the events at the end of the world from a child's wonderful and playful perspective: "You mean he'll be able to ski?" (M 240). Binx's "Yes" is not just a pious consolation to grieving children but an affirmation that results from his week's search.[24] Having become aware that "everyone is dead," he discovers that after the end of his world, he and his family are alive (M 99). Binx can proclaim the doctrine of the last day when Lonnie will be restored to life because the moviegoer has seen the vitality of his brother's love, witnessed his own last day, and felt that he himself has been made new. By the novel's end Binx's personal apocalypse finds its fulfillment in an eschatological faith. In the epilogue the moviegoer no longer refers to movies, for he lives not in front of a camera but before God and his family. Binx has at last begun to achieve the consummate form of good acting.

PERCY'S FIRST GENTLE MAN

THE LAST GENTLEMAN

I   Although not a dedicated moviegoer, like Binx Bolling, Will Barrett glimpses a cinematic revelation in one of those odd moments of time gone askew that afflict him throughout *The Last Gentleman*. Emerging from the subbasement of Macy's, where he works as a humidification engineer, the young Southerner in New York suddenly perceives the surge of commuters on Seventh Avenue as if they were photographed in an old-fashioned movie. They even seem to walk faster, "like the crowds in silent films" (*LG* 45). Will's vision of the past as motion picture dramatizes the essence of an older order, when people showed that they knew exactly what they were doing by their serious faces and purposeful strides. So sure about how to act, they performed each action with the manners that were an archaic equivalent of the movie star's gestural perfection. Will views the pedestrians of the 1960s as walking with the same certainty as did the gentlemen and ladies of a bygone age, whose ranks the wayfarer hopes to join.

Emily, the custodian of the genteel code in *The Moviegoer*, imagined that Binx belonged among just such a well-bred company; but during her climactic confrontation with her louche nephew, she realized that he was not one of those "certain people, gentlefolk I don't mind calling them" who display a "native instinct for behavior, a natural piety or grace" (*M* 222). No gentleman, just a disappointing and ungrateful scapegrace, the moviegoer was finally dismissed by his imperious aunt for bad manners. If a gentleman seems rare in the placid and prosperous days of Emily's Eisenhower era, he has become obsolete in the turbulent 1960s of *The Last Gentleman*. The title character of Percy's 1966 novel is thus an anachronism. He is determined to be a gentleman, perhaps the last of his breed, the sole survivor of the Old South. As Will Barrett undertakes a moral odyssey across America, he confronts and rejects various codes of gentility until he at last discovers how to live as the end and epitome of his line by a daring reinterpretation of his family's tradition. Beginning almost as a reactionary, the wanderer converts the values of the old order into the virtues of a radically new age. Will progresses from being outdated to being apocalyptic, from the last upholder of past ideals to a seeker of the time to come. By the end of his journey he acts not so much out of noble obligation and dutiful courtesy as out of an urgent love for those lost near the ends of their worlds. The last gentleman becomes the novel's first gentle man.

Will's transformation of a cultural ideal into a spiritual discipline begins with a casual and chance revelation. Like Binx Bolling, Will comes to himself through a visionary moment that ends his old way of life and discloses the beginnings of a new lifetime. Having purchased a highly sensitive telescope, Will anxiously scans Central Park for some sign of his future. The Tetzlar serves the same function as the movie camera eye that Binx formed with his thumb and forefinger to focus his sight on his possessions. It allows Will to recover a world hollowed by the "ravenous particles," the moviegoer's malaise turned into a deadly fallout (*LG* 26). These particles rain a devouring everydayness on people, objects, and events that consumes whatever has become commonplace. The telescope saves the ordinary from being unnoticed. It does not simply extend the range of Will's vision by bringing the faraway close at hand; rather, it increases the very intensity of his perceptions. Although the instrument always has the possibility of interposing itself between Will and his cosmos rather than returning him to it, the young seer generally avoids the mistake of the stargazing Dr. Bolling. Whereas Binx's father transcended the earth in studying the heavens, Will uses technology to defeat such extraterrestrial abstraction. The telescope sets the world at nought through the immensity of distance, and then it startles Will into consciousness by giving the scene back larger than ever before. In place of pallid actuality, it reveals a "brilliant theater bigger and better than life," the equivalent of the resplendent reality manifested to Binx Bolling at the movies (*LG* 76).

Will's telescope locates him in New York as a seer by helping him to recover not just a view but himself as a viewer. And when by good luck he happens to spy the Handsome Woman and her lovely young friend at the beginning of the novel, he gains a view of his own peculiar destiny and doom. Will imagines that to live any longer is to love Kitty. Several weeks later, Will learns from the *New York Times* that Ground Zero on a map charting the effect of nerve gas on the metropolitan area is the precise place in Central

Park where the two mysterious women sat. The park bench marks the place of catastrophe, where Will receives a private answer to the same question that disturbed Binx's sleep: "Was it possible, he wondered, that—that 'It' had already happened, the terrible event that everyone dreaded" (*LG* 47). On a day early in summer in Central Park, the apocalypse approaches not for everyone but for Will Barrett.

At "Ground Zero," Percy's early title for the novel, Will's old world begins to end.[1] For the past twenty-five years Will has lived as the postmodern everyman described in *The End of the Modern World*, the source of the second epigraph in *The Last Gentleman*. Romano Guardini's typical citizen of the late twentieth century is "mass man," the abstracted and anonymous technician who "acts almost as if he felt that to be one's self was both the source of all injustice and even a sign of peril."[2] Percy's titular engineer has never fully been himself but has stumbled through life in a paralyzing daze of temporal disintegration. He has either forgotten his past in attacks of amnesia or remembered it too keenly in overwhelming spells of déjà vu. Infinite desires claimed whatever time was not plagued by the vagaries of memory. Watching and waiting, Will lived not just for the future but in the future, in a world of perpetual possibility. Since he feared that any action, however insignificant, might compromise his potential identity, Will cultivated obscurity in New York and reduced daily existence to a series of nonevents. He languished in eternal ambivalence, even managing to occupy Dr. Gamow's "ambiguous chair," designed to reveal the psyche of his patient by the position which he chose, ambiguously—neither sitting nor reclining, neither facing his therapist nor quite turned away. The present was always deferred, a suspended tense where nothing crucial ever happened because it was besieged by a capricious past or pledged to a completely open future.

Since Will could not act decisively for himself, he became the most theatrical of actors, another moviegoer after Binx's own heart. Like Barth's Jake Horner, who likewise shifted his hands and arms while sitting before the Doctor because he wished to exclude none of his innumerable options, young Barrett perceived a bewildering array of possibilities and simply assumed a multiplicity of roles in random succession.[3] So mercurial was his identity that Will tended to become like everyone else in a group. While at college, he stuck his hands in his pockets after the best Princetonian fashion. On a ski weekend with some coworkers he forgot the South completely and even began to speak like his fellow Ohioans. As the most urbane of New Yorkers, he went to the Metropolitan Museum, attended the Philharmonic, and consulted a psychiatrist. Will was as protean as Huck Finn, whose travels he later imitates, yet he demonstrated no selfsame identity underlying the constant transformations. There were so many Will Barretts that there was no one Will Barrett, but only a performer, a would-be Barrett, hiding behind the desperate pretenses.

Will's vision of Kitty in Central Park changes him from a playactor into an actual person. The well-advised narrator understands this final metamorphosis as not merely a psychological transformation but as a spiritual conversion experienced in apocalyptic terms: "If a man lives in the sphere of the possible and waits for something to happen, what he is waiting for is war— or the end of the world" (*LG* 10). Will interprets the surprising revelation of Kitty as the sign of his personal apocalypse. If the seer once imagined that every option should always be available to him, he now realizes that "he was not destined to do everything but only one or two things" (*LG* 4). If he thought that he had to be everyone, his identity ever shifting and unstable, he discovers that he must only be Will Barrett. At that instant he begins the recovery of his name, for Percy always a sign of the self, which climaxes at the end of the novel. Will regains the power of his own volition, a decisive sense of purpose equal to that of the old-time pedestrians envisioned on Seventh Avenue. Will now knows what to do. No longer like everyone else in the group, he embarks on a course of action that he alone decides: the pursuit of Kitty as a Percyan wayfarer. Percy almost disregards Barrett's longed-for love by the end of the novel, but Will's initial vision of her is so momentous because it begins his search for a way to live in the ruins of his once-postponed life. Will will be himself.

Although the narrator flatly observes that most people would have forgotten the chance sighting of a lovely girl in a week, Will cannot forget his love at first sight. The amnesiac remembers her as a sign because the coming of the end in Central Park fits into the disconcerting pattern of his eschatological life. Will thrives on misfortune. His imagination of disaster makes him wonder, "*do I not also live by catastrophe? I can smell it out every time. Show me a strange house and I can walk straight to the door where the bad secrets are kept. The question is: is it always here that one seeks one's health, here in the sweet, dread precincts of disaster?*" (*LG* 113–14). Will's hallucinatory moments of racial memory and recurrent bouts of self-forgetfulness often make the time at hand come to an end as the present fades into a felt moment from family history or suddenly drops into wrenching oblivion. Disorientated by time, Will feels like the sole survivor of a bombed building, who sees the world afresh (*LG* 11). As the narrator in chapter 1 completes some of the fictional gaps in the life of the young man so afflicted by *Lücken*, his disjointed past almost seems a series of variations on apocalyptic themes. More violent than the very ordinary opening, these various episodes show how Will continually becomes aware of himself and others through the grace of catastrophe.

As he was returning the previous summer with Midge Auchincloss from the Newport Jazz Festival, Will drove into the heart of hurricane Donna. The disaster freed them, for the storm cleared away the noxious particles that had earlier reduced their affection to abstracted embraces. When Will and Midge no longer lived during an ordinary weekend but in the whirlwind of the last day, they achieved a singular intimacy. They could finally talk to each other and noticed that the table in the diner, where the two of them sought refuge, suddenly seemed worth two hundred dollars. Their misadventure made what was most negligible gain in value because it was seen against the background of possible annihilation. Will's paradoxical awareness that in the worst of times lies the best found a wondrous manifestation in the child they discovered lost in the storm. The infant, "a cherub striding the blast, its cheeks puffed out by the four winds," combined the tenderness and terror of Macbeth's naked newborn babe (*LG* 24). Heralding the last day and embodying the miraculous newness at the heart of apocalyptic disaster, this child of catastrophe reappears as Jamie newborn through baptism at the end of his life, and then as Will newly begun at the end of the novel.

Disaster once again helped Will to recover the lost world a week later when a worker crashed through the skylight at the Metropolitan Museum. Will noticed that although the painting by Velázquez was displayed to its best advantage, none of the spectators could really see it. The very perfection of its setting made it invisible to barely conscious visitors with blinkered eyes. Instead of revealing the work of art, the Metropolitan's ideal environment concealed the painting by providing no context in which it could be viewed. Will tried to reclaim the masterpiece obliquely by watching a family of viewers stare at it with glazed looks, but no one could break through the terrible ordinariness. The "cataclysm" (*LG* 27) transformed the onlookers from passive consumers of another's aesthetics into active participants in their newly beautiful world. Powdered by the glass from the fallen window, these momentary pillars of salt escaped unscathed in the midst of disaster like the infant in the storm. Only after the bystanders had been shocked out of their insentience could they laugh and cry and even show some concern for the injured workman. And Will, who supported the worker as he caught his breath, finally saw the work of art as if he had just passed the master's studio and peered in the front door.

Although Will's glimpse of Kitty lacks the devastating force of his earlier apocalypses in the storm or at the museum, it too is a moment when sight is so intensified that it reveals normally unseen significance. The shock of vision illustrates the narrator's observation that over the generations the violence so characteristic of the Barrett family had gradually turned inward. The destructive renewal caused by the hurricane and the crash of glass also occurs in Will, but the cataclysm takes place in his consciousness. His romance by chance at Ground Zero virtually copies the movie convention of "meeting cute" that Binx desired and that Percy describes in an apocalyptic scenario from "The Man on the Train": "When the Bomb falls and the commuter picks his way through the rubble of Fifth Avenue to Central Park, there to take up his abode in an abandoned tool shed à la Robert Nathan, everything depends upon his meeting *her* and meeting her accidentally" (*MB* 90). In Nathan's Depression-era *One More Spring*, a failed shopkeeper happily meets a golden-hearted streetwalker after both have tried to steal food from the kitchen of a casino. As winter turns into a maudlin spring, the pair discover love in a toolshed in Central Park. Will Barrett's casual observations in Central Park seem as full of promise as the beginning of Nathan's New York idyll. The earlier visionary moments of Percy's last gentleman never led beyond themselves. Like Binx's wartime observation of the dung beetle, they remained keen instants of perception eventually lost in everydayness. Will's "meeting cute"—his improbable and passionate discovery of Kitty two thousand feet away—may ultimately be as illusory as any of Hollywood's fortuitous rendezvouses, but it provides the necessary impetus for seeking a way to live at the end of his world.

I I   In these last days Will decides that he can best realize the willful identity discovered at Central Park by acting like the last of his family line. "Here you are in love with a certain person and bound south as a gentleman like Rooney Lee after a sojourn in the North," he grandly and sweetly resolves on the way to following Kitty and her family home (*LG* 135–36). As a gentleman, he decides to practice a southern form of secularized faith whose cardinal tenet is veneration and imitation of the patriarchs. If Will comes to himself as a person whose decisions define him, he simply rediscovers what the exemplary Senator Underwood said long ago to Will's father: "when you grow up, decide what you want to do according to your lights. Then do it.

That's all there is to it" (*LG* 348). Being a gentleman requires more than simply consummate manners: the courtesy that makes Will address everyone as ma'am or sir, the amiability of a man's man that makes Mr. Vaught want to invite him on a hunt or to a poker club, as well as the gallantry of a ladies' man that makes Mrs. Vaught enjoy bantering with him. Living as a gentleman also demands an underlying manner that supports all of these social virtues, an integrity characterized by clarity of vision, decisiveness, and self-determination. Like the movie stars whom Binx impersonated, Will's family provides exalted ideals for how to act. Typical of the forthright tradition was Will's great-grandfather, who "knew what was what and said so and acted accordingly and did not care what anyone thought" (*LG* 9). Assuming that truth and virtue were so obvious and incontrovertible that they need not be defined, the deliberately generalized portrait emphasizes that boldly following one's unquestionable convictions is basic to being a gentleman. So sure was Will's great-grandfather that upon once meeting the grand wizard of the Ku Klux Klan in a barbershop, he challenged the official to a duel. But the Barretts gradually lost the energy of this absolutism. Will's grandfather would also have dared the grand wizard if only he were convinced that it was the right course. And Will's father felt the strain of honor so intensely that even to walk down the street on a September morning became an exercise in the rigorous choreography of a gentleman.

The initial ability of the great-grandfather to act with such assurance declined into his son's ambiguity and his grandson's irony. Defiance yielded to doubt and finally to the despair of Will's father, who saw every deed except suicide as futile. The only action possible was to end all possibility of action. Will came to Central Park as the uncertain heir to this outworn and self-consuming tradition. His father's concern for what others thought became in the lost son a basic ambivalence about what to think at all. If irony both affirms and negates, Will transformed his father's double vision into the lifestyle of a nonentity. Since he had just as many reasons for as against doing something, he lived at Ground Zero, the cancellation of the self by the self. Will's opening apocalyptic vision reverses the steady enervation of the will in the Barrett family. Lancelot Andrewes Lamar, Percy's later fierce gentleman for the latter days, perfectly understands the connection between personal action and social ethic when he explains manners as guaranteeing "that no one will not know what to do" (*L* 149). Seeing a lady, Will now knows what to do: he resolves to act with the savoir faire of a gentleman. And so he searches for a course of action honorable in the tradition of his ancestors. The sometime amnesiac must live in the present as if it were the past that pursues and claims him throughout the book in sudden flashes of imaginative memory.

Will's decision to continue the family example of being a gentleman may seem especially ludicrous when viewed against the grim background of ominous events and violent upheaval in *The Last Gentleman*. The beginning of the novel heralds this pervasive doom by dramatizing the opening lines of "The Second Coming."[4] At Central Park, where one of many statues depicts a medieval youth with a hawk perched on his hand, Will waits to photograph the peregrine falcon, but it never appears. The falcon does not hear the falconer. In the 1960s when things fall apart, the center does not hold at Central Park, where Ground Zero marks the place of catastrophe, not coherence. Although the uneasiness in *The Moviegoer* always hinted at disaster, the bloody tide has already begun to be loosed in *The Last Gentleman*. The near riot in Levittown when Will is mistaken for a blockbusting real estate agent threatening the white ghetto, the campus melee over the admission of the university's first black student, the harassment of the festival staged by the Writers' and Actors' League for Social Morality, the mysterious use of Fort Ste. Marie as a prison for dissidents, the lurid light over Dallas—all point beyond Binx's private sense of malaise to widespread civil unrest and anticipate the social chaos of *Love in the Ruins*.[5]

Percy's fiction seeks to reflect this disorder by breaking out of the deliberately imposed imaginative limits used to narrow and intensify the focus of *The Moviegoer*. As Will travels from the Northeast to the Southwest, *The Last Gentleman* surveys a wider American landscape, introduces a larger cast of characters, and chronicles a longer period of wayfaring than did Percy's meditative rendering of Binx's little life during one week in New Orleans. Because of this new expansiveness the apocalypse seems less a personal crisis and more a steadily growing but unrecognized national emergency. Its persistent pressure further loosens Percy's typically disconnected, capacious plot. Although *The Last Gentleman*, like its predecessor, follows a search, its picaresque action is more varied, episodic, and unpredictable. This greater fragmentation imitates Will's own chaotic consciousness, filled with jumbled events and jarring gaps, as well as the country's increasingly disjointed psyche. Because Will journeys through a crazy America, which seems even crazier to readers when seen by this 1960s Idiot, Percy's comedy also becomes more extreme. His use of a knowing, ironic narrative voice still causes much of the novel's humor to be based on the intelligent perception of incongruity so favored by Binx. Yet the point of view is more often the young and addled Will Barrett's, and the world appears slightly more askew to his earnest and ingenuous gaze. Percy's baffled seer meets boldly drawn characters whose lunacy reflects lives distorted by the ravenous particles. Since they typically and wrongly assume that Will knows the plot of their lives when he wanders in medias res, he naïvely gets involved in escapades that frequently climax in absurdity or the painful humor of slapstick. The novel's slightly perverse comedy results from a good-natured seeker with good manners confronting a society without gentleness or generosity. Will does not know why Mort Prince's pugnacious neighbors accuse him of being a scheming interloper, or why the university campus seems overrun by maddened figures racing through the dark. Rather, Percy's hapless hero simply stumbles into adventures already in progress, only to get punched and knocked to the ground. Often Percy leaves the reader as ignorant and confused as Will about the precise reason for such violence, so that the silent despair of *The Moviegoer* seems to have been replaced by the country's age of unreason.

If *The Last Gentleman* creates a vivid sense of the approaching disaster, it occasionally risks diffusion and disintegration, particularly in the lengthy section at the Vaughts' household. Since Percy agrees with Cervantes that the "road is better than the inn" (*MB* 89), his natural fondness for the quest rather than for stasis may explain the somewhat halted pace of chapter 4, in which Will is less a wanderer than at any other time in the novel. *The Last Gentleman* lingers too long in this grand home of a very unheroic family without creating enough pointed scenes. It is distracted with portraits of servants like David Ross and John Houghton that seem set pieces with a thematic but not dramatic validity. And the action too often falters after threatening to start whenever Jamie inevitably changes his mind about beginning some new plan. This interlude seems especially dilatory because afterward, except for the diversion at Uncle Fannin's in Shut Off, the novel builds to a series of decisive adventures—Will's mysterious visit to Val, the catharsis of his homecoming, Jamie's severe and poignant death. Although these episodes have their parallels in *The Moviegoer*—Binx's conversations with Lonnie, memories of his father, visit to his half brother at Touro Infirmary—the critical moments in *The Last Gentleman* have a desperation and desolation never as intensely felt in their earlier counterparts. Val's bleak school in the ruins lacks the idyllic atmosphere of the Smith fishing camp; Will's return to Mississippi brings to an anguished climax the search for a father, which is never central in *The Moviegoer*; and the final hospital scenes in *The Last Gentleman* starkly depict the death of a youth that is only mentioned by

Binx and anticipated by Kate's horrified reaction in the last pages of *The Moviegoer*. In *The Last Gentleman* Percy seems to have moved the fictional world of *The Moviegoer* closer to a wilder and more dangerous edge.

Although living as the last gentleman in such an uneasy land seems preposterous, Will eagerly chooses doomsday over everydayness. "It was not the prospect of the Last Day which depressed him," the narrator explains, "but rather the prospect of living through an ordinary Wednesday morning" (*LG* 23). However, the South to which Will returns after his sojourn in the North seems an optimistic land intent on denying apocalypse. The urban North looked bombed out to Will, and he felt happy and at home there because he could detect the miserable lack of home and happiness underlying its busy prosperity. But in the South Will discovers an indomitable happiness instead of the ominous indications of spiritual malaise to which his sensitive radar was attuned in the North. The new earth in his homeland is the backcountry landscape leveled down, filled in, and built up. In this City of Man, all the cheerful, wealthy men and glad, captivating women have forgotten defeat and do not even believe in disaster. Will hoped "to return to the South and discover his identity, to use Dr. Gamow's expression" (*LG* 79), but the regional examples he finds in both past and present are usually as reductive as his psychiatrist's cliché. This native son of Mississippi, who once exploded a Princeton monument to the Union dead, finds himself a Southerner never at home in the South.

Will meets the most egregious citizen of the country-club South in Kitty's father. Chandler Vaught burlesques Will's ideal of being a gentleman in a decade when gentility is out-of-date. As if trying to restore a vanished age of chivalry, he lives in a castle of jagged, purplish brick across from the sixth fairway and behaves with excessive cordiality. But Mr. Vaught wishes simply to exploit the façade of an earlier culture for his own selfish ends. Whereas Will's bonds with history frequently draw him back to visit Civil War battle sites, the past for Mr. Vaught provides only quaint paraphernalia—Rebel colonel's hats and walking canes—for his car salesmen. Underneath Mr. Vaught's apparent conviviality Will discovers a hidden malice, a fierce heart which his racist son-in-law conceals with less charm. Lamar Thigpen longs for the old times when the family retainer did a buck-and-wing for his master's entertainment and no blacks were ever admitted to the university. The aggressively amiable New South of the Vaughts does embody one of the chief virtues of the gentleman: it is sure of itself, unlike Will at the beginning of the novel. Son Thigpen's friends, for instance, are "very much themselves with themselves, set, that is, for the next fifty years in the actuality of themselves and their own good names. They knew what they were, how things were and how things should be" (*LG* 265). Will seeks such absolute conviction throughout the novel, for it enabled his ancestors to act nobly in times of crisis. But just as the South has transformed its customs into costumes, and geniality into guile, so its certainty has become a stifling smugness.

Mr. Vaught can provide Will with no adequate example for how to act like a gentleman in the 1960s because he lacks the necessary sensitivity to disaster that might disturb his self-satisfaction and give him the urgency to act with honor. Although the wealthy patriarch occasionally laments the corruption of the world and the ingratitude of his family, he never even achieves the tragic melancholy of the equally disappointed Emily Bolling. Mr. Vaught only plays at being an old-time Southerner, for he has aestheticized the apocalypse. At the sixth hole fairway, Mr. Vaught and company adopt a tone both "pessimistic and pleasurable. The world outlook was bad, yes, but not so bad that it was not a pleasant thing to say so of a gold-green afternoon, with a fair sweat up and sugared bourbon that tasted as good as it smelled" (*LG* 192–93). Although these sportsmen of the New South recognize the possibility of doom, they merely indulge in Weltschmerz as they wash disaster away with drink and enjoy the taste of both in leisurely fashion. Mr. Vaught revels in the prospect of destruction, but he is never quickened to respond. However, the entire gentlemanly tradition to which Will belongs derives its vigor from confronting the crises that Mr. Vaught only savors with sweetened sorrow.

The antiquated manners of Chandler Vaught's South become mere mannerisms precisely because they have no relevance to any larger order beyond his considerable self-interest. For Will's forebears, manners reflected not just the niceties of social intercourse but passionate moral convictions, a gestural perfection of ethical implications played out in the face of doom. Will's ancestors seemed most gentlemanly when they lived on the verge of catastrophe because the possibility of disaster made decisive action possible and especially honorable. Will remembers that Senator Underwood paid dearly for his virtue. His own great-grandfather risked his life in defying the grand wizard; and his uncle, the high sheriff, once stood on the top step of the city jail and warned the crowd that he would kill the first person who tried to incite any violence. These legendary figures, who virtually live in Will through sudden moments of cultural memory, demonstrate that every gentleman must live each day as if it might be his last and act as if he were at the end of his world.

Will seems to discover such a worthy risk in his apocalyptic romance with

Mr. Vaught's daughter, Kitty. During the course of the novel he tries to develop new ways of understanding and appreciating her, to live in the final days described in the novel's epigraph from Guardini's *The End of the Modern World*: "Love will disappear from the face of the public world, but the more precious will be that love which flows from one lonely person to another." Yet Will and Kitty fail to achieve this final intimacy, a love for a new era, because he is too much his father's son, and she becomes too much her father's daughter. Will cannot escape the simplistic romance of the gentlemanly tradition, and Kitty settles for the equally saccharine banalities of the newly gentrified South.

Before Will saw Kitty he knew only the love that must disappear from the face of the public world in Guardini's vision of apocalyptic romance. He might sit with his head in the lap of Carol Schwarz around the fire at a Bear Mountain ski lodge, but at such an ostensibly pleasant time he "felt a familiar and disastrous sinking of heart. . . . People seemed to come to the point of flying apart" (*LG* 21). The attack of heartsickness made Will feel the chaos and catastrophe of relationships at the end of the modern world when the psychic center does not hold despite the apparent coziness. Will's initial vision of Kitty in Central Park exposes the silent desire and frustrated communion of his previous passions. He sees in Kitty himself, even "his better half" (*LG* 8), the person to whom he must come if he will ever become himself. These anxious lovers seem uniquely suited to each other because they are both so unsuited to the rest of their too-facile world. The bemused engineer who has trouble remembering might repeat the confession of the shy ballerina who has trouble speaking, "I am not what I want to be" (*LG* 62).

In these crazed times, Will realizes that "love is backwards too. In order to love, one has not to love" (*LG* 69). Will and Kitty's romance seems to thrive in such upside-down times when love becomes paradoxically negated and renewed because it renounces the age's conventional means of expression. Since the Percyan apocalypse dawns in the consciousness of his characters rather than in the cosmos at large, it causes a restructuring of relationships. Trying to live in a radically new world, Will cannot be satisfied with the customary forms of love but must discover it as if for the first time. Will eschews formal dates with Kitty in the belief that he should not go to see her but simply come upon her. And Percy stages their entire courtship as a series of chance encounters and accidental separations as if its haphazard course were governed by the strategies in "The Loss of the Creature" (*MB* 46–63). Since the ordinary has become so invisible, Percy's essay recommends stealing upon it unawares. The odd angle of vision, the unfamiliar approach to the familiar, can restore the lost cosmos just as it can renew the abstracted person. Will does not so much see as constantly rediscover Kitty, beholding her for the first time again and again and again. His romance seems most original and promising in such moments when he appears to have left behind the comforts of his roles. When Kitty rescues him during an amnesic fit in Washington Heights, or when Will unexpectedly visits her in the Mews apartment, he admits his instability and need for her with an honesty that sounds more like Kate's openness than Binx's reticence. Yet as the last gentleman, Will compromises such potential freshness of feeling by deciding to woo Kitty "in the old style." The last of his breed does not propose what he decorously considers "country matters" but foresees a life of idealized romance: "He loved her. His heart melted. She was his sweetheart, his certain someone. He wanted to hold her charms in his arms. He wanted to go into a proper house and shower her with kisses in the old style" (*LG* 71).

Will's old-fashioned romance may seem new because it rejects the distorted sexuality of other loveless hearts in the novel. Son Thigpen glumly fornicates, Sutter Vaught celebrates the morality of pornography, and novelist Mort Prince panders to popular taste by making superficially pious connections between sex and the sacred. Will chooses a gentleman's courtship rather than a love that is dispiriting, obscene, or sanctimonious. But in following the tradition of his ancestors, he forswears a possibly more daring apocalyptic identity: "No more for him the old upside-down Manhattan monkey business of rejoicing in airplane crashes and staggering around museums half out of his head and falling upon girls in hurricanes. Henceforth, he resolved, he would do right, feel good when good was called for, bad when bad. He aimed to take Kitty to a proper dance, pay her court, not mess around" (*LG* 174). Will plans to exchange a life exultant in its awareness of the eschaton for ordinary and conventional everydayness. Although Percy's misguided suitor earnestly seeks a more proper way to love, he cannot merely adopt the manners of the gentleman; he must reinterpret them at the end of the modern world. For Percy, sexual love cannot be reduced to sweetness or wantonness, for it involves a profound sharing of consciousness greater than either of these extremes. Will's archaic code simplifies and sentimentalizes what should be an apocalyptic romance.

Will's chivalry hides the unspoken sexism and sexual license of the whole gentlemanly tradition. "Go to whores if you have to," Ed Barrett advised his son, "but always remember the difference. Don't treat a lady like a whore or a whore like a lady" (*LG* 100). Will tries to live by his father's clear distinctions but fails. Either the last gentleman treats Kitty with the politeness appropriate to a southern belle and then finds her too much of a whore, or he expects her to respond in kind to his passion and then is disappointed when she seems too much of a lady. He needs to see her as Kitty, not a species created by the masculine imagination; however, the traditional dichotomy is reinforced because Will suffers from the abstraction that Sutter diagnoses as the age's epidemic. Seeking to relate to the world only through his mind, the engineer turns love into courtesy or lust.

This dualism, as old-fashioned as it is modern, causes comic disaster when Will and Kitty meet for a late-night liaison in Central Park. While sirens, fires, and gunshots announce the upheaval of the end, the lovers retreat from the terrors of the city to the green world of the urban pastoral. But the last romantics do not discover the union of the lost and the lonely in the Guardini epigraph because they do not understand the unity of love. In Central Park the puzzled youth first tries to be gentlemanly toward Kitty until he is overwhelmed by the sexuality of this "great epithelial-warm pelvic-upcurving-melon-immediate Maja" (*LG* 111). When he finally responds to her overtures, the earth goddess is transformed into a sick and frightened waif; and he can only berate his thoroughly improper conduct after later learning that Kitty had been suffering from exposure to paint fumes. Throughout the novel Will and Kitty constantly alternate between such extremes. She is by turns demure and provocative just as Will is desirous and respectable; the two are forever at odds, and love at such poles becomes impossible.

If Will's courtship of Kitty simplifies love, it also threatens to ensnare him in a maudlin and mundane romance. He drifts toward fulfilling his cloying dream of "marrying him a wife and living a life, holding Kitty's charms in his arms the livelong night" at "a cottage small by a waterfall" (*LG* 187, 166). Kitty plans to buy the Mickle place as just such a hideaway, a picturesque prison of a home by "a ferny dell and a plashy little brook with a rustic bridge" (*LG* 285), where Will could succeed the recent eccentric tenant and settle down as the local lunatic. As the good daughter of Poppy Vaught, Kitty is glad to play the lady of the New South to Will's odd gentleman of leisure. Whereas Will feels progressively disorientated in the South, his once timid and gauche beloved feels only more at home. Pretty Kitty soothes away doom with her sweet clichés and eliminates the necessary renewal with a pet's domestic complacency. She seeks not to be genuinely new but merely contemporary. Kitty embraces the ravenous happiness of the South's latest reconstruction to become a chipper coed, slangy sorority sister, and modern bride. She tempts Will to deny his apocalyptic vision: to reject his conviction that the bad are the best of times and to accept the age's official optimism, which is much easier than apocalyptic hope beyond hopelessness. This Kitty, "fond and ferocious and indulgent," is as dangerous as a lion precisely because she offers a snug life of suburban gentility (LG 286). But Will increasingly balks at being wed to such a fiercely and falsely sanguine world. When the last gentleman is caught up in the murderous fury over admitting the first black student to the university and is knocked unconscious at a Confederate monument, he feels with his own head how the New South has not overcome its old hatreds. Still in a daze, Will turns his back on such civilization and decides, like Huck Finn, "well, I'm not going back because I've been there" (LG 294).

||| When the slightly stupefied Will wanders into a bleak mission in the pine barrens of Tyree County, Val Vaught seems to have expected him. More completely than any other character whom Will meets during his search, this news bearer lives out the apocalyptic rhythm of destruction, expectation, and renewal, and so she can show Will how to live up to gentlemanly ideals that he never dared to imagine. Val heard her old world as Chandler Vaught's daughter end in a moment of revelation at the Columbia library. While writing a paper on Pareto, she met a nun who told her that she looked half dead and wondered whether she would like to be alive. The evangelist repeated the gospel's summons to discipleship, "come with me," and offered the moribund linguist the life-giving Logos itself. Val heeded her call, and in six weeks took instruction, received the sacraments, and made her first vows. Although the skeptical bishop of Newark, New Jersey, required Val to submit certification that her family was free of all insanity, she explains that her alacrity simply resulted from the good faith of a student of language, "all I'd done was take them at their word" (LG 300).

Val puts language at the service of the last day. Like her brother Sutter, she looks to the exhaustion of Christendom, when she hopes "that the air would be cleared and even that God might give us a sign" (LG 378). The nun has established an outpost for such divine semiotics at her school, where she awaits the disappearance of the South's latest idols while looking to the full and final coming of God. Surrounded by cancerous trees, Val's mission stands in such terminal disrepair that it seems barely to have survived the end of the world. Will views its assortment of surplus army buildings and Quonset huts as "a lunar installation . . . a place of crude and makeshift beginnings on some blasted planet" (*LG* 302). Sutter likens the forlorn settlement to "one of those surviving enclaves after the Final War" and rejects his disappointed sister as a woman who has dressed for the bridegroom that never arrived. Imagining Val amid the maids who expect the Parousia in Matthew's parable (Matt. 25:1–13) or attend the marriage of the Lamb at the close of Revelation (Rev. 19:7; 21:2), he claims that she acted "as if the world had ended and she was one of the Elected Ones Left to keep the Thing going, but the world has not ended, in fact is more the same than usual" (*LG* 378). In his despairing apocalypse Sutter sees only what has not come, while Val looks beyond the devastation to the One who came, comes, and is coming again. Val's academy is not an eschatological retreat but a place where the kingdom of God already dawns. Since the apocalypse is not just personal but communal, she heralds this revelation by teaching speech to children who have been raised in silence. The Second Coming begins with their first coming to the word.

Val brings her Alabama pupils to Percy's "delta factor," the point at which they break into the world of language like Helen Keller learning at the pump in Tuscumbia, Alabama, that *water* names the clear liquid flowing over her hand. By giving her silent students the word—*pencil, hawk, wallet*—she gives them back the entire world that she affirms as well as their very selves as Adamic namers. Val compares her students to Adam on the first day, for when they come into consciousness through language, they achieve a new creation. Apocalypse ends where Genesis begins—in a garden, and Val enables her pupils to rediscover Eden in the ruins of their school. But their celebration of the world through signs only marks the beginning of a further revelation. When they can see creation as new and good, they are ready to hear the good news. In the progression typical of the Percyan apocalypse, their coming to themselves and into the world culminates in their coming to God. Recognizing herself, the student who was told that she looked almost dead, in her children, Val describes how their education finds its consummation in their salvation: "They were not alive and then they are and so they'll believe you. Their eyes fairly pop out at the Baltimore catechism (imagine)" (*LG* 301). The teacher's credibility, one of the chief requirements of the Percyan news bearer (*MB* 135), leads to her students' eager acceptance of her religious creed. Val empowers them to see—first, the world, and then, the truths of faith, so that her disciples hear with amazement the new name or the good news. They gain the equivalent of a renewed earth and heaven through living in the world and under God.

Val seeks to bring the same new life to her young brother. Whereas the Tyree children are dead without language, Jamie is physically dying and equally ignorant despite his searching mind. When her pupils point and ask questions, she gives them a name. She hopes to do the same for her abstracted brother, who still does not know the answer to such fundamental questions as "why he came here, what he is doing here, and why he is leaving" (*LG* 210). Val would instruct him as she does her students, for their catechism actually offers a primer filled with answers to these fundamental mysteries. But since Jamie will not listen to her, she ordains Will—first at her parents' home and then later by phone in the hospital—so that a "fellow technician" (*LG* 65) and searcher can teach her brother that the end is not the entropy that has fascinated the youth as an aspiring scientist and now claims his deteriorating body. Will, the indifferent believer, becomes a reluctant apostle by resentfully accepting her charge. It leads him to the novel's final scene of catastrophe, in which he acts like a gentleman somewhat after Val's own heart.

Although Valentine Vaught often seems to lack all gentleness, she struggles to convert her obduracy of heart into a form of gentility more appropriate to her name. This harridan freely confesses that despite her love of Christ, she still wishes her enemies to fry in hell. In the language of Lonnie's catechism, she has a habitual disposition to hatred. When Will first sees the truculent nun she is feeding her chicken hawk a packet of viscera, perhaps fit revenge on her "chicken-hearted" bishop, and immediately before Will leaves, Val asks him to pray that she might receive the grace "not to hate the guts of some people, however much they deserve it" (*LG* 297, 303). Percy refuses to sanctify the barbed religious with the easy transcendence of bland piety; instead he presents her as fervently engaged in her own spiritual wayfaring. Hating the age as much as Sutter, Val came to love her Lord and so to recognize her wrongful lack of love for her enemies. She is a Christian in spite of her own spiteful self. Val's membership in the ever-arriving eschatological kingdom does not annul her prejudices and frustrations but makes them no longer the permanent limit on her love. Whereas Sutter disdains the Baptists, Methodists, Seven-Up men, and scientists with whom his sister associates, Val transforms what he dismisses as a compromise into the very sign of her salvation. Partly out of financial need but chiefly out of spiritual exigency, the self-dispossessed daughter of a tycoon must embrace the representatives of the unsavory age she rejects.

Because she labors to show love in the ruins, this hard-hearted nun represents a new breed of gentlewoman. She still retains enough lineage in the older order to make her worthy of so honorable a title. When Val first met Will at her parents' castle, she told him that she had once heard his father address the DAR, "a strange bunch of noblewomen," on their responsibilities for civil rights. Although Val disagreed with the reasons behind the elder Barrett's campaign for racial justice, she clearly favored him over the opposing bigots. "He was right about one thing, of course, character," she admits. "You don't hear much about that either nowadays" (*LG* 208). Val's pet hawk, a variant of the royal bird that Will sought to photograph in Central Park, graces her strong-willed character with the nobility of the gentry. Sharing the boldness of the attacking falcon and of Will's mythic ancestors, Val Vaught seems as if she belongs to that earlier era when his great-grandfather "knew what was what and said so and acted accordingly and did not care what anyone thought" (*LG* 9).

Val follows the older tradition only to restore its central ideal to its rightful source. For her, as for Chaucer and Dante, "Criste wil we call of hyme our true gentilesse."[6] Her caged hawk witnesses to the spirit of holiness and wholeness that dwells amid her school at the world's end. When the apparent center does not hold in a wildly spiraling age, this falcon does hear the falconer. Val converts gentlemanly daring into what Guardini envisions as a primary virtue of the eschatological era, "a courage of the heart born from the immediacy of the love of God as it was made known in Christ."[7] Hence she challenges listeners not to duels but to "stop stealing or abusing Negroes, go confess your sins and receive the body and blood of Our Lord Jesus Christ" (*LG* 213). And she teaches her Tyree children out of a desire to give them back the world rather than from the possible haughtiness of noblesse oblige. Unlike Ed Barrett, who worked for the disenfranchised but not with them and always above them, Sister Johnette Mary Vianney labors alongside her students and under God. She makes her school on the grounds of the deserted Phillips Academy, which Will's father might even have attended, into a haven where the least aristocratic members of society can take their places in creation without losing themselves in the cosmos. Here where privileged sons once learned Greek and military science, the poorest in body and spirit come alive through language. Out of the old and in the ruins, Val creates a new order that transforms education into revelation, and gentility into the radical love of the Gospels.

At the Tyree school Will experiences no astounding conversion like Val's spontaneous change of heart at Columbia. In fact, he listens to this nun not because he is interested in her work at the end of the world but because he is a gentleman. "A complex system of scoring social debts kept him from leaving," the narrator explains (*LG* 299). Since Will cannot offer her much money, he pays her the courtesy of attention, but he repeatedly faults this disreputable lady for failing to live up to his rigorous standards. He is slightly "scandalized" by her attention to the hawk (*LG* 297), suspects that her "costume" indicates that she is "some sort of off-brand nun, perhaps not yet certified by the higher-ups," and finds her religious name "barbarous" (*LG* 298). Determined to be proper even if she is not, Will tries to reject Val's commission to attend to the dying Jamie as an example of the same Catholic impudence that his father opposed. Although such defiance seems necessary to preserve the independence of his ancestors, Val's mandate is actually the means by which the last gentleman will not just honor but actually surpass the code of the Barrett family.

I V   Ed Barrett left his son the consummate model for how to live and die like a gentleman. As Will wanders across America and back in time, he tries to understand the shade of his father, first through memory and finally through revisiting the family home in the Mississippi Delta, where Ed Barrett committed suicide. Amid the ruins of the gentlemanly tradition, Will recovers one of the sources of his own apocalyptic vision and reappraises his desolate patrimony.

Lawyer Barrett followed the tradition of his ancestors by acting with what Edwin Cady has defined as the hallmark of the gentleman: "the self-discipline of tender-minded persons for the furthering of social and cultural 'values.'"[8] His clients were the least likely to pay. He dared to address the DAR on the noblesse oblige owed by these American blue bloods, and when he lived out his lecture by helping blacks, Catholics, and Jews, he was accused of betraying his class. Unlike the jovial Poppy Vaught, Will's gallant father lived fully aware of the end. Will repeatedly remembers his parent walking in the dark and listening to Brahms, the "very sound of the ruined gorgeousness of the nineteenth century, the worst of times" (*LG* 100). While the ruffians who might murder him cruised silently in cars without headlights, Lawyer Barrett stood defiant in the face of possible disaster. Through sheer moral conviction he forced his opponents in the fight for social justice to leave town. The elder Barrett became the perfect member of his caste by fulfilling the civic obligations that his less enlightened contemporaries shirked, yet he revealed the limits of a gentleman's social activism by explaining to his son that he betrayed no one and actually had little concern for the people he defended. Although the most honorable man in an increasingly dishonorable age, Will's father lacked the necessary bondedness with those rejected by society and with the son he abandoned. Instead, he lived in the aloof preserve of his own transcendent virtue. But by acting like a gentleman in what he saw as the last days of the Old South, Lawyer Barrett set the pattern for how his own son, the last gentleman, would try to meet the end with the same noble righteousness.

In the 1960s Will follows his father's example most clearly by serving as a champion of civil rights. Just as his great-grandfather defied the grand wizard and his father defended the freedoms of black people, Will fights against racism, at first without even knowing it. When he accompanies a black-faced Forney Aiken to the home of novelist Mort Prince, an irate pack of Levittown householders mistakes young Barrett for a blockbusting real estate agent from New Jersey. Will takes offense at their hostile tone. Although he is puzzled about the reason for their insolence, the would-be hero wonders, "could it have come at last, a simple fight, with the issue clear beyond per-adventure?" (*LG* 143). Will hopes that the menacing crowd will finally give him the opportunity to act with the assurance of a gentleman. Although Forney later refers to the fisticuffs as if it were part of a valiant campaign, Will's attempt to follow the example of his forefathers is a travesty of the tradition. He suffers from a not very chivalrous attack of hay fever and the indignity of being punched in the nose by a maniacal hausfrau. Yet what makes this burlesque battle truly insignificant is that the honorable naïf does not really understand the social issues involved. Will is fairly certain that he has been insulted, and such an affront justifies a fight among gentlemen. But he does not realize that his foes are a band of suburban segregationists. Since he finds it impossible to "keep his anger pure and honorable," he duels more out of pique than noblesse oblige, championing no cause but his own (*LG* 144). The great moments in the lives of his ancestors resulted from seeking both self-justification and social justice. Not only did they act decisively in times of personal crisis, but they also acted for the sake of others. At Levittown, however, Will seems only a cocky young man looking for a fight.

Will demonstrates that being a gentleman requires more than just private

outrage when he meets Forney later during the arts festival in his hometown of Ithaca, Mississippi. After a redneck deputy pursues Forney and some
fellow artists to the Dew Drop Inn, routinely hits its black owner with a
blackjack, and humiliates the last gentleman by snapping the fly of his pants,
young Barrett relives all the tense urgency with which his forebears confronted bigotry and threats to their own integrity. Yet in these worst of times
Will feels best: "for once things became as clear as they used to be in the old
honorable days" (LG 325). He avenges both himself and the stricken Sweet
Evening Breeze by knocking Beans Ross unconscious and devising a plan for
the artists' escape. But even when Will at last acts with all the certainty of a
gentleman in the epic town of his ancestors, his virtue is compromised. He
strikes Beans Ross not when the officer assaults Sweet Evening Breeze but
only after the deputy has insulted Will's manhood and leered at the girlfriend
of a visiting actor. Unlike Val, who serves the most forsaken black children
of Tyree County, Will does not respond out of outrageous love. Rather, the
activist is a true son of his earnest and equitable father, the best of his very
limited line.

Although the wayfaring Will seems to find a moral haven in Ithaca, he
discovers in his hometown that the hereditary example can be fatal. While
visiting the old family home, he meets in memory the phantom of Lawyer
Barrett and finally recalls the details of the parent's suicide that he has been
fleeing on his travels. Despite his nobility and dedication, Ed Barrett was
ultimately false to Percy's apocalyptic vision. He was ruined by his own detachment and despair. Will's father devoted himself so completely to being
a gentleman that in the end he found a shotgun blast the most gentlemanly
accomplishment of all. The tension between his ethical imperative and his
pessimistic view of the times at last became self-defeating, so he decided on
his own last day and performed the ultimate act of ending his world. Instead
of the honorable action in the face of doom, Ed Barrett chose the honorable
action that was his own doom, the noble death of a stoic—suicide.

Like Dr. Bolling, Lawyer Barrett allowed his potentially apocalyptic vision
to degenerate into the tristesse of an overripe romanticism because his rarefied idealism was not balanced by a rootedness in this fallible world. Whereas
Percy's eschatology views the beginning of re-creation as the discovery of
communion amid the ruins, Will's father was unable to see anything after the
coming dissolution. Although he drove his opponents out of town, Lawyer
Barrett conceded that they had actually won, for their moral corruption had
become characteristic of the age. Since the servant of the law never labored

out of love, he found no reason for continuing to exist in an imperfect society. He intended his suicide as a deliberate rejection of a future in which manners were replaced by public defecation and fornication. But his death actually expressed a more profound pessimism, not toward the coming age but toward himself. Will's father succumbed to the perpetual strain of "living out an ordinary day in a perfect dance of honor" (*LG* 10). He killed himself because he could not bear alone the burden of living as the last gentleman.

As Will stands before the Barrett home, he performs the "deliberate exercise of freedom" that Percy describes in *Lost in the Cosmos*: a return to "the evacuated, bombed-out homeplace" which through absence and abandonment has "magically acquired a certain solidity and integrity of its own" (*LC* 151). Will realizes the error of the old gentlemanly tradition as he gazes at the scene of its wreckage in his own family. Since his father could not live in a corrupted age, he conducted his final duel with himself, the only fit match in his sublime kingdom, and freed himself from all taint of disrepute. He died for his abstracted and impossible ideals rather than live in a flawed age for the sake of his needy son. Having relived the anguished evening of his father's suicide, Will rejects his fatal inheritance. Instead, he rediscovers the solidity and integrity of the world in an iron hitching post circled by an oak standing before his family home: "It was not in the Brahms that one looked and not in solitariness and not in the old sad poetry but—" (*LG* 332). Will turns away from the melancholy art of his father's deathly tradition and attends to what Louis Rubin calls those "human qualities growing out of continuing existence in time, never perfect, never complete and self-sufficient in themselves, but always in vital relationship with ongoing experience."[9] Whereas the gentlemanly tradition was so inaccessible that it could not be touched except in death, Will realizes that he must look at hand, "here, under your nose, here in the very curiousness and drollness and extraness of the iron and the bark" (*LG* 332).

In this astonishing reappropriation of the immanent realm, Will discovers a presence so tangible that he cannot think of it apart from this particular example; he can only testify to its gratifying proximity. His father could not live here—in confining duration, at this limiting locale—but sought the otherworldly escape of deathly perfection in the gunshot blast that has resounded throughout Will's life. The partially deaf engineer wrings out his ear as if listening for the first time to a possible counterpoint to the romantic strains of his parent's gloomy solitude. Although Ed Barrett's discriminating taste honored culture with the faith that Guardini considers characteristic of the modern age, his suicide typified the tendency of postmodern culture that Guardini fears in *The End of the Modern World*—the dangerous use of power and freedom for destruction.[10] Rejecting his father's pessimistic poetry and music, Will hears the summons of the individual moment, literally at hand in the hitching post, manifestly here. From his opening revelation Will has been looking at what is immediately present and palpable before him. It is the uniquely concrete, the moment new and strange and now, which will locate him in this world and save him from taking refuge in his father's lovely darkness. Since he must live as a gentleman and not die as one, he seeks for some other way than the bloody and self-defeating idealism of his forebears by which he can make his way in the singularly compelling world that stands out before him.

V   Will flees the Old South of his father, just as he had earlier renounced the New South of the Vaughts, and follows Sutter into the bleak western desert where he truly becomes the last gentleman. He lives up to the example of his ancestors by pursuing a properly honorable quest: he seeks to rescue the dying Jamie from the reckless plans of his shameful older brother. But Will also sets out on an apocalyptic mission to discover the revelation known only to the ruined Sutter, the secrets that will enable a lover to live at the end of the world. Throughout the novel Dr. Vaught has steadfastly refused to play the role of news bearer to Will's island castaway. "Fornicate if you want to and enjoy yourself," he admonishes his aspiring disciple, "but don't come looking to me for a merit badge certifying you as a Christian or a gentleman or whatever it is you cleave by" (*LG* 225). The abstracted doctor realizes that the engineer simply wants to receive formulas from on high rather than assume sovereignty over his own life. Yet if Sutter abjures the role of apostle, he embodies his own form of bad news that travesties the gentlemanly traditions of the Old and New Souths. This unethical ethic teaches Will by its futile cultivation of irreconcilable extremes. Sutter's nihilism not only confirms Will's own eschatological vision but also compels the would-be apocalyptist to search beyond the doom of a desperate suicide.

Sutter's life celebrates the catastrophe that the modern world repudiates. Since the New South values material success, Sutter has abandoned a propitious career as a physician to become an assistant coroner, a position he later deliberately and scandalously loses. The doctor makes some of his most astute diagnoses by recognizing the happiness amid disaster and the disaster of too much happiness. Sutter once confined to a terminal ward a patient depressed over the necessity of feeling cheerful, while he suggests that the Deltans, the blissfully complacent fraternity brothers of Son Thigpen, may not feel as cheerful as they seem. He rejects one of the novel's chief images of prosperity—his father's Chevrolet dealership—to drive an Edsel, according to Jamie a constant reminder of the debacle of the Ford Motor Company. Sutter intimates to Will, who always feels bad in the best of times and who takes pleasure in "the voluptuousness of bad news," that his paradoxical emotions may be entirely appropriate in an age out of joint (*LG* 274).

As an apocalyptist of despair, Sutter even imagines that he recognizes the archfoe of the end times. "If I were a Christian, I shouldn't hesitate to identify the Anti-Christ," he announces. "Leigh Hunt" (*LG* 217).[11] The sniping doctor has fittingly turned a picture of Abou Ben Adhem caring for urchins into a target for pistol practice. Sutter finds Hunt guilty of an insidious humanism. The poet glorifies Ben Adhem by allowing his name to lead all the rest in the angel's book because the Arabian physician loved humanity best rather than God. Percy's sardonic physician takes aim at such humanitarianism even as he considers taking his own life because he cannot live for anything more ultimate. The marksman accurately recognizes that such romanticized benevolence signals a critical moment in the West's "entire melancholy procession of disasters." Since Hunt praises a man "who is extremely pleased with himself for serving man for man's sake and leaving God out of it," he represents a shift from the primacy of God to the vaunted self-sufficiency of humanity. And so the poet reduces the Deity to "a capricious sentimental Jean Hersholt or perhaps Judge Lee Cobb who is at first outraged by Abou's effrontery and then thinks better of it" (*LG* 217). God becomes like the actor who played Shirley Temple's grandfather in *Heidi*, or like the star of *Twelve Angry Men* who is the last juror to change his verdict to an acquittal. Hunt's holy philanthropy is a more egotistical version of salvation by good works. His apotheosis of the compassionate doctor exalts the human ability to heal its own malaise and eliminates the suffering and saving godliness of the biblical God. The Lord is remade not simply in the creature's image but in a Hollywood persona's so that he is left with only the corrupted panoply of the Creator. Love degenerates into sentimentality, mystery into whimsicality, and majesty into the privilege of changing his mind.

If Sutter's version of Hunt celebrates Western civilization's impotent divinity and arrogant humanity, the present age simply continues the reign of the Antichrist. Although virtually everyone in Percy's New South fears the Lord and goes to church on Sunday, God is present only in the most enfeebled and conventional of ways. He is relegated to being the ubiquitous plastic savior on car dashboards while he is everywhere absent from the lives of believers. Under the present caricature of a deity, Christianity has become a handmaiden to humanism, just one of the World's Great Religions to provide useful psychological insights, according to the enlightened engineer. On the radio Dizzy Dean encourages attendance at one's house of worship for a "rich and rewarding experience" that gets faith lost in profitable self-actualization (*LG* 186). The ultimate self-made man, the entrepreneurial Chandler Vaught, has saved himself, or at least several fortunes. Like Hunt's blessed physician, the New South has left "God out of it" and so honors all the idols of piety, prosperity, and personal enrichment. Hence, Sutter yearns not for the customary Second Coming but for the *apousia*, the going away of a God not worthy of the name.

The most avid disciple of Abou Ben Adhem in the world of *The Last Gentleman* is Sutter's ex-wife, Rita Vaught.[12] Kitty considers her sister-in-law the most unselfish person she has ever met, and her philanthropic work among the Indians has all the hallmarks of one who loved her fellow man best. As an officer of the third-largest foundation in the world, she would be a fitting candidate for the Jean Hersholt Humanitarian Award, Hollywood's tribute to the actor who headed the Motion Picture Relief Fund. Her modernly humanistic marriage sought "the right balance of adult autonomous control and child-like playfulness," but only doomed itself with pop psychology clichés (*LG* 246). Sutter objects that like all secular saints Rita canonizes herself, for her lay sanctity actually conceals the love of self that is the spirit of the Antichrist. Her deft maneuvers to obstruct Will's romance with Kitty show how, as with Emily Bolling, her patronage serves her own pride. At the novel's end, when Kitty seems to prefer the roles of cheerleader and wife-to-be over that of devoted protegée, Rita selects Myra Thigpen as the next victim of her generosity. Although Rita practices her faith in self-fulfillment with the high-minded dedication of Will's ancestral tradition, she serves neither God nor even "man for man's sake," but her own glorified ego so that her name may be set above all the rest in her angelic reckoning of life.

Sutter denounces Rita's liberality as "fornication of spirit" and turns from it to fornication of the body (*LG* 117). The libertine understands the crisis in Western civilization that haunts all of Percy's writing. The individual as knower, represented by the modern scientist, suffers from a radical dichotomy in which the self does not live fully in the world. Rather, the mind has abstracted itself to dwell far above mundane, human concerns while the world and the body left behind become a collection of specimens, examples, and coordinates. In such gnostic dualism, the incarnate God must be as irrelevant as Hunt's divinity because humanity seeks self-transcendence as it denies or perverts the flesh. The Southerner in the 1960s lives in no particular region or century and under no God: the aloof and musing Will Barrett, who plans to engineer his life according to the principles of modern science; Jamie, a scientific prodigy who would escape the breakdown of his body by pondering set theory and entropy; Rita, who offers Jamie a humane life of beauty and joy so that he need never experience his own mortality. Although Binx Bolling detected this same division between scientists and romantics, Sutter gives the rift between transcendence and immanence the urgency and importance of catastrophe. It has populated the world with the living dead. Sutter must be a coroner, for the only operation possible in such a devitalized land is a postmortem. But as an autopsist, Sutter can only analyze the casualties of this disaster; he cannot reverse it, even though the doctor imagines that he has found a way to restore the lost life of the body.

Sutter makes a religion out of being a perversely Chesterfieldian gentleman. When he disappears into the desert with Jamie, he leaves Will, his would-be son, a conduct book that expounds his views as a moral pornographer through a series of coroner's case studies.[13] Like his sister, Sutter recognizes that Christianity hallows the greatest abomination, what he terms "the Scandalous Thing, the Wrinkle in Time . . . God's alleged intervention in history" (*LG* 307). Paul saw such an affront—the Lord of all time subjecting himself to human mortality—as centered in the *scandalum* or stumbling block of the cross (1 Cor. 1:23). The disgraced, incarnate savior is the least gentlemanly of gods. As a connoisseur of all that is dishonorable, Sutter even approves of his sister's ungenteel conversion because he does "not in the least mind scandalizing the transcending scientific assholes of Berkeley and Cambridge and the artistic assholes of Taos and La Jolla" (*LG* 308). But then the embittered scientist faults Val for compromising her outrage by accepting the very groups whom she might have offended.

Sutter does not understand that his sister works and loves in a world that has so much to detest precisely because of the divine indignity at the heart of her faith. Instead, the apostle of profligacy reduces the scandal of Christianity to pure scandal. He proclaims what Guardini calls the "radical unChristianity" of the postmodern era as a way of rejecting the faith of his sister and the faithless secularism of the New South.[14] Seeking to save his incorporeal world, Sutter announces lewdness as his sacrament, a new rite of

absolute immanence calculated to mock both piety and propriety. The icono-
clast travesties religion by advocating a sexual parody of the Eucharist and
perverts manners by extending the gentleman's acceptable sexual license into
pure licentiousness. Like Van Norden in "The Gramercy Winner," Sutter
views carnality as enabling the abstracted self to reclaim the flesh and the
whole realm of experience from which it has been exiled. Every lady becomes a whore, "pure immanence to be entered" by the transcendent mind
(LG 345).

Since Sutter's gospel of sexual scandal offers only one more sign of the
ruins rather than a guide to a past or future way of life, it cannot teach Will
how to be a southern gentleman or a Percyan apocalyptist. Although Lawyer
Barrett counseled against ever treating a lady like a whore, Sutter obscures
the difference by viewing all women as partners in his lust. Just before killing
himself, Will's mannerly father foresaw a time of fornication so nonchalant
that it would be done in public. Surrogate father and potential suicide, Sutter
proclaims fornication as the sole means of recovering humanity's lost awareness of its immanence. This flagrant carnality mocks the apocalyptic vision by
replacing love in the ruins with lechery and by reducing prophetic pessimism
to mere despair. Such indiscriminate couplings as Sutter's liaison with Jackie
Randolph on the golf links twenty minutes before her bridge luncheon or his
rendezvous with a nurse on duty parody the Guardini epigraph about love at
the end of the modern world. Lonely people meet not in love but in lewdness.
Although Sutter envisions such daring and deliberately chosen coitus as an
antidote to the paltry lives of the present, the moral pornographer discovers
that his escape from such impoverishment is short-lived and ends finally in
the same spiritual destitution. Since pornography "manifests itself in the abstracted state of one self (male) and the degradation of another self (female)
to an abstract object of satisfaction" (LC 10), it actually intensifies Sutter's
displacement. The objectified self intersects with another self become object
in a pantomime of intersubjectivity, but they are left with only a sorrowfully
depleted physicality.

When sex fails to provide deliverance, Sutter turns to suicide, as did
so many of the wearied sensualists whose bodies he examines after death.
Throughout the novel he seems to court disaster. He once took Jamie out
to the desert where they nearly died of thirst, he has deliberately lost his
job, and he practices marksmanship for his own death. Yet even such possible self-destruction does not lack all justification in this age of abstraction.
Sutter led Jamie into the wilderness because he feared that his brother was

going to be dispossessed of his own death, allowed to die in comfort without ever knowing what was happening to him. Like Kate Cutrer, he is fascinated with suicide because "the certain availability of death is the very condition of recovering oneself" (*LG* 372). Although most of the Vaughts try to deny the inevitability of Jamie's death, Sutter confronts the eschaton on a personal level as a way to quicken his vitality. In a century when the autopsist sees large areas of life increasingly surrendered to the hegemony of science, suicide remains the one domain that is indisputably his own. But if Sutter rightly despairs of his transcendent age, his fatal alternative is the ultimate act of transcendence. It brings no apocalyptic renewal but only reduces the coroner to another corpse for scientific investigation. When Will visits Sutter at the dude ranch in New Mexico, he rightly sees his discredited mentor for the first time as "the dismalest failure, a man who had thrown himself away" (*LG* 381).

While the first part of Will's journey is dominated by the memory of Lawyer Barrett, the second part is directed by Will's search for the elusive Sutter. Neither the father in his gentlemanly idealism nor the father figure in his desperate eroticism provides an adequate model for living in the world. Lawyer Barrett chose to kill himself rather than live in an age of lewdness; Sutter Vaught contemplates suicide when the lewdness that he embraces fails to return the scientist of the body to his own sloughed-off flesh. Unable to live at the end of time, both would end their lives, for they can only live by what is absolute. "Where he probably goes wrong . . . is in the extremity of his alternatives," Will muses about Sutter, although the verdict applies to his father as well. "God and not-God, getting under women's dresses and blowing your brains out. Whereas and in fact my problem is how to live from one ordinary minute to the next on a Wednesday afternoon." As an aside the narrator wonders, "Has not this been the case with all 'religious' people?" (*LG* 354–55).

When Will visits the hospitalized Jamie in the final scenes of the novel, he glimpses an answer to the religious problem of how to live in every mundane minute. Will fulfills the gentlemanly ideals of his family so completely that he makes contact with the Scandal to which Val has dedicated every day of her life. He begins to recover the faith that James McBride Dabbs in *Who Speaks for the South?* suggests was seriously undermined by the southern cult of propriety.[15] Although its code of behavior respected each person as a guest in the universe, Dabbs contends that southern religion faced the danger of degenerating into manners that lacked all connection with what really matters, a cultivation of social graces without any awareness of the need for divine grace. Percy himself has recognized a distinction between "that courtesy which one Christian awards another by virtue of the infinite value he assigns to the other's person" and the southern ethos based on "a minuet of overture and response . . . an economy of gesture which in its accounting of debits and credits, of generosity given and gratitude expected . . . is almost Oriental." [16] The southern emphasis on how things were done and said risked turning its religious life into noble gestures and courteous deeds devoid of any larger sustaining context.

Dabbs views such a reduction of faith to formality as signifying that "this world was not clearly rooted in another." [17] Since it severed the bond to one's ultimate concern that Percy understands as the root meaning of religion, this attenuated gospel became a purely public and superficial ritual. And conversely, much as Will remembers the illustrious deeds of his precursors, the great moments of life were preserved as images by memory and story but in a free-floating suspension that created heroes but never saints. *The Last Gentleman* depicts the result of the South's inability to realize "within its temporal forms its eternal spirit":[18] Chandler's mock geniality, Kitty's genteel tradition for the 1960s, Ed Barrett's gentlemanly suicide, Sutter's genitality. After continually trying to imitate the Barretts of family lore, Will moves toward resolving this inherited dichotomy between society and spirituality, immanence and transcendence, the riches of this time-place and their covert roots in eternity: he discovers the radical bonds that provide meaning in his life.

Will meets the eschaton in the hospital room where Jamie lies dying. Percy stresses the sheer physicality of death—the swollen face, the skin blotched with purple, the stink of defecation—so that this scene becomes a graphic equivalent of the bombed-out cityscape at the end of *The Moviegoer*. The flesh in ruins marks the end of the road for this wayfarer who has never known how to live in his own body. Like Barth's terminal Jake Horner, who witnessed the bloody death of Rennie Morgan at the end of *The End of the Road*, Percy's last gentleman beholds the messy horror of mortality. Yet whereas Horner remained paralyzed by his own inability to act decisively, Will lives most fully up to his name by deciding to act. Although the blank and silent landscape of New Mexico tempts Will to abstraction, the eschaton in the world of the body rebukes such idealism as a naïve retreat from the agonies of incarnate existence; and it reveals the inevitable corruption of the carnal life that Will desired while buffeted by "an abstract, lustful molecular wind" at the Alamogordo Motor Park (*LG* 375). Ground Zero is not in New York but in New

Mexico, where the first atomic bomb was detonated at Trinity Site. Yet only after such exhaustion and destruction in Santa Fe, when the futility of Ed Barrett's sublime manners or Sutter Vaught's subhuman mores is exposed, can Will discover the holy faith necessary for living in the ruins.

Before the end Will treats Jamie with a courteous camaraderie. As these friends and fellow travelers have pursued adventures like two men of the world, they have developed some sense of the brotherhood earlier shared by Binx and Lonnie. When Jamie is hospitalized, these gentlemen rely on manners in the face of the ultimate dishonor, "the bare-faced embarrassment of getting worse and dying." Will grieves, "How is this matter to be set right?" as if his honor and courage and high style could correct the fatal wrong just as he and his family have always righted social injustice (*LG* 390). Jamie's death is the last duel for the last gentleman. Like the Gramercy Winner at the end of his own contest, the helpless Will is daunted by the sheer finitude that most of the Vaughts ignore and that his father and Sutter honor in despair. His ethical idealism cannot win a battle against mortality, and he can only mourn the indignity of defeat: "It was like getting badly beat in a fight. To *lose*. Oh, to lose so badly" (*LG* 390). Yet even amid the humiliation of the hospital room, Jamie and Will win privileged moments of private communion by belittling catastrophe through heroic discipline and restraint. Jamie tries to suffer with soldierly fortitude. And Will properly considers asking him about baptism, "absolutely the last question to be tolerated by the comradely and stoic silence generated between the two of them" (*LG* 394).

Death is awkward enough for Jamie and Will without discussing salvation. To speak of baptism would abandon good taste and jeopardize their fragile truce with mortality, compounded of shared looks, card games, and tacit avoidance of ultimate questions. Although each of the pair has placed himself in the service of the other, Will's inability to mention receiving the sacrament demonstrates how the extravagance of their friendship is limited by decorum. Yet baptism may offer what both gentlemen need. As Ted Spivey has shown, Will has been seeking some ritualistic initiation into transcendence throughout the novel.[19] And Jamie finally went with Sutter to Santa Fe because he was convinced that something would happen in the West.[20] Hoping to escape the emptiness of his family and to discover some new place of his own, the restless wayfarer may envision little more than a life of freedom and simplicity along the beach or in the woods. However, when his illness turns plans for recreation into catastrophe, Val challenges Will to bring him the genuine re-creation proclaimed in the good news of the gospel.

Will's love for the dying youth causes him to realize and then redefine all the possibilities of being a gentleman. Having long sought an occasion to act with as much conviction as his ancestors, Will finds that the crisis of the eschaton fills him with new power and authority. Hence the normally polite engineer thunders at the nurse who has ignored his requests to attend to Jamie's fibrillating pulse, "You hear me, goddamn it, . . . or else I'm going to kick yo' ass down there" (*LG* 394). The speech with its marked southern accent hardly seems to come from Will at all; rather, it booms with the mighty, self-assured voice of his family's tradition. No longer lost in possibility, Will dares the formidable Queen Bess look-alike with all the scornful defiance of his great-grandfather's challenge to the grand wizard. The heir to the Barrett code suddenly feels that "segments of time collapsed, fell away," so that he lives as if in the past and virtually becomes one with his forefathers. Will does not even seem to be acting on a will of his own as he is "transported magically into the corridor," a much more hospitable nurse at his side, until the "next thing he knew he was speaking in a businesslike and considered manner" to the resident and chaplain, informing them of Val's request (*LG* 395).

Ever the gentleman, Will explains that he conveys this strange message because "it seemed proper to me" (*LG* 395). At Jamie's deathbed he never loses his sense of decorum. He is scandalized at Father Boomer's use of a plastic cup for baptism, as if the priest's expediency lessened the sanctity of the rite rather than attested to the holiness that consecrates the most profane products of twentieth-century engineering. He is embarrassed when Sutter later gives the priest his congé so perfunctorily that the prosaic minister is reduced to being just another serviceable vessel of sacramental life. Yet the last gentleman goes beyond the limitations of manners to discover a loving communion of wills with both Jamie and Sutter. He violates hospital protocol by asking whether his dying friend will ever regain consciousness. He does not simply relay Val's request but listens with his "good ear" (*LG* 402) to the priest's proclamation of the good news, and he finally takes part in the baptism. Serving as an interpreter between Jamie and Father Boomer, Will repeats the youth's whispered words for the priest to hear and shares so deeply in the neophyte's life that he intuits his barely expressed thoughts. Will tells of Jamie's will to believe and love.

Will's bonds with Jamie and, later, with Sutter seem more decisive than the last gentleman's uncertain romance with Kitty. His southern sweetheart is noticeably absent from the final scenes of the novel's ruins, as if she were part of the old order that must be abandoned. From its first pages *The Last*

Gentleman gives Kitty a greater prominence than Kate often seemed to have in *The Moviegoer*. But although the novel begins with Will's love at first sight and traces his haphazard pursuit of the woman glimpsed in Central Park, she virtually disappears after they are separated by the racist mayhem at the university. Afterward, Will often thinks of Kitty with typically sweet platitudes, calls her from Dallas, and tells Sutter at the dude ranch that he has just talked to her on the phone and that they are getting married after "things are more settled" (*LG* 380). He will become personnel manager for her father's glum car lot and establish himself as a happy and useful member of the community. But these plans are not just more tentative than the married love at the end of *The Moviegoer* and *Love in the Ruins*; they are more unconvincing.[21] After Will's communion with Jamie and Sutter, a cheerfully boring life with Kitty, in which religion means only agreeing on the same denomination and the new place is just the house with the best view, hardly seems possible. Whereas Kate and Ellen live through disasters with their end-of-the-world lovers, Kitty has not participated in the catastrophe of Jamie's death and has even escaped the campus violence unharmed and unchanged. Will's mention of his telephone reconciliation with his utterly conventional beloved seems less the result of dramatic necessity than of Percy's reluctance to abandon his ideal of romance in the ruins. Yet Percy's fictional heart is clearly not in such spurious love, for the novel finds a more promising sign of the apocalypse in the last gentleman's gestures of new bondedness with Kitty's brothers.

The dialogue of these final scenes dramatizes the hope of the Guardini epigraph that love may flow from one lonely person to another at the end of the world. When Father Boomer asks Jamie to pray for the living, he identifies Will as "your friend who loves you," and as Sutter holds his restless brother still, Jamie tells the priest who has been holding his hand, "Don't let me go" (*LG* 406). "Dr. Vaught, don't leave me," Will implores after Jamie's death (*LG* 409). Speaking with customary courtesy, Will addresses Sutter by his title. He is always a gentleman, but his achievement at the end is to be much more as well. While conveying respect for another person, manners may also protect the self by hiding feelings behind formality. In this last conversation Will lets passion speak louder than propriety as he admits his supreme need for the doctor who planned to commit suicide soon after his brother's death: " 'Dr. Vaught, I need you. I, Will Barrett—' and he actually pointed to himself lest there be a mistake, '—need you and want you to come back. I need you more than Jamie needed you. Jamie had Val too' " (*LG* 409). Will offers love to those in the ruins—a dying youth and a suicidal doctor—

and in the process of bringing them new life glimpses the possibility of his own new life. Refusing to hide behind stoic silence or gentlemanly reserve, Will exposes himself in the intense ache of his want. He strips himself of all the protective conventions of social intercourse by substituting for his typically mannered language—careful of contractions, favoring periphrasis and a slightly formalized diction—a naked declaration of dependency. Once hardly aware of his identity, Will uses speech and gesture to make his name and person virtually synonymous with his need. He reveals a will to love that would give Sutter a will to live for a new brotherhood.

Will's loving affirmation of his need requires as much boldness as any of his ancestors' heroic feats as gentlemen. Will had been amazed at how directly Val could speak to people, for he interpreted her interest in their salvation as papist hauteur. But Val's apparent effrontery actually expresses an uncommon intimacy. Her only presumption is simply to bypass the normal waste of words in order to speak a frank language of love. Such pointed speech, like the nun's question to Val whether she wanted to be alive, or Val's mandate to Will, dares to be so deeply personal that communication becomes communion. The whole tradition of the gentleman militates against such confidences by emphasizing public gestures and social respectability. At the end Will at once violates and consummates the ideals of his family by his wild risk of the heart. The novel ends with the hope that after catastrophe—Jamie's death and the disastrous attempts of Will and Sutter to live in pure immanence or transcendence—such daring openness will characterize life in the new age. For a time, it seems to have saved Sutter. Will has convinced the doctor to heed his call, "Wait," a word that echoes eight times throughout the final scene. The repetition testifies to the necessary patience and expectation that Percy's apocalyptists must always demonstrate as they give time for the future to come ever more fully. Unlike the engineer's irresolution at the beginning of the novel, this waiting is based not on passive isolation but on the promise of communion. Sutter rejects the fatal despair of Will's father, who refused when his son cried out for him to wait on the night of his suicide. Instead, the father figure offers a tentative gesture of hope. When the last gentleman thinks of one last question to ask Sutter, he runs after his car with great, joyous strides because, in the last line of the novel, "the Edsel waited for him" (LG 409).

Like the screen images of the movie stars that so captivate Binx Bolling, the career of the gentleman is composed predominantly of gestures, highly visible and impeccably executed. But living as if one were always in public may cause the heart to be hidden behind such triumphs of style as Chandler's worldliness, Lawyer Barrett's despairing stoicism, or Sutter's fatal carnality. At the end of *The Last Gentleman*, Percy shows manners deepened by mystery as his searchers make gestures of ultimate concern that express the unseen love amid the obvious ruins. Jamie's grasping of Father Boomer's hand, Will's confession of need, and Sutter's final consent to wait reveal them living not for outward show but on a level so personal that they become gentle men. Such apocalyptic cordiality embodies the heart of Will's inchoate faith. Its informal and unorthodox expression arises from feeling the ligatures that form the beginning of all religion for Percy, the primal connections that may unite humanity with its most passionate concern. Will's ties join him to the mystery beyond himself so that he gains what Thomas LeClair calls "a sphere of focused possibility, turned ever so little toward God."[22]

After the baptism the puzzled Will asks Sutter, "What happened back there?" (*LG* 407). Will does not entirely understand the significance of the ritual, but he perceives that something has, in fact, happened. In "How to Be an American Novelist in Spite of Being Southern and Catholic," Percy almost answers Will's question about what happens at such riddling times throughout his fiction. He writes that a novelist with "a necessary sensitivity to the hidden dimensions and energies of his characters" must recognize "the presence of the mystery which may always erupt in their lives and which for want of a better word we may call grace. Neither he nor his characters may know why certain things happen as they do."[23] Such immediate contact with what seems beyond words naturally baffles the well-bred young man who wanted to engineer his life. Sutter speculated in his notebook that even if Will heard Val's gospel about religious wayfaring, the technician would only reduce it to a psychological stimulus to make him feel better. Just as Will once rejected making "a personal decision for Christ" by fleeing from summer camp (*LG* 13), in the hospital room he does not embrace salvation with any of the conventional signs. But the felt crisis of Jamie's death keeps Will from turning faith into an abstract therapy and reveals it as a loving bond with the mystery by which one lives and into which one dies. He enters into what Simone Vauthier aptly calls "a circulation of meaning and being" as Father Boomer brings God's news to Jamie, and Will then bears Jamie's response to the priest.[24] Much as he touched some vital presence during his epiphany at his father's house, Will feels the inexplicable dynamics of self-transcendence well up amid the giving and the receiving of the sacrament. Having participated in proclaiming and hearing the news, he lives at the intersection of what is most fundamentally human for Percy. Only through such bondedness can Will ever become completely open to the divine message of Val and Father Boomer.

Although only Jamie is baptized, both Will and Sutter seem ready to be reborn through their final reciprocity. Conversion in Percy's fiction, as in the Gospels, means just such a "turning toward," entailing not mere assent to dogma but a more profound reorientation of the heart. The promise inherent in the last scene of the novel depends on the counterpoint between Jamie's earlier reception of baptism and the overtures of Will and Sutter toward Percyan communion. Their graciousness toward each other bespeaks the first acts of grace in lives radically religious by their very bondedness. Their dialogue intimates the Word beyond the words, the ultimate Logos of Percy's fiction, which is love. Father Boomer questions Jamie about what he believes or hopes to believe; in his own version of the catechism, Will interrogates Sutter about what he intends to do. The priest tells the dying youth that God, who is his end, loved him so much that he sent his son to die for him; and out of love Will tells the suicidal doctor of his need for him to stay alive. "I, Will Barrett, . . . need you"; the last gentleman names himself as if intimacy provided the context for realizing his identity (*LG* 409). Minutes earlier, Father Boomer had christened Sutter's brother "Jamison MacKenzie Vaught." For Percy, the act of naming is an almost religious proclamation and reception of the word that reveals the heart of reality, uniting both speaker and listener as cocelebrants of creation (*MB* 257). Baptism consecrates Percy's archetypal act of language; it is the sacrament of naming. Amid the ruins of the ancestral tradition, Will Barrett will bear his name as a new kind of gentleman. Will will be one of the gentle-hearted.

5

THE CENTER DOES HOLD

LOVE IN THE RUINS

I   *The Moviegoer* and *The Last Gentleman* were novels for a late day in America but not for its last hour. The confessions of Binx Bolling and the wanderings of Will Barrett intimated a land of the dead and doomed. *The Moviegoer* portrayed an age in which an exhausted humanism and devitalizing scientific objectivity produced a silent and secret despair, while *The Last Gentleman* hinted that the ominous disquiet of its predecessor was already flaring into violence. But although both novels sensed the possibility of disaster in the everyday life of America, neither envisioned the imminent destruction of the nation as does Percy's 1971 novel, *Love in the Ruins: The Adventures of a Bad Catholic at a Time Near the End of the World.* If Percy earlier discovered the apocalypse in the private, revelatory drama of consciousness, he seems to restore it to a grander, perhaps even global, perspective in the novel whose subtitle looks to the approaching cataclysm. *Love in the Ruins* begins on July 4 of the near future as Dr. Tom More awaits the end of America in the next two hours. Yet despite its waggish celebration of Independence Day as the Day of Doom, Percy's most overtly eschatological novel is as much antiapocalyptic as it is apocalyptic. Only after exposing the possible perversions of the eschaton and comically undermining the very tradition in which it is written does this dire fantasy end by affirming love amid the ruins.

Percy turns to science fiction in *Love in the Ruins* because the genre gives him the imaginative freedom to envision more boldly than ever before the debacle that seemed to be drawing near in his previous novels. Even before he wrote the pensive and picaresque comedies of *The Moviegoer* and *The Last Gentleman*, Percy had considered drafting a science fiction fantasy.[1] He must have sensed something of the truth in David Ketterer's claim that the apocalyptic imagination "finds its purest outlet in science fiction," since both look to a time when "man's horizons—temporal, spatial, scientific, and ultimately philosophic—are abruptly expanded." Ketterer even traces an arche-typal science fiction plot—the actual or threatened destruction of a dysto-pia, the aftermath of catastrophe, and the vision of a new world—inspired by the Book of Revelation.[2] Since speculative novels frequently depict the whole doomed panorama of the physical world, their cinemascopic view en-ables Percy to show how late is the hour, how drastic the crisis. He projects the catastrophe previously internalized in his apocalyptists onto an America near the close of the century. The deteriorating scenery of this highly ex-ternalized novel thus reflects what its dissolute seer typifies in all of society. The countryscape provides a screen for an enormous last picture show that locates the dilapidated and amorous prophet amid the very palpable ruins of a loveless world.

In a tribute printed only a month before *Love in the Ruins* was published, Percy praises one of the finest works of science fiction, Walter M. Miller's *A Canticle for Leibowitz* (1959), for having "hit on the correct mise-en-scène for the apocalyptic futuristic novel." Percy views the reader, like some double of his own fictional apocalyptists, as secretly longing for the collapse of such a city as Phoenix, the desert setting of Miller's novel, into the ruins, or for "the greening of America, vines sprouting on 42nd Street."[3] In *Love in the Ruins* Percy also imagines, with the consummate attention of a set designer, the appropriate mise-en-scène for his novel at a time near the end of the world. He chooses not the wasteland but the garden grown wild. Paradise Estates, where Tom More lives, is meant to be an urban planner's new earth, but this pseudoapocalyptic order is actually far to the east of Eden. In the greening of America, sumac sprouts on Tom's front lawn; vines curl around his statue of Saint Francis, poke their way through the patio wall, and sneak into the country club to twist around bottles on the bar; a green growth makes store roofs resemble the Hanging Gardens. Tom More laments over the menacing profusion of this antipastoral world, "our beloved old U.S.A. is in a bad way" (*LR* 17).

Because of its utopian pretensions the America of *Love in the Ruins* is a latter-day Babylon, the archcity of evil in Apocalypse (Rev. 17–18). Reve-lation uses the image of Paradise to suggest the pristine splendor of the new age, but the vines that wind their way over the novel's terrain reveal the human-made garden as a decadent version of the divine order of cre-ation established in Genesis 2 and gloriously restored in Revelation 21–22. Chaos threatens the modern attempts at re-creation; the boundaries be-tween the cultivated greenery of Paradise Estates and the nearby swamp have begun to disappear. Yet if the vines disclose the demonic origins of this supposedly Edenic order, they also provide a peculiar pleasure, as Percy himself recognizes in his homage to Miller's novel. Covering the world lost to scientific abstraction and thereby recovering the earth in all of its strangeness, the lushness signifies nature's mysterious subversion of humanity's proudest schemes to create its own paradise. Binx Bolling looked forward to a time after the end of the world when the survivors would "live as merrily as children among the viny ruins" (*M* 231). As the vines encroach upon the dystopia of *Love in the Ruins*, they promise a renewed earth when the engineers in the City of Man cease to play God. The green grows in judgment but also in hope.

The vines that transform the ideal community into a paradise of snakes reflect in the natural order the chaos that dominates every aspect of life in *Love in the Ruins*. The fragmented America of the novel dramatizes the Yeatsian vision of the end first sounded in *The Last Gentleman* and now echoed by Tom More: "Things fall apart; the centre cannot hold."[4] Signs of the city's disrepair surround the doctor as if he were living amid the breakdown of E. M. Forster's "The Machine Stops" (1909). None of the many appliances in Tom's own household any longer works. The landscape of Paradise Estates is so littered with the rusting wrecks of abandoned cars that Tom blames the entire decline of America on the fact that "things stopped working and nobody wanted to be a repairman" (*LR* 63). But things do not simply fall apart in *Love in the Ruins*. They fly away helter-skelter as if in a cosmos where centripetal force has been abolished. In the centerless world of the novel, all institutions and individuals lack that selfsame integrity whereby opposites complement and correct each other, the whole cohering as a harmony of mutually sustaining contradictions. Rather, each has become divided into pairs of absolute and incompatible extremes. In *Love in the Ruins* the tensions that Binx pondered in the contrast between science and romanticism, and that Sutter felt still more strongly in the rift between transcendence and immanence, have become so exacerbated that they sunder the whole world of the novel.

When the center does not hold, the anarchy loosed causes a polarization of the country's political, social, religious, and psychic life. The Republicans have become the rigidly conservative Knothead party, whose members suffer from apoplexy and bowel disorders, while the Democrats have been driven to form the fiercely liberal Left party and are prone to abstraction, morning terror, and impotence. The diseases reflect Dr. Percy's modern symptomatology of the comedy of humors—the Right, all blood and choler, and the Left nothing but phlegm and bile. Society and religion are just as drastically split. Bantu revolutionaries, discontent with their roles as mammies and gardeners, have fled to the swamps to organize a rebellion that will turn July 4 into a new kind of independence day. The Catholic church has been divided by schism into the conservative American Catholic church, the radical Dutch Reformers, and a disheartened remnant loyal to Rome and led by one of Percy's typically unremarkable priests, Father Smith. On the anniversary of its birth, the fractured United States has lost title to its very name.

Since the world is rushing to its end in *Love in the Ruins*, Percy's most explicitly apocalyptic fiction relies more on the stylization typical of Revelation than on the precise and poetic realism used in the novel's less visionary predecessors. While trying to call Sharon at the end of *The Moviegoer*, Binx noticed the drawings of lonely lovers penciled in the phone booth; yet no character in the novel, even Binx at his randiest, existed purely as a twisted sketch of body and soul. Figures on the often unsteady circumference of *The Last Gentleman* became more absurd and exaggerated, but in *Love in the Ruins* Binx's erotic graffiti and Sutter's casebook of coroner's reports have come alive as the loveless grotesques of Tom More's America. All the graphically deformed hearts of the novel find their collective likenesses in the cartoons of desire that decorate the walls of the Howard Johnson's where Tom hopes to spend July 4. Just as John's Apocalypse portrays a cosmos filled with herald angels and monstrous beasts, *Love in the Ruins* simplifies and schematizes its amorists into comic-book illustrations of what Tom diagnoses as angelism-bestialism. Percy's apocalyptic aesthetics do not depict human characters inhumanely, but they do reveal the essential inhumanity of characters who live in a supposedly humane world. Even the novel's rare saint is graced with a terrible beauty. Samantha, Tom's dead daughter, was distorted by suffering into a Picasso icon until death finally transformed her into an affectionate ghost who haunts his heart. In such a world without cohesion, these caricatures do not so much act as overact. The subtleties of the moviegoer's gestural perfection and of the gentleman's discriminating manners are replaced by broad and bold performances that drive the novel toward violence and farce or the violent farce of black comedy. The hour is so ultimate and Percy's fiction is now so extreme that conventional verisimilitude suitable to lives in medias res has no place in a world without mean or middle.

If Percy favors an art of controlled chaos to depict how the center of America and of Tom More no longer holds, the chaos sometimes exceeds his control. The imaginative violence risks eliminating the mysterious implications of behavior and resonant interchanges between people that form the heart of Percy's fiction. In the two-dimensional world of the novel, almost all action takes place out front and on the surface, but it can occasionally turn into the tedious busyness of mere movement. Percy finds more dramatic significance in the social implications of Tom's stepping an ambiguous foot too far into the Little Napoleon with Victor Charles than in all the exact and abundant details of Tom's many journeys by foot, his stealthy attempt to surprise the sniper in the pro shop of the clubhouse, or his ingenious escape from Saint Michael's. Unlike the psychic and spiritual travels of Binx and Will, Tom's activity at times exists for its own sake.

Since Percy depicts a future when the self has collapsed, characters naturally resemble the case studies that Dr. More includes in his narrative. However, in this microcosm of America, Percy creates no one of sufficient stature or complexity—like Kate and Emily in *The Moviegoer* or Kitty, Val, and Sutter in *The Last Gentleman*—to engage and be engaged by Tom in the very depths of selfhood. If *Love in the Ruins* is a triumph of spectacle, its misshapen souls are not people but part of Percy's cracked and crazy mise-en-scène. Although consciousness, for Percy, depends on a knowing with, on a dialogue of heart, mind, and soul, Tom has no central confidant in whose intimacy he can really become himself by talking out his identity. Perhaps Percy even recognizes the limits of the apocalyptic monologue, of reducing the fictional world solely to the sound of one voice that is never really challenged or affirmed by another character in colloquy, for in *Lancelot* and *The Thanatos Syndrome*, his two later first-person novels, he uses Fathers John and Smith as listeners, critics, and fellow searchers. Tom seems to be speaking into a tape recorder to leave a warning for future generations, yet Percy never consistently maintains this pretense or seriously explores the possibility of the reader as audience to such a confession. Tom has no one but his own extravagant and exhausted self.

Perched above a cloverleaf of intersecting highways, which divide the novel's landscape into four quadrants, Tom More is at Will Barrett's Ground Zero, the unstable center of a nation in disarray.[5] Over him hovers a bird balanced on a column of air that suddenly slants off in the direction of the swamp. The falcon from *The Last Gentleman* has become a marsh hawk whose flight pattern is broken by the centrifugal forces that disorder the whole world of the novel. Like Binx and Will, Tom is a seer. Not only does he see the end more clearly than anyone else in the novel, but he also understands its hidden causes and has finally discovered a cure for the ills of the age. Tom even includes himself among those who have "seen visions, dreamed dreams" (*LR* 106), the prophetic company anticipated by Joel (2:28) and witnessed by Peter on Pentecost (Acts 2:17). His grand self-evaluation is comically appropriate because, as Lewis Lawson observes, the major portion of Tom's narrative (*LR* 61–352) is a kind of dream vision, a retrospective of the disastrous last four days as re-viewed by the sleeping More, in typically apocalyptic fashion, from his point of transcendence above the interchange.[6] Yet if Tom is a visionary, *Love in the Ruins* begins with no initial revelation like Binx's sighting of his possessions or Will's glimpse of Kitty. Rather, since the world seems to be hurdling toward immediate destruction, Percy has accordingly speeded up the entire course of Tom's personal apocalypse. The novel opens not with the leisurely and low-key account of how the seer comes to consciousness but with an intense and urgent *now:* "Now in these dread latter days of the old violent beloved U.S.A. and of the Christ-forgetting Christ-haunted death-dealing Western world I came to myself in a grove of young pines and the question came to me: has it happened at last?" (*LR* 3).

There was still time in *The Moviegoer*, so Percy could begin with Binx's reception of his aunt's summons, start once again with the survey of his uneventful life in Gentilly, and then begin a third time with the memory of the signal event that disturbed his peaceful morning routine, the real beginning of his last days. Since Will Barrett hardly lived in a temporal world, *The Last Gentleman* opened with a Percyan version of the fairy tale's "once upon a time": "One fine day in early summer . . ." (*LG* 3). But from the headnote on the first page, which announces the hour as 5:00 P.M. on July 4, *Love in the Ruins* seizes the moment now. There is virtually no more time, for by seven o'clock Tom expects catastrophe. Hence the modest and muted lines that introduced *The Moviegoer* and *The Last Gentleman* quicken and intensify to become the rushing words of a periodic sentence in which the speaker barely has time to pause on a hasty *tour d'horizon* before the whole scene vanishes.

Since *Love in the Ruins* begins with unprecedented urgency, the coming to self becomes identical with recognizing the coming end. Consciousness in this novel is knowledge of encroaching disaster, for the apocalyptist "finds himself," according to Walter Schmithals, "only when he comprehends *when* he is living."[7] Tom comes to himself when the question comes to him whether the cataclysm has finally happened. This moment of awareness is not Tom's first. As his narrative doubles back to recount the events of the preceding weekend and his past life, it reveals that Tom has not been a stranger to himself or the eschaton. Rather, the opening sentence simply affirms what the rest of the novel dramatizes: to be Tom More is to be aware of the end. This consummate selfhood is so distinctive because almost no one else in the novel even seems worried about the ruins in America. When Tom points out the vines cracking the sidewalk to a neighbor, the Boeing engineer prefers to ignore them. Tom's mother, a reputed prophetess who has predicted four of the last five assassinations, uses her clairvoyance not to warn of the end but to make successful real estate deals. Tom alone has an eschatological identity as if his very being were predicated on the apocalypse.

Tom's anxiety at the beginning of the novel results from his awareness that the end may be announced by any one of three possible disasters: the murder of the president or vice president, a revolution by the Bantus, or the misuse of his own lapsometer, which might trigger explosions in the salt marshes and widespread psychic disturbances. Looming over the dreamy review of the July 4 weekend, these threats intensify the novel's ominous atmosphere by making plot more important than it had ever been in Percy's earlier fiction. Percy acknowledges in "From Facts to Fiction" that he began *The Movie-goer* intending to abandon the traditional concept of plot in order simply to present a man in a situation. *The Last Gentleman* continues this existential narration from its very beginning as it comes upon Will's predicament in Central Park and then follows the loosely connected episodes of his quixotic adventures. Actually, these novels are very deliberately plotted, but the pattern of the movement remains hidden behind the apparent randomness of the search and only becomes clearly visible at the ends that bring the journeys into focus.

Love in the Ruins likewise begins with the classic Percy predicament, an individual at some critical place and time, but the situation becomes almost as important as the man in it. The novel starts not on an ordinary Wednesday morning or on a fine summer's day but on the evening of the possible last day, and then reviews what led to this near disaster. Hence, all of the action from Tom More's birthday to America's falls under the shadow of the July 4 eschaton. As Tom meanders toward the end that Percy's prologue has anticipated since the beginning, he increasingly gets swept up in the rush of apocalyptic events and imagines himself the hero in an eschatological melodrama. *Love in the Ruins* is so dependent on plot that, as Max Webb has shown, Percy uses the extremely conventionalized design of the thriller, a form particularly suited to apocalyptic fiction.[8] The genre defined itself after World War I, the Armageddon that haunts Tom in both *Love in the Ruins* and *The Thanatos Syndrome*, for it expressed in fiction the unstable modern age of global crises caused by vast and shadowy powers of evil. In the thriller, the Book of Revelation is played out by confidential agents as they pursue, spy on, and flee from each other on secret missions that might determine the fate of the world. "No other work of fiction depends so heavily on mood and situation," says Ralph Harper, who views these edgy works of art as a series of existentialist casebooks. "The thriller is situational fiction."[9] Although the genre's emphasis on events sometimes causes *Love in the Ruins* to give too much attention to sheer activity, Percy adapts the techniques of the thriller because they enable him to write about a man placed in a situation that might end all situations, a "bad Catholic at a time near the end of the world."

As apocalyptic herald to a world that prefers to deny the possibility of disaster, Tom understands why the center is no longer holding, "It's not even the U.S.A., it's the soul of Western man that is in the very act of flying apart HERE and NOW" (*LR* 115). The cause of public catastrophe goes back to a spiritual crisis. Tom recognizes that every faction in politics, society, and religion testifies to a more profound, underlying split in the psyche that More can gauge with his lapsometer. More's high-tech device for delivering judgment on his doomed age records the electrical activity of specific areas of the brain and correlates the readings with similar reports on patients who suffer from varying degrees of abstracted terror and murderous rage. If such a crudely mechanical conjunction can ever be possible, More's Qualitative-Quantitative Ontological Lapsometer diagnoses the maladies of the soul through the signs of the body. In a splintered world it unites state of psyche and encephalographic measurement to expose the age's lapsed unity of being. Tom identifies this peculiar extremism as chronic angelism-bestialism. More's name for the epidemic indicates that, at least since the time of Descartes, humanity has increasingly come to exist as flesh devoid of spirit, scientific intelligence divorced from body. The novel's self-centered lovers lack a coherent center beyond themselves that will keep them humane enough so they do not become anthropoids and humble enough so they do not become angels. They are paradoxes who prefer not to be paradoxical.

Since Tom sees the end more clearly than any of Percy's earlier visionaries, he has even formulated a theological interpretation of history, like John in Revelation. Living at the eschaton, apocalyptists understand both the past and the future. They see into and throughout time so that events reveal their true significance in a pattern that only becomes evident near its completion. John views Domitian's persecution of Christians not as a meaningless moment for despair but against the background of God's triumph that begins and ends in Jesus. Likewise, from his lookout point at the start of *Love in the Ruins*, Tom More sees the destiny of the nation as governed by its cooperation with divine Providence. His religious understanding of the country's past resembles Faulkner's tragic myth of American history, except that Percy's apocalyptist casts himself in the role of new world redeemer. Blessed by the Lord, America was the "new Eden," which Tom envisions as existing in the time outside time. God gave its citizens "Israel and Greece and science and art and the lordship of the earth," and finally a test (*LR* 57). The trial required the country not to violate the black person, but America turned angelism-bestialism into a national institution by creating a society of overlords and enslaving an entire race as its beasts of burden.[10] As punishment for this original sin, the United States suffered its own expulsion from Paradise. The roller coaster's "old historical machinery" began to clink as the timeless land of promise entered the temporal world. Tom now feels the chain that catches and "carries us back into history with its ordinary catastrophes, carries us out and up toward the brink" (*LR* 3, 4). Trapped inexorably in time, America is shaken by the convulsions of the present age as if feeling the ominous clackety-clack before its precipitate doom. Tom imagines the course of his nation's history as spanning from Genesis to Apocalypse. At the end he offers himself as the country's deliverer: "I can save you, America! I know something! I know what is wrong! I hit on something, made a breakthrough. . . . You are still the last hope" (*LR* 58).

Tom More promises the Disunited States the unity of being that Northrop Frye discovers in apocalyptic glory. Frye explains that Revelation uses the Body of Christ as "the metaphor holding together all categories of being in an identity." The entirety of creation—mineral, vegetable, animal, human, and paradisal—converges in him as the new Jerusalem, the eucharistic bread and wine, the Lamb of God, the heavenly bridegroom, the Tree and Water of Life. As revelation turns into participation, the seer comes to share in such wholeness, so that "there is only one knower for whom there is nothing outside of or objective to that knower, hence nothing dead or insensible."[11] Frye's epistemological apocalypse envisions the kind of all-embracing harmony needed by Tom's age, for its chronic angelism-bestialism reduces the human person to either the knower or the known. Out of his very fragmentation Tom dreams of an end to such dualism. Just as the end of Revelation celebrates Eden anew, he also wonders, "What if man could reenter paradise, so to speak, and live there both as man and spirit, whole and intact man-spirit, as solid flesh as a speckled trout, a dappled thing, yet aware of itself as a self" (*LR* 36). To be a creature and to be conscious, Hopkins's stippled fish and the reflective fisherman, is Tom's apocalyptic goal, one the other characters, angels or beasts, cannot even imagine.

Although Tom sees further than anyone else in the novel, he never sees far enough beyond himself. Judged by John Edward Hardy "in many ways the most attractive of all Percy's heroes," Tom More is appealingly genial and generous.[12] America may be divided by the most self-serving factionalism, but this truly good doctor tends without prejudice a love couple, a murderous Bantu, and the swaggering guard at Paradise Estates. Yet Tom's service is too often compromised by his own ambitions. His plan to heal the century really hides a mad messianism, heard above in the shrill egotism of the incessant first-person pronoun. Rather than averting disaster, Tom's attempts to be a secular Christ for a scientific age only make the end seem more imminent and himself appear damnably like the Antichrist. When Tom dozes on the evening of July 4, the clownish nightmare of the preceding holiday weekend shows precisely how Tom's apocalypticism has degenerated into such vainglory. Over the last four days the would-be savior has sealed the loveless direction of his life by selling his soul to his own devilish double.

| | The satanic Art Immelmann would have seemed totally out of place in the ruminative chronicles of *The Moviegoer* or even in the antic comedy of *The Last Gentleman*. But he is an almost inevitable figure in Percy's "Adventures of a Bad Catholic at a Time Near the End of the World," for apocalypse traditionally envisions a decisive confrontation with diabolic powers.[13] Demons overrun Percy's novel. Tom discovered the principle on which the lapsometer is based when heavy sodium radiation "had driven the demons out of the mad patients and into the doctors." During his confinement to this same hospital for the possessed, Tom hears the patients "moaning and whimpering like souls in the inner circle of hell" (*LR* 27, 28). Father Smith, one of Dr. More's fellow madmen, attributes the pervasive living death to the work of devils, whose reign Tom also acknowledges by July 4: "Principalities and powers are everywhere victorious" (*LR* 5). The evil spirits of Paul's Letter to the Colossians (2:15) triumph as the spiritual sickness of the modern age.

Immelmann's appearance seems like the last loosing of Satan in the novel's already devil-ridden world (Rev. 20:7–10). The cunning Art follows a legion of con artists in American apocalypses that, according to R. W. B. Lewis, have played the false prophet in Revelation 13 and duped their victims into darkly comic days of doom.[14] Over the holiday weekend Percy's Mephistopheles tempts More to be the messiah in a series of three scenes that parody Christ's trials in the desert. As the rakish Tom listens to a record of Don Giovanni's descent into hell, he himself slips closer to the pit represented by the infernal More Qualitative-Quantitative Ontological Lapsometer. Calling it MOQUOL, Art laughs that the acronym sounds like a hole in the ground. He tries to get this Faust to stumble into the pit by offering financing for the lapsometer, a 75 percent return of profits, and the glory of possibly saving America. More resists Art's first appeal to pride out of his own professional arrogance, for he is convinced that the Director will support his research in redemption. Two days later, he rejects Art's funding a second time, even though the tempter lures Tom with the promise of improved technology. Immelmann offers to convert the lapsometer from a diagnostic to a therapeutic device so that it would become not just an instrument for revelation or judgment, like Binx's movie camera or Will's telescope, but one for actual re-creation.

When Tom's interview with the Director fails to win his expected triumph, he succumbs to Art's third temptation. After Art treats the disappointed scientist with his own modified invention, Tom knows a fiendish version of the Percyan coming to consciousness. In this mock apocalypse Tom sees his hand for the first time in fifteen years and senses an unknown harmony. Art demonstrates how the lapsometer can stimulate the musical-erotic area in the brain so that "in the same moment one becomes victorious in science one also becomes victorious in love. And all for the good of mankind!" (*LR* 213). At Art's feet while the trickster sits on the "throne" of a men's room shoeshine chair, Tom, unlike Jesus in his third meeting with the adversary, pays homage to a devil who also quotes from Scripture (*LR* 209).[15] Art reveals to Tom how the lapsometer can heal psychic imbalances through a discovery that Tom himself made twenty years ago. This disturbingly familiar con man, who knows about Tom's secret research and even about the shortcut from his office to the old Southern Hotel, speaks as the demonic alter ego of the overly confident psychiatrist. Art tempts Tom to be less than More could be. He promises victories in science and love that will only intensify the polarization of the time under the guise of a spurious unity.

As the paradigm of the modern age, Tom already devotes himself to a musical-erotic life, where the abstract is experienced concretely and the concrete is known abstractly. Art wants to turn Tom into a caricature of himself.

More, the Don Juanish doctor, would make his sole end the passionate pursuit of knowledge and women. Although such a goal might seem to reintegrate humanity, it only fragments the self even further. Since music is "the abstract experienced as the concrete, namely sound," the Mozart to which Tom listens is only an aesthetic representation of mathematical truths (*LR* 213). Its beauty ultimately appeals to the individual as knower and scientist, the intellectual Dr. Tom More. At best, life on the musical level produces the euphonies of scientific humanism. The pure mind pursues such abstract knowledge as designing the lapsometer for the sake of advancing learning and improving the quality of life. "Isn't it better to feel good rather than bad? . . . Isn't it better to be happy than unhappy?" Art asks Tom in this new religion's catechism of better living through technology (*LR* 215).

Art's optimistic doctrines assuage the dread and discontent that may be fit responses in an age about to end, and his glorification of abstraction ignores a more comprehensive kind of knowledge. Even while tempted by Art's sophistry to embrace a life of omniscience, Tom recalls a wisdom beyond the most searching forms of scientific inquiry: "Knowing God is knowing all things" (*LR* 214). Percy's literal *diabolus in musica* tempts Tom with a knowledge of things but not of God, an angelic comprehension of creation rather than an encounter with the Creator. Art's temptation to live in the musical sphere is finally the temptation of Art.[16] Whether enjoyed as an aesthetic or intellectual paradise, this supernal realm offers a heaven of enlightenment in which the supremely transcendent mind uses its powers to make itself happy and feel good.

If the musical life provides only another form of the angelism that More knows so well, Art's eroticism is a less offensive name for bestialism. He encourages Tom to love a woman neither loyally for herself nor purely out of lust but as a representative of the whole world of women, "faithlessly but truly" (*LR* 213). Since each woman is just a particular example of an abstraction, she is cherished intensely but not exclusively. This unrestricted love may seem to resolve the tension between immanence and transcendence, for Tom loves each as typical of the category and so loves all. But it actually fosters the same hollowed carnality that Sutter Vaught found so disappointing because eroticism becomes only a frenetic way of making love to an idea. His love for all women impugns his love for each woman as well as his love for the All. Just as Tom suspects that his mind will discover knowledge only in God, so he realizes that his heart ultimately longs for divine passion. But Art

142

tempts him to deny that "love is God, because God is love," by suggesting instead that "love is music," as may be expected in the idolatry of the musical-erotic kingdom (*LR* 214). The charlatan's panacea only heightens the already existing divisions in the world of the novel by turning the sick away from the God that must be known and loved in other people.

Tempted by Art to become the savior, Tom More becomes a messiah in ruins, the very image of himself that he unknowingly glimpses in the Little Napoleon just before his first visit from Art. He sees at the bar what looks like the portrait of a Spanish Christ with deep-set eyes, a pox on his face, and vacuoles in his chest. The holy picture represents "the new Christ, the spotted Christ, the maculate Christ, the sinful Christ." Whereas the old Christ died to save the world from sin, Tom imagines that the "new Christ shall reconcile man with his sins. The new Christ lies drunk in a ditch" (*LR* 153). The grimy icon that Tom celebrates is actually his own disheveled reflection in the pockmarked bar mirror. Since he had just stumbled into a ditch while trying to walk to the Little Napoleon, the alcoholic doctor envisions himself as a boozy send-up of a savior. After gaining new power from his contract with Art, this once-feckless Christ can begin his ministry by casting out the age's devils, curing all of its infirmities with his lapsometer, and even delivering an elderly patient from death. Tom may imagine himself a savvy redeemer for a technological century, but he actually performs the devilish work of Art Immelmann by reconciling humanity with its lapse from God. The sins of angelism and bestialism become quite justifiable if disguised under the more enticing name of the musical-erotic life. Although Paul preached that Jesus who was sent "in the likeness of sinful flesh . . . condemned sin in the flesh" (Rom. 8:3), Tom becomes a savior who, despite all of his desire to heal the broken time, only confirms his own and the age's profound sinfulness. Tom replaces Incarnation with the sentimental humanism—Christ is just a brother in sin—that Sutter Vaught traces back to Leigh Hunt's devaluation of God. If More's Lord is nothing more than a glorified version of his own wretchedness, this new Christ is no Christ but the Antichrist.

Father Rinaldo Smith tries to oppose such bedeviled messianism by living out an entirely different apocalyptic vocation. Although he too senses catastrophe, he becomes not a deluded savior but an eschatological prophet who attends to God's words and visions. Once struck silent during his sermon at Mass, he mutters that demons have jammed the system. Since the doctors are less attuned to such spiritual interference, they confine this mad messenger to the acute wing of the hospital where the crazed Tom was once a patient. The priest, who is also a ham radio operator, hears the spiritual disorder caused by the same psychic plague that Tom hopes to heal. The static results from a satanic assault on language. It is heard in the diabolic doublespeak of Art Immelmann and of all the glib experts who reduce love and death to mere physiological processes facilitated by the most indiscriminate and intrusive technology. Father Smith tries to broadcast the good news amid such babel. Leaving a mysterious message at Marva More's lovely estate, he summons Tom to his slave-quarter chapel, where he greets him with a request for a bell. Father Smith wants not the electronic carillon at St. Pius XII's, whose tones proclaim for five miles the self-aggrandizing religion of the very rich, but the church's traditional and humble instrument that rings out against demons, sounds the angelus, and calls worshippers to Mass. The priestly news bearer already cuts through the dissonance with his own voice by offering a special message for Tom, a warning about physical and spiritual peril. He cautions the doctor that he should leave his house, perhaps to reside amid the slave quarters, and casually invites him to confession. The evangelist slyly calls Tom to give up all that he has so that he may gain all that he really needs.

Father Smith has not only the ears to hear but also the eyes to see. Although Tom falls asleep as America seems about to be destroyed, Percy's aged and undistinguished priest regularly keeps a bleary-eyed vigil in his fire tower. As a watchman for the forest department, the impoverished curate works for a living while working out his salvation. Father Smith scans the ground for blazes set mostly by people who are frustrated at being the victims of world conspiracies. Yet the prophet also surveys the skies for "signs and portents" (*LR* 6) like those beheld in Apocalypse. While fulfilling the injunction in Mark to watch for the Lord who comes at a sudden and unknown hour (Mark 13:32–37), Father Smith also watches out for the well-being of his flock, a blessedly diverse congregation in an otherwise polarized society. At this late hour of national and spiritual crisis, he performs the kind of dreary and unpretentious labors that the aspiring Dr. More must accept as his own vocation. In Percy's works, to seek is to begin finding; the sentinel scouts the heavens and discovers the kingdom of God coming on earth. In his mundane ministry Father Smith fights his own demon of alcoholism, administers the sacraments, brings solace to the sick and imprisoned, and buries the dead. But although Tom pledges to bring the clergyman a bell, he rejects the priest's appeal to move and the invitation to confess his sins. Instead of such love in the ruins, Tom helps to cause the conflagration for which Father Smith has kept watch.

Having signed the contract that virtually gives Art possession of his soul, Tom looses the henchman of Satan to wreak destruction. The devilish funding officer begins by making the Pit, a mock-serious, highly theatrical disputation between opposing doctors, live up to its infernal name. Immediately following Tom's covenant with Art, the chaos of the Pit makes visible the psychic catastrophe caused when demons of angelism and bestialism are released in the modern world. Tom expects the duel in the Pit to end in the victory promised him by Art. As scientist-lover, he hopes to triumph in the musical-erotic realm by defeating Dr. Buddy Brown, his professional enemy and rival for the affections of Moira Schaffner. Yet Tom's exhibitionism is undermined by a less selfish motive. In a debate with Brown he argues to save the scandalous Mr. Ives from the tranquilized death in life routinely imposed on the elderly until they choose a euphoric suicide. Tom's questions reveal the keen vitality of this geriatric linguist, who by exploring a reputed fountain of youth in Tampa has located the same fountain of language that Helen Keller found at the pump in Tuscumbia, Alabama. Mr. Ives has discovered a medal with a proto-Creek glyph on one side and a salamander on the other, a sign united with what it signifies, which has enabled him to crack the baffling code on the Ocala frieze. By defending the meaning in the life of a linguist who searches for the Logos, Tom advocates a position that Brown earlier labeled as patently religious: opposition to the euthanasia practiced at the Happy Isles Separation Center. Tom has not yet totally accepted Art's creed of happiness at all costs or the pervasive misnomers that hide death behind promised bliss. But when he uses the lapsometer to reveal Brown's natural lewdness, the devil's disciple unintentionally gives his patron the power to burlesque his own example. Just as Tom seems about to win a genuinely religious victory for life, Art frantically begins a pilot program to create pandemonium by an unlicensed distribution of More's lapsometers.

The amphitheater of the Pit becomes an infernal circle whose center does not hold. As the doctors, students, and nurses aim their new toys at each other, they release evil spirits of vague rage and abstracted lust until they writhe like a den of vipers. Over the jumble of raised fists and spread legs presides Art Immelmann, the genius of the musical-erotic life, who waves his arms like an old-time band leader. However, his frenzied orchestra only produces cacophony. The hysteria of the Pit serves as a microcosm for the novel's whole discordant world where obsession is just another name for diabolic possession. Virtually all of the novel's demoniacs appear in this panoramic scene, and once the chaos has erupted, Percy focuses on each in a series of abrupt and disconnected vignettes that capture a world in fragments. "But, *liebchen,* all we're doing is what you yourself suggested," Dr. Helga Heine reminds her "love" (*LR* 235). Tom has created a hell on earth.

From the centerless center of the Pit emanate the confusion and calamity that threaten to make America's birthday its last day. Although Tom cancels his agreement with his damnable partner, Art appears at the doctor's office on July 4 as his new associate, ready to treat patients with the lapsometer. And throughout the day he is sighted on television, in town, at the Love Clinic, before the Behavioral Institute, everywhere causing havoc with Tom's invention. The last loosing of Satan threatens to cause an inferno as the sand of the Paradise Estates golf course begins to burn and the smell of brimstone fills the air. The impending holocaust is only the sign of a more widespread psychic collapse, for the polarization of the individual plays itself out in a society divided against itself. Tom hears reports of riots in New Orleans, fights between students and the National Guard, clashes between the Lefts and the Knotheads, and the persecution of the Jews. The demonic Art has become the very spirit of his demented nation.

If Tom More's scheme to become the savior of the age nearly destroys it, his pride also causes his own self-ruin. Despite his professed concern for the salvation of the world, his real goal is his own glory. In his grandiose imagination, Tom fears not the coming catastrophe but its untimely arrival, which might prevent him from receiving the accolades of the scientific community after his article has been published in *Brain*. The eschaton must conform to the timetable of his cerebral egotism. Hence, by the evening of July 4 the narrow-sighted doctor notices that his field of vision has been reduced to the slit of a gun turret. The jeremiad of his splendidly rhetorical opening sentence turns into a joke as the prophet offers an incongruous portrait of himself sitting "against a young pine, broken out in hives and waiting for the end of the world," in need of epinephrine at the eschaton (*LR* 3). Although Tom claims that an allergic reaction to his steady consumption of gin fizzes has caused his near blindness, he has lost the apocalyptist's comprehensiveness of vision because of his sorry self-celebration. Two hours later, when the bunker is on fire, an ominous cloud hangs over the swamp, and his three ladies may be in danger at the Howard Johnson's, the new Christ nods off, closing his eyes for a catnap in the face of catastrophe. Tom's vanity has left no room for visions other than his own dreams.

| | | Having failed to create a utopia, Tom's salvation comes at last from discovering that love has been corrupted almost everywhere he looks and can only be found in the most unlikely place—amid his own self-ruin. The brave new world of Percy's near future has sought its own version of Raphael Hythloday's ideal realm through institutionalizing both the ruins and love in the twin perversions of the Fedville complex: Gerry Rehab and the Love Clinic. The novel's heartless utopians live at the grim end of the glorious evolution traced by Ernest Lee Tuveson.[17] If pessimistic interpretations of Revelation were gradually transformed into the Enlightenment's faith in an earthly paradise of inevitable human perfection, science's very attempts to perfect love and death have brought America nearer to doomsday. Whereas utopia once grew out of apocalypse, now apocalypse grows out of utopia. Both Gerry Rehab and the Love Clinic travesty Francis Bacon's hope that the close observation of the scientific method might enable humanity "to write an apocalypse or true vision of the footsteps of the Creator imprinted on his creatures."[18] Although Bacon (like Tom More) at least dreamed of reintegrating mind and nature, rational faculties and empirical senses, his intellectual descendants have completely lost sight of the Creator and have only furthered the dissociation among his loveless creatures.

Dedicated to eliminating the despondency that ensues when every need is supposedly satisfied, the Geriatric Center either conditions the elderly into accepting their fate of ceramics and square dancing or sends them off to the suicidal felicity of the Happy Isles Separation Center. Although Gerry Rehab denies the ruins, it actually promotes a more deadly alternative. It encourages the aged to flee despair, which for Percy is often the beginning of insight, by losing themselves in therapeutic triviality or in merciful death. Such abuse of the elderly reflects the far wider lovelessness that fractures the United States. *The Last Gentleman* looked to a time at the end of the modern age when, in Guardini's epigraph, love "will disappear from the face of the public world." In *Love in the Ruins* Percy's America lives in such a void, even though it supports an institution purportedly devoted to the study of love. The Love Clinic demonstrates how love is ruined when sundered by the dualism that afflicts every other area of life in the novel. Solemn scientists, hidden in their viewing rooms, monitor the sexual performances of their matter-of-fact clients through a battery of sensors, tapes, cameras, and computers. The Love Clinic simply perpetuates angelism-bestialism by dividing the unity of love into bodies achieving orgasm and intelligences taking notes. Human sexuality becomes just a paid scientific experiment, and objective research degenerates into clinical and sometimes comic voyeurism.

The love couples seek an unfettered alternative to the mechanized sex of the Love Clinic. Percy's updated version of the 1960s counterculture looks for a pastoral apocalypse reminiscent of Charles Reich's greening of America.[19] Watching his father desperately trying to extinguish the smoking bunker that has ruined his golf tournament, the disaffected Chuck Parker announces that he is "glad to have seen it. . . . Seen the end. You're looking at it, Doc. The game is up" (*LR* 366). He views Tom as a hero in the development of what Reich calls Consciousness III, for the scientist's doomsday machine has supposedly brought destruction to the whole wicked lot of technocrats and patriots who would prevent America's renascence as a national commune. Chuck invites Tom to become the shaman of a new, whole earth where everyone lives on love, Choctaw cannabis, and the fruits of the field. Tom's beloved on this green planet would be the vacant Hester. This human tabula rasa reveals that the simplicity and naïvete of the love community hide a perilous abstraction. Totally devoid of a past, Hester lives out the break between the old order and the age to come so completely that she has removed herself from history to become an embodied expectation. However, the Percyan apocalypse returns mortals to the fullness of time, as Tom discovers in the epilogue, and its new order is never so innocent, easy, or idealized as this land of Cockaigne. Survivors must not only watch, they also must work, especially at love, more like Hester Prynne than her anonymous descendant, who is so lost in the cosmos that she has no last name. Hester and the love couples turn apocalypse into a retreat from the difficulty of love and the necessity of labor in order to escape into a world of dreamy beatitude.

The novel's spiritual landscape is littered with wrecked relationships like those embodied by the Love Clinic or the love couples. The result is that love seems to have disappeared from the face of the private as well as the public world. As Tom seeks to discover love amid these ruins throughout the weekend, he occasionally glimpses the communion that can only flow between lonely individuals at the end of Guardini's modern world. Tom readily admits that he loves Max Gottlieb and that Max "loves me because he saved my life" (*LR* 108). Max sutured Tom's wrists after his suicide attempt, and later in the hospital saved his manic-depressive colleague again by simply giving his illness a name that would dispel its terror. Tom knows the only name for such healing language, "That, sirs, is love" (*LR* 110). Max continues to treat Tom with the same affection throughout the novel, even when the savior with his lapsometer must seem most desperate and deluded to his neobehaviorist friend. As if living out his name, Gottlieb shows a love in the ruins that overcomes philosophical disagreements just as much as the love of Victor Charles, deacon at Starlight Baptist, overlooks racial differences. Having once cared for Tom in the hospital, Victor rescues the helpless doctor after he has fallen unconscious in a ditch, and later tries to warn him about possible danger. Tom imagines himself asking Victor Charles and Leroy Ledbetter, the generous but bigoted owner of the Little Napoleon, the same question that Christ put to his apostles, "Do you love me?" (John 21:15–17). "They love the new Christ," he concludes in a fantasy of reconciliation, "and so they love each other" (*LR* 153).

More loving than Leroy but never loving enough to make his black friend feel at home in the Little Napoleon, Tom appeals to Max and Victor by his very vulnerability. He unabashedly opens himself to them in his ruin. But he cannot find such love with his wife and mistresses because he cannot reveal his unseen hurt, his lapsed self, to cartoons of women who hardly seem to have hearts of flesh. From the collapse of his marriage with Doris to his present round of empty assignations, Percy's frustrated lover knows only the abstraction and aestheticism of carnality. Only when he faces these amours as the ruins themselves, and not as alternatives to the ruins, can he ever discover the beginnings of a possibly consummate passion.

Doris's spiritualization of love helped to bring Tom's marriage to an end and his world to ruins. Once a lovely apple queen with whom he shared a prelapsarian splendor in the long-ago past of the old Auto Age, Doris fled from the horrid physicality of their daughter's death to a world without bodies. Here she remade many of the features of apocalypse according to her own angelic mind. She converted the revelation received in humility into a gnostic "yearning for esoteric doctrine," and she pursued this heavenly knowledge by becoming a "priestess of the high places" (*LR* 64). As a scientist of the spiritual realm, Doris sought a new earth in her airy gazebo atop a spiral staircase while living as far removed from the actual earth as any abstracted researcher at the Love Clinic. In this haven of transcendence Doris sought love above the ruins with the spiritual confidence man, Alistair Fuchs-Forbes. She surrendered a possibly healthy discontent with the present world for the rarefied salvation of her guru, with whom she committed "solemn spiritual adultery" (*LR* 71). Alistair wooed Doris away from the flesh, so subject to the corruption and death that she witnessed in her daughter, by teaching her that "the physical is the lowest common denominator of love" (*LR* 66). As Doris became more ethereal, Tom became more sensual, until their marriage reflected the omnipresent dualism of the novel's world.

Doris finally fled the ruins of her home for Alistair's Eden of meditation and primitive manufacturing at Cozumel. Although she hoped to find the lake isle of Innisfree and build a stately mansion for her soul in this exotic paradise, she met her death in a life of romantic clichés that delivered her from all the sordid things of the world. Doris's scorn for the physical universe blinded her to the cosmic semiotics of apocalypse itself. Marveling at the sheer profusion of objects mentioned in Revelation, Guardini observes that Apocalypse manifests "the divine word concealed in created things. These become pure and free. The inner voice is protected; the outer remains uncontaminated. Thus all things become luminous, their message audible."[20] Because Doris abandoned creation, she missed the things that talk, objects that suddenly open to revelation, a visionary appreciation radiantly captured by Percy in the novel's epilogue.

Tom turns from the ruins of love with Doris to seek love in the ruins with Moira and Lola and finally Ellen. Since Percy's libertine loves not a woman but Woman herself, he can court Moira without contradicting his passion for Lola because he really loves neither but rather the whole category that each represents. Often appearing similarly undeveloped or superficial, Tom's frequently criticized trio of women has little independent existence in the novel. Since they seem more like outlines than fully realized characters, Percy's romance depicts love and lovelessness but not really lovers in the ruins. Rather, the novel's three feminine ideals reveal more about Tom than about themselves. Like the spiritual self-projections met in dreams and allegorical visions, they live in this apocalypse as signs of the heart, as highly stylized embodiments of the novel's title. Each shows Tom a way of loving in the ruins.

Tom faces the ruins of the country and his own personal life in the forsaken Howard Johnson's where he and his three women await the end. "Love, where is love now?" Tom asks himself when he tours the moldy rooms of the motel that form a gallery of obscene graffiti (*LR* 136). The motor lodge's crumbling roof, moss-draped balconies, and swamplike swimming pool offer dilapidated tribute to a world where love has lost to destruction and degenerated into such caricatures as the penciled organs repeated on the walls of its rooms. Tom attempts to reverse the loss on a small scale by turning the

wreck of room 203 into a bower to wait out the eschaton with Moira Schaffner. Cleaning the walls and floors, providing his own supply of canned food,
bourbon, and Great Books, he tries to create a fallout shelter to protect body
and mind from the coming devastation. But since his plans for such civilized lechery actually bring the wreckage with him, Tom More's search for
love in the ruins differs little from Tom Rath's. In *The Message in the Bottle*
Percy dismisses Sloan Wilson's man in the gray flannel suit for having sought
"refuge in the standard rotation of the soap opera." Rath's wartime dalliance
in a ruined villa simply repeated "the acceptable rhythm of the Wellsian-
Huxleyan-Nathanian romance of love among the ruins" (*MB* 99). Percy exposes the sentimentality of such melodrama by reducing More's version of
the same soap opera to lusty low comedy as Tom and Moira are joined by
Ellen and finally Lola. As he hurries from bedroom to bedroom of these differently demanding ladies, like a lascivious farceur whose antics are given
new urgency because it is the world's last scene, Tom must manage a *ménage
à quatre* in which there seems little possibility of love. All of his improvements
belie the fact that the apocalyptic new place is no place in the disintegrating
Howard Johnson's. It is literally utopian, for his love nest is only the scene of
the same old carnality felt by the flappers and salesmen who frequented the
motel in Moira's imagination.

More's rank desire amid the decay burlesques the poem to which Percy's
title alludes, Browning's "Love among the Ruins." Overlooking a pasture
that has claimed a once-great city, Browning's narrator gazes at a crumbling
tower overgrown with caper, where his lady awaits him. "Love is best," he
concludes among the ruins that give the poem the apocalyptic atmosphere
that Birkin noted in *Women in Love*.[21] Tom More would agree, but at the beginning of the novel, as he looks down from the intersection at the wrecked
and vine-covered Howard Johnson's, not one, but three ladies expect him.
The title is played out with a comic vengeance, for Tom discovers love only in
the ruins beyond the ruins—not in the horribly pleasant disorder of the motel
but in the still further collapse of his own spent psyche. "Love is always possible, even here in the ashes of my forty-five-year-old life. Something stirs,
a phoenix," he muses about a rendezvous with Lola (*LR* 176). Lawrence's
totem emerges to suggest how intimately connected are love and ruins. In
Percy's fiction love arises from the ashes if the disaster clears away the self-
confinement that obstructs openness to another. Yet Tom More refuses "to
be sponged out, erased, cancelled, made nothing" like Lawrence's phoenix.[22]
He prefers self-gratifying fornication to the radical self-immolation neces-

sary for renewal. Indeed, Percy's Don Juan makes catastrophe titillate his amorous ego by turning it into a surrogate partner. A would-be suicide, an alcoholic who drinks gin fizzes although he is allergic to them, Tom flirts with destruction. He has even enjoyed his daughter's death as a "delectation of tragedy" (*LR* 374). As long as disaster is kept at a distance, affecting his wife, his daughter, even his health, but never his very self, he is in love with the ruins.

The decay of the Howard Johnson's provides the appropriately romantic setting for pursuing this ruinous love with Moira Schaffner on July 4. Although Tom still appreciates "ordinary summer evenings, cicadas in the sycamores," Moira cannot enjoy such commonplace pleasures (*LR* 130). Tom complains that she is a "romanticist and I'm not. She lives for what she considers rare perfect moments," like visiting ghost towns and jungle ruins (*LR* 130). Despite all of the amenities that Tom provides for their motel room, part of its charm for Moira lies in its disrepair. Like the artists of the broken-column school of painting, she aestheticizes disaster. She loves picturesque detritus and must live as if in the crumbling landscapes of Rosa, Guardi, and Desiderio. However, unlike Val Vaught, who works in the ruins as a rejection of the age's numbing death-in-life, Moira simply finds the more concrete form of disintegration lovely in itself or an incentive to love. "Ruins make her passionate," Tom explains. "Ghosts make her want to be touched" (*LR* 133). Ruins do not create a space for renewal so that love can abound once all the old ways of not seeing and not knowing are destroyed. They represent no real end to this woman who lacks any historical sense or appreciation of personal catastrophe. Deserted saloons from the old West and the monuments of collapsed civilizations only provide Moira with a stimulating backdrop for a kiss.

Moira turns love in the ruins not only into a love of decadence but also into a decadent form of love. Despite the promised kismet of her name, the secretary from the Love Clinic is more a fatal than a fated love. Manufactured out of exacerbated sensations and a childish gaiety in being scared, her love lacks the patient endurance that would enable it to survive daily toil and testing. Rather, it thrives on the highly attenuated plateau of intense sensibility, the catch in the breath and pang in the heart of consummate feeling. Since she lives for the perfect moment of aching loveliness, Moira romanticizes not just the ruins but also love itself. "Are you going to delight me? isn't this the time? aren't things falling out just right?" she seems to ask Tom (*LR* 133) in the voice of those who seek "the fragile utopias of the right place and the right person and the right emotion at the right time" (*MB* 22). Moira's vision of the new life is just such an exquisitely sentimentalized daydream. Placing little credence in the catastrophe that Tom foresees, she looks forward to a home in Paradise Estates where she will follow her Uncle Bud's example and raise golden banties while the attractively avuncular More conducts his research. Her fantasy offers nothing genuinely new, only the present order heightened by a rare emotional connoisseurship and enlivened by dabbling in rusticity. Moira transforms apocalypse into one more perfect and apropos rotation, just as Lola Rhoades, Tom's other love, recasts it as a theatrical repetition of the southern past.

Lola offers Tom the full possibilities of the musical-erotic life. Although she lacks More's eschatological awareness, not believing "that anything could go wrong with the U.S.A. or at least with Texas," Tom's musician mistress embraces the chance to turn her off-stage hours into Wagnerian opera: "Lola will do for you! We'll make music and let the world crash about our ears. Twilight of the gods!" (*LR* 342, 316). Since the musical is the erotic to such a siren of the cello, Tom and Lola will survive the Götterdämmerung by making music and making love. She hisses tunes in Tom's ear, plays a passacaglia on his spine, and makes him sing as if he were her very own instrument between her knees. Lola's response to catastrophe is to fiddle while America burns. Becoming musicalized and eroticized, apocalypse simply intensifies her love of art and art of love.

After the world crashes around her, Lola will host a new Arcadia at Tara, her mansion modeled exactly after the plantation in *Gone with the Wind*. Her idyll tempts Tom to envision a new Eden inspired by Margaret Mitchell and H. G. Wells. This Scarlett O'Hara of the latter days seeks to restore early times in her agrarian paradise. Placing her faith in the earth, she avows, "When all is said and done, the only thing we can be sure of is the land. The land never lets you down" (*LR* 279). In this new world of the Old South, Lola and Tom will cultivate their garden, listen to music, and sip the bourbon of nostalgia, Early Times. She will show horses or play concerts. He may work on his time machine in the laboratory made from the garçonniere and become so forgetful of time that she must remind him to eat his collard greens and corn bread. Lola's version of love in the ruins promises a sweet union of aestheticism and abstraction, sensuality and science, played out amid antebellum grandeur to the sunny strains of Haydn and Dvořák. Yet if Lola looks to the past for an image of the future, her restoration of a genteel and bucolic South is as apocryphal as Moira's love for all things lovely. Tara re-creates a movie set and so copies a copy. The hill on which Lola's country house stands has been manufactured by dredging a swamp; even its columns are deliberately flaked to reveal the underlying brickwork. Although apocalypse revives traditional images as metaphors of a glorious era to come, it never seeks merely to imitate the past. Lola, however, turns southern history into Hollywood artifice by tempting Tom to participate in a cinematic fantasy that stars herself as Vivien Leigh.

All of Lola's efforts to re-create Dixie ultimately seek to abolish the only past that is meaningful—not the ersatz pastoral of a vanished South but Tom's recollections of an older, almost mythical order, his own past as the father of his dead daughter, Samantha. Imagining his new life with Lola, he thinks himself fortunate to be able to howl down the Halloween moon with his paramour and then retire to his lab for abstract inductions, "free of ghosts, exorcised by love and music" (*LR* 339). But Tom must actually confront the spirit of Samantha, who haunts him in memory throughout *Love in the Ruins*. Lola's musical-erotic pastime annuls this spectral past by canceling the pain of the remembrances that sadden the heart. "What needs to be discharged," Tom concludes, "is the intolerable tenderness of the past, the past gone and grieved over and never made sense of" (*LR* 339). His past with Samantha is a heartfelt history of vulnerability and subsequent hurt when love came to ruins. Although in retrospect it seems to have meant too much, cost and confused him too much, Tom must seek a sign for the future amid the poignant devastation of the past. Yet he prefers to escape the sorrows of such genuine passion by listening to the lustful notes of his musical-erotic mistress, for she offers a highly sensual intensification of life at the present moment.

While Tom lies in bed with Lola at the Howard Johnson's, he hears exactly what role music plays in his new life with this bewitching artist: "Music ransoms us from the past, declares an amnesty, brackets and sets aside the old puzzles. Sing a new song. Start a new life, get a girl, look into her shadowy eyes, smile" (*LR* 339). Since the tempo of music aestheticizes the present tense, it delivers Tom from earlier pain and failure by always rewarding him with the sound of the instant at hand. Rendering memory as fleeting as its vanishing notes, the cellist's strains invite the listener to a new life free from the burdens and challenges of either his own or southern history. Lola's musical-erotic divertissement promises the joyous renovation of apocalypse, but its exclusive concern with the allure of immediate possibility offers a pleasant hedonism that ignores the more concrete ruins of the past.

Tom's intolerable memories of his daughter remind him that love lies not in the motel rooms that he turns into trysting places for Moira and Lola but in earlier ones all across America where he and Doris stayed on trips with Samantha. Always quick to try the Slepe-Eze vibrators on the bed, like the one humming in Tom's room at the Howard Johnson's, Samantha is continually recalled by her father, a recurrent presence from a past of love. "Why does desire turn to grief and memory strike at the heart?" he wonders (*LR* 138). The reason is that love is dolefully lacking in the present eroticism and lost in the ruined past. Yet if passion dissolves into mourning, the piercing recollections are salutary. The heart's remembrances expose the fraudulence of what passes for love and challenge Tom to recall an earlier unity with his family and within himself that originated in his communion with God.

I V   Just as America once seemed to enjoy an Edenic past, Tom once found paradise in Paradise Estates. Even then Tom was rather selective; his world centered on Samantha—not graceful but graced—and God. His fondest memory was of walking home after Mass, "caring nought for my fellow Catholics but only for myself and Samantha and Christ swallowed, remembering what he promised me for eating him, that I would have life in me, and I did" (*LR* 13). Although nostalgia obscures some of the difficulties and divisions of such an idealized life, Tom knew a rare harmony in this microcosm before the fall. On a summer evening sweetly American in its barbecue and time for Walt Disney, he enjoyed all pleasures as good. The bosky flavor of bourbon had not yet led to alcoholism but distilled the taste of the day itself. Eroticism still meant making love with his wife beyond the azaleas, in a garden rather than in the ruins. The piety that later cooled into loving God after women, music, science, and whiskey drove him to sing with passion "Holy God We Praise Thy Name." For a time the center did hold.

Loving the world without being lost in it, Tom rejoiced in the concord where extremes were not exclusive and reconciliation prevailed over polarization. He found the symbol and source of this coherence in the Eucharist, which gave this American Adam life by his own admission. So central and centering was the sacrament of Percyan communion that Tom recalls how even before Samantha's birth, when he and Doris traveled the highways, he left their lodging on Sunday morning to receive Christ's body. The motel was situated in some anonymous nowhere, which Tom visualized as a mere abscissa and ordinate on the graph of the interstates extending indefinitely in all directions. Doris did not accompany him but remained in the realm of mathematical abstraction as the priestess of high places. Leaving this "geometry of Holiday Inns and interstates" and "descending through a moonscape countryside," Tom traveled from a lofty orbit to a place where the eternal mystery was made concrete and particular—a small, side-street church that he attended as if for the last twenty years, hearing the bemused priest talk of such prosaic matters as the turkey raffle and Wednesday bingo (*LR* 254).

The Eucharist once united the transcendent and the mundane worlds which have become so fragmented and corrupted in *Love in the Ruins*. After sharing in such food, Tom could return to Doris's rosy flesh, as if the body of Christ made possible a wonderful appreciation of his own wife's body. Doris could never understand the significance of the sacrament to Tom. Since she regarded religion as an affair of the spirit, she failed to realize that the Eucharist actually saved her husband from such angelism. Although even then Tom was tempted to view the self as detached from the world, the supreme scientist was restored at Mass to the earth, his own body, and his wife's flesh. It "took nothing less than . . . eating Christ himself," Tom admits in language bluntly physical that avoids such euphemism as "receiving communion" for the starker image of feeding on God, "to make me mortal man again and let me inhabit my own flesh and love her in the morning" (*LR* 254). As the liturgical celebration of God's Incarnation, the Eucharist once again united humanity and divinity. If God became flesh and assumed in the sacrament a form as ordinary as bread, the abstracted doctor had sanction for his own incarnation. Tom felt that during Mass he "touched the thread in the labyrinth" and found his way out of the maze that otherwise led to life as a minotaur, the bestial self divided against its more sublime counterpart (*LR* 254). Communion once brought the union whose loss causes Tom and the world to be in ruins.

This centered life of faith began to disintegrate with the breakdown of Samantha's body, so wracked by neuroblastoma that one eye had been pushed "out and around the nosebridge so she looked like a Picasso profile" (*LR* 373). Both More and his wife sought to escape the pain of being human by living at extremes. Whereas Binx and Will found that the horrible deaths of brotherly wayfarers were passageways to their own spiritual maturity, the Mores experienced in Samantha's agony the kind of fall that the lapsometer was designed to measure. William Rodney Allen suggests that in Percy's fiction a child's death "reveals the characters of those left alive, who see the tragedy either as proof of the absurdity of the universe or as a paradoxical indication of God's mysterious but loving design."[23] Samantha's ruin gave the Mores a license not to love. "That's a loving God you have there," Doris scoffed at Tom, never forgiving either her husband or the Deity (*LR* 72). As his wife retreated into the speculations of her disembodied religion, Tom in despair began drinking, embraced lewdness as a lovely refuge from the grotesque, and finally stopped eating the sacramental flesh of Christ.

The Eucharist embodied wholeness of being, but Tom knew only the deformed body of his daughter, the flesh in ruins. The lapsed believer made the contorted form of Samantha, rather than the God who became flesh, his image of human nature and chose to live in the wreckage of his own carnality rather than in communion with the incarnate Lord. Instead of feeding on Christ, Tom turned to a delectation of tragedy, enjoying sorrow for its own sweet taste and for the dispensation that it gave for his debauched life. Samantha's horrid mortality justified More's own corruption so that the doctor became a caricature of bodily appetites as distorted in life as his disfigured daughter was in death. At the climax of *Love in the Ruins*, Tom seeks to transcend this selfish pleasure in destruction. "Is it possible to live without feasting on death?" he wonders, as he judges all the years of delight in disaster since Samantha's end (*LR* 374). Once given life by the Eucharist received at the masses with his daughter, Tom died with his child seven years ago. However, the heartbroken father is called back to life by a sudden memory of Samantha, who reminds him of what he has lost, and by Ellen Oglethorpe, who appears immediately thereafter in the ruins with love.

Tom More's account of what seems a disastrous July 4 ends with a series of disjointed scenes amid the smoldering golf course in which he reencounters many of the novel's riven selves as if they were all random bits of his broken world. Into this welter comes the gently inquiring voice of Samantha, "Papa, have you lost your faith?" (*LR* 373). Tom remembers the timely question first heard while his daughter was dying but now asked with new urgency in the ruins of July 4. Like Lonnie in *The Moviegoer*, she speaks out of the disintegration of her own body with faith and love. The schoolgirl who used to clap Sister's erasers has been transformed by suffering into her father's spiritual mentor who questions, advises, and admonishes. Samantha is the divine enigma. Chubby, acned, jilted on the night of her prom, and terrible in death, she teaches her wanton father that love need not appear lovely. She speaks only of Tom's salvation with such unaffected wisdom and stark fervor that his feverish eroticism is exposed by her pure intimacy.[24]

Samantha warns that her father may be culpable of the unpardonable sin against the Holy Spirit: "If God gives you the grace to believe in him and love him and you refuse, the sin will not be forgiven you" (*LR* 374). Her frankly theological language sounds strangely fresh amid the novel's scientific and psychological babble.[25] Like Val's speech, it voices a love of God that avoids pious sentimentality by its total concern for others. Samantha dares to confront her father with ultimate questions and challenges him to believe in response to God's grace. This pearl of great price found at last by her father's heart reminds him that love must find its consummation in God. Tom's memory of his daughter's charge reveals that her death did not just dramatize the bare and awful horror of the eschaton in each person's life. Rather, it provided a sign of how love was indeed possible in the ruins.

Tom begins to embody this apocalyptic ideal when he offers a prayer of contrition to the daughter who reminded him about the sin beyond forgiveness: "Samantha, forgive me. I am sorry you suffered and died, my heart broke, but there have been times when I was not above enjoying it" (*LR* 374). Tom sinned against Samantha by using her ruin to take pleasure in his own, but he now begins to discover a life beyond such gratifying dissipation. Samantha's insistence on loving God turns her father away from his indulgent self-collapse and toward recovering the revelation that he glimpsed once before when he was near the end. In the hospital the previous Christmas after trying to kill himself, Tom was filled with lust for the nurse on night duty and then in remorse prayed, "Dear God, I can see it now, why can't I see it other times, that it is you I love in the beauty of the world and in all the lovely girls and dear good friends, and it is pilgrims we are, wayfarers on a journey, and not pigs, nor angels" (*LR* 109). The ex-suicide felt that central to his life, the very limit of his keenest longings, was the love of God. Percy's more overt apocalypticism in *Love in the Ruins* reveals more clearly than in his previous novels the religious direction of his seer's search. Even in the epilogue after the end of his world, Binx Bolling is reluctant to speak about religion; and Will Barrett, still more hesitant, does not seem to understand how at Jamie's baptism he has touched a sacramental thread in Tom More's labyrinth. Percy has always been as cautious as his visionaries in using religious language, but the late hour of this novel allows a more radical affirmation. Tom realizes that his wayfaring is a passionate pilgrimage to an endearing Lord. God is Tom's beginning; his presence was mediated through Samantha, first in seemingly paradisal splendor, then in the love of her wracked body. Tom creates his own wreckage by loving the world and women in place of God, not the Creator through his creation. After remembering his ardent daughter's advice, he is returned at the end to the love of God in all things by the nighttime nurse who had inspired his lust last Christmas, Ellen Oglethorpe.

Ellen's mere presence in the Howard Johnson's makes Tom realize how shabby are all his efforts at eroticism. She exposes the ruins in all of their ruin so that Tom's redoubt no longer seems the haven of love that he imagined, and she challenges More to recognize a passion that is not just carnal but also moral. This "ripe Georgia persimmon not a peach" is as sensuous as Lola or Moira; "she fairly pops the buttons of her nurse's uniform with her tart ripeness" (LR 155). Ellen adds to this burgeoning vitality a Presbyterian rectitude that intensifies rather than inhibits her sexuality. Like Spenser's Britomart, she embodies "a kind of chaste wantonness," which allows her to be so prodigal with herself precisely because she is so strict in her starched white uniform (LR 155). Since Nurse Oglethorpe understands that love entails responsibility and obligation, she makes the erotic inseparable from the ethical.

In chaotic times Ellen performs the essential function of protecting, serving as center, preserving. She tends to the disheveled doctor at times almost like a mother, buttoning his collar tab, slicking his eyebrows, telling him to tuck in his shirt, as if summoning Tom out of the ruins to a new sense of personal order. Realizing that "the best that's in you is so fine," she encourages and frequently chides, until Tom More lives up to his namesake, the saint about whom Ellen knows nothing (LR 250). She speaks with the voice of his own missing conscience, quite literally when she is heard only on Tom's Anser-Phone, while he dances to the mephisto waltz of *Wine, Women and Song* on the morning of July 4. As he knocks back a drink of bourbon and soothes his psyche with a charge from his lapsometer, Ellen's tiny, insectlike voice chirrups from the tree where he has hung his pager. The buzz of his own Jiminy Cricket calls to him over the hedonistic anthem of his musical-erotic life. Percy keeps this self-assured woman from seeming too self-righteous by Tom's delight in her love, until Ellen gradually becomes more than just the peppery private secretary of her employer's scruples. Although the nurse is at first an unforeseen interloper in Tom's July 4 affair with Moira, Ellen's commonsensical questioning—"First. Do you intend to marry? . . . Are we going to go back to work?"—reminds Tom of the intimacy that he once enjoyed with Samantha when he quizzed her letter-perfect on her catechism (LR 350, 351). "She liked for me to ask and for her to answer," he recalls.

"Saying is different from knowing" (*LR* 350–51). The latter lacks the shared affirmation of naming that can make every dialogue a profession of faith. Mere knowledge, the scientist discovers, is not enough as both Samantha and Ellen turn question and answer into a naming game of love.

Tom used to ask Samantha why God made her; Ellen's queries are much more practical. Although the daughter of missionaries, she does not believe in God and is even embarrassed by religious questions. "Rather does she believe in the Golden Rule and in doing right," Tom says. "What does God have to do with being honest, hard-working, chaste, upright, unselfish, etcetera" (*LR* 157). Like most of Percy's women, Ellen is not as intensely and knowingly religious as her questing male counterpart at the end of the world. Rather, pragmatism makes her reduce religion to praxis: an ethical humanism that lacks the ardor of Lonnie and Samantha, the spiritual suffering of Kate and Val. Although Ellen is fond of calling More "Chief" and acting as his girl Friday, doctor and nurse rarely seem to achieve the true communion that Percy is fond of seeing in Defoe's castaways. Since this self-reliant woman is so completely the ground of her own moral being, Ellen is not conscious of being lost and so never meets Tom with the same degree of vulnerability. Samantha reminded her father that God had given him the prevenient grace to love and believe, but Ellen empowers herself to achieve her own excellence. Yet if her brisk efficiency in leading a virtuous life makes her a guide for the conscience but not for the soul, Ellen's emphasis on obligation is precisely what the reckless More needs. The failed physician and lapsed Catholic must return to his practice—the everyday duties of being a doctor and a disciple. Tom concludes that her good works and his faith might have enabled the two of them to save Christianity; instead, their achievement is less grandiose. They simply save each other.

Tom finally discovers love in the ruins not in the decaying Howard Johnson's with Moira and Lola but on the smoking golf course with Ellen. When the long-awaited eschaton arrives, it dawns in the most unexpected manner, in the wrong place and hour, for the very nature of apocalypse defies all categories of space and time, which at best provide only metaphors for its coming. After Tom slips out of Lola's bed on July 4 and returns briefly to Ellen, she tells him that Art has sent a message about some climactic event, a mysterious "it," which will occur that afternoon. He promises such urgent signs of the end that like the coming of the Son of Man (Mark 13:16), the moment will not even allow going back to get one's coat (*LR* 343). Tom is not quite sure what is going to take place, but he goes to the highway interchange, where he can see the four sections of the novel's cordate world, to watch and wait for the catastrophe that he expects to happen by 7:00 P.M. Despite the stifling odor of brimstone and the swirling smoke of the golf course, the apocalyptic catastrophe is nothing more spectacular than Tom's final rejection of Immelmann and his loving acceptance of Ellen.

Amid the ruins Tom meets Immelmann for a final battle. Art tempts Tom to deny his very identity as an apocalyptist by inviting him to flee disaster. Art is the presiding genius of the novel because, like all of the utopian dreamers, he refuses to face the wreckage, preferring to ignore or idealize destruction rather than confront the spiritual polarization that caused it. So, Art appears once more to lure Tom back to the motel, or even to Denmark, the devil's musical-erotic home base. Whereas Art summons Tom away from the debacle, Ellen invites him to confront it on a daily basis in a life of significant toil. Her prescription that he resume the duties of a doctor might seem just another version of the work ethic or, what Tom fears as even worse, a return to his old life of mysterious terror and longings, if Ellen's call to labor did not also include a call to love. "I believe in you completely. . . . I'll help you. We'll do it," she promises (*LR* 365). And when Art returns again to claim Tom as his own, she virtually becomes his savior. She accepts Art's previous offer to serve as his traveling secretary so that the paralyzed Tom might go free and perhaps even be goaded into action. Ellen can consider working for the devil because her high-minded practicality keeps her immune from his spiritual corruption. Since she does not understand the religious life, she cannot really be tempted away from it. But despite her nonchalance in rescuing Tom by abandoning him, her ransom prompts More's love to emerge like the phoenix out of the smoking bunker.

After remembering Samantha's injunction to love and believe, Tom witnesses this salvific memory become a reality as Ellen casually and inconspicuously tries to save him from Art. Tom's awareness of human and divine love impels him to save Ellen from Art's arms. As the devil advances on them with arms outstretched like Christ at Sacre Coeur in New Orleans, a mock messiah of musical-erotic pleasures, Tom realizes his infernal nature. And the doctor gains new resolve when his seemingly defeated nurse challenges him by suggesting that they follow Art to Copenhagen. But the "new Christ" cannot defeat the devil as the martial Lord of hosts does in Apocalypse. The strangely debilitated hero of Percy's apocalyptic thriller cannot even move to do anything conventionally heroic. Stunned by his own insufficiency, Tom can only pray, naming the devil in a petition for exorcism that also names his own patron saint: *"Sir Thomas More, kinsman, saint, best dearest merriest of Englishmen, pray for us and drive this son of a bitch hence"* (*LR* 376). More does not refer to the con man as "Dr. Immelmann," as Ellen had just named him, but exposes his foe's true identity by the properly improper epithet. Art, who has been unusually sensitive to the charged language of oaths and curses throughout the novel, is dumbstruck and vanishes into the smoke. Tom has cast out the father of lies by the sheer power that resides, for Percy, in bona fide language, especially in the hallowed speech of prayer.

When Tom calls upon his ancestor and spiritual guide, he finally recognizes his own dependency on the More, and so he begins to become like More. Sir Thomas More embodied the life of love that his descendant has turned into a pursuit of unfulfilled longing for women, knowledge, and whiskey. "Why can't I follow More's example, love myself less, God and my fellowmen more?" he challenges himself (*LR* 23). In an age characterized by the "layman's canonization of scientists," Saint Thomas More reveals to the aspiring Dr. Tom More an alternative to such secular sanctity (*LR* 7). He is an especially appropriate patron for his apocalyptic namesake because, as Percy noted in a 1963 essay, it made the saint happy "to think on the four Last Things."[26] Having delighted in meditating on his own personal eschatology, he demonstrated such love at his execution that even his own end became amusing. His American descendant recalls that More "was merry in life and death and he loved and was loved by everyone, even his executioner, with whom he cracked jokes" (*LR* 23). The martyr could jest because he knew that his end was not the ending. Tom's own farcically apocalyptic narrative often strives for this same gallows humor. However, the American More transforms his ancestor's joy into a more manic black comedy and perverts the saint's ability to show love in the ruins by his own infidelities at the end of the world. Only on the evening of July 4, when Tom More, unable to move on the grounds of the golf course, faces his own spiritual collapse and the prospect of love once again ruined in Ellen's loss to Art, does he finally begin to live up to his name. Ellen asks him whether he imagines that he is a saint, but Tom rightly rejects the title. No Saint Thomas More, for the alcoholic immediately wants a drink, yet no more the old More, heart full of longing but not of love, Tom discovers the long-expected apocalypse in the most unexpected place, his own life. By showing selfless love for Ellen, he finds his end in his identity and his identity at the end.

Although Tom has awaited God's imminent judgment from the first page of *Love in the Ruins*, the disaster never happens to America but only to Percy's apocalyptist. The catastrophe is comic in heaven and on earth. By beginning with Tom in a dark forest and ending with his recovered vision of Paradise in the epilogue, Percy makes More's quest into a divine comedy. He hears the glad tidings of redemption described by Ralph Wood: "Christian faith is nowhere more comic than in this eschatological confidence. No matter how grim the immediate prospect, no matter how great the likelihood of being calcined in a nuclear bonfire, the Gospel announces that history's final destiny has been graciously fixed."[27] But since the eschaton is personal rather than national, the counterpoint to the Dantean joy of Tom's *vita nuova* is laughter at the end that never ended. The novel becomes an end-of-the-world joke in which the apocalypse degenerates into absurdity, and the anticipated eschaton falls apart into anticlimax.

Percy creates this humorous doomsday by continually evoking apocalyptic themes and motifs only to undermine and trivialize them. Throughout the novel loom all the omens—the encroaching ruins, Ellen's report of civil disturbances, atmospheric portents, the burning golf course—that seem to herald the last day. But the specific moments in the supposedly unfolding apocalyptic drama are all rendered ridiculous. Percy's clownish angels and beasts tumble through low-comedy capers and stumble through melodramatic escapades so that the explosion of the last day finally sputters out into ludicrous misadventures. Days of wrath become days of laughter in the way that R. W. B. Lewis has found characteristic of modern apocalyptic fiction.[28] Hence, the Bantus plan only a burlesque rebellion that depends on the capture of the Christian Kaydettes and their arsenal-toting, karate-trained mothers, all en route to the national baton-twirling contest. Tom views the burning sand as a possible harbinger of apocalyptic conflagration, yet Charley Parker, the golf pro, merely laments that the city may lose the chance to host the Camellia Open next year. The rift between the Lefts and the Knotheads deteriorates into a bout of name-calling by two enraged doctors. The devil is routed not after pitched warfare but through a sinner's helpless invocation of a saint. In Percy's self-consuming apocalypse, what should be the most extreme moments of the eschaton keep turning into the preposterous incongruities and exaggerations of knockabout farce.

The ultimate absurdity of *Love in the Ruins* is that the end of the world never happens. Robert Plank defines "the End" in apocalyptic science fiction as meaning "essentially the dying out of mankind, or of that part of mankind that formed the significant characters' world."[29] The entire genre depends on the destruction wreaked by technology or by such natural catastrophes as celestial disturbances, extraterrestrial invasion, biological anomalies, and geological upheavals. But the mock apocalypse of July 4 concludes with no real disasters, only a series of nonevents. Neither the president nor the vice president is assassinated at the political rally as Tom had feared; More's lapsometer neither saves nor destroys the world, and despite its early promise the Bantus' revolt fails to gain control of Paradise Estates. Even when the rebels seem victorious five years later in the epilogue, Percy exposes the new social order as hardly apocalyptic. The Bantus have won not through violence but simply through buying Paradise with the profits from the oil discovered on their swamps. However, nothing has really changed; an aristocracy based on property and prejudice still governs society. Individuals remain torn by angelism-bestialism, and without this fundamental reintegration of the bipolar self, all apocalypse is only an appearance.

Love in the Ruins seems, then, to be an apocalypse in ruins. But if the last day ends in laughter, Percy's conclusion chastens Tom's pretensions and emphasizes More's own life as the realm within which apocalypse actually occurs. The boisterous humor does not conflict with the comedy of salvation but prepares for its joyous ending. On July 4, the day of no doom, Tom More faces the ruins of his own ego and the wreck of his musical-erotic fantasies. Neither savior nor very accurate seer, he at last discovers a love that promises a more human embodiment of the life of God. W. Warren Wagar writes that many speculative writers "reduce St. John from prophet of God's word to just another science fiction writer,"[30] but Percy reverses the demotion by restoring his technological fantasy to its roots in spiritual renovation. The only apocalypse in *Love in the Ruins* is the one Percy's seer never clearly envisioned: the revelation that the real center does hold.

V   Like the epilogue of *The Moviegoer*, Percy's fictional equivalent of life beyond the end, the finale in *Love in the Ruins* depicts Tom's new world after his saving disaster. By deliberately not providing the anticipated end to which all the adventures and complications inevitably should have led, Percy creates a catastrophe out of not creating a catastrophe. And that comic mishap makes possible the truly happy conclusion of the novel. Like each of the preceding chapters, this last section focuses on a single day in the life of Tom More, but without the violent extremism of the July 4 weekend five years earlier. Percy abandons much of the exaggeration to which the novel has accustomed the reader and simply records the ordinary events as seen from Tom's calm center. After so much distortion, the simplicity of this ending reclaims a sense of the elemental goodness that fills Tom's world after the end.

The newness of this life is emphasized by the five-year interval that separates this final section from the rest of the July 4 weekend. Dependent on God and others, Tom now lives beyond the crazy vortex of Independence Day. In the course of *Love in the Ruins* apocalypse is announced, undone, and finally restored to its rightful place in the life of Percy's visionary. On Christmas Eve a more serene Tom More reflects on the attraction of the eschaton throughout history as well as in his own life. While hauling up that morning "a great unclassified beast of a fish," he thinks of "Christ coming again at the end of the world and how it is that in every age there is the temptation to see signs of the end." Tom himself fell victim to that peril by nearly allowing his vision of doomsday to lead to his own destruction. Now with the forbearance of a searcher who is ready to look for the mysterious *ichthys* instead of becoming the rough beast himself, the fisherman concludes, "there is nevertheless some reason, what with the spirit of the new age being the spirit of watching and waiting, to believe that—" (*LR* 387). The tentativeness of this broken sentence, which barely intimates the Parousia, indicates that Tom lives not in the era of Christ come again but in a time of anticipation and preparation. Uncertainty and understatement replace More's earlier confident predictions. Tom heeds the warnings in the Gospels and Revelation always to be open-eyed. But unlike his watch five years ago, he keeps this vigil with greater humility and patience so that while looking to the future he does not live outside the present.

Before this epilogue Tom never seemed to have any time for such attentiveness to the moment at hand. By beginning on July 4 at 5:00 P.M. and then recounting the events of the preceding three days, Percy brings virtually the entire novel under the threat of the eschaton. All of the action is subsumed by More's urgent and overarching first word: *Now*. But this *now* does not name a pure present, for it is always in hostage to the future. Tom's awareness of the end claims every instant so that the action seems to occur in a kind of narrative fast forward, a speeded-up version of the present in which each second races toward disaster. Percy's epilogue makes clear that one of the greatest benisons in Tom's new age of waiting is that at last there is time. The Christmas Eve coda begins with present participles—"Hoeing collards in my kitchen garden. . . . Waiting and listening and looking at my boots"— that tell of time almost stretched out by the progressive action as the deed is done, redone, and then done again (*LR* 381). Just as a film in slow motion makes every second last longer because each is separated and suspended, apprehended and appreciated, so Percy makes the instants of Tom's workaday world seem quantitatively increased. Time is not running out, as Tom once believed; rather, he has "all the time in the world" (*LR* 383). The apocalyptist himself recognizes this shift from the frantic rush of minutes to the moment known in all its plenitude. He recalls that "in the last age we planned projects and cast ahead of ourselves. We set out to 'reach goals,'" but now "there seems to be more time, time for watching and waiting and thinking and working" (*LR* 382).

Since Tom has more time but fewer things, he gains a renewed sense of the world. Having been strangely disencumbered of his inheritance from Doris, he can now cherish the abundance that he once overlooked. Although he only has a small practice and lives with his family in former slave quarters, he feels as if he had been given everything, "like God's spoiled child," Adam once again (*LR* 383). Tom attends to and treasures the sound of chinaberries striking his tin roof, the taste of roast beef at the club, the vision of winter light filling up his garden, and especially the feel of soft, oiled new boots with which he can continue his life as a Percyan wayfarer. This sensuous bounty found in poverty's bare simplicity differs from his former surfeit of objects and experiences in the old world of Paradise Estates. The needy More has actually become more wealthy because he has discovered what Giles Gunn calls "the astonishing numinousness of things as they are . . . the rich liminality" of creation.[31] As Percy continually makes the natural kingdom disclose a supernatural landscape, Tom lives at the very threshold where lordliness dwells deep in a Louisiana morning and a bayou borders on being a sanctuary for the spirit.

Outside the apartments built like an English charterhouse, Tom hears the call of the kingfisher. And every dawn, feeling as authoritative as Kingfish Huey Long, the halcyon oarsman runs his trotline across the vapory marsh. Having suffered like the infirm monarch of the Grail legend, Tom has regained life as one of Percy's sovereign wayfarers. "Water is the mystical element!" this hale fisher king proclaims, a doctor who mistakenly thought that he could heal himself (*LR* 382). In such a sanctified country the divine presence is announced even when it is glimpsed by those without eyes to see. At the end of the novel, bird-watchers Fran and Colley Wilkes make a rare sighting of the legendary ivory-billed woodpecker and cry, "We found him. . . . He's alive! He's come back! After all these years." "Who?" Tom wonders as he recalls his earlier meditation about Christ's return (*LR* 387). Although the Wilkeses, who celebrate the Bantu god of the winter solstice rather than Christmas, do not hope for the Second Coming, they yet affirm the prospect of the Parousia in this ornithologist's parody. Called by blacks "the Lord-to-God," the fabled bird heralds the holy spirit of Tom's apocalyptic life. In his new age More comes closer to achieving this blessed dimension of time on the wing, the still second of Hopkins's sacred creatures, when the momentary is at last momentous. If the center once did not hold, the epilogue owes its coherence to Percy's God, whom Ted Spivey well describes as "the unseen energy that reunifies disparate elements of life."[32]

Although heaven and earth seem to have drawn closer together in this wondrous coda, there is still no finality in these last pages. Percy's apocalyptists never achieve a perfected state of being in their new world, but they do gain a clearer orientation, a life of coming and becoming, progressive, provisional, and never so definite that it cannot be lost. In the epilogue Tom still longs for knowledge, alcohol, and women. If the scientist seems less obsessed about winning fame and more concerned with healing a broken humanity, he continues to work on his lapsometer. After not drinking any bourbon for six months, in the last scene the alcoholic steals six drinks in as many minutes. Tom finds Ellen golden and glorious as she prepares breakfast in the morning sunlight, but he also admires the lickerish Mrs. Prouty. Percy prevents Tom's coming to self and God from ever turning into a facile attainment, achieved once and forever enjoyed. Rather, his new life involves prayer, observance, discipline, suffering, and regression. As watcher and waiter, Tom lives in the time between. He must make his way neither in the old age of abstraction and appetency nor in the sure consummation of the Parousia, but in a period of preparation and expectation shared by all who observe Christ's first coming.

Ellen, busy in the kitchen during the first section of the epilogue as in the last, never seems a full part of the novel's final harmony. Since Tom's wife still lives by her "ancient Presbyterian mistrust of *things*, things getting mixed up in religion," she does not understand how bread, wine, oil, water, salt, and ashes may provide sacramental encounters with God (*LR* 400). Ellen's wariness, as Tom realizes, may be a wise defense against the magical piety of bleeding statues and the sale of indulgences. However, it keeps her from sharing in the graced appreciation of nature and human nature that gives the epilogue its quiet delights after the bustling plot of the July 4 weekend. Unlike Kitty in *The Last Gentleman*, Ellen has confronted catastrophe and even helped to save the would-be saint from a musical-erotic life, but she does not consciously and completely participate in the holy kingdom that seems to be the particularly male province of Tom and Father Smith. And so, despite their domestic intimacy, the Mores are never as unified in body and heart as they may seem because the sexes continue to be separated in spirit. The love of Tom and Ellen makes it possible for Tom, but not Ellen, to live in a world of extraordinary unity, where opposites converge in the life of consecrated flesh—the Eucharist and the feast of the Incarnation.

Although the temple has not yet become God (Rev. 21:22), the chapel where Tom at last receives the Eucharist conjoins the godly in a holy communion. Services overlap in the building shared by Jews, Protestants, and Catholics. Such casual rapprochement makes unnecessary any ecumenical movement, for religious differences, although not resolved, have been accepted into a larger economy of salvation. Catholics take part in Protestant hymns; Tom joins the Jews on their Sabbath in waiting for the Lord. Since apocalypse is political, according to Walter Wink, because it offers "new paradigms of man's authentic existence in community," this religious remnant may be one of the best hopes for America in a novel that began on July 4.[33] Before attending Christmas midnight Mass at the chapel, Tom goes to confession. Although he recognizes his sins, Tom feels no sorrow, and he imagines adulteries that he has never actually committed. Father Smith counsels that when he is plagued by similar thoughts in his watchtower, he views the brushfires as the outer circle of hell, where his sins are being punished. But when the sinner who is so proud of his lusts balks at any likeness between himself and the gray celibate, the wily priest leads Tom by a different path to this private purgatory.

Confession is a Percyan sacrament of dialogue in which God's words expel the demons that once threatened to make speech impossible for Father Smith. The cleric leads the unremorseful sinner to feel contrition by getting him to look beyond what he has done or might do to what he must do. While repeating "forgive me" the confessor chides Tom that being a better doctor or priest and showing kindness, especially to one's family, are more important than the carnal fantasies of middle-aged men. The priest's apologies for such frankness create the properly rueful spirit in Tom. " 'You're right. I'm sorry,' I say instantly, scalded," as the fires of penitence that burned Father Smith now touch Tom, even if he hastily qualifies the sorrow as only shame (*LR* 399). Although the apocalyptist once announced a new messiah who would reconcile humanity with its sins, Tom is at last reconciled with God, and he rejects his sins by accepting the signs of the shriven. Ellen looks askance after Tom dons sackcloth and sprinkles his hair with ashes, yet the ancient tokens of repentance actually reflect a new unity within himself as well as with Ellen's distrusted world of things. This spiritual integrity finds its fulfillment in the sacramental meal, "I eat Christ, drink his blood" (*LR* 400). Having forsaken the self-divisive angelism-bestialism, Tom once again feeds on God rather than "feasting on death" (*LR* 374).

Tom eats Christ's flesh on the day that honors God's becoming flesh. Percy makes the novel's last day not July 4 but December 25; Christ's birthday, rather than America's, is celebrated at the end as children explode firecrackers. Just as John's image of the woman in labor connects his vision of the last things with what has been interpreted as the sign of Christ's birth (Rev. 12),[34] Christmas implies the promise of the apocalypse in *Love in the Ruins*, and later in *Lancelot*. Five and a half years before the novel began, riots broke out on Christmas Eve, the first signs of the coming end. On a later Christmas Eve, Tom first met Lola, developed the lapsometer, and noticed the vines twining around the liquor bottles at the country club bar. On July 4 Tom escapes from Saint Michael's rectory, where he had been imprisoned by the Bantus, to the strains of the carillon's Christmas music. These reminders of the Nativity continually look beyond the ruins of the novel to the hour when the Incarnation finds its consummation in the Parousia. The union of Logos and flesh, remembered on the feast of Christ's first coming, manifests the unity needed in the polarized world of the novel and finally achieved to some extent by Tom More. In the end the scientist seems to accept his own incarnation—to live in the flesh as one seeking and meeting God. On Christmas, God comes to Tom, and Tom comes back to God. He encounters the Deity not only in the Eucharist, the sacrament of Incarnation, but also as a pervasive presence in the day itself.

As Tom barbecues a turkey early in the morning while his children sleep and his wife prepares the stuffing and sweet potatoes, he realizes, "It is Christmas Day and the Lord is here, a holy night and surely that is all one needs." In a dance, "cutting the fool like David before the Ark," he celebrates the divine tabernacling among men and women on December 25 and in his own life (*LR* 402). Percy's wayfarer is at last the joyous sovereign of his own life because he honors with a choreographed psalm a more ultimate Sovereign to whom he is bound by a new covenant. Tom's capering before the Lord who dwells amid humans perfectly defines the scope of the Percyan apocalypse. God comes not to judge all of America but to be present in a scene of household good cheer, the closest that Percy's Thomas More ever comes to utopia. Tom makes the holy day a sign of how he will live out Percy's apocalyptic ideal when on the last page of the novel he and Ellen go to bed on Christmas morning, settling down for "a long winter's nap." The cozy scene of secular incarnation on December 25 recalls a moment created by another Moore, Clement Clarke, in his "A Visit from St. Nicholas." Tom no longer sleeps in the ascetic convent bed of chaste white iron favored by Doris, nor does he make love "under a bush or in a car or on the floor or any such humbug as marked the past peculiar years of Christendom" (*LR* 403). In the new brass bed, a Christmas present to a goodwife who does not completely understand the significance of the feast, Tom comes a little closer to finding what the day celebrates—in the ruins, unity, and at last, love.

6

ROUGH BEAST AND BETHLEHEM

LANCELOT

I   The end that has loomed over Percy's fiction from its very beginning finally explodes and implodes in *Lancelot*. Percy's most violent apocalypse explores the very limits of an already extreme genre. Although its domestic focus may seem much less expansive than the national scope of *Love in the Ruins*, and its hour not as urgent as Percy's futuristic age when machines no longer work, *Lancelot* is actually a novel for an even later day. Tom More's dreaded end blazes at last in the devastation of Belle Isle, which turns a would-be messiah into a mad and murderous Antichrist. And that highly theatrical catastrophe is the sign of a spectacular collapse deep in the heart of Lancelot himself. Whereas much of *Love in the Ruins* is a highly external novel, whose physical decay and psychic caricatures make visible a panorama of America's doom, *Lancelot* internalizes the most frightening scenes in the drama of the end. The apocalypse becomes the self's reduction of the world and time to ashes as all history is consumed in Lancelot's self-referential story. If, as Northrop Frye claims, "the apocalypse is the way the world looks after the ego has disappeared," Lancelot rewrites Revelation so that it becomes the way the world looks after all but the ego has disappeared.[1]

Percy's knight of the last days carries apocalypticism beyond the outrance of its own form until nothing seems to be left of its vision except the void that is Lancelot—the outrage of his black comedy, the annihilation of his grotesque revenger's tragedy, the exhaustion of his commanding narrative voice.[2] The final revelation of Lancelot's tale is a virtual negation of its visionary tradition: there is no revelation. Yet if *Lancelot* reads like an apocalypse in the process of self-destruction, Percy creates a still and steady center that keeps the novel from falling apart in the figure of Father John. After listening to Lancelot's tirades, he intimates in thirteen words as simple as *yes* and *no* a more radical version of the apocalypse than Lancelot can ever imagine.

Ultimately, Percy's Lancelot proves to be a prophet manqué, while the true bearer of apocalyptic news is another Percy, the priest known since youth as Percival.

Confined to the Institute for Aberrant Behavior, like John exiled to Patmos, Lancelot regards himself at the beginning of the novel as the most fortunate of seers. "Have you noticed that the narrower the view the more you can see?" he asks Father John, who frequently looks out his cell window (*L* 3). By choosing a first-person narrator, Percy almost makes *Lancelot* nothing more than a narrow view, the speaker's intensely focused but extremely limited vision from the window of the self. The prophet looks scornfully at the present, whose corruption he sees emblazoned in the pornographic poster of a local theater. He attempts to see into the future through two dreams—one of a picnic after living in an abandoned desert house with a mysterious woman, the other of a man standing with his rifle above the Shenandoah Valley, watching and waiting—which prophesy his life of patient expectation with the "New Woman" after the end of the world (*L* 37). But Lancelot spends most of his vision in re-viewing the past as he recounts the events that led to the explosion at Belle Isle. He explains to his visitor, "Seeing you was a kind of catalyst, the occasion of my remembering. It is like the first time you look through binoculars: everything is confused, blurred, unfocused, flat; then all of a sudden *click*" (*L* 13). He hopes that seeing again what he once saw will lead to revelation by bringing him "closer to *it*, the secret I know yet don't know" (*L* 62). Lancelot begins a visionary quest to remember and reconstruct his version of the apocalypse; however, his completed confession reveals the faultiest hermeneutics. He does not read his own life by the Book of Revelation, but the Book of Revelation by his own life. He absorbs the apocalypse into himself so that he enacts its divine drama within the confines of his own mad imagination.

Lancelot recalls first glimpsing the eschaton a year ago when he saw by chance his daughter's blood type on her application to summer camp and suspected that Siobhan could not possibly be his child. The catastrophe of coming into consciousness makes the father and husband see the end of the world in the end of his world. The apocalyptist, who will become a scientist of transcendence, realizes that his discovery of the blood type I-0 portends as much disaster as an astronomer's sighting of a comet in the heavens. The apocalypse is domesticated; at 5:01 on an autumn afternoon, the eschaton is infidelity.

from his negative accomplishments into a reverie of poetry, painting, and the curiosities of local history. The young Lancelot's espial of his father's venality revealed to him the total failure of his parent's life in a single, pleasant, and terrible look, which brought the son the end of the world that his sire had feared: "At the sight of the money, a new world opened up for me. The old world fell to pieces—not necessarily a bad thing" (L 42). The discovery of dishonor relieved Lancelot of honor's burden. He saw that the venerable order of the gentleman had ended, while the new and very private cosmos of the secret sinner had begun, where fathers are thieves and wives are whores.

| | As angel of the end, Lancelot pronounces doom upon the corrupt world revealed in these visions of his false father and faithless wife. At times his judgment resembles Binx's melancholy exposure of his half-alive city, especially when Lancelot recalls the townsfolk who live "in a dim charade, a shadowplay." Their world of the cave is suddenly illuminated by the "resplendent larger-than-life" figures of the movie company much as the starstruck wayfarers near Canal Street found transitory salvation in seeing William Holden (L 152). More often, such despair at the paltriness of life animates Lancelot's indictment with disgust. If Percy imagines the potent delta factor as Helen Keller's "magic Excalibur which she found in Alabama water" (MB 45), the lord of Belle Isle turns words into his knightly weapon for avenging the infidelity of his mock Guinevere. The moral outrage of Lancelot's wildest utterances often makes him resemble a biblical prophet. Like John the Baptist, the desert dweller who denounced Herod's adultery and heralded a new age, he castigates the sexual sinfulness of his era. And like Hosea, also cuckolded by his wife, he cries, "I'll prophesy: This country is going to turn into a desert and it won't be a bad thing. Thirst and hunger are better than jungle rot" (L 158).[3]

Lancelot's fierce and single theme echoes one of John the Divine's opening letters to the seven churches of Asia. The epistle admonishes believers at Thyatira, "Notwithstanding I have a few things against thee, because thou sufferest that woman Jezebel, which calleth herself a prophetess, to teach and to seduce my servants to commit fornication, and to eat things sacrificed unto idols" (Rev. 2:20). The censure imagines the infidel queen, who worshipped Baal and tried to kill all of Yahweh's prophets, as the representative of ritual rather than sexual offenses. But if taken literally—as Percy's seer always reads his world—the charge expresses the prophetic condemnation of Lancelot Lamar. He might almost be referring to John's accusation when he complains, "Your God seemed much more jealous of false idols, golden calves, than his people messing around with each other" (L 16). Unlike the Lord's wrath, Lancelot's jealousy is more aroused by adultery than idolatry. Since Percy's prophet typically overlooks the spirit in only seeing the flesh, he cannot understand how faithfulness to God may guarantee fidelity in marriage.

Lancelot excoriates the nation's current sexual immorality in caustic orations that carry Tom More's diagnosis of angelism-bestialism in *Love in the Ruins* to monomaniacal extremes. The fleshly corruption represents not just an ethical failure but an existential fall. Having come to consciousness, Lancelot sees how his age does not live in full awareness of its sovereign powers—self-reflection, volition, self-determination—but has become an animal in heat. Lancelot denounces every form of what he regards as sexual misconduct in his attack on "the great whorehouse and fagdom of America" (L 176). Every child, he cries, grows up to rape or be raped. Although Lancelot claims that making love should bring an ecstatic awareness of what is infinite, the nation has perverted it into a source of sin, particularly in its movies. Disbelieving in Hollywood's ability to hallow actions, Lancelot denounces the entire movie company at Belle Isle as bad actors. He is the film critic par excellence. The cast lacks not simply talent but the "resplendent reality" that Binx always tries to imitate outside the theater (M 16). In a novel buffeted by winds, the actors "were hardly here at all, in Louisiana that is, but were blown about this way and that, like puffballs, in and out of their roles" (L 112). Janos Jacoby, the film's codirector and Margot's current lover, "had been an actor too and so didn't know what he was" (L 110). Lancelot's daughter copies the mannerisms of the actress she loves. Raine Robinette, her screen idol, seems a perplexing mélange of roles; "what is she?" Lancelot wonders, "actress? flirt? wanton? nice affectionate girl?" (L 149). The off-screen lives of the filmmakers are as empty as their performances on film, for they debase sexual love whether before or behind the camera.

Lancelot comes to view Margot as the leading lady of this American Babylon, the Great Whore whom he as apocalyptic deliverer must destroy. He considers his wife worthy of such vengeance because for a time she seemed the one person with whom Lancelot could discover love in the ruins. Much as when he later learned of her adultery, his first meeting with Margot caused one of the rare times when he "left life's familiar path—I being a creature of habit even then, doing the same thing day in and day out" (L 75). Attracted by this hoopskirted beauty who helped to welcome tourists to Belle Isle, Lancelot abandoned his usual routine of watching the evening news for reports of disaster so that he might lie with her in the pigeonnier—sex in a cluttered and befouled garden shed that used to be a dovecote, if not quite love amid the ruins. His delight in Margot continually inspires ecstatic celebrations of sexual love as his narrative repeatedly turns into impassioned lyric. Their physical union was at the center of an immense affair with the world in which the once-abstracted Lancelot spent his time and took his place. After restoring the seigneur of Belle Isle to life, Margot also restored his mansion to its former beauty. Just as Lola had planned to remake Tom More, Margot converted the pigeonnier into a study and cast Lancelot in the role of Jefferson Davis writing his memoirs at Beauvoir, although her husband, the man to whom nothing had happened, claimed that he had nothing to remember. But despite her renovations to the house of Lamar, Margot was not so much an apocalyptist as a "Texas magician" (*L* 82). Her dazzling metamorphoses always concealed something spurious and self-centered and desperately sad. Margot transformed herself as well, from the belle of the nouveaux riches to the chatelaine of Belle Isle, and finally, since her whole life was a magical act, into an actress, student of the film wizard Robert Merlin.

Margot's busy transformations and impersonations attempted to answer the same question that burdens Lancelot and all of Percy's seekers, "What to do with time? . . . what was she going to *do*?" (*L* 121). She made of this need to act a career that parodied the new freedom that Lancelot later gains when he discovers her adultery. If the alcoholism and impotence of her listless husband were the symptoms of his total failure to act, Margot acted at acting, until her real life and film roles became interchangeable. At the town library that has become a movie set, Lancelot watches his wife engage in simulated sex as she works in the film directed by her current partner in adultery and produced by her former lover. He finds Margot as false a performer as she is a wife, for she does not really act but only impersonates an actress. Even when the apocalyptic fury of the hurricane threatens and Lancelot proposes that they escape to a new life in North Carolina or at least lie down in the belvedere while the storm clears away the misery of their marriage, she rejects the offer in favor of a life on film. Having played Lancelot's wife, Margot announces that she is leaving for a chance to star as Ibsen's Nora.

The hollow acting and sexual performances of Margot and the film crew dramatize how the world of *Lancelot* needs a savior, the coming again of the Christ near whose birthday both the destruction of Belle Isle and Lancelot's memory of it a year later occur. But the novel's "new Christ" is the actor with whom Margot makes mock love in the library (*L* 153). Troy Dana is a decadently empty version of the moviegoer's messiah. His handsome looks, glowing eyes, and instinctive sense of grace have easily turned him into the town's cynosure, but the more disillusioned Lancelot exposes the movie-star savior as a fake. Dana's radiant appearance actually conceals "a blank space filled in by somebody else's idea." Merlin explains, "I created Dana—Dana himself is nothing, a perfect cipher," as empty as the zero on Siobhan's application to summer camp (*L* 147). Dana exemplifies not so much negative capability as pure negation. This lord of light is simply a moviemaker's optical illusion, a void who depends on the screen for his very existence. Only in the film does Dana play the role of reconciler, yet in Percy's steamy send-up of Tennessee Williams's *Orpheus Descending*, the salvation degenerates into an earnest example of Hollywood sentimentality. Although the mysterious stranger is immolated by the town rabble, he saves the townsfolk from their prejudices and sexual inhibitions so that every possible southern stereotype may be united in the final reel. In the novel's bleaker off-screen world, the vapid Dana is incapable of playing "the new sunlit god come to save this sad town" (*L* 150). Reconciling no one, he only helps to corrupt Lancelot's daughter Lucy, who wants to join Dana and Raine in a household for three.

Since reconciliation seems so illusory, Lancelot seeks a more violent regeneration. When he parts with both Elgin and Merlin, they shake his hand and give him a level-eyed look, which in cinematic parlance means that "we understand each other and have been reconciled, perhaps by the Christlike stranger played by Dana." Lancelot perceives the hypocrisy of redemption on and through film. He knows that "nobody understands anyone else, and nobody is reconciled because nobody knows what there is to be reconciled" (*L* 200). Tom More's new Christ would reconcile humanity with its sins, but reconciliation lacks all meaning to Lancelot, who finds God absent and sin unable to be seen. Earlier, Lancelot claimed that he had a choice of ignoring someone, killing him, or shaking his hand (*L* 149). But the sign of the gentleman has lost all significance, and the movies record only a mockery of manners when actors part with the ritual of supposed friendship. Since the messiah has failed, Lancelot becomes the self-appointed scourge of the present time, who seeks to reunite the gestural perfection of Binx Bolling's movie stars with the ethical code of Will Barrett's ancestors. Having lived in the ignorance of abstraction for twenty years, Lancelot will kill so that he may once again be reconciled when he shakes hands.

Lancelot's diatribes against this damned age become increasingly virulent as he remembers more about the last days and nights at Belle Isle. Despite its violence *Love in the Ruins* rushed toward apparent doom with a cheerful lunacy that made the novel outrageous but never savage. Tom More's essentially good heart and Father Smith's sage counsel provided the sane perspective that kept the chaos from ever becoming overwhelming. The comedy was madcap but never frighteningly mad like the humor in *Lancelot*. Seeking to be utterly alone in the self-enclosed world of his story, Lancelot is supremely and incontestably sardonic. As he comes closer to explaining the mysterious end of Belle Isle, his initial good breeding turns into the ultimate display of bad manners that always results when divine mystery is denied. This ungentle man seems to translate into speech his own discovery that the great secret of life is violation. Lancelot's tirades have their precedents in Binx's last judgment on himself and his age, Sutter's analytical notebook, and Tom's laments; but what is often elegiac in the moviegoer, objective in the coroner, and hysterical in the psychiatrist becomes in Lancelot a lawyer's hateful and horrifying indictment of his age.

Although Lancelot's torrents of words give the novel the "Lear-like effect" that Janos Jacoby also seeks for the storm in his movie (*L* 197), Percy's fiction keeps from being blown apart through an opposing centripetal force that controls and counterbalances its own gales. Unlike *The Last Gentleman* and *Love in the Ruins*, *Lancelot* is severely restricted in scope: in a small room with one window its narrator recalls the past for a single listener. Lancelot's memories tell of a domestic tragedy, more like Othello's than Lear's, whose plot unfolds with greater singleness of purpose than do the more loosely structured episodes of its predecessors. The small cast of this drama is integral to the full-blooded action of the plot and never includes characters who only live as digressions or merely embody abstracted ideas.

At the seemingly heartless center of this chamber piece, Lancelot's voice animates the novel. But if the knight at times appears as sharp as a two-edged sword, like the tongue of the Son of Man in Revelation (1:16), Percy constructs Lancelot's narration so that it finally undoes itself. As the terrible prophet obscenely denounces the obscenities of his time, he notices that even the self-possessed Father John blanches before his ferocity.[4] By the end of the novel the priest poses the most direct challenge to the supremacy of Lancelot's vision, but the rabid speaker discredits himself long before the telling last pages. Although this southern cousin of Roger Chillingworth is obsessed with discovering the sinful truth, he misses the sin of his own obsession. And although Lancelot attempts to restore a lost sacredness to sexuality, the reformer finally becomes so angelic that he commits murder and sexual abuse without even a flinching protest from his own flesh. As deliverer of eschatological judgment, Lancelot finally stands judged by his own standards. Because *Lancelot* risks the extremes of apocalyptic art, Percy keeps working to concentrate its focus and correct its recklessness. The result is that his most audacious novel is also one of his most finely controlled fictions.

I I I   Convinced that the present age is hopelessly depraved, Lancelot announces the apocalypse not just in his home but for all of America. "The only thing I'm sure of," he declares, "is that the past is absolutely dead. The future must be absolutely new. This is true not only of me but of you and of everyone. A new beginning must be made" (*L* 62). This apocalyptic conception of history solves Lancelot's problem with the flow of time. His technological mind imagines that the "past devours the future like a tape recorder, converting pure possibility into banality. The present is the tape head, the mouth of time" (*L* 106). Acutely conscious of *tempus edax,* Lancelot can see only a used-up past, disappearing present, and inevitably wasted future. Lancelot decrees that the intolerable and useless past should be annulled because it contains his own sins, his father's graft and ineffectiveness as a husband, and his mother's probable adultery. As the tense of the forever promising Will Barrett, the future contains the attractive blank of pure potentiality, yet Lancelot views it as constantly being transformed "into the shabby past" (*L* 107). The prisoner is so aware of the present that he compares his cell, a small room with a single opening onto the world through which the temporal ribbon flows, to the devouring tape head of time, the instant that eats all others. Like Tom More who speaks into a tape recorder at the apparent end of his world, Lancelot lives as a voice that is always talking because it is just as rapidly vanishing into the silence of the ruined past. Since every tense seems inhospitable, Lancelot needs some dimension beyond time in which he can live.

Apocalypse seems to show Lancelot how to overcome this disappointing temporality. After the end, time itself—or at least the old, uncertain way of experiencing it—has reached its conclusion. The new Jerusalem no longer needs the sun or moon to light the days and nights, for God illuminates eternity (Rev. 21:23). Lancelot seeks to live by such a supernal light of his own devising. He turns apocalypse into a way of escaping the workaday world to which the genuinely Percyan apocalypse always returns his visionaries. The godlike Lancelot would transcend time by becoming his own sun and moon rather than labor with others in mortal fellowship below the heavens. His apocalyptic fantasies obviate any awareness of the wastefulness of time, consuming but never fulfilling any purpose. Lancelot simply does not have to confront the ruins or his responsibility for them because the eschaton abolishes the past or perhaps burnishes its memory to provide heroic images for the new order. Lancelot need only remember what will come. His version of the apocalypse preserves the pure possibility of the future while bestowing upon it a new glory, and it redeems the present moment, lets Lancelot know the answer to the "mystery" of "What is one to do with oneself?" by making him the herald of the last day (*L* 106). He must only watch, wait, and work for his vision of the end.

Lancelot's private apocalypse enables him to formulate a comprehensive interpretation of history. Like Tom More, he stands at the point outside time from which all tenses become comprehensible. Lancelot's memories of Lucy, Margot, and Anna inspire him to identify three epochs—a romantic period, an era of indiscriminate sexual coupling, and an age of imminent catastrophe—and to divide the course of America into three phases: the American Revolution won at Yorktown, the Second Revolution lost at Appomattox, and the Third Revolution, the new life of Lancelot and his disciples in the Shenandoah Valley. Since America viewed both of these earlier wars as apocalyptic, Lancelot's virtuous confederacy of the future will fulfill the nation's chiliastic ambitions. In May 1777 the historian Jeremy Belknap regarded the American Revolution as proof that the "proud horn of the seven-headed beast" would never rule in this land (Rev. 12:3). This judgment was echoed by many preachers who identified British rule with the reign of the Antichrist and who later envisioned a millennium of political and religious freedom, confidently described by Ezra Stiles in *The United States Elevated to Glory and Honor* (1783). But eighty years later a postlapsarian America was again anticipating the end of the world. If the Union joined Julia Ward Howe in hoping that God would trample the grapes of wrath (Rev. 19:15), the South of the Second Revolution might have agreed with one writer in the *Christian Index* who viewed northern churches as the infamous Whore of Babylon. This apocalyptic redaction of the War Between the States culminated in J. W. Sandell's *The United States in Scripture* (1907). It interpreted the entire upheaval through the Books of Daniel and Revelation and looked to a time in the future when God would vindicate the cause of states' rights.[5]

Lancelot, the last patriot and true son of the Confederacy, continues this theological exegesis of history by planning to wage a holy war to secede from a corrupt land.

Although Lancelot imagines that the United States will find its consummation in his private state of grace, his conception of the new republic invalidates him as an apocalyptic prophet. Whereas Revelation makes it clear that only God can say, "Behold, I make all things new!" (21:5), Lancelot arrogates the right of divine renewal by offering "not a vision sent to me by God but my own certain vision of what is going to happen" (L 221). This architect of a new Old South has not learned what Lewis Simpson has emphasized as one of the most important lessons of the Civil War: "the fallibility of any redemptive order set up in human history."[6] Although at the novel's end Lancelot concedes that he will give God time to chastise the age, his ultimatum simply transforms the Divinity into an extension of himself. If God fails to punish the sinful nation, Percy's apocalyptist will assume command but be even more ruthless than Jehovah. Lancelot is nothing more than a twentieth-century Zealot who imagines that the kingdom of heaven can be taken by storm. Founded by violence, Lancelot's new age will unite southern gentility and religion in a theocracy of manners. His Third Revolution, begun in the year of the American Revolution's two hundredth anniversary, will herald a "new Reformation" that makes fierce honor into an essential article of faith (L 177). The new saint is the model general and gentleman, Robert E. Lee, and the heavenly defender of this well-bred land is Michael with the flaming sword. They will set the pattern for an age of uncompromising rectitude that will value stern discipline, tight-lipped sobriety, and simplistic clarity. Although in Lancelot's own recent past his mother seemed an adulteress and his father a swindler, whores and thieves will easily be distinguished from ladies and gentlemen in the less ambiguous future.

Lancelot considers himself the last gentleman. He does not practice the code of his father, whose good manners declined into hypocrisy and milk-soppery. Rather, he follows the violent mores of his great-great-grandfather or of Will Barrett's self-assured ancestors. Lancelot may demur at the barbarism of his forebear, who out of wronged honor once cut his opponent from ear to ear and then dismembered his body: "I do not think men should butcher each other like animals. But it is at least a way to live. One knows where one stands and what one can do" (L 155). Yet despite his reservation Lancelot adopts this brutal ethic when he slits Jacoby's throat and possibly even mutilates his corpse. The values of the southern past, whether in their

strict propriety or noble savagery, attract Lancelot for the same reason that
they appeal to Will Barrett in his nonage. They offer these would-be cava-
liers—the latter bewildered by choices, the former embittered by the immorality that such choices make possible—a clearly prescribed standard of
behavior that solves the problem of what to become by dictating a way to be.
But if Lancelot discovers the same "readiness to act" (*L* 157) that Will admires in his fabled relatives, he turns this existential freedom into an absolute
intolerance of the freedom of others and finally into violence against all who
do not act as he demands.

Lancelot's merciless cult of good form lacks the splendor of apocalyptic
renewal. Its martial virtues are paltry, middling, even minimal. While John
sees the establishment of a spectacular new order after the great catastrophe,
Lancelot, who has described himself always as moderate, offers only a modest renewal. His vision of a time when "the violent bear it away" promises too
little (Matt. 11:12). Crusaderlike courage and inflexible dogmatism are easy
compared with the demands of *caritas*. Percy exposes this Spartan reformation in the unheard question of Father John to which Lancelot replies, "What
did you whisper? Love? . . . Don't talk to me of love until we shovel out the
shit" (*L* 179).[7] Lancelot's Third Revolution will fail for the same reason that
his domestic apocalypse has already come to nothing. In prison he wonders,
"But what went wrong with the other new life last year? I must find out so I
won't make the same mistake twice" (*L* 108). Although Lancelot causes the
fall of the house of Lamar in order to usher in a new morality of good manners, his mistake is that, unlike Father John, he does not talk of love. Instead,
he reduces the apocalypse in America and at Belle Isle to his own egotistical
consummation.

I V   After his initial discovery of Margot's unfaithfulness,
Lancelot sets out on a quest to discover further revelations. He is more an
evil seeker than a holy seer. He will earn his apocalyptic vision rather than receive it as a graced moment, freely given to one like John, whose compassion
and endurance make him a worthy witness (Rev. 1:9). The sinful Lancelot
hopes that the climax of his search will be nothing less than the sight of sin,
"the sweet secret of evil . . . the dear darling heart of darkness" (*L* 216). He
even justifies his pursuit of the unholy grail by suggesting that such a view
of corruption may reveal its ultimate opposite, the Deity this age of niceness
has forgotten. Lancelot looks for such revelations in bedrooms because the
apocalyptic vision is such a privileged insight that it reveals secrets only in

seclusion, in the most extreme retreat where the seer encounters what is beyond the self. John seems almost removed from the already remote Patmos
when he enters the door to heaven and becomes privy to an unimaginable
future (Rev. 4:1). And Lancelot views the sanctuary of bedrooms as enclos-
ing a similar rapture of transcendent intimacy. In the innermost recesses of
these hallowed chambers, amid the private parts of the body's temple, occurs
what he can only describe as "unspeakable" and "incommensurate . . . a
unique ecstasy, ek-stasis, which is a kind of possession" (L 16, 21). Lancelot
senses the awe that Earl Rovit sees as an essential response in anyone who
even considers the apocalypse: "How can you think about an apocalypse with
one mind—with a rational intelligence that is designed to make precise ex-
clusions of anything that is chaos. You can't even talk about an apocalypse
univocally. . . . It eludes the single-chorded voice."[8] Lancelot intends to see
the hidden truths about which he cannot speak, to glimpse the holy of holies
in the penetralia of the flesh.

Although Lancelot imagines that he is a visionary, Percy exposes him as a
disappointed voyeur. All of Percy's seekers thrill at learning about disaster,
but Lancelot's pleasure is peculiarly sexual. He watches the evening news
as a viewer would "a lewd act come to climax" (L 72), and his discovery of
his own bad news, Margot's adultery, arouses his "worm of interest" (L 21).
Despite railing at the obscenity of The 69ers, Lancelot's own experiment in
cinema verité produces what he dismisses as a "dirty movie" (L 180). Since
the eschatological prophet is only a pornographer, he fails to achieve his ultimate apocalyptic vision. "Why did I discover nothing at the heart of evil?"
has been the disturbing question that Lancelot has wanted to ask Father John
from the beginning. "There was no 'secret' after all, no discovery, no flick-
ering of interest, nothing at all, not even any evil," he concludes (L 253).
Lancelot ends by admitting not that he failed as a seer but that there was
nothing to see. Having missed the sight of his own adultery, butchery, and
incendiarism, Lancelot is a more purblind visionary than even Tom More. If
he finally discovers nothing and no evil, the reason is that he can neither get
beyond the facts of the flesh nor read the signs of his own spiritual perversion.

Apocalypse communicates on an anagogical level, but from the beginning
of his quest Lancelot has only wanted to understand on a logical level. He
continually applies the methods and reasoning of modern technology to areas
such as sex and the sacred, which by their nature transcend purely objective approaches. And he is continually frustrated in pursuing his peep shows
because he reduces the *mysterium* to nothing more than the mysteries inves-

tigated by his favorite detective, Philip Marlowe.[9] Trying to know sexual sin for certain, he first sends Elgin to spy on the movie company at the Holiday Inn, but such observation yields the empiricist nothing really conclusive, only the raw data of times, names, and room numbers. Since Lancelot views the present as the tape head of time, he appropriately resorts to the most elaborate audiovisual equipment possible to produce a videotaped documentary on the most immediate forms of concupiscence. Hidden cameras monitor five bedrooms at Belle Isle, yet even this erotic home movie does not clearly reveal the carnal truth to him. Instead of filming the undistilled evil of lust, the devices record only hazy red images and incomprehensible dialogue, a low-budget skin flick in scarlet for this lewd moviegoing successor to Binx Bolling. What Lancelot does detect, with his abstracted mind that increasingly views everything through the eyes of a geometer, are triangles. In the first film, he watches the love triangle involving Margot, Merlin, and Jacoby; in the second, he notices "pubic triangles [which] turn like mobiles, now narrowing, now widening," and the "rough swastikaed triangle" made by the bisecting bodies of Raine, Dana, and Lucy, "a six-arm Shiva" reproduced as a stick-people triangle in the text (*L* 191, 192). Fond of drawings himself in essays such as "The Delta Factor" and "A Theory of Language" (*MB* 3–45, 298–327), Percy uses the triangle to represent the semiotic relationship involving name, object, and namer. The deltas of Lancelot's double feature enact sexual travesties of this archetypal act of linguistic intercourse. The trinities turn into signs of the omega over which Shiva, Hindu's phallic god of destruction, presides.

Lancelot's gnostic adventures climax when he spies for himself and sees nothing. No longer using video equipment, the moviemaker becomes his own probing movie camera for the Gothic film of his imagination as he walks through Belle Isle and surveys the bedrooms of his remaining guests. His final scenes of sexual assault and murder make him guilty of the worst form of acting in a world of bad actors. Yet even as the avenging apocalyptist holds Janos Jacoby before slashing his throat, he is aware of "nothing except the itch of fiberglass particles" under his collar (*L* 253). Lancelot ends in a hellish version of Kierkegaard's aesthetic stage. Since he lives at nerves' end, he recognizes only a stimulus and his irritated response. Lancelot knows no sense of sin but merely pure sensation, the only feeling left when all human feelings have been lost.

Lancelot chafes under a reflex action rather than enjoying his long-sought revelation because he has abandoned the office of visionary to become the

most reductive of scientists. He sees, but he does not see into facts and beyond feeling and by faith. At breakfast the day after he discovers his wife's
adultery, he describes with appropriate detachment his reactions to a fly
crawling across his watchband and triggering a hair on his wrist: "The hair
moved its root which moved a nerve which sent a message to my brain. I
felt a tickle" (L 88–89). But such physiological terms cannot describe the
essence of adultery, surely the mystery of mysteries for Lancelot since it
couples the two areas that he regards as transcending all categories: sex and
sin. Nevertheless, Lancelot reduces his wife's infidelity to the simplicities of
such action and reaction. He reasons that "her fornication, anybody's fornication, amounts to no more than molecules encountering molecules and little
bursts of electrons along tiny nerves" (L 89). The consummate behaviorist
makes adultery virtually no different from feeling a fly on his wrist.

At its best, scientific observation can provide Lancelot with images and
information. These findings may later be judged as sinners or sin itself, but
such a verdict can only be reached by applying religious standards totally
outside the measurement of science. Having desired to film "who moved,
toward whom, with whom" (L 145), Lancelot records only a motion picture
of pure movement—figurines who constantly seem to blend together and be
blown apart in an electronic wind, a high-tech gale out of Dante's infernal
second circle. The filmmaker glimpses but cannot decode the semiotics of
sin. To see true darkness of heart requires a form of second sight impossible
for Lancelot because he is far too restricted by the surface of reality. Such a
literalist is the very opposite of the apocalyptic seer, for he knows only what
is at hand, up close, in front of his face. Without a religious imagination, any
attempt to photograph sin can yield nothing more than the patterns of electrons flowing on Lancelot's screen. Since the materialist has reduced sexual
intercourse to just such electrical activity, he rightly sees on the videotape
a vision of one of matter's basic constituents. The grace of greater insight
might have enabled Lancelot to detect in their charge the negativity of his
own soul.

Such sin in his heart prevents Lancelot from seeing the sinfulness of sin
elsewhere. In the worst form of intellectual pride, Percy's twentieth-century
Ethan Brand turns people into parts of his production company.[10] Lancelot
reduces Elgin to his ancestral status as slave by using the MIT student as
his personal cinematographer, and he casts the Hollywood film company as
real-life actors in his apocalyptic melodrama. But he overlooks his own unpardonable sin because he is so obsessed with ferreting out wickedness in

others, and he never recognizes their ungodliness because he is so benighted by his own. Hence, at the end of his quest Lancelot sees nothing of sin but not the nothingness of sin. He is blind to Julian of Norwich's revelation that sin "has no kind of substance, no share in being, nor can it be recognized except by the pains which it causes."[11] Sin is known only by that which it negates, for it has no independent essence, no sign but the resultant suffering. The shock of confronting this void might have pointed to the end that the knight of the unholy grail supposedly sought, the absolute being of God. But Lancelot, who prefers not to speak of love, misses the invisible nonbeing at the heart of darkness, at the heart of himself.

Since Lancelot's quest ends in a nonrevelation, Percy stages its climax as a parody of the Apocalypse of John. As the end finally approaches, hurricane Marie crashes at last, its lightning flashing like camera bulbs between darkness audible and palpable. Whereas the planter in the film produced at Belle Isle enjoys "the apocalyptic fury of the hurricane," Lancelot delights in more private forms of devastation (*L* 196). He believes that storms neutralize the malaise so that victims become free to act (*L* 164). So, it is appropriate that hurricane Marie appears as a travesty of Marian iconography to inspire his wicked finale. Holding a surreal vigil in his pigeonnier during the world's last night, Lancelot beholds his own variation on John's bejeweled and scarlet-clad woman whose cup brims with abominations (Rev. 17:3–6). The sensuous, scandalous Our Lady of the Camellias proffers a knife so that Percy's knight can be her champion. This southern version of the fallen woman, a mistress with the manners of a lady, is the quester's archetypal image of her ambiguous sex. She reminds Lancelot of a whole class of graceful, voluptuous women who have outlasted all the stories about their sexual disgrace. The apparition wears a strangely out-of-season, flesh-colored camellia, its center a protruding mass of stamens and pistils, yet she explains away Lily Lamar's adultery by comparing it to Camille's grand passion for Robert Taylor. Our Lady epitomizes all the ladies of the novel who in Lancelot's eyes are really secret whores, especially Lily, who is as carnal as the visitor's camellia, and Margot, who is as provocative as Marguerite Gautier. As Belle Isle becomes a movie set for genuine sexual betrayal, Lancelot's vision of Garbo's greatest role dramatizes the opposites that Percy's crazed gentleman can only explain as the self-contradictions of female hypocrisy: overt sexuality and Hollywood sentimentality, voracity and gentility, lewdness and romantic love.

Whereas the harlot in Revelation, drunk on the blood of martyrs, must be stripped of her finery and burned, Lancelot's lady incites him to seek the vengeance that ends with the explosion of Belle Isle. She thrusts the Bowie knife at her servant and challenges him to enact what he later proclaims as the great secret of life: violation. Making the archenemy of Revelation his evil mistress, Lance obediently leaves the pigeonnier and uses his weapon, phallic or knightly, to violate Raine and do violence to Jacoby.[12] Since he has viewed both Lily and Margot as wives and mothers who are also whores, Lancelot has actually been paying tribute to this ambivalent patroness throughout the novel. At the end, the chevalier consummates his fealty. As dweller in the Sodom of America, he practices Our Lady's rapacious sexuality by sodomizing Raine after he notices that she wears his daughter's sorority ring. As avenging cuckold, he vindicates the honor of southern womanhood by destroying Margot, the apocalyptic whore of Belle Isle. Because Percy's knight considers woman "the omega point of evolution," Lance finds his end neither in the Christ of Revelation nor in the evolutionary culmination of Teilhard but in the pure violence of his deadly name (*L* 223).

Spurred by his mock madonna, Lancelot unwittingly becomes the surrogate for the seven-headed, ten-horned beast on which the Whore of Babylon sits. While the cuckold stares down at Margot and Janos coupled in a cathedral of a bed, he sees them as "the strangest of all beasts, two-backed and pied, light-skinned dark-skinned, striving against itself, holding discourse with itself in prayers and curses" (*L* 239). The avenger achieves the apocalyptic triumph of capturing the Beast as he calmly squeezes the lovers together in a deathly embrace (Rev. 19:20). By calling them "It," Lancelot can justify his own jealous and self-righteous revenge on the horrible creature with two backs that also enraged Othello. But the true brute in this end-of-the-world drama is actually Lancelot himself, the husband with horns who murders Janos without any emotion. Sinning in his quest for knowledge of corruption more grievously than those he caught corruptly engaged in carnal knowledge, Lancelot receives a devilish apotheosis. When the gas that he has piped into the house suddenly explodes, he is sent "wheeling slowly up into the night like Lucifer blown out of hell, great wings spread against the starlight" (*L* 246). Lancelot's self-serving revision of Apocalypse imagines that he has been catapulted out of an imprisoning inferno rather than expelled from the heaven of Belle Isle (Rev. 12:9–10). His belief that *l'enfer c'est autrui* prevents him from realizing that the hell is himself. Although *Lancelot* climaxes in the fiery last judgment averted in its predecessor, the catastrophe means nothing if it does not herald that still-greater catastrophe, discovering love in the ruins. Percy's unregenerate narrator seems left with nothing—no knowledge, no unholy grail, not even any feeling—just the enduring chill, the Dantean hell of utter negation.

V   *No* is not the last word of the novel. After visiting the "lost people" in "the region of the dead" mentioned in the epigraph from the *Purgatorio, Lancelot* ends with Percival's affirmation. Although Percy's lost seer never achieves Tom More's glimpse of Paradise in *Love in the Ruins,* the novel's very open-endedness prevents Lancelot's nihilism from seeming conclusive. Rather, the final pages intimate a completely opposite vision of the apocalypse, which may bring hope to Percy's bleakest fiction and his darkest prophet. There is yet the possibility that the love of Anna and Father John may save Lancelot from the ruins and at last lead him to revelation.

Anna seems to correspond to the third stage of catastrophe in Lancelot's sexual theory of history, for he recognizes that the woman in the next room has lived out the apocalypse in her own spiritual quest. After she dropped out of Agnes Scott College, Anna sought the supposed "New Life" of an artists' colony in California, which Lancelot defines as only a more daring repetition of the past. When she became discontent with this rotation, she abandoned the latest version of aestheticism for still another new life as a social worker in New Orleans. But after the disaster of gang rape and fellatio, Anna withdrew from the violence of the time into silence and the fetal position. Since her sexual assault was a violation of the very principle of orality, the end of her world was translated into an end to words. All speech seemed senseless after such an unspeakable outrage. Lancelot views his inarticulate lady as a "survivor of the catastrophe and the death of old worlds" who has been strangely purified by her ordeal (*L* 37). It has enabled her to transcend the usual stigma of woman as secret whore by becoming the "new Virgin" (*L* 159).

Lancelot's virtual monologue contains the story of an attempt to create a new world of dialogue with this first woman of the future. Like Percy himself, who laments that "language undergoes a period of degradation, words wear out,"[13] Lancelot realizes that the familiar signs have been exhausted: "To *make conversation* in the old tongue, the old worn-out language. It can't be done" (*L* 85). Hence he undertakes a semiotic apocalypse to create a paradise of language where he can recover the pristine significance of the Adamic namer. In his old world of enjoyable eroticism, Lancelot celebrated the prenuptial communion that his mouth found in "that sweet dark sanctuary" between Margot's thighs (*L* 171), but while trying to communicate with his assaulted and silent lady, the linguist develops a totally different form of intercourse that depends on neither sex nor speech. Lancelot reduces language to the cipher, Ground Zero, and then re-creates speech as a new set of ciphers. *Lancelot* is nothing but speech. However, the counterpoint to its narrator's outpouring of words, alternately lyrical, angry, and wistful, is another unspoken series of signs. In Percy's grimly comic variation on the movie cliché of falling in love with the girl next door, Lancelot taps on the wall of his room in an attempt to converse with the neighboring Anna. Each letter of a word is represented by a number of knocks that corresponds to its position in the alphabet. This system of sounds seems a fit method to make contact with a woman whose ravishment has paradoxically restored her virginity, for the abstracted code preserves speech from the violation of the body inevitable in a vile and violent world where everyone either rapes or gets raped.

Lancelot's difficulty in communication is strangely typical of what Percy has called "the community of discourse" in contemporary literature. In *Diagnosing the Modern Malaise* Percy compares characters in modern fiction to "two prisoners who find themselves in adjoining cells as a consequence of some vague Kafka-like offense. Communication is possible by tapping against the intervening wall. Do they speak the same language?" [14] Binx Bolling and his half brother faced the same potential loneliness in *The Moviegoer*; however, the speech of Lonnie Smith, pronounced only with great difficulty and with great love, kept words from being worn out. When questioned by the youth, Binx found it "possible to tap back: yes, I love you" (*M* 162). Lancelot tries to undertake a similar renewal as he taps out such a rudimentary sentence as "*Who are you?*" (*L* 35). He seeks to restore words to their original import by paring away all that is indirect and extraneous, simplifying sentences into the barest of signs so that the remaining essentials recover the easygoing, forthright dialogue that he remembers sharing with his first wife, Lucy. Lancelot's tapping signals the effort of an embittered polemicist to rediscover on the most elementary terms—speech stripped to the point where it is simply sound—a sense of the fundamental decencies in an age of obscenity.

The attempt fails. Tapping lacks the rich humanity of talking. A system of communication based on the numbered repetition of sounds demonstrates the same dangerous transcendence of the incarnate world that Lancelot has shown in spying on his wife's adultery and later in heralding the day of doom at Belle Isle. Lancelot's linguistic code is as primitive as the ethical code of pitiless justice and stern virtue that he hopes to establish through his new American Revolution. The cryptographer even seems to recognize its inadequacy, for he eventually speaks to Anna in a chastened form of language. It gives voice to an oddly poignant yearning for what is truly primary in speech as well as in gesture and attitude. With Anna he only wants "to come close but keep a little distance between us, to ask the simplest questions in a new language—*How are you*—just to hear the sound of her voice, to touch the tips of her fingers, to hand her through an open door ahead of me, my hand pressed lightly against the small of her back" (*L* 86). Imagined with such tenderness, Lancelot's militant age of good manners seems as if it could be a time of the gentleness implicit in being a gentleman.

As Lancelot periodically interrupts his memories of Belle Isle to inform Father John of his small and tentative advances in knowing Anna, their unassuming romance is played out against the background of the cataclysm at Belle Isle. She responds to his tapping. He gives her a kiss, the Hershey's kind, putting the candy into her mouth, which she has lately used for eating and finally rediscovered for speaking. They talk. All their actions are as understated as the past was melodramatic. Just as Father John draws Lancelot out of his speechless prison, Lancelot likewise calls Anna forth into the world of language. At the same time he is beginning indirectly to explore the only means to his own freedom. Although virtually all his words to Anna and Father John are filled with self-justification and self-glorification, the very act of speech may lead to Lancelot's emerging beyond his silent self-sufficiency into genuine communion with another. Percy's solipsist can escape his self-created confinement only if he can use language to affirm Anna as *Homo loquens* (*MB* 17) rather than to level the world and live in his own fiction. Lancelot proposes that they settle on the fifty acres Anna's father left her in Virginia, an "island between two disasters," the North and the South (*L* 219). He hopes that the new world will begin in the virginal land left amid the ruins.

Although both Lancelot and Anna are "aware that an end had come and that there had to be a new beginning," Anna does not agree that the great secret of life is the pleasure of violation (*L* 251). The knight's lady of catastrophe is not in love with the ruins. Since she has discovered a life beyond her personal disasters, she rebukes Lancelot for being so obsessed with her rape, "You goddamn men. Don't you know that there are more important things in this world? Next you'll be telling me that despite myself I liked it" (*L* 251). Anna's defiant response at the end of the novel indicates that having recovered the use of language, she has also recovered her very self. If her rape was a sexual attack on her ability to speak, Anna can now vent her outrage at the obscene prophet and self-righteous assailant. Lancelot cannot accept her healthy perspective; he believes that if she could only shoot enough men in revenge, she might join him in his new life of ladies and gentlemen. Percy's extremist is always more comfortable with his simplifications of women—his first wife out of a Poe ballad, his Jezebel of a second wife—than with their intractable ambiguities. Since Lancelot recasts his loves to enhance his own gentlemanly self-image, his narrative portrays none of his ladies in her fully human complexity. Yet the women of Percy's novel can never be entirely reduced by Lancelot's misogyny. Just as his memory of Lucy on the tennis court reveals a less ethereal version of his lovely dead bride, and Margot's last words suggest that she is more than a category, Anna exceeds Lancelot's dire imaginings.

Despite Lancelot's rancor, Anna has not become a vengeful female chauvinist but a possible guide, like Beatrice, out of his purgatorial prison.[15] Her last words, as reported by Lancelot, reveal how, along with Father John, she converts language into an expression of love. Holding Lancelot's hand, she tenders him a haven in her family's two-hundred-year-old barn in the Blue Ridge Mountains of Virginia. After Margot's attempt to coop him in the pigeonnier, the prisoner distrusts this offer of a manger and even fears that the anticipated new life will only be a repetition of the past. However, in his apparently final conversation with Father John, Lancelot seems to hope that his lady will share his future. And the priest, who knows Anna well, indicates that she may join him in the country's birthplace as the new Eve to his American Adam. The apocalyptic linguist needs her love to see that his lady is truly the first word that she speaks in the novel. Anna pronounces her name, which means "grace."

Father John affirms the same life-giving logos. At the end of the novel when Lancelot asks whether his friend has anything to tell him, the confessor simply says, "*Yes.*" The last word is Percival's. His enigmatic reply bespeaks a fellow searcher who can help to initiate Lancelot into the central mystery for all of Percy's knights of faith: the Holy Grail is not glimpsed in fitful visions of transcendence but embodied in daily communion. Just as Father John has been doing throughout his visits, Lancelot must give, sympathize, and invite the sensitive responses of other hearts. Although Percy's continuing allusions to chivalric romance echo and invert the work of such writers as Chrétien de Troyes, Dante, Malory, and Tennyson, *Lancelot* seems closest in spirit to the twentieth-century apocalypse of *The Waste Land* as it pursues the knightly quest amid the ruins.[16] After the cities of the world fall in "What the Thunder Said," Eliot's poem reaches the dry land of death around the

Chapel Perilous. Having announced the apocalypse through his own search for the unholy grail, Lancelot has come to a bare cell and hopes that America will become as barren as the desert. In his own wasteland, he needs to feel "a damp gust / Bringing rain" and to hear the enigmatic words of Eliot's thunder.[17] According to some versions of the medieval legend reported by Jessie Weston, if the seeker asks questions about the sacred objects finally beheld at the Grail Castle, the Fisher King will be healed, the rains will flow, and renascence will emerge from the ruins.[18] Percy's physically and spiritually impotent lord of Belle Isle will only be healed in this place at the end of his world if he opens himself to the priestly physician who lives out the meaning of the Grail. Although Lancelot earlier claimed, "I know what I need to know and what I must do" (*L* 254), he appropriately ends the novel by asking questions of his visitor, a true vessel of grace, and listening to the mysterious monosyllables of what the priest says.

As Father John at last looks directly into his eyes, Lancelot seems to read his listener's mind with the shared knowledge of their former camaraderie. His queries articulate the priest's own thoughts, for Father John keeps replying "yes"; even his one "no" is actually its opposite, an agreement to Lancelot's negation. Lancelot's questions show that he has gained a threefold knowledge: he knows that he does not know everything, he begins to know in communion with Father John, and yet he confesses that the priest still knows more than he has said. Although Lancelot promises, "One last question—and somehow I know you know the answer" (257), that inquiry leads to another and then to a final one. The starkly affirmative last word of the novel promises that after Lancelot has stopped talking long enough to listen, there may come to him in the space of silence the Word beyond all of his words. Since Percy believes that all language affirms the connection between speaker and listener, Father John's "yes" sounds the single word that underlies the intimacy of all dialogue, an eloquent and loving affirmation of the Logos itself.

Until these final pages, Percy's priest spends most of his time in a ministry of listening. He speaks occasionally, but his responses are only known through the indirect means of Lancelot's reply. Yet Father John is not just a shadowy set of enigmatic inferences about whom it is impossible to say anything certain, for Percy consistently makes his words, actions, and reactions point to his vocation as a bearer of God's news. Indeed, Percy's minimalist depiction of the priest is the fictional sign of his spirit. Father John does not need the self-aggrandizement of a dramatic monologue because he lives in his self-effacement, so reduced to his essentials that he becomes a cipher totally expressive of the mystery that is Other. His felt presence—caring, questioning, confirming—prevents the violence of Percy's fictional techniques from turning the novel into the most despairing of apocalypses. Father John intimates the only possibility of Lancelot's deliverance from the prison of his own language.

If Binx Bolling exists in the meditations of his written confessions, Lancelot, like Tom More, is solely a voice. But whereas Percy's other first-person narrators address an imagined audience, Lancelot speaks to an actual listener, although he prefers to ignore him. The novel almost seems a dialogue of one, as if the mad monologuist would hardly leave room for any other speech that might challenge his verbal supremacy. Afraid of silence by his own admission, the sullen Lancelot fills up the quiet blanks of his days with the noise of television's bad news and then with the voice of his own hate-filled gospel. Percy's fiercely unrelenting speaker is a narrative black hole whose first-person account seems to absorb all language into his own loveless rhetoric. "Don't talk to me of love until we shovel out the shit," the soliloquist warns when his friend tries to interpose a barely spoken word (L 179). Lancelot protests throughout his reminiscences that he does not know what *love* means, or he qualifies its meaning by redefining it as the exhilarating carnality that he savored with Margot. His plans for a re-creation of speech and society reflect the same egotistical desire to dominate words and the world rather than to make both the expressions of dreaded love.

Obsessed with shoveling out the excrement, the eschatological prophet who does not speak of love sees only the end products of a filthy era. Lancelot's invective turns language into the tool by which he clears away the refuse of twentieth-century America. His own speech, however, actually adds to the waste matter of the age, for he spends the entire novel overusing and abusing words. The prophet's logorrhea and obscenities wage a verbal assault on language and the Logos itself. His narrative voice, which overwhelms the occasional replies of Father John, attacks the communion that speech should bring. And his profanities, which express absolute contempt for all things carnal, sin against the sacred Word that Lancelot scorns for pitching its tent in the place of excrement (L 238).

In *Lancelot* Percy carries the techniques of apocalyptic fiction so far that they eventually collapse and so leave the way clear for their complete opposites, a more affirmative way of heralding the future. Like all misanthropes,

Lancelot unwittingly reveals his far greater miscreancy even as he lambastes his household of unforgiven trespassers. Since the invective and derision of his self-authored monodrama have such a hollow center, they finally implode and bring down Lamar's house of fiction around its own vain mastermind. Lancelot's ire is finally overpowered by Percival's irenic spirit; his denunciations by Father John's twelvefold assertions; his violence and brutal humor by his friend's silence and faith. The priest's quiet vigils grow more resonant with each day of Lancelot's vituperation. He follows Percy's own dictum in "The Message in the Bottle" that when everyone is saying "come," perhaps the best summons to discipleship is to say nothing (*MB* 148). Such wordless testimony compels with its own oblique power. Its pure receptivity actually invites Lancelot to utter his own wrathful words, yet its patience and humility articulate a way to live once the prophet's choler has been exhausted.

Percy's silent listener is the sine qua non of the entire novel. There is no *Lancelot* if there is no Father John, for he makes all of Lancelot's speech possible by first enabling him to see. Like Anna, Lancelot once refused to talk to anyone. He finds, however, that the sheer presence of the friend he loved, not the mechanical sight of Elgin's movie camera, grants him the most beneficial perspective. "But when I saw you yesterday," Lancelot tells his visitor, "it was like seeing myself. I had the sense of being overtaken by something, by the past, by myself" (*L* 5). Percival enables Lancelot to reflect on the past and to be reflected in the present as the seer glimpses his own image in his fellow quester after the Grail. This vision gives the narrator his voice. Lancelot's first words to the priest are "Come into my cell. Make yourself at home," and he ends the opening interview with a request, "Will you come tomorrow?" (*L* 3, 6). Father John's coming causes Lancelot's own coming to self again. When the confined knight again sees his once-beloved semblable, he can review and retell the unspeakable past to a confessor accustomed to hearing what seems beyond language. The communion born of being friends, schoolmates, and former companions at whoring leads Lancelot to remember his own wife's infidelity in an age so lewd that "young men don't have to go to whorehouses any more" (*L* 14). Since the murderous cuckold prefers to forget, his narrative frequently evades, minimizes, falsifies, and digresses from the past; nevertheless, Percival patiently questions and redirects the knight-errant's erratic story so that he can at last be a true seer and speaker. Lancelot initially views his own history as it was reported in the newspaper headlines that present him as a grief-stricken husband who heroically tried to save his wife from the flames of Belle Isle. Yet by the end of the novel the priest's constant attention and examination lead the sinner to behold and confess the truth.

Having helped Lancelot to recover the past, the taciturn Father John also reveals to his friend a future based on extraordinary love in an ordinary life rather than on glorified legalism in an inglorious City of Man. Although he aspired to be a visionary, Lancelot has only become the incarnation of the evil that he sought; he is a damned John the Divine. Percival is Lancelot's own apocalyptic double, a second eschatological prophet truly named John. The priest agrees with Lancelot that "we are not going to make it this way. . . . It's all over. . . . There must be a new beginning" (L 256–57). And like his fellow seer, Father John recognizes the apocalypse only after some crisis in his own life. After his return from missionary work where he hoped to surpass Schweitzer, he at first seemed so sad and preoccupied that Lancelot regarded him as "a screwed-up priest or a half-assed physician. Or both" (L 10). Lancelot intimates that his listener's rival loves for God and a woman may have brought the failed clergyman, who has taken up counseling, to such spiritual ruin. Father John's sardonic look indicates that perhaps he shares the same doubt and dissatisfaction that Percy's naysayer vents in his tirades.

Lancelot does not know whether his priestly confidant has been named after the Baptizer or the Beloved Disciple, but this John honors both of these New Testament news bearers.[19] He listens and speaks with the prophet's sense of advent and with the evangelist's radical witness to the Word, the essence of which is love. In Lancelot's bare cell the herald's voice hints at a new order for the prisoner's arid soul. When Father John's words are finally allowed into the text on the novel's last pages, his spare use of language about the end and at the end is a startling affirmation of the Logos spoken in genuine dialogue. Whereas Percy's fantast uses speech to create his own autonomous world of the apocalyptic imagination, the priest bears the divine Word in the communion of everyday conversation. Since this Johannine language establishes the fundamentally religious bonds with another and with God, the Percyan nuncio accomplishes the goal that Lancelot sought. His words about newness—one negation and twelve affirmations into which is compressed a vision of the old order's doom and the new one's dawn—restore words to newness. None of Lancelot's harangues sounds with quite the same force as his friend's pregnant and decisive "yes" and "no."[20]

The word spoken by Father John is the gospel. Percy dramatizes the most telling difference between Lancelot and Father John by their attentiveness to the good news. As seer and messenger, Lancelot is obsessed with bad news. During the 1960s he lived for the latest tragedy on the evening news, and he finally made the headlines by achieving a miserable stardom in the newspaper stories about the tragedy at Belle Isle. From his cell he broadcasts splenetic bulletins about America's imminent collapse, but his plan for the future is so heartless that it becomes the ultimate bad news. "Why so pale and sad?" he cries to his friend. "After all, you're supposed to have the good news, not me" (*L* 84). Lancelot is more right than he realizes, for Father John embodies the gospel by bearing the good news. Although the eschatological prophet does not disagree with Lancelot's awareness of a spiritual crisis, the priest offers a new beginning. It is inspired not by Lancelot's fusion of Roman *virtus* and medieval chivalry but by the glad tidings of the evangelist.

The word most closely associated with Father John is the word repeated endlessly in the gospel of John: *love*. At an early meeting Lancelot despairs when the apostle speaks of love: "That is easy to do. But do you wish to know my theory? That sort of love is impossible now if it ever was. The only way it will ever be possible again is if the world should end" (*L* 55–56). During the course of the novel the world does end for Father John, and then begins again in love. His change from casual to clerical clothes and his new willingness to pray for the dead at the cemetery give a sign of how his own inmost collapse has led to a personal apocalypse. Listening to Lancelot's pitiless narrative, the discouraged priest rejects the vision of the crabbed prophet that he might so easily resemble and dedicates himself to a more beneficent way of living in the ruins.

After the passing of the old order, Father John is ready to center his life on a love so radical that he will labor in a small Alabama church. Lancelot jeers at his friend's new world in which he will "preach the gospel, turn bread into flesh, forgive the sins of Buick dealers, administer communion to suburban housewives" (*L* 256). The final conversation between the two friends makes it clear that the apocalypse must be based on either Father John's or Lancelot's vision. Percy does not sentimentalize the life that his priest chooses, for Lancelot makes it seem ordinary and unattractive after their previous knightly adventures. But this failed actor-director really does not know the difference between spiritual drama and Hollywood melodrama. Lancelot never can decide whether such deeds of his friend's as leaping off the *Tennessee Belle* in the middle of the river or jumping "from unbeliever to priest, leapfrogging on the way some eight hundred million ordinary Catholics," are reckless stunts or leaps of faith, "the ultimate show-off thing or the ultimate splendid thing" (*L* 61). Lancelot lives for the kind of spectacle that he suspects Father John might have produced. His destruction of the Lamar mansion turns the gestural perfection of Binx Bolling's screen idols into the means for creating an end-of-the-world extravaganza. Father John renounces such showmanship by a freely made choice that defines a life in the most literal sense of setting forth its ends. The ultimate splendor of this eschatological livelihood comes from incarnation rather than film acting.

Often seeming distracted and abstracted, Percy's priest assumes the everyday burdens of the flesh in a life of service at an Alabama parish that recalls Val's ministry of the word in the same state. Whereas Lancelot has unknowingly become the unholy grail that he sought, Percival finds the Holy Grail in the communion given and received, where the center of the most daily life possible is the Divine. He believes in the "time-place god" (*L* 31), like the Creole women whom Lancelot, nearly a lost soul himself, watches decorating the graves for All Souls' Day in the small and simple tasks of faith.[21] In the end and as a beginning, the priest's bleak vocation is far preferable to Lancelot's angry age of self-righteousness because it posits a love so great that it does not despise the uninviting. Father John modestly implies that such godlike concern must be at the heart of the era to come.

Lancelot cannot agree. Living only for tragic and triumphant scenes, he fails to perceive the newness of such a common glory. "Isn't that just more of the same?" asks the apocalyptist whose own new earth promises only a violent repetition of a gentlemanly past (*L* 257). Since he cannot tolerate the inexcessive, Lancelot mocks his friend's generosity of spirit as "God-bless-everything-because-it's-good-only-don't-but-if-you-do-it's-not-so-bad" (*L* 177). Father John dedicates himself to a paradox that is divinely comprehensive, not compromising, but Lancelot protests that such a contradiction reeks of mediocrity. Although Lancelot claims to approve that the cathedral in the Vieux Carré is set in the midst of a sinful city, he never really accepts that God may dwell amid ungodliness, or that "love should pitch its tent in the place of excrement" (*L* 238). By his objection to Yeats's "Crazy Jane Talks with the Bishop," the self-consecrated Lancelot rejects not just the complexity of sexual love but also the entire gospel of John that proclaims the divine tabernacling among men and women.[22]

Although Lancelot Andrewes Lamar explains away his Anglican namesake as his father's attempt to gain Episcopalian sanction for such a knightly praenomen, the seventeenth-century divine bears witness to how Lancelot misses Christ's daily second coming because he sins against the first. Andrewes, who made the feast of the Incarnation one of the central themes of his life, preached in his "Sermon on the Nativity, 1611" what might well be a reminder to Percy's failed prophet: "It will not be amiss to tell you; the word that is Hebrew for flesh the same is also Hebrew for good tidings—as we call it, the Gospel; sure, not without the Holy Ghost dispensing it. There could be no other meaning but that some incarnation, or making flesh, should be generally good news for the whole world. To let us know this good tidings is come to pass He tells us, The word is now become flesh."[23] But Lancelot, who watches children build Christmas bonfires before he brings his own fiery destruction to Belle Isle, finds all flesh filthy, claims that his gospel is pornography (*L* 224), and desecrates the primal Word to whom all of the bishop's words give glory. This evangelist of despair promises only a blank and pitiless Second Coming. As Shelby Foote recognized in a letter to Percy, the novel ends with Lancelot "stalking toward Bethlehem after all the mayhem he committed upon those children of perdition."[24] But his priestly friend, who will announce the gospel and turn bread into flesh, incarnates an alternative to the future of the rough beast. Lancelot will discover the glad tidings of the true apocalyptic hour only if in the words spoken after the novel's last word he can say, like John the Divine, "Amen!" (Rev. 22:21) or, like Father John, "Yes."

7 THE REVELATION OF ROMANCE

THE SECOND COMING

I Although the Book of Revelation often seems like the nightmare of the whole sleeping world, its vast and terrible images should not obscure the fact that the Apocalypse of John is also a love story. John's greeting praises the One to come as "him that loved us, and washed us from our sins in his own blood" (Rev. 1:5). The returning Lord warns the community at Ephesus because "thou hast left thy first love" and promises those in the city of fraternal love that he will humble their enemies so that they will "know that I have loved thee" (Rev. 2:4, 3:9). The divine guest knocks on the door of the lukewarm Laodiceans and will have supper with anyone who responds with an invitation. At the end of Revelation, the intimacy of that messianic meal finds its consummation in the wedding feast of the Lamb (Rev. 19:9–10). John's canticle of canticles celebrates the Second Coming as God's marriage to a lovely and loving new creation. More joyously than any of Percy's other novels, *The Second Coming* espouses John's vision of the passion that lies at the heart of the Parousia. Percy's apocalyptic comedy is a romance for the end of the world in which human love serves as a sign of the divine love at its source. Having come to himself, Will Barrett comes to Allison and in the end to the God whose gradual coming into his own life he almost overlooked.

In his second coming in Percy's fiction, Will resolves to bring the manners of the gentleman to the mystery that he only began to understand at the end of *The Last Gentleman*. Recalling the tradition that claimed so much of Will's allegiance in *The Last Gentleman*, Kitty says that in the past, "if you fell out with somebody, you didn't smile at them and go around behind their backs. You called them out and had it out with them." Will recognizes that this honor code still governs his own life but as an introspective and self-destructive ritual: "That's right. We call ourselves out and have it out with ourselves. Famous one-man shoot-outs" (*SC* 142). His father's suicide was such a self-duel, and in *The Second Coming* he devises his own religious version of this noble combat. He will either call God out of hiding and have it out with his holy opponent or have his own shoot-out with himself. Planning an absurd variation on the divine wager, Percy's last gentleman redivivus comes to discover a faith like Pascal's, "God felt by the heart."[1] As Will follows Lancelot's chivalric course, he begins his life again by helping a disturbed young lady recover from the violations of a senseless age. In a private retreat both couples discern how language may lead to love. Yet whereas *Lancelot* ends with a riddling dialogue that may eventually direct Percy's lost quester to the salvation mediated by Anna and Father John, *The Second Coming* concludes with Will's elated speculation on the apocalyptic semiotics that have surprised him in Allie and Father Weatherbee. After having dramatized his epigraph from the *Purgatorio* by imagining the utter depths of Lamar's dark soul, Percy makes his own graced second coming to *Lancelot* by rising from the region of the dead in *The Second Coming*.

Will begins the process of coming and coming again through two bewildering visions in which the past repeats itself in the present. His memories lead first to a sense of his identity and, later in the novel, to love. Although Will often seems to wander through *The Last Gentleman* like the amnesiac hero of the movie seen by Binx Bolling, the older Barrett now remembers everything. He inhabits a semiotic universe in which all that "he saw became a sign of something else," an emblem for memory (*SC* 51). Since any moment may be the point at which time doubles back upon itself, Will often seems to live in two tenses at the same instant. He at once attends to what is happening as it happens with that intensified awareness characteristic of Percy's seers after revelation, but he also comes back to the past that keeps coming back to him. Will's quest is to discover the significance of these sudden moments when time is reversed and reprised, these mysterious second comings. Indeed, virtually the whole novel is contained in the two recurrences mentioned on the first page.

Like John's apocalypse, Will's initial revelation occurs on a Sunday. However, although he lives in the most Christian city of the most Christian state in the most Christian country, the site is not one of the thirteen churches in Linwood, North Carolina, but one of the favorite sanctuaries in Percy's secular city: the verdant pastures of the golf course. In *Novel Writing in an Apocalyptic Time* Percy glances at the significance of this green world when he explains that he is interested neither in "the sociological horrors of the old South" portrayed by Faulkner and Caldwell nor in the urban decay of the New South, but in "the more elusive apocalypse of the country club, the quaint Vieux Carré, the 5,000 happy midwest tourists who visit a tastefully restored mansion on the River Road."[2] The professional gentry of Percy's South live in a world of such consummate charm and style that catastrophe seems absurd amid this abundant well-being. Yet it continually breaks into these ideal environments, challenging the blithest spectators and consumers to turn renewal into something more than another building project. The apocalypse in *The Second Coming* dawns elusively on the very grounds where Chandler Vaught in *The Last Gentleman* enjoyed sweetened bourbon and even sweeter despair, the highly mannered world of the golf course. As Will eyes the position of his golf ball, he suddenly sees the brilliant fairway go black and then reveal an apparently insignificant event from thirty years ago with such clarity that the present is only the past re-presented. Once while walking home from school along the railroad tracks, he saw Ethel Rosenblum practicing her cheerleading in a "wedge-shaped salient of weeds . . . shaped like a bent triangle, the bend formed by the curve of tracks" (*SC* 7). The memory is the kind of appropriate accident to which Allie later gives the name of romance. The middle-aged man tumbles to the ground much as he threw himself to the earth out of anguished desire for Ethel Rosenblum when he was fifteen. On the golf course Will suffers a fall of the most fortunate sort. This collapse brings his world to a crash but also reveals the possibility of finding love in these ruins.

While Will gazes at the sky from the bunker into which he has stumbled, he notices a towering cumulus cloud, which ordinarily he would not have given a second look. Like all of Percy's visionaries who come to consciousness, Will is forced by the downright novelty of his position to notice what is normally ignored: a strange bird flying past, the multicolored granules of fertilizer on the green, and the cloud whose top "went boiling up higher and higher like the cloud over Hiroshima" (*SC* 3). At the beginning of *The Last Gentleman*, Will glimpsed Kitty by chance at the point marked Ground Zero, but that romance at the end of Guardini's modern world ended in unpromising ambiguity. At a later hour Will sees another young woman over whose memory loom the mushroom vapors that have become the twentieth century's sign of the apocalypse. And this vision eventually leads him to his end, to Kitty's own daughter, Allie.

Will's memory of Ethel Rosenblum standing in the weedy triangle is a nearly dead man's sight of the delta of Venus amid the bodyscape of desire.

Much as Lancelot watched the spinning pubic triangles in his erotic home movies, Will realizes that the three-sided parcel of land was a "public pubic sort of place, to make a sort of love or to die a sort of death" (*SC* 162). While Allie kisses Will later in the novel, her invitation further maps the sexual geography of this "wedge-shaped salient of weeds": "Your tongue is welcome but you, that is, the salient you, would be even more so" (*SC* 328). Will's memory of this rank triangle is at once an accusation and a promise. The delta-shaped plot of land should be the place where the conjunction of Percy's delta factor occurs, but in the present as in the past Will does not feel linguistic or sexual communion, merely a sign of frustrated passion. Filled with desire at the romance of the rose in bloom among the weeds, he drops to the ground in unfulfilled longing for Ethel Rosenblum. The collapse typifies the dead end of his loveless life, a dying fall which he finally reverses only at the end of *The Second Coming*. At another wedge, an empty corner of grass by the Holiday Inn, he rejects the temptation to kill himself in order to live for Allie's love.

From the beginning of the novel, Will's memory calls him to this intimacy. Will and Ethel never knew such love, nor even the fellowship of language, its prerequisite in *The Second Coming*; at best they engaged in coolly impersonal, clipped conversations. As Will remembers a typically empty exchange about summer vacation, his name is mentioned for the first time in the novel. The reader learns what Will recovers thirty years later in recalling Ethel at "this unnamed unclaimed untenanted" spot: his identity is his name (*SC* 8). In coming to consciousness, he claims title to himself, resumes his own tenancy. Although Will Barrett has not thought amorously about women since long before Marion's death, he suddenly regains his will. His name signifies the whole spectrum of desire from love of women to longing for God, what Dr. Ellis later diagnoses as *wahnsinnige Sehnsucht*. Will's yearning is salutary, for desire is the measure of what his life lacks. Although he is often told "You won it all," Will's memory of Ethel reveals that he has nothing but urgent need and passionate insufficiency (*SC* 70). His being is desire; he lives to will.

As a retired and wealthy widower, Will once seemed to face a future bounded by the green of the golf course. But his vision of Ethel Rosenblum amid the landscape of longing disturbs his plans to perpetuate the present leisurely game of life. Since the will of desire restores to him the "will be" of time to come, he comes to want such a love and such a place for his future. Over the years Will calls to Ethel to join him in homesteading this weedy delta, where his life has met its eschaton: "Here's the place for us, the only place not Jew or Gentile, not black or white, not public or private" (*SC* 8). The repetition and antithesis of Will's summons echo Paul's description of Christ as the locus where opposites disappear (Gal. 3:28), for, like Tom More, Will comes to discover that his desires converge in God. Although his wife was an old-style Episcopalian who lived her faith through an astounding liberality toward the needy, and his daughter, Leslie, is a born-again Christian, Will is an agnostic. But almost immediately after Ethel Rosenblum reappears in memory, he begins asking questions about the apparent disappearance of the Jews from North Carolina. He later remembers Marion's belief that the survival of the Jews was a sign of divine Providence and that their exodus to Israel would be an omen of the apocalypse. Uncertain about the significance of the Jews, Will begins a search for proof of God's existence and for portents of the coming end. Although Will's overpowering vision of Ethel foreshadows his approaching fall, only amid this very self-collapse does he discover the romantic and religious passion for which he has been searching.

If Will's first coming to self on the golf course quickens the life of his heart, his second coming through memory reveals the forgotten death at the heart of his life. The next day, while Will is bending under a fence to retrieve a golf ball, a vibrating wire echoes a moment from more than thirty years ago that was the most important event in his life. Will cannot fully interpret this sign and prefers to resist and reject its significance. He keeps returning to this memory throughout the novel, sometimes in brief illuminations and casual associations, frequently in extended reconstructions of various incidents, so that he seems constantly coming to understand himself through coming upon the past. In Percy's great narrative circles, Will repeats the story in his mind, questions his memories, and recalls new details, which will only be reexamined and revised once more. And Percy's recursive novel leads the reader to participate in these roundabout discoveries. On the first page the Percyan narrator mentions that Will experienced "two odd incidents" on the golf course: the sudden fall and the memory of a forgotten sound. But then the novel amusingly ponders Will's suicidal depression at the farce of life before it loops back to present his tumble in more detail. After veering away in chapter 2 to focus on Allie, Will's double, the narration returns to the second odd incident at the beginning of chapter 3 when Will has sliced out-of-bounds. But it turns away once again to tell about his erratic golf game, and only after repeated windings does it finally curve back to the moment at hand when Will hears the strand of fence singing. The narration spirals with previews, visions, and reviewings. *The Second Coming* is a book made out of continual second looks.

The thrumming of the barbed wire reminds Will of the twanging that he heard as a twelve-year-old when he followed his father under a fence in a Georgia forest. As the past resounds in the present, Will begins to remember the signal day when he experienced catastrophe but not revelation, and when he met his eschaton but did not know it. On the hunting trip Will and his father were wounded by Lawyer Barrett's Greener. He recalls that after being shot he crashed to the ground just as he has again fallen some thirty years later after remembering Ethel Rosenblum. Both memories challenge his golfer's complacency by awakening desire. Will longs to know: Why did his father reload his double-barreled shotgun after only one shot? Why did he miss the second single, although he was an expert marksman? Why did Will hear only three shots but afterward count four spent shells? Before this moment Will believed that "there is no mystery. The only mystery is that nothing changes" (*SC* 51). His memory of the hunt, however, intimates the mystery that changed everything in his life.

The catastrophe of the hunt marked the violent climax to the efforts of Will's father to live by repetition. Since Ed Barrett's melancholy stoicism in *The Last Gentleman* had only intensified to become a mad hopelessness in *The Second Coming*, he went on the hunt to escape his despair for the present and to return to the myth of the southern past. Percy's richly Faulknerian prose suggests that Will's father tried to live as if he were in "The Bear."[3] The boy and the man hunted in the very woods where the elder Barrett had once gone on a great hunt, perhaps even a fabled hunt, with his own father. They spent the preceding night in the same hotel where Will's father had stayed long ago as a youth. Lawyer Barrett sought the consummate hunt of southern legend as some sustaining fiction in his dark world without gentlemen, but he could not make his life an extended second coming of the past. He discovered that the hotel was simply not the same, the guide was inadequate, and the dog was poorly trained. The failure was catastrophic.

Immediately before Will and his father separated in the woods, the boy heard his father say "shit" for the first and only time "in exactly the same flat taped voice airline pilots use before the crash: *We're going in*. Shit" (*SC* 55). Barrett's expletive was the sign and sound of the end. This single last word spoken before both were wounded betokened certain crash—of planes, of Will to the ground, of Will's life to Ground Zero. Moreover, as Will later learns from Ewell McBee, his father's name for the end typified his entire ex-cremental vision of life. The elder Barrett once said that a soul is just a man, and a "man is born between an asshole and a peehole. He eats, sleeps, shits, fucks, works, gets old, and dies. And that's all he does. That's what a man is" (*SC* 176). Since Will's father reduced humanity to a series of biological functions, "shit" was the appropriate outcry at the last day. Sensing a lifetime of dung and death, he smelled the same merde that Binx and Dr. Bolling de-tected in their malodorous age. Ed Barrett's eschatological vision could see no more than a scatological sign.

As Will tries to understand the catastrophe of the hunt for the first time, he assumes that his father sought to communicate the sad misery of his own waste-filled life. He suspects that the apparent accident was actually an at-tempted suicide, planned to save the son who was so much like his father: "*he had a secret and he was trying to tell me* . . . that one day it would hap-pen to me too, that I would come to the same place he came to" (*SC* 62). In Will's misreading of the signs, Ed Barrett wanted to turn the sorrowful disaster of his life into a means of revelation. He would avert catastrophe by catastrophe. The paternal seer with glittering eyes that seemed to look ahead into the future was offering Will a proleptic image of his own inevitable de-spair because he hoped to prevent his son from coming to the same place in the Dantean woods of his life. Will imagines that the failed suicide was his father's attempt to obviate this second coming.

Will's interpretation of the hunting accident allows him to achieve a spuri-ous reconciliation with the father whom he now recognizes as a would-be savior. But although he misunderstands what J. Gerald Kennedy terms the "semiotics of memory," he begins to realize how his father secretly loved and lived by death.[4] Will remembers how on the hunt his father nearly loved him to death. Although the elder Barrett violently rebuked Will for carrying his gun the wrong way while going under the fence, the chastisement also re-flected the concern of a fond father for his son's safety. The parent later held his shotgun with one arm and hugged his son with the other, even addressing Will as if he were the Greener, "*You and I are the same*," in a confession of his own propensity to turn love into violation (*SC* 55). Will believes that this fatal love culminated in his father's attempted suicide. Loving his son and death, Ed Barrett tried to save the youth by seeking to end his own life. If Will glimpses a vision of eros in his sight of Ethel Rosenblum, his memory of how his father virtually courted destruction reveals the central force in his father's life, in his own repetition of that death-haunted career, and in his entire morbid age as thanatos.

Although Will has not thought of the past in years, his repeated musings on the hunt bring into focus the love of the end that dominated Lawyer Barrett's life. His southern honor code made his obsession with death into a respectable pastime, for it licensed his great hunts and even greater hates. Since Ed Barrett could hardly walk down the street without wanting to shoot someone, he could kill, if not his world of enemies, at least animals with vicarious pleasure. War gratified his murderous passion. And so Will's father took from an SS colonel a Luger and a black cap with a *Totenkopf* insignia, the skull beneath the skin on which his eyes were always fixed. His suicide consummated this love affair with death. Having failed to kill himself in the forest, the hopeless gentleman succeeded the next time in the attic of the family home and made a second coming with the same shotgun but with both barrels appropriately loaded.

When Will later finds the gun in a broom closet in his upstairs study, he looks at it for the first time in twenty years with almost visionary understanding. He realizes that his father declared his own eschaton and made his suicide the Second Coming. By taking the Greener into his mouth, Ed Barrett aimed at "the ecstasy of love" in the only form that he could imagine it, a double blast that would achieve the double task of destroying his whole old world and achieving the final, supreme orgasm. Suicide became a form of sexual intercourse at the end of his world. Deceptive toward his wife, who could only view the shots in the forest as a hunting accident, and ambivalent toward his too-similar son, Barrett regarded love as dead in his own life, and so he made love to death in an apocalyptic climax:

> And what samurai self-love of death, let alone the little death of everyday fuck-you love, can match the double Winchester come of taking oneself into oneself, the cold-steel extension of oneself into mouth, yes, for you, for me, for us, the logical and ultimate act of fuck-you love fuck-off world, the penetration and union of perfect cold gunmetal into warm quailing mortal flesh, the coming to end all coming, brain cells which together faltered and fell short, now flowered and flew apart, flung like stars around the whole dark world. (*SC* 148–49)

Lawyer Barrett transformed love and death into sex and suicide, and then he united the two in his own bizarre version of the Parousia. Gun in mouth, the Greener only a mechanical extension of himself, he parodied self-induced fellatio in the horridly spectacular double come of his own singular death. Sexual intercourse could only produce *le petit mort,* but Will's father intensified "the little death of everyday fuck-you love" by his suicide to create "the coming to end all coming," his own superlative second coming of self-love and self-destruction. Much like Lancelot, he declared the end, but whereas Lawyer Lamar would at least preserve himself and a world of small-scale virtues, Lawyer Barrett performed an even more radical act of annihilation. His "ultimate act of fuck-you love fuck-off world" destroyed self and society so that his apocalyptic egotism found its fulfillment in a blaze of nihilism. In a single moment of destruction and renewal, his brains were blasted around the attic to blossom and burn in the night.

Will's memories of his father's attempted and actual suicides give him the necessary insight to judge his own deadened life and the living death of his age. The stricken son realizes that he tried to escape his father's fatal love by rejecting all that the elder Barrett's life embraced. Will left old Mississippi for New York, tried to believe in the Christian God because his stoical father could not, and sought refuge from gentlemanly violence in "an ordinary mild mercantile money-making life . . . mild sailing, mild poodle-walking, mild music-loving among mild good-natured folks," much like Binx's "modest" existence in Gentilly or Lancelot's "moderate" routine at Belle Isle (*SC* 72). The lawyer lost his future and his name in his career; he administered the property of his clients and executed wills. Living out this death, Will is startled to recognize how negligible was his vocation: "I can't believe I spent all those years in New York in Trusts and Estates and taking dogs down elevators and out to the park to take a crap," an entire lifetime reduced to the ordure that his father saw so clearly (*SC* 73). Lawyer Barrett at least felt the passion of his anger. Yet in trying to "turn 180 degrees away from you and your death-dealing" (*SC* 72), Will substituted a mediocre life that was never really his own but only a fashionable collection of the activities supposedly pursued by prosperous and cultured New Yorkers. Hence, the son has turned 360 degrees away from and around back to where his father stood. At the beginning of the novel he finds himself standing in the woods and thinking about his parent's attempted suicide in the forest—the second coming.

I I   Whether as the death in life that Will knew in New York or as the life in death that his father cultivated in Mississippi, Will's memories reveal the doom that reigns not just over his family but over the entire era that he calls the Century of the Love of Death. As the prophetic judge of this baleful age, Will notices that virtually all of the living dead believe in some bizarre version of the Second Coming. Percy's novel takes its title from the scriptural image of the Parousia, originally a Hellenistic term for the coming and presence of kings and gods. As Sigmund Mowinckel explains in *He That Cometh*, the eschatology of the Old Testament grew out of Israel's experience that Yahweh was a Lord of action who came by his own choice to reveal himself. He came in the great events of Israel's history; he came yearly in cultic festivals; and even after the destruction of the nation, he would come to save not just Israel but the entire world.[5] Christians discovered this climactic advent in the figure of Jesus, and in images borrowed from Daniel's vision of the Son of Man (Dan. 7:13–14) they looked to the Second Coming of Christ, the Parousia that would bring the fulfillment of his saving presence (Rev. 1:10–20). Although the early followers of Christ expected this return any day, its immediate territory in Percy's fiction is the everyday. "From a Christian existential point of view," Lois Parkinson Zamora explains, "Christ's Second Coming is not to be construed as an event to be waited in the future, but as the future coming into and constantly renewing the present."[6] Before Will Barrett comes to recognize the unexpected intimations of this theophany in his own life, he must confront the absurdity and even the spiritual jeopardy of his own and others' eschatological visions. Percy's comedy laughs at various delusions about the Second Coming and reveals still more serious perversions of the eschaton in order to herald a more radical way of living at the end.

Although the minister Jack Curl claims that he is "less interested in signs of the apocalypse than in opening a serious dialogue with our Catholic and Jewish friends" (*SC* 136), he tries to persuade Will to accept his modish version of the faith of Will's fathers. "Don't you think you belong here in the church? With your own people. This is where you're coming from" (*SC* 137). Like Curl's Episcopalian social gospel, Leslie's Pentecostal faith offers answers more readily than it encourages Will's quest and questions. Will's grimly ardent daughter converts the Second Coming into being born again through a spirit-filled encounter with Jesus Christ, but Will finds that as a charismatic Christian she hugs too readily and speaks of love too glibly. Will notices too little love in his resentful chauffeur, who looks to membership in the post-Armageddon reign of the 144,000 elect anticipated by Jehovah's Witnesses. Yamaiuchi fills Will with such rage that he considers striking the insolent servant, as if he believed in Lancelot's apocalyptic vision "that in the end the world yields only to violence, that only the violent bear it away" (*SC* 171).

The Second Coming is so potent and pervasive a metaphor in Percy's novel that even characters who profess no formal religion travesty the Return of the title. Will meets Jimmy Rogers on the golf course, "coming at him with thumbnail screwing into his back, coming close as a lover, eyes glittering with love-hatred" (*SC* 70). In his former schoolmate's gleaming eyes and ambivalent emotions, Will seems to meet his father come again, who also united sex and violence in the "screwing" of his apocalyptic suicide. Rogers practices the milder form of the con man's one-upmanship. Along with the Hugers, he seeks only to "screw" Allie out of her inheritance—as Kelso accurately describes the scheme (*SC* 261)—so that he can gain the island off Georgia for Arabs to develop, but the deal seems an ominous sign to Will Barrett, who has become concerned about the disappearance of the Jews. Marge Cupp envisions the novel's title as a more benign return to the womb of the ocean. Teaching children how to swim before they even learn to walk, this apostle of New Age religion preaches "her California principle" as an alternative to the more violent forms of "screwing" in the novel. She believes in "leaving the sad failed land life behind and leaving it soon enough and young enough before it screwed you up for good, and going back to the original environment" (*SC* 160). The evolutionary cycle culminates in a watery second coming.

Will Barrett judges Marge's faith in a new age of Aquarius to be as absurd as Kitty's belief in astrology and the laws of karma. Although she too seeks the revelation of mysteries, Will's first love turns apocalyptic disclosures into the faddishly occult, and the semiotics of revelation into the signs of the zodiac. In her return to Percy's fiction, the brazen Kitty bears no resemblance to the uncertain young lady whom Will first courted in *The Last Gentleman*; instead, she has become a sun-bronzed and braceleted golden girl. Kitty reborn reinterprets the Second Coming as reincarnation. In her attempt to explain Allie's psychic withdrawal as the inevitable working out of karma, she has sought a clairvoyant to discover her daughter's past life as a Civil War courtesan-spy. She boasts that twenty years ago she could even have predicted Will's own second coming. This savvy prophetess foresaw that he would have "to undergo trial and exile before you finally won. . . . Your destiny is the Return" (*SC* 286). Will easily detects the boredom and perfunctoriness of Kitty's beliefs and judges her to be another Californian like Marge Cupp; but more difficult to dismiss is her fatal sexuality. She is always coming at and on to Will. Repeatedly maintaining that she shares his independence and unpredictability, she offers herself as a kind of soul mate, Will's self come again. Even Will imagines that through sex Kitty "would echo him, print him out, trace his shape like radar. He could read himself in her" (*SC* 172). This provocative and predatory example of Tom More's bestialism makes Will think of women for the first time since his memory of Ethel Rosenblum. Kitty invites him to consummate that vision of desire by coming to her at three o'clock in the summerhouse. "I wanted to tell you where I'm coming from," she says to explain why she has playfully grabbed him. ". . . I'm fixing to beat Marion's time" (*SC* 165).

Kitty transforms their possible coming together in the flesh into an eschatological climax. As one Scorpio to another, she confides to Will that Pluto, the god of the underworld who governs both the positive and negative aspects of sexuality, is now entering his own sign, which is also their sign. She exalts this conjunction of eroticism and destruction to national significance by reminding him that when two fully evolved "Scorps" unite, they can save or destroy a country. Kitty and Will become mythical deities enacting a carnal apocalypse that will determine the very course of history. But if Will's father found sex in death, Kitty offers only death in sex. Her feline heat is no more than "tomcattin'," her own description for Will's stay with a young woman that she does not yet know is Allie (*SC* 282). Although she is under the patronage of Pluto, Kitty offers no chthonian renewal, for her cupidity is an indistinguishable mixture of greed and lust. Constantly touching and tugging at her old beau, she also places her hand on Marion's Louis XV secretary in an appreciative gesture that reveals to Will her true end. This devotee of Pluto, god of wealth as well as sex, regards Will as just another object to be stroked and his possessions as desirable extensions of their attractive owner.

Although Will never delivers anything like Lancelot's masterly philippics, the Percyan narrator occasionally formulates sustained passages of indictment that epitomize Will's constant exposure of these many silly second comings. After summarizing the creeds of various guests at his house, Will concludes that the time is either a new age of faith or an age of madness in which everyone believes everything (*SC* 158–61). Yet such crazy latitudinarianism does not sanction a sane unbelief. Will's critique of his foolish century includes two examples of unbelievers whom he finds even more insane than the believers. Despite their cheerful accommodation to a godless world, both Lewis Peckham and Ewell McBee love death almost as much as did Will's father.

Peckham seems to represent the best of humanism in these last days. Will senses that this lover of the arts and discerning reader of signs would be clearheaded enough to save a remnant from the destruction of war and racial violence by leading a group to the cave at Lost Cove. Yet he faults Peckham for never going beyond the culture and compassion of humanism to consider the possibility of belief. Peckham's faithless faith—an aestheticism that has ripened into a suicidal, Rupert Brookeish fascination with the end— reminds Will of his father's romance with Nazi Germany as the reich built by the sons of Goethe. Will cannot understand why his parent, who often spoke of Weimar, never mentioned nearby Buchenwald, where "the horrified Patton paraded fifteen hundred of Weimar's best humanistic Germans" to witness the inhuman sights for themselves; "is not this in fact, Father, where your humanism ends in the end?" he wonders (SC 132). The ghost of Will's father haunts Lewis Peckham's godless religion of high culture just as his spirit comes back again in the menace of the novel's other unbeliever, Ewell McBee. His very name suggests that he, not Will Barrett, is the true son of Lawyer B———. Having nearly shot Will in his garage just as Lawyer Barrett wounded his son in the forest, McBee appears in a white cloud reminiscent of the fog from the Georgia hunt and speaks with such anger that he, as much as Will's father, deserves to be named "the last hater" rather than the last gentle man (SC 179). Like his spiritual father whom he describes as a pistol ball, Ewell makes physical and psychic violation the very heart of his being. The poacher threatens not just Will's body but also his spirit by perpetuating Lawyer Barrett's reduction of the soul to the sum of the body's functions. As an incentive to invest in his erotic home video business, McBee offers Barrett the chance to spend an evening with the star of *Foxy Frolics*. "A little pussy never hurt anybody. You like pussy as much as I do," he tempts, while Will thinks of his own very likable Kitty (SC 178). Although their physical resemblances attest that "Brother" Ewell is what Will could be, Will decides that if the soul is virtually soulless, he would rather kill himself.[7]

The novel's believers and unbelievers are all denounced in the letter that Will sends Sutter before seeking his own justification for faith. Placed almost at the center of the novel, it presents a comprehensive verdict on his age. If the believers are intolerable, the unbelievers are insane. Those who place faith in everything from religion to astrology "think they know the reason why we find ourselves in this ludicrous predicament yet act for all the world as if they don't" (SC 190). Worse are the unbelievers who never even realize the essential farce of existence and so never require an explanation. Increasingly deranged himself, Will wonders about such a crazy question as whether

Groucho Marx is dead because he knows that the blackest comedy is a life in which death gets the last laugh. But the clowns of unbelief ignore the jest of mortality by grinning inanely like Allie's father, purveying ethnic humor like Jimmy Rogers, and telling knock-knock jokes like the daffy Dr. Duk. Or they perform such a ludicrous rite as sailing little balls through a windy mountain meadow, silently understanding that playing golf "was after all preposterous but that they had all assented to it and were doing it nevertheless and because, after all, why not?" (*SC* 48). Unbelievers in Percy's sorrowful comedy speak and act absurdly but never face the Absurd. These existential farceurs are unreligious because they do not consider the possibility of the radical bond to reality that for Percy may confer meaning in life. While unbelievers have never come to consciousness and so never search, believers who appreciate the cause of life's farce have never turned their first coming into a lifetime of preparing for the second.

Will Barrett delivers such a final judgment against his age because he comes to understand that Ed Barrett has helped to cause the catastrophe of his life. While he inspects the Greener that his father used in his great hunts, Will realizes why his parent used four shells but shot only one small quail. After firing at the bird and before trying to kill himself, the elder Barrett risked a leap of unfaith by deliberately trying to kill his son. He hoped to make of the gun's double-barreled blast the kind of second coming that he achieved for himself years later in the attic of the family home. Will suspects that he might have always known that the accident was an attempted murder but simply did not know that he knew it. His new revelation is a Platonic recollection, a second coming to consciousness, of how his father loved death so much that he wanted to share it with the son he loved as well. As Mary Deems Howland reads the apocalyptic drama of Will's psyche, the victimized son comes to identify "the warlike God of the Last Days with his father," who seemed to be "the author of one's life *and* death." [8] The hunting mishap was not a warning of the suicidal end to which Will's life might come; it was meant to be the eschaton itself.

Suddenly feeling at ease, "as if somehow I were now free to do what I am going to do," Will gains the authority to kill himself (*SC* 147). His death will at once complete what Lawyer Barrett intended in the forest and repeat his sire's own fate. He will twice be his father come again. But if his parent's suicide was simply an eschatological act, the son resolves that his own attempt will be a fully apocalyptic gamble. Will considers his father's death wasted because such an end proved nothing; however, he decides to turn the possibility of his own extinction into an experiment in revelation. Ed Barrett was sure that there were only two alternatives—the numbing death in life that he despised and the violent life in death that he desired. His agnostic son aims to discover whether there might yet be a third possibility: life itself, the life of God. He carries Pascal's wager to its illogical extremes and resolves to bet all on God. Although Pascal warned against the extravagances of the seventeenth-century millenarians, Percy's twentieth-century apocalyptist decides that either he will die of starvation in Lost Cove or God will prevent his suicide by revealing the divine presence through a sign.[9]

If Will's dangerous game typifies how apocalyptic delusions often double as the self's own grand desire for destruction, his psychological imbalance reflects a deeper and more desperate case of spiritual arrogance. He becomes as ridiculously self-absorbed as the rest of the believers and unbelievers whom he denounces as insane because he seeks through his own trickery to triumph over his father and God. Lawyer Barrett's suicide proved nothing and lost the family his insurance policy, but the more ingenious son surpasses his father by a suicidal wager that may euchre Prudential out of one million dollars or answer the most important question of God's existence. Pascal paid homage to the *deus absconditus,* but Will asks God to come out of hiding. "No, not asking. Requiring," he presumptuously asserts (*SC* 192). Otherwise, God can go out of existence for all practical purposes since Will views the divine failure to give a sign as proof that there is no deity. The Parousia must occur when Will in his conceit so wills it. Like Lancelot's, Will's gnostic pride tempts him to become a scientist of the sacred, for he turns his own possible suicide into an investigation of the apocalypse. He repeatedly thinks of his venture in Lost Cove as if the abstracted intellect were conducting research into the mechanics of mystery. Called by the narrator "the engineer," his familiar title in *The Last Gentleman,* Will plans what he considers "the ultimate scientific experiment" and asks Sutter to publish the results in the learned journal of his friend's choice (*SC* 180, 186). Will naïvely overlooks the paradox that if Pascal's wager was a rationalist's attempt to show the logic of belief in God, it was formulated by a scientist and mathematician who continually recognized the limits of reason. "God prefers rather to incline the will than the intellect," Pascal realized. "Perfect clearness would be of use to the intellect, and would harm the will. To humble pride."[10] Seeking God through his mind rather than through the inclination of his name, Will sets himself up for the fall that will humble pride.

Although Will's experiment fails to prove his hypothesis, it succeeds in a way that he never imagined. He learns that Lost Cove is no laboratory yielding definitive conclusions about God but a problematic realm where he loses himself only to find himself. Amid flashbacks and fantasies, Will discovers what Lancelot can never understand: the attempt of reason to seek ultimate revelation confounds itself when lawyerly logic and scientific methods confront a world of mystery that they are ill-equipped to measure. But it is within these baffling precincts that the novel's cunning God may act. By merest chance Will develops a toothache that forces him to abandon his experiment. Whether the toothache "was God's doing or ordinary mortal frailty, one cannot be sure" (SC 213). The Percyan narrator prefers to reserve judgment, yet in a novel where God frequently seems to work through simple and silly bodies, both alternatives may be correct.

Percy's amusing deflation of Will's grand expectations reveals his folly in imagining that the Second Coming will occur in some literal rendition of the Book of Revelation: a judgment by fire that will consume the earth now overrun by demoniacs (SC 197–98). If Will receives any sign, it is an achingly comic comeuppance, a humorous token to a foolish man from an ironic God. In his letter to Sutter, Will fancied himself like Jacob, who wrestled an answer out of the Deity. However, he neglected to mention that the patriarch's blessing was preceded by a wound in the hip that made him lose the contest. Much as his Old Testament predecessor received the benediction of a new name after suffering defeat, Will Barrett finally realizes the meaning of his name in the last words of The Second Coming; but first this would-be champion needs to sense his own shortcoming. His divine struggle climaxes when he feels in his flesh the humbling yet saving pain of his creatureliness. As engineer and scientist, Will lived in his head, but the ache in an upper canine, feeling like a "hot ice pick shoved straight up into his brain," drives him where he must go—out of his mind. So sick that he vomits, the gnostic quester is forced by the body to come back to the body. "What does a nauseated person care about the Last Days?" the narrator wonders amid this laughable chastisement (SC 213). Will's nausea is not Roquentin's sickened response to the horrors of existence but a violent physical corrective to an existence that has become too abstracted. It cures him of a more dangerous sickness unto death and restores him to the incarnate world where Percy's God may truly be known.

Driven out of his head and out of the cave, Will stumbles upon an eschatological climax. After a free fall through brilliantly colored light, he crashes to confront "the great black beast of the apocalypse roaring down at him, eyes red, jaws open and ravening" (*SC* 226). Percy's fatuous visionary beholds a wry version of Revelation that mocks his pretensions even as it hallows his aspirations with the irony of a *felix culpa*. Unlike John, he does not enter heaven through an open door (Rev. 4:1–2); he plummets through the "tacky heaven" lit by Allie's stained-glass window (*SC* 226). The Great Beast that threatens to devour him is only a dog, perhaps even a ludicrous hound of heaven. His pride humbled, Will falls, but into grace, for he tumbles into an Edenic greenhouse and soon falls fortunately in love. Having conceived of his experiment as a cry to end God's game of hide-and-seek, "Come out, come out, wherever you are, the game's over," Will discovers the most unexpected sign. The answer of the *deus absconditus* to his childish call for "allie, allie in come free" is Allie (*SC* 192).

I I I   Allie is Will's second coming. Since the same apocalyptic rhythm has shaped her search, Percy's doubles find their consummation in each other. And this love leads to the clearest intimation of God's entry into their lives. Percy's previous apocalypses have suggested that his seers' natural revelations reach a tentative completion when the divine goal is discovered as already beginning in human communion. But although his novels have often portrayed friendship and even possible discipleship among men, his fiction has only convincingly recorded how his typically male wanderer comes to love a woman in Binx's tortuous wayfaring with Kate. The rest of Percy's last ladies never seem to have come as fully to themselves as his last gentlemen. Since they lack such a quickened consciousness, the romance always threatens to falter, or it never seems entirely fulfilling. In "The Gramercy Winner" and *The Last Gentleman* Allison and Kitty virtually disappear from the novel as Scanlon and Sutter become increasingly important as male apostles. Later women live for what they represent. Ellen is more of an end than a heartfelt character in *Love in the Ruins*, and Lancelot's Anna, a study for Allie, at best remains a symbolic possibility.

The Second Coming is a virtual second coming for Percy as a novelist. Having envisioned the sexist narrator of *Lancelot* in all his awful fury, Percy makes Allie come to the fore in a way unlike that of any other woman in his fiction since Kate Cutrer.[11] He thus creates his most fully imagined romance, his most lovingly embodied and completely conceived revelation of the union at the very heart of selfhood. Allie becomes so central in this apocalypse that she shares with Will the novel's double focus. Will's plunge into her life-giving greenhouse formally divides the novel into two parts. In the first section, odd-numbered chapters are told from Will's point of view by a sometimes intrusive narrator, while even-numbered ones are seen through Allie's eyes by an invisible observer. She acts as Will's beginning and end in the second part, for Allie tends to him in chapter 1, and Will thinks about his future wife on the last page of chapter 5.

The structure of *The Second Coming* reveals how romance consummates in the Parousia. Virtually the whole novel tells the story of how Will and Allie together come to each other and then come together again. Shortly before seeing her for the first time, Will meditates on such apocalyptic crossings: "Lives are lines of force which ordinarily run parallel and do not connect." But occasionally, and especially in times of catastrophe, lifelines are bent, and he might meet someone by grateful surprise, the way Jimmy Rogers appeared to help him when Will had a car accident on the day Robert Kennedy was assassinated. When time itself is wrested out of joint and probability is skewed, what normally might have been regarded as adventitious becomes casually appropriate. Will raises this principle of the odd and graced encounter to the apocalyptic level: "Perhaps, he thought, even God will manifest himself when you are bent far enough out of your everyday lifeline" (*SC* 67).

Before Will even knows of Allie, he senses her advent in his life. Percy's successor to the confined Lancelot feels like a man in prison for years who suddenly hears steps approaching his cell: "Someone was coming" (*SC* 70). Will at last meets this imagined visitor when he slices out-of-bounds on the golf course that circumscribes his conventional life. The error causes a minor convergence of parallel lines and their parallel chapters, which later climaxes when he tumbles through Allie's roof after seeking a sign of God.[12] Will's progressively oblique course ends in romance, but also, as he suspected, in the surprise of divine revelation. After the end of *The Last Gentleman* his lifeline was too perfectly straight, too directed by unwavering everydayness, to lead to God. The whole first part of *The Second Coming* depicts how he is steadily bent out of his regular course through sudden epiphanies, questions about the Jews, searches for signs, and finally an experiment in revelation that reads like a playful *Divine Comedy*. Will leaves the dark forest of the opening chapters to make a descent into the underworld that is actually an ascent to the overworld, since he enters Sourwood Mountain one thousand feet above the more familiar entrance to Lost Cove. After he spends time inside the purgatorial mount, Will falls into heaven, where he beholds no vision of a rose in bloom, but a paradisal greenhouse and the novel's successor to Ethel Rosenblum nonetheless. Coming to Allison by falling through the multicolored light of her stained-glass window, Will enters a farcical wonderland, on the other side of the ordinary world of the golf course, where madness is divinest sense. In this crazy country presided over by Percy's own version of Alice, speech takes the form of gnomic riddles, and a girl who has escaped from a sanatorium quite matter-of-factly hoists a Grand Crown stove.[13] His daily lifeline by now not just gone askew but completely left behind, Will comes to Allie and to God.

Allie's presence causes a joyous redefinition of Percy's increasingly vehement apocalypticism. In *Lancelot* Percy made such radical use of the techniques cited in "Notes for a Novel about the End of the World" that he virtually exhausted the direction in which his novels had been moving. Percy still relies on such fictional violence in *The Second Coming*, but it is more restrained and constantly undermined. Although Will Barrett scoffs at believers and unbelievers, his harangues lack Lancelot's ferocity; and the saner, somewhat amused third-person narrator undercuts them further by pointing out Will's folly in acting like "some crackpot preacher in California" (*SC* 198). Like his predecessor, Will sets out on an outrageous quest, yet Barrett's search for a holy sign rather than for the unholy grail is not so much appalling as absurd. The seer who rails at the farce of life gets trapped in a consummate moment of low comedy and physical humor: lost underground and discomforted by nausea and a toothache. The real shock of *The Second Coming* is not Will's perverseness but that his very willfulness becomes despite himself his backward way of coming to God. In Percy's wonder-working plot Will's comic catastrophe is not simply an existential joke in a godless world but the painful prelude to his salvation.

Part 2 of *The Second Coming* begins where *Lancelot* ends: Percy's apocalyptist discovers the possibility of love with another woman from a sanatorium. Percy repeats the eternal patterns so favored by Shakespeare and Spenser—death and regeneration, a journey into the green world and then back to society, coincidences that would be unreal if they did not point to a more astonishing reality—as he creates a prose romance about romance at the end of the world. Apocalypse is the ultimate romance, a sublime marriage of plot and artistic form. It celebrates God's espousal of creation by carrying to its extreme what Northrop Frye calls "the mythos of summer" to create a dream world where time, logic, and the laws of nature are suspended.[14] The unique urgency of the eschaton makes all action consummate and makes all characters find their culmination in the extraordinary ideals of allegory.

Sharing the highly colored aura of such supreme fictions, Percy's twentieth-century love story mingles the actual and the imaginary in the way that Richard Chase recognizes as characteristic of much American fiction.[15] Although *The Second Coming* is never as stylized as the Book of Revelation or even *Love in the Ruins*, the reconciling marvels of the romance tradition grace Will and Allie's very unconventional romance in North Carolina. Percy makes their chance coming together and coming to God seem at once natural and wonderful. "A fit by chance is romance," decides Allie, in a definition that reflects her own appreciation of lifelines bent by luck as much as it points to the surprising form of Percy's fiction (*SC* 84). Nothing could be more fortunate or less likely than Will's crash into the greenhouse of his own double and his first love's daughter. Yet what might otherwise be just a comic improbability seems so appropriate and thereby even more amazing because it marks the intersection of lifelines that, unknown to Will and Allie, have been converging throughout the novel. Percy's alternation of chapters between his two fictional centers shows how their courses are already approaching each other, for Allie's life follows the same apocalyptic pattern as does Will's.

If Will's clamant memories begin the quest that brings his present life to an end, Allie has no memory at the beginning of the novel. A recent victim of electroshock therapy, she suffers from the same amnesia that sometimes ended the last gentleman's world in oblivion. However, she does possess a substitute for memory: a notebook of instructions and information that she prepared before escaping from the sanatorium. This book of revelation reminds the stunned young woman of her lifetime of catastrophe. Like Will, Allie is the victim of "violence masquerading as love," which R. D. Laing believes at best creates "a half crazed creature more or less adjusted to a mad world." [16] Allie surrendered sovereignty over her own existence for a life dictated by the expectations of authorities who supposedly loved her. She became whatever they wanted her to be. Allie lived by the book—first, her texts for school, which she studied to please her father, and later, the sex manual that she followed to satisfy her commandant of a boyfriend, Sarge. She finally revolted against this external conformity through the disaster of her apparent mental collapse. Hoping to escape the "outside I, the me you see, the meow-I," the superficial copycat life of feline satisfaction represented by her mother, Kitty, she tried to go down to "the inside deep-I-defy," where she could define a more profound self by defying the crazy world (*SC* 89).

Allie's seeming madness judged the world that she allowed to coax her into compliance and then privately destroyed it by a psychic apocalypse. She gained a new freedom; a psychotic young lady did not have to eat with others or seem to make sense. But the new order for Percy does not lie in the remade world of madness. Allie's rebellious "I-defy" risked creating only a solipsistic paradise rather than the kind of communion that she later discovers in the greenhouse with Will. When she overheard her parents and Dr. Duk as they selfishly arranged the details of her life, Allie realized that confinement at Valleyhead had actually ended all possibility of defiance. Like Will, she had lost her own future. But Allie regained the freedom of her will when she decided to flee the still-greater catastrophe of further electroshock therapy. "*Fried is crucified*," she thought about this new calamity, even though she found it strangely fascinating (*SC* 103). She enjoyed "the familiar sweet doomstroke in her throat. What is this sweetness at the horrid core of bad news?" (*SC* 88). Allie's consent to another series of shock treatments would be as suicidal as Will's decision to repeat his father's death. Both Allie and Will are entranced by disaster, but whether the head is shot by a bullet or with electricity, the result is similar: either ultimate death or the death in life of being merely like everyone else.

The threat of such catastrophe revealed to Allie that at last she could act. She proposed, "What if *I* make the plans for me? What then? Is there an I in me that can start something? An initiating I, an I-I" (*SC* 105). Whereas she had previously used her freedom for negation, the world defied and annihilated in madness, Allie resolved henceforth to use it for initiation and re-creation. Like Kate Cutrer, she made the great discovery of her life: "I was *free* to act" (*SC* 40). Her notebook records the details of her stratagem to escape from the sanatorium, for as with Lancelot's preparations to destroy Belle Isle, Percy lets the sheer minutiae of plotting convey the sovereignty of self-determination. Instead of having her life planned by others, Allie would now plan for herself.

After the end of her old servile world, Allie's task throughout *The Second Coming* is to discover a new order by first coming to herself and then to Will. Still dazed from the last shock treatment before her escape, feeling like the sole survivor of a plane crash, at the beginning of chapter 2 she exists in the aftermath of disaster. The misfortune that Allie dreaded and desired has left her at once devastated and self-possessed. Since each sight and insight startle her with their luster, she can follow with unusual attention a single ant as it navigates with its leaf-sail along the sidewalk. As Percy slows down the entire process of coming into consciousness, Allie seems to make the transition from being unconscious to being hyperconscious in every instant that she feels. But Allie must go beyond reappropriating her senses to recover a whole way of being in the world. She remembers failing ordinary living once before, and so she needs to learn the fundamentals that hardly seem learned at all, the given facts of her present existence. From an old calendar, a brief conversation, and her driver's license, she learns those key triangulation points for Percy's wanderers—time, place, and name. From her notebook she learns who she was. Written by her past self to her present self as a survivor of catastrophe, it helps her to achieve a temporal reintegration. "I have to know enough of where I've been to know which way I'm going," she tells herself (*SC* 93). Knowing the past for both Allie and Will points the erratic way to their future.

Allie must progress from the private conversation of this notebook to communion with others. She begins by rediscovering all the rubrics for going through life and getting along with others that normally go without consideration. Can one save a place on a public bench? How does one interpret a conversation when everyone seems to speak in code? Is it possible to walk on a sidewalk without walking into someone else? The questions are rudimentary, but they point an answer to the single underlying question faced by every Percyan castaway: "What would she do with time? Was there something she was supposed to do?" (*SC* 31). She must find a place. She must learn to use language, the wanderer's first step toward love. And taking pleasure in her newly oiled boots, as *Homo viator* she must perform the activity that for Percy defines human existence as well as his own first name: she must walk.

Allie continues her peculiar pilgrimage when she walks to the Kemp estate and discovers a new place amid the wreckage of the greenhouse. The hole in the roof, pottery in shards, and Virginia creeper growing through broken windows make her garden home resemble a leftover setting from Tom More's dilapidated world. But whereas Percy's roué tried to transform room 203 in the Howard Johnson's into a romantic hideaway from the end of the world, Allie finally discovers genuine love in the ruins of her inheritance. First, she must clean it out and make it her own, turn the act of claiming a bequest from her Aunt Sally into a means of reclaiming herself. She writes in her notebook, "*I am here,*" for the house locates her in the world and serves as a sign of her basic Percyan identity as a someone who now lives somewhere (*SC* 85). Allie's restoration climaxes in the hearth's consecration of her home. She dismantles the Grand Crown stove found amid the debris of the old Kemp home and transfers it to her greenhouse by a complicated system of ropes and pulleys. If the novel almost turns into a how-to manual for hoisters, Allie's labors prove that although she once failed ordinary living, she is now at home in Hopkins's world of "gear and tackle and trim." Hanging from a rope so that it seemed as if "it had descended from another world," this *machina ex deo*, rescued from the ruins and polished by Allie, comes at last to rest in her home as the grand crown of her renovation, the lares and penates of her newly sovereign life (*SC* 110).

Allie hopes that in the sanctuary of her greenhouse she can "make a new start with words" and recover the distinctively human ability to speak (*SC* 82). Language is so closely associated with becoming herself that the first word she speaks in the novel is her own name. And since the cosmos according to Percy "is segmented and named by language" (*LC* 99), in relearning speech Allie is gaining all the world anew. She first risks only questions, but she later tries statements and finally commands—for Lancelot as well as for Allie the verbal expression of one's authority as Percy's sovereign wayfarer. However, Allie is confused by the distortions in everything that she hears and speaks. "Something happens to words coming to me from other people. Something happens to my words. They do not seem worth uttering. People don't mean what they say. Words often mean their opposites" (*SC* 82).

Allie discovers this duplicity when she first comes to Linwood in chapter 2. In a pair of scenes she meets a walker and a runner who welcome her to the religious and sexual meanings that come together in the novel's title. A sidewalk evangelist inquires whether Allie has ever had a personal encounter with her Savior and asks her to "a little get-together we're having tonight. . . . Won't you come?" (*SC* 33). Allie considers the request a personal invitation but then realizes from the woman's professional cordiality that the offer is no more immediate and individual than any billboard advertising the best gasoline. The colporteur does not mean what she says just as Richard Rountree, who has been saved by running, does not understand what Allie has meant. When she innocently evades his invitation to eat at a favorite stopping place by saying "I don't know where I'll be staying tonight," he comes on to her and asks her to share the night with him in a mountain shelter (*SC* 35). In *The Second Coming* the polarization of the modern world that has so preoccupied Percy in all of his writing takes the form of a radical split in language between signifier and signified. Words work at cross-purposes, and what is named is never what is really willed.

Percy himself attempts to renew language by creating for Allie a modified version of schizophrenic speech, a code filled with second comings. In the course of her aphoristic sentences, sounds keep returning through assonance and alliteration, and meaning is doubled through wordplay. "No buzzin cousin" she tells Dr. Duk as she rejects further shock treatments that violate her as much as does "a bang by the gang," a visit from her exploit-ative parents (*SC* 90). Such unintelligible talk simply proves to the Hugers that she has suffered a psychic breakdown. They do not hear that her rhymed and rhythmic speech actually sounds her rejection of the worn-out idiom of her old life and articulates her attempt to reinterpret language for a more meaningful age. Her words express not an absence of significance but a com-pressed richness and imaginative allusiveness. But if Allie is to achieve her goal of succeeding at ordinary living, she must learn to converse in the ordi-nary speech that she so capably uses when talking to herself in her notebook. She cannot, however, merely return to the old way of comprehending words. So, like Percy himself, she explores the very basis of discourse as she tries to reach a renewed understanding of language for her rediscovered world.

Since Percy believes that all language affirms the being of oneself and another, the beginning as well as the end of Allie's search is *love* (*MB* 295). In the notebook written before she escaped from Valleyhead, she reminded herself that her parents "love you as well as they understand that word, or as well as most people love. Come to think of it, who or what do you 'love'? Do you 'love' them? What is 'love'? I am saying the word aloud" (*SC* 39). In questioning the word, she questions the entire mystery represented by its sounds. Like Percy, Allie finds an ontological affinity between the sense of a word and the sensuous apprehension of it, so that she virtually tastes *morsel* and touches *rubbish* (*SC* 89). Words themselves seem to have bodies as if lan-guage were a virtual incarnation of existence. Although her repetition of *love* could reduce it to a bare vocable, Allie does not rob the word of its meaning but hears her way to its heart: "It sounds like something dark and furry which makes a lowing sound" (*SC* 39–40). She can only express the essence of the word by metaphor. Unlike her parents, who understand *love* as the imposi-tion of their selfish wills for her well-being, Allie gets beyond the violation that passes for love to an intuition of its warmth and tenderness. It is the felt knowledge of love that will finally reveal to her a new understanding of *love*, language, and all the world.

Will comes to the same end where the word is understood at last when made flesh. Like Allie in having suffered from the outrages of parental love, Will carries her questioning of the word to a more skeptical extreme. Much as Allie had written in her notebook, he writes to Sutter about his feelings for his daughter: "I've always been suspicious of the word 'love,' what with its gross abuse and overuse. There is no cheaper word. . . . I don't really know what 'love' means except as it applies to one's feeling for children" (*SC* 196). Will learns what *love* means through his romance with Allie. They first speak to each other after an accident that foreshadows Will's later crash: his golf ball smashes her window in a minor catastrophe that leads to a dual revelation. "I felt concealed and revealed," she admits; Will likewise realizes that "she was seeing all of him because all at once he became aware of himself as she saw him . . . she was as familiar to him as he himself" (*SC* 76–77). These eschatological doubles stand disclosed in shared privacy and mutual secrecy; each is unveiled in the intimate look of the other. As Will comes upon Allie for the first time, he senses how love completes his coming to consciousness.

Will the golfer, whose own language Dr. Vance Battle thought peculiar, finds the speech of this comely girl in the woods strange, "as if she were reading the words on his face" (*SC* 76). His presence helps to make her speech possible, since for Percy the simplest act of naming is done for another. It serves "to affirm the thing as being what it is for both of us." [17] Will seems to give her words, literally so at his second coming, when the self-reliant laborer rejects his help in moving the stove but accepts his advice about what to use: a creeper. Allie knows the mechanism but not the word, and Will notices how she thanks him for it as if she had received a present. It is, in fact, a present, for he tells her that she need only speak the word at Washau Motors, owned by Will, and she will get the device that she names.

Signs of presence, words re-present. Between Allie and Will language comes to life, so that a word almost conveys the concrete reality of a thing. And the thing is affirmed by the word that gives it form. Will and Allie achieve Percy's version of the linguistic renaissance that since Emerson has sought to "pierce this rotten diction and fasten words again to visible things." [18] If Will helps Allie to name what she knows, she helps him to know through the name. When Will looks at his daughter, Leslie, a speech therapist, he thinks about how the unnamed "girl in the woods might see her. In her nutty way with words, she would have seen Leslie in her name *Leslie* and now he too could see her, had always seen her as a *Leslie*" (*SC* 159). Will hears in the very sound of her name "a secretarial primness" that perfectly suits his business-like daughter (*SC* 160). Allie changes the way that Will looks at language. Having given him back the word, she has made him hear it as never before, so that he at last envisions its meaning.

When Will learns the identity of the anonymous young woman in the woods by chance from Kitty, he feels that her name naturally fits her. It affirms and confirms his image of her as if by the logic of necessity the word for this mystery could not be other than Allie: "Allie. Yes. That was her name. That was Allie sitting on the stoop of the greenhouse reading the fat pulpy *Captain Blood*. Allie" (*SC* 167). Percy's prose places language at the service of language. Will's redoubled stream of assertion, naming, and asseveration emphasizes how speech is a way of saying yes to being. Allie senses the same bond between name and person during her chance discovery of Will's identity from the attendant at Washau Motors. "How did the name go with him? How to take the name?" Allie wonders. "She tried to locate him in the name" (*SC* 201). Since Percy's speakers find a local habitation in their names, his listeners enjoy the surprise of revelation when these proper nouns are heard from and by the heart. Names inform most profoundly when they express the forms of their bearers. As the paired lovers of *The Second Coming* find the titles of their own identities not just in themselves but in each other, Allie discovers her future in Will, and Will finds his all in Allie.

Allie's coming to herself and to the world through language anticipates a final coming to God. The tractarian indirectly pointed to this end when she handed the novice in Linwood a pamphlet that asked, "*Do you want to make a new start? Have you ever had a personal encounter with our Lord and Saviour?*" (*SC* 33). Returning to life in mid-autumn spring, Allie feels the essentially religious

> . . . urge, wrestle, resurrection of dry sticks,
> Cut stems struggling to put down feet

that Roethke described in one of his own greenhouse poems:

> What saint strained so much,
> Rose on such lopped limbs to a new life.[19]

As she comes to flourish in her verdant world, Allie does not try to track down God as Will the hunter does, but she obscurely senses that her self-realization must find its end in divine revelation. She typifies all of Percy's questers who do not so much intuit a transcendentalist God in themselves as discover that they can only be themselves when living before and under God. Like Will, she finds that the coming to God, which completes her coming to self, is by way of coming to another. As she repeats Will's descent into the underground of the psyche, Allie believes that at last in the greenhouse, "I can already feel myself coming down to myself" (*SC* 93) and imagines that she is collapsing from a giant red star to a white dwarf. In the past she tried to be whatever anyone wanted her to be, expanding and fanning out like that "great gaseous fake of a star," Betelgeuse, Dr. Duk's particular favorite, until she lived to please the entire universe (*SC* 93). Her use of drugs and withdrawal from the world were attempts at "going down down down toward *it*," which she hoped would be the central core of selfhood but which only led to the terminus of a psychic breakdown (*SC* 94). However, she now realizes that such radical means of reclaiming her identity as a white dwarf only created the illusion of achieving this second coming.

In the greenhouse Allie feels that she is approaching a crystallization of self rather than the amorphous distortion of being everything to everybody. Her goal shines as her own favorite star, Sirius, "diamond bright and diamond hard, indestructible by comets, meteors, people. Sirius is more serious than beetle gauze" (*SC* 93). In the apocalyptic comedy of *The Second Coming*, the serious becomes associated with the ultimate opposite of the absurdity known alike by believers and unbelievers: God. "*Go-ing, go-on, Gawain, go-way, gong, God, dog*," Allie babbled when Kitty discovered that her daughter had retreated into a private hideout near suicide like Sylvia Plath's Esther Greenwood. Offering a possible interpretation of her apparent nonsense, Allie proposed, "maybe dog-star = Sirius = serious = God" (*SC* 94). By going down to her own star Sirius and going away from her catlike mother, Allie goes on a quest for the Deity. Although a nameless dog, which "came down from the trail, straight across the ruins," offers Allie affectionate company in the greenhouse, "woman's best friend" also provides a fitting anagram for what has already found her (*SC* 82). Percy, like James Joyce, enjoys the peculiar connection between the verbal mirrors for the canine and the divine. The dog-star is her private sign in schizophrenic speech for the coming God whom she seeks.

As a Percyan wayfarer, Allie seems to have embarked on her own version of the Negative Way. While the vestal maiden tends her "cathedral of a stove" in a greenhouse as large as an ark, she hopes that such deliberate rejection of the insane world may lead her to a place of psychic recovery and spiritual discovery (*SC* 203). But although such denial may be necessary for Allie's initial reclamation of self, it is ultimately not by going down but by coming to that she achieves her goal. Dr. Duk warns that her stellar implosion may cause her to become a black hole, the self as nought, only a great vacuum that sucks up the world and finally consumes itself. Allie risks the same suicidal fate that lures Will. If she achieves the diamondlike indestructibility of Sirius, she may not gain a new self in the presence of God; instead she may lose herself by becoming as deadly and self-destructive as the pistol ball that McBee likened to

verb. Will's speech to Allie eroticizes language; the word is one with the action. As Will reveals his past to Allie while they lie together, she does not so much listen to what he says as sense how he says it. She hears only fragments of his life story, phrases resonant of Will Barrett's apocalyptic quest like " 'our new language' . . . 'how to reenter the world'(?), 'by God?' 'by her?' (!!!!!!)." Instead, Allie feels the meaning of the words through the sexuality of his speech. "Though he hardly touched her, his words seemed to flow across all parts of her body. Were they meant to?" (*SC* 262). When discourse becomes a form of intercourse, words are understood as acts of love.

Will and Allie's sexual apocalypse becomes one with Val's linguistic renovation in *The Last Gentleman*. The pair in the greenhouse come together just as do signified and signifier, namer and listener, when the nun teaches her silent students to speak. Both of these revelatory conjunctions show the world as new and never the same, for it is seen and named in love. After their lovemaking through language, Will appropriately asks Allie about Val. Although Allie is inclined to forget, she clearly remembers the aunt who visited her when she first became sick and who now teaches at a school run by the Little Eucharistic Sisters of Saint Dominic. Will is astounded that Allie recalled "that outrageous name. The Little Sisters of what?" (*SC* 263). The outrageous name in an entire scene about the names of love calls attention to itself even without Will's amazed emphasis. It signifies that Val has continued her life of the holy ordinary in which bread becomes God and teaching turns into revelation. And Percy intimates that through their love Will and Allie come to share a similarly religious life. They discover what Leslie's sentimentalized Parousia, Marge's retreat from the wreckage, Kitty's sexual coming, Ed Barrett's suicidal consummation, and Will's own selfish experiment in revelation all failed to embody—the Percyan apocalypse of loving and laboring amid the ruins.

Percy's understanding of religion as the "radical *bond* . . . which connects man with reality . . . and so confers meaning to his life" makes it possible for both speech and sexuality to provide a link with the realm of the sacred (*MB* 102–3). To be human, for Percy, is to pursue connections.[21] Since words and flesh are the ways by which his seekers connect themselves to the world and to others, they point to the most fundamental bond for Percy: religion. If God's Word became flesh, then both language and incarnate love may lead to the divine image at their source. Percy uses a metaphorical consecration to show how the communion between Allie and Will is a sign of God's coming into their lives. Will becomes Percy's version of Lawrence's

Man Who Died. When Allie sees him for a second time, she notices that his eyes resemble those in "a trick picture of Jesus," now shut, then open, "dark then bright with eye sockets like a skull" (*SC* 106, 107). After the man who nearly died crashes into Allie's greenhouse, he repeats the fate of Lawrence's crucified hero before discovering Percy's God Who Lives. Although Will reminds Allie of artists' depictions of Jesus taken down from the cross, he is restored to life through Percy's priestess of Isis in a greenhouse that the injured patient compares to a church. Like Lawrence's holy lovers, both have rejected a world where sex is in the head to come together finally in a firelit celebration after which the man newly risen to life must depart.[22]

Percy retells Lawrence's late novella as a prelude to revising its purely erotic theology. Since Will pursues not a mythic god of the blood but Father Weatherbee's God who entered history, the vital energy of the body is not an end in itself but a sign for the intense generosity of the divine giver. Percy does not primarily view the sacred as the sexual, yet the sexual is definitely sacred to him. "Jesus Christ," Allie exclaims as a ball of lightning comes rolling down the center aisle of the greenhouse where they share a makeshift bed (*SC* 264). Amid the glory of an apocalyptic storm, the God who became flesh comes again when love approaches incarnation. Eric Jones believes that "Percy shows no sign, gives no hint, that the second coming of Christ will ever occur or should ever be expected," but the Parousia only fails to dawn according to the naïve interpretation that Will foolishly adopted.[23] There is no dazzling hierophany, no climactic conflagration to destroy an age possessed by the demons of thanatos (*SC* 197–98). Rather, Percy's title brings the whole novel under the prospect of the ever-arriving apocalypse. His progressively realized eschatology makes the Second Coming not just an absolute end but a possibility to be recognized every minute. God is always coming. Percy's romance echoes Karl Rahner's meditation on the Parousia in affirming that the divine approach is neither "past nor future, but the present, which has only to reach its fulfillment. Now it is still the one single hour of Your Advent, at the end of which we too shall have found out that You have really come."[24] The Second Coming dawns as the archetype and end of all the various comings in the novel—to consciousness, to words, and especially to love. Each shares in the final coming of and to God. By making his end "the double Winchester come of taking oneself into oneself . . . the coming to end all coming," Lawyer Barrett turned the Parousia into a suicidal rejection of the speech and sexuality that find a center in another. But the signal image of the Second Coming implies that Allie and Will might discover in their salvific love a bond so religious that it becomes a sign of God's ongoing advent.

Although Will comes back to life in the greenhouse, he misses the consummation promised in the novel's title until he leaves Allie and then comes back to her. Most of the scenes during his first stay in the greenhouse are told entirely from Allie's perspective. Will often seems curiously detached, his speech rehearsed like a lawyer's address to a jury. Even while the couple lies together, he suddenly interrupts the increasing physical intimacy by announcing his decision to depart, tend to some obligations, and then return. Will does not overlook all the revelations of Allie's love. He realizes the limits of his knowledge through Allie's fondness for asking unanswerable questions, and he recognizes the necessity of caring for other people in the future, especially the woman who cared for him in the greenhouse. However, Will still has not freed himself from his deadly alliance with his father and still does not know that he has been given in Allie much of what he yet seeks to find. When Will leaves Allie, he agrees to assume official responsibility for her in the legalese that signifies how lost he still remains in his role as servant of the law and son of Lawyer Barrett. Allie seems just another client in his practice devoted to Trusts and Estates. The lawyer must turn the romance, which has so far been a "fit by chance," into a choice of the heart and will.

V   The rest of *The Second Coming* tells the story of Will's second coming to Allie. He must rediscover the bondedness that Allie discovered with him in the bower at the end of the world. If Percy structured part 1 as a series of alternating and parallel chapters devoted to the gradually converging lifelines of Will and Allie, he conceives of part 2 as a circle to depict Will's coming back to Allie. After their love in the greenhouse in the first chapter, Will moves away from Allie until he finally returns to her in chapter 5. As Sue Mitchell Crowley observes, Will follows the movement of Withdrawal and Return, a historical motif that Arnold Toynbee views as reaching its spiritual climax in the Second Coming.[25] Will is always in a state of coming, and his way—progressive and incomplete—necessarily includes diversions and indirections, which are yet themselves part of being a walker in Percy's world. Will's destiny is the Return, as Kitty predicted, but when he leaves her daughter in part 2, he realizes that prophecy in the wrong way. After glimpsing the possibilities of new language and love in the glass house, he returns to his old order only to find that he really cannot quite return.

Dancing beside his German-engineered Mercedes parked near the golf course, Will celebrates how Allie's love has made him see by contrast the many names that death takes in the Century of the Love of Death. Will's ceremonial naming begins to dispel the thanatos syndrome by unveiling the negation of life embraced by a century fatally fond of misnomers. This exposé then becomes Will's way of expelling his own personal demons, because death can no longer hide under the guise of religious, social, or political institutions. At the end Will understands that such death is the very manifestation of the devil in his time, for only the "father of lies" could have conceived "all the deceits and guises under which death masquerades" (*SC* 272). Leading the list of false faces worn by the father of lies is the form of death practiced by his own father: death in the guise of love. This perversion gives its name to the whole century; the other fatal varieties, which follow it in Will's litany, only repeat this parental desire for destruction. Will unmasks his sire and uncovers all of his deadly doubles as if at the end of Melville's *The Confidence Man* all the con men were finally revealed as variations of their diabolic master. After such a denunciation Will cannot return to his old world of everyday deaths, but he seems not quite willing to accept an apocalyptic life. In part 2, *The Second Coming* doubles back upon itself so that after leaving Allie, Will seems again at a beginning, but it is not really new. He vacillates between the equally fatal extremes of suicidal despair and scientific bliss, yet he is saved on both occasions by Allie. Her presence in sign and memory seems to infuse the life of this half-dead man who sees a semiotic universe and remembers everything significant.

Much of Will's travel in *The Last Gentleman* was an exercise in repetition, which culminated when he stood before his father's house and faced the ruins that dominated his memory throughout the novel. In part 2 of *The Second Coming*, Will tries this same strategy and nearly duplicates his father's morbid apocalypticism. Since his hereditary love for death threatens his newly discovered passion for Allie, he resolves to go back to Georgia to gain a deadly title to the parcel of land where his father sought to kill him. Nunally's swamp by name and location is the antithesis of Allie's greenhouse. From the beginning Will's past and future have been connected to a significant venue and a becoming young woman; the successor to the weedy delta and Ethel, as well as to the greenhouse and Allie, is now a marshy tract and Will's first love, death. Will goes to Georgia because he suspects that his interpretation of his father's attempted murder-suicide has not been searching enough. He has long regarded the catastrophe as a shocking moment of self-awareness after which he knew all and could never be surprised, a coming to self that left him inured for life. But Will realizes that he has not escaped with his life at all, for he has actually been living out a prolonged death: "His life—or was it his death?—he had left behind in the Thomasville swamp, where it still waited for him" (SC 296). Will seeks to find personal sovereignty in suicide. Since he has been dead ever since the hunting trip, he plans to reclaim both his life and his death through the life in death of killing himself. Will hopes to discover in the swamp a travesty of the union offered him by Allie. At his end he will become a second version of Lawyer Barrett, who once tried to kill his son in the swamp and who later killed himself. The sexual communion of Will and Allie is replaced by the suicidal convergence of father and son.

Will is saved from this fierce and fatal bond by a vision of Allie. Having found through love the essential Percyan principle of connection, she herself becomes signified as Will glimpses from the bus window "a single gold poplar which caught the sun like a yellow-haired girl coming out of a dark forest" (SC 297). The lovely sight reminds Will of the moment when he first saw the blonde Allie as a mysterious figure behind a sunlit poplar. Whereas he earlier felt "a sweet certainty" that he would find his end at the post oak in the Georgia woods, he senses while looking at the radiant tree "a sharp sweet urgency, a need to act, to run and catch. He was losing something" (SC 296, 297). Will recovers the freedom to do and decide characteristic of Percy's apocalyptists when they gain revelation. He rushes off the bus, hardly even knowing why but dimly recovering Allie re-presented through memory and represented in metaphor.

Will's recollection of an unnamed young woman in a forest serves as the vehicle for his perception of the tree. Since the human as coupler tends to connect things and "through the mirror of the one see the other" (MB 308), he embodies the present in the past by seeing the luminous poplar as reflecting his golden love. But if his eidetic memory of this dryad at first provides only the mediating term of a comparison, she is the eventual end of the simile. The tree points to Allie. Without her Will feels "a sense of loss, a going away," the very opposite of the coming that creates the apocalyptic rhythm of the novel (SC 321). He loses all in her absence—sense of self and search for God—until memory, imagination, and desire all suddenly coalesce in the image of Allie. She keeps coming back to Will, replacing his fatal memories with saving visions, becoming part of his semiotic world, until Will at last comes back to her in the flesh. Her love is the alternative to his love of death as well as the living death to which Will later surrenders himself in the hospital.

Hurled out of the express bus by a driver furious at making an unscheduled stop, Will crashes to the ground once again. He wakes to the fallen world of Duke University Hospital, whose scientific regimen unfortunately keeps patients from recognizing that their lives are their own. Without Allie, Will abandons all authority and responsibility to others, much as she had earlier done at Valleyhead. And just as the Hugers hope to control their daughter's wealth, Leslie and Jack Curl see Will's helplessness as a chance to win the Peabody fortune for their own well-intentioned schemes. Will's life is planned completely for him. Because he is troubled by an extremely sensitive and unstable pH, he must be monitored constantly and his medicine adjusted accordingly. Scientific abstraction understands the search for love and God only as the symptoms of an imbalance in body chemistry. Tom More's lapsometer was based on the same infernal principle: unwavering well-being is always preferable to ultimate desire. The treatment works. Will virtually loses his will and forgets all about the Jewish exodus, Ethel Rosenblum, and a sign from God. Saved from the possibility of an apocalyptic life by the old, everyday order, Will is fittingly treated as one of the elderly. He is confined to a home for the aged, where he may even be allowed to sign up for the Seniors tournament after his convalescence. St. Mark's, the successor to Gerry Rehab in *Love in the Ruins*, makes residents feel obsolete by lulling them with meals, medicine, and Morning Movies so that, every material need supplied, the patients actively do nothing. But the gospel of such enlightened humanism cannot really heal Will's soul, and he is happily delivered from this world of the living dead by the second coming of Allie.

Will may have forgotten Ethel Rosenblum, but his longing for Allie cannot be destroyed. Although he no longer enjoys total recall and cannot even walk to her greenhouse, the heart's recollections make Allie continually come back to him. He looks to her coming, yearns to see her face. "Talk about a nostalgia trip," Jack Curl exclaims as he shows Will the senile model-train enthusiasts who return to childhood amid the diesels and locomotives in the sunlit attic of St. Mark's. On a nostalgia trip of his own, the wayfaring Will suddenly "for some reason thought about Allison standing in the sunlight," the golden-haired apparition in the forest whose very element is the mechanical world (*SC* 310). And he thinks of her again just before he finally flees St. Mark's. Allie's coming to mind is a virtual liberation for a man who once lived by memory. Reviewing the hunt, he concludes for a second time that he did not survive at all: "He killed me then and I did not know it. I even thought he had missed me. I have been living, yes, but it is a living death because I knew he wanted me dead" (*SC* 324). Since his own death was willed by his father, Will's whole life became a will to destroy his life; he was the death wish. But after pursuing suicide, and then the debilitating everydayness of St. Mark's, he again recalls his vital passion. Just as Will's remembrance of Allie saved him on the bus from becoming the parental will to die, it again rouses him from the nursing-home routine designed to destroy his will to live. The memory of love overpowers the memory of death; Allie is his will.

The second coming of Will to Allie marks the consummation of their love. When she sees her onetime guest approaching the greenhouse, Allie thinks that he resembles a visitor from Atlantis or Atlanta "because of the way you came through the woods like you were coming from elsewhere not there. . . . I mean it is a question of where you are coming from." Will laughs at her question about his origin because it sounds so colloquial—"like man, where are you coming from"—but the phrase is peculiarly her own as if even Allie's most ordinary language intimated the title of Percy's novel (*SC* 327). Although Will tells her that he came from the hospital, he has also come out of love. He now turns his willy-nilly first coming into a willful decision of the heart. Not simply a repetition, Will's return is a second climax that fulfills the promise of their earlier intimacy. The young lady whose mother wanted to send her back to the sanatorium and the middle-aged man who has just escaped from a convalescent home find love here in the apparent ruins of their lives. While apart, he lapsed into fatal conformity and she regressed into silence and solitude; now they come together in mutual dependency. Will has a tendency to fall, but her proven virtue is hoisting. Allie often forgets and speaks a language strange to others, but he remembers everything and appreciates her oblique conversation. Each supplying the other's lacks, they discover romance out of fitting each other by chance. "Our lapses are not due to synapses," Allie recognizes as she rejects all the attempts to make them whole by shock therapy or hydrogen ions. He agrees, "No, they are as they should be," for love makes even their reciprocal frailty into the most congenial fitness (*SC* 329–30).

Will and Allie find their ends in each other. But much as Art Immelmann appears at the climax of *Love in the Ruins* to tempt Tom a final time, Will confronts his father's seductive voice of love in death even after he has returned to his life of love. "Come, it's the only way. . . . Come, believe me, it's the ultimate come . . . the second, last and ultimate come to end all comes," Ed Barrett beckons his son to a suicidal Parousia (*SC* 336–37). Like Tom's infernal confidence man, this revenant perverts language by giving the death to

239

which he summons Will a variety of false names: romantic triumph, stoic exit, inherited destiny, old age's dignified alternative. Having long ago established a depraved connection between love and violence, he now severs word from meaning and confers upon *suicide* a more appealing definition. Will opposes the simple and repeated "no" against the alluring rhetoric of his father's invitation, until the negative gains in force to become an exorcism. He hurls away the Luger and Greener and, calling "Come here. . . . Come here," turns back once again to his own life-giving love from the greenhouse, Allison (*SC* 338). "When she came against him from the side," Will has found the haven that his father's suicide had destroyed in Ithaca. "Entering her was like turning a corner and coming home" (*SC* 339).

Although Will was always somewhat abstracted during his first stay with Allie, he participates more fully in their love during his second coming. Percy now uses both points of view to depict this deepened form of communion, first pledged in the greenhouse and later celebrated in the Holiday Inn where they flee to escape pursuit by Kitty. Whereas much of their former exchanges tended toward discussion and explanation, Percy now uses a stripped-down form of dialogue for constant, naked affirmation. Typically in short phrases and often without speech cues, so that the words seem to belong to both, their conversation constantly doubles back on itself, coming and then coming again, what each says always seconded by the other:

> "No. I don't know. Now."
> "Yes. That's better. Now."
> "Yes, it is." Her skin was like silk against him.
> "There you are," she said.
> "Yes."
> "It's you."
> "Yes."
> "You against me, yet not really opposed."
> "Yes. That is, no."
> "Put your arms around me in addition."
> "They are around you."
> "They sure are." (*SC* 338–39)

Words are all the time recalled, rephrased, and repeated, as if Will and Allie shared a linguistic circularity.

This simplified form of speech, a private interchange of echoes, serves not for complex discourse but for the kind of pure celebration that Amos Wilder frequently hears in the rhetoric of apocalypse: a fondness for exclamation and acclamation as language partakes of the glory that it proclaims.[26] Reclaiming the words that Lancelot could only use for ridicule, Will and Allie save speech for rejoicing. The affirmative *yes* (the word favored throughout the scene) and deictic *there you are* assert and confirm in responses of ongoing reciprocation. In such speech, negative can become positive; Will's *no* becomes the homonym *know* and then the diphthonged *now*, affirmed by Allie's *yes*. Or a positive can become negative: "Yes. That is, no." This comprehensive love enables Will to be against her but not really opposed. If Allie once sensed a fundamental harmony between noun and verb, sex and love, such unity is turned into words by their dialogue of one.

Each discovers the oneness of truth amid its multiplicity. "The truth is . . . I wish to speak to you of several things," Will tells his love, whose name means "truth," upon his second coming (*SC* 327). In these scenes where troth is constantly pledged, *truth* reverberates throughout their colloquy. And immediately before Will leaves her for a final time in the novel, promising to come back in an hour, their conversation circles back to the single truth of love. As Will holds Allie and speaks to her from his heart, she asks about the connection between word and meaning, which she earlier found so fragmented, "Is what you're saying part and parcel of what you're doing?" (*SC* 355). This correspondence between speech and significance prompts Allie to consider a still more inclusive form of unity as if intuitively following Percy's own way in *The Message in the Bottle.*

The subtitle of Percy's collection of essays, *How Queer Man Is, How Queer Language Is, and What One Has to Do with the Other,* points to a connection between disconnections: the split psyche of the modern world and the reduction of language to mere labels for experience. If the name can be understood as affirming the speaker, listener, and object, Percy hopes that such verbal bonds may be the beginning of a wider restoration to lost harmony. Since Will and Allie have achieved this linguistic apocalypse through their love, they discover an integrating vision of the heart of life. "Tell me the single truth," Allie asks Will, "not two or more separate truths, unless separate truths are subtruths of the single truth. Is there one truth or several separate truths?" He responds to her philosophical inquiry by simply telling his love what she has helped him to learn, "Both. . . . The single truth is I love you. The several subtruths are: I love your dearest heart. I also love your dear ass, which is the loveliest in all of Carolina. . . . These are separate truths but are also subtruths of the single truth, I love you" (*SC* 355). Tom More sensed a similar unity in the epilogue of *Love in the Ruins*, but because of her distrust of things, Ellen never seemed completely a part of it. Percy's success in *The Second Coming* is to make the unity more convincing through making it more comprehensive. Both Will and Allie come to the congruence where love forms the unifying center of truth. Having earlier delivered a litanylike indictment of the many names of death, Will achieves precisely the opposite in his blazon of Allie. The single truth may assume many forms, but all are the many names of love. And this passion, as the novel's title implies, looks to an eschatological consummation. *The Second Coming* embraces a theology of sexuality. Longing for another becomes part of the search for the God whom Revelation envisions as the coming bridegroom.

Will and Allie's world of apocalyptic romance places them at the beginning of a re-created order in which the old and familiar universe is reappropriated as if new made. Percy's lovers can never escape the world in a private hide-away but must always come back to the ruins and work for renewal. Hence, time and place again form the intersection where Will and Allie must live. After staying in a cave, a greenhouse, and a motel, they decide to get a more definite address in the future. "There will be plenty of time," says Will, who once expected the approach of Armageddon (*SC* 331). Since he has regained the future, Will knows the answer to the problem faced by all of Percy's seekers who confront their lifetimes: what to do? "It had come to pass, for reasons which neither could have said, that he now knew what needed to be done and could say so and she could heed him" (*SC* 342). The reasons are unknown because they are not the rational considerations that show how the odds favor gambling on God's existence or risking elopement from a sana-torium, but the more mysterious ones appreciated likewise by Pascal, the heart's reasons beyond reason.[27] Only love lets Will know what to do and Allie know how to respond. He proposes marriage, itself conceived in appro-priately apocalyptic terms. Sounding a little like Allie, Will admits that while many marriages seem disastrous, "we might not only survive it but revive it" (*SC* 343).

Since the literary form of romance typically looks to a grand concordance in its sundered world, the renewal that begins with Will and Allie's own romance widens to include a promising overture toward communal regen-eration. At the end of *The Second Coming* Percy's lovers seem at the center of an apocalyptic community where the aged and outcast are made new, and the novel's living dead come back to life. Their plans to complete Allie's green-house and develop her property through building affordable log cabins gather in all of the novel's exiles: Kelso, the retired Associate, many of the infirm at St. Mark's, and a construction crew composed of society's nonconformists. Although this building scheme may appear silly and sentimentalized, its very unreality makes it suitable to a novel where improbabilities continually seem like miraculous possibilities. Because it is as farfetched as the love of Will and Allie, this ragtag assembly of the poor in spirit, rather than Leslie's proposed "love and faith community" financed with her mother's estate, may help day by day to prepare the groundwork for the much grander city of God beheld in Revelation.

The conclusion of Revelation foresees a time when humanity will see God face-to-face in a world resplendently sacred (Rev. 22:4). Will never achieves such a beatific vision, for Percy's apocalyptists do not live at the point of absolute consummation but at the end that is always just beginning. Having looked for signs of God throughout the novel, in the last pages Will keeps glimpsing the divine image through its human embodiments: Allie, Father Weatherbee, and a puzzling pair of orderlies at St. Mark's. Just as at the end of The Moviegoer Binx meditated on the possibility of God's baffling presence in the black businessman's reception of ashes, at St. Mark's Will ponders another example of mystery in manners. He watches two black attendants reassure a frightened woman, a true southern lady like one of his aunts, about a trip to the hospital, where she fears she will die. "You gon be fine, bless Jesus," one aide comforts like a mother, while a Sugar Ray Robinson lookalike hoists the patient onto the stretcher "in one swift gentle movement" and promises her a second coming to St. Mark's (SC 348).

Will finds logic inadequate to explain the apparent contradiction of the orderlies' behavior. Their small acts of kindness seem at odds with their hidden intents. The workers' hearty smiles may conceal a private joke, and their solicitude may be mocked by the looks in their eyes. Will cannot separate such possible lies from the probable love. Sugar Ray's gentleness demonstrates that perhaps Will is not the last gentle man, and his authority in guaranteeing the old woman's return places him in the ranks of Percy's news bearers. The paradox of charity before which reason breaks down, rather than a revelation in a cave, gives Will an unexpected view of God's mystery. He is driven to conjecture how it all adds up "in the economy of giving and getting . . . that they, the orderlies, who had no reason to give her anything at all, gave it because it was so little to give and so much for her to get? 2¢ = $5? How?" (SC 349). Will cannot calculate how the giving of the proverbial two cents should have the effect of seeming to cost so inordinately much more. Such inequality simply does not tally in the economy of giving and getting to which he as an estate lawyer is especially accustomed. It is only comprehensible in the economy of grace. "Does goodness come tricked out so as fakery and fondness and carrying on," he muses, "and is God himself as sly?" (*SC* 349). Fond of quoting Joyce about the artist's use of cunning and guile as license for his own trickery as a novelist, Percy intimates that Will may have penetrated beyond the professional benevolence of hospital routine to an enigmatic apprehension of the divine nature.[28] Like Percy's artificer in fiction, God himself is sly.

Slyness may not be one of the conventional attributes of God, but the epithet exemplifies Percy's long quest to renew religious language. It is what piqued Binx Bolling in "God's ironic revenge" for his indifference to signs and in the "dim dazzling trick of grace" at the corner of Elysian Fields and Bons Enfants (*M* 146, 235). The adjective pays tribute to the immense gap between human expectations and the unfathomable indirection of divine manifestations. What Will discovers at the end of *The Second Coming* is a God of surprises who keeps appearing in ways that Percy's seeker never anticipated. Eluding the hunter's petty schemes to track him down, he yet stages a casual, purely unforeseen theophany. This wily God is extraordinary in his very ordinary revelations, and so he goes often unknown. He does not really hide but simply discloses himself in the places where questers are too proud and fatuous to look. Will searches for the Deity in the dimmest of Platonic caves and finds a more telling sign of him in the ambiguous generosity of two assistants in a hospital. Five dollars does not equal two cents, nor do God's and the orderlies' actions make sense, except in a mysterious love beyond everyday logic. Her heart beating in her neck, the old woman's head seems to nod assent to Will's silent question about divine cunning "as if she understood and agreed, yes, yes, yes" (*SC* 349). A sly God does indeed dwell in fondness—in the affections of the heart and in the apparent foolishness of old age, in Allie and Father Weatherbee.

Father Weatherbee is the Creator's and his creator's joke, for he seems the least likely person to serve as a Percyan news bearer. He should speak with authority, but a red bleb punctuates all of the words of this timid priest, who would rather be left to play with his railroad cars than preach the gospel to the novelist's "man on the train." Yet Will's radarlike sensitivity to people and his new perceptions about divine mystery enable him to recognize in the ruins of this evangelist a Kierkegaardian apostle to his own limited genius. Father Weatherbee's fascination with the Seaboard Air Line is at least rivaled by his wayfarer's faith in Apostolic Succession. Jack Curl thinks such a tradition "sounds more like the ancestor worship of his Mindanao tribesmen. . . . A laying on of hands which goes back to the Apostles" (SC 311). Will spent the entire novel paying nearly fatal homage to his ancestor, the father whose violent laying on of hands at the beginning of the hunting trip marked Will from boyhood with a love of death. After trying to be Ed Barrett's violent successor through suicide, the wayward son will consider a different form of filial piety and follow a padre hallowed by apostolic succession. "You'll be in his hands while I'm gone. And damn good hands they are, better than All-state," Curl tells Will as he hands him over to the ancient priest upon whom hands have been laid in consecration (SC 311).

Coming to Father Weatherbee in the very last scene of the novel, Will comes to a new godly father as well as to the Father in God. And God comes to Will through this wreck of a priest who, as if participating in the apocalyptic renewal of the old world, becomes again a bearer of good news. For fifty years this worn and weathered messenger proclaimed the gospel to the people of the Philippines. Although this former missionary to spiritual island dwellers now utters only fretful cries and questions, Father Weatherbee suddenly regains the Word in order to deliver an indictment of America as the most generous yet most selfish and unhappy of lands. Despite one bloodshot eye and another that spins like a wheel, he too is a seer, and his critique of the nation very much seconds Will's own. Percy's engineer, however, senses that the priest knows even more than he does. Will opens himself to further revelation by declaring that he is "willing to be told whatever it is you seem to know" and "will attend carefully to what you say" (SC 358). The seeker announces that he and his future wife are ready to take instruction in the faith, but they will not necessarily believe all of the church's teachings like uncritical conformists. Having found the world renewed in the word restored with Allie, Will awaits the Logos itself. The Second Coming concludes with the imminent coming of God's word to Will, whose partial deafness in The Last Gentleman is finally replaced by the ears to listen with discernment.

As a sign of his new orientation, Will asks Father Weatherbee to perform the ceremony at his wedding to Allie. The sacrament testifies to the concourse of human and divine love that Will is discovering. Seeking God, he finds Allie and learns through their romance the sign of and summons to a divine passion. In the wedding of the Lamb, John envisions God's final union with the world, a time when "the entirety of new creation will be in a state of love."[29] The lovers of The Second Coming share in the beginning of this re-creation, as Will suspects in his last question to Father Weatherbee: "Do you believe that Christ will come again and that in fact there are certain un-mistakable signs of his coming in these very times?" The only possible signs in the novel are not the traditional portents but the apocalyptic semiotics announced in Will's own life. When the priest replies with his fearful eyes, "What do you want of me?" Will reflects on the holy significance of the daft Father Weatherbee and the gratuitous Allie (SC 360).

Until this last paragraph, Allie is surprisingly absent from the conclud-ing pages of *The Second Coming*. Her religious quest has always been less explicit than Will's; even when Percy's gambler recounted his apocalyptic wager during his first stay in the greenhouse, Allie paid more attention to the emotional rather than the intellectual significance of his words. Yet although her love has intimated the divine presence in Will's life, Percy never shows or implies any mutual discussion about the decision that both will take instruc-tion and participate in a church-sanctioned wedding. Will remains strangely mysterious about such plans when, for a final time in the novel, he leaves the woman who has so clearly been a source of sacramental life to him. Before Will searches out Father Weatherbee, he merely explains to Allie, "I have one errand to run," and offers to leave his future wife and her dog at the motel (SC 356). Since Allie has seemed more like the spiritual daughter of Kate Cutrer than of Kitty Vaught, such preparation for possible entry into the church might be an understandable continuation and consecration of her deeply intuitive journey toward faith. But if Allie seems unaccountably forgotten, the beloved woman from the greenhouse is so central that she sud-denly comes back to Will's mind and comes together with Father Weatherbee during the last lines of the novel.

Father Weatherbee's frightened and whirling eyes remind Will of Allie's wide gray ones, and the priest's sticklike bones make him think of her boy-ish arms with their strong hands. "What is it I want from her and him, he wondered, not only want but must have? Is she a gift and therefore a sign of a giver? Could it be that the Lord is here, masquerading behind this simple silly holy face?" (SC 360). Will's final revelation is that although the Second Coming has not yet reached its conclusion, it has already begun in the daily arrival of the divine presence. The sublimely foolish Father Weatherbee dis-closes the face of the Divinity to Will, much as when Jacob, Will's biblical father in faith, discovered that seeing his brother in all his graciousness could be like gazing on the very countenance of God (Gen. 33:10). The generous Allie points to the Lord as the sacred giver, whose free and unexpected love she mediates. "Am I crazy to want both, her and Him?" Will continues to question (*SC* 360). The two are mutually inclusive; in coming to Allie, Will finds God coming into his life. Humanity's approach to the Deity accords with the Lord's own advent. "No, not want, must have. And will have." Will's desire turns into necessity and finally into absolute determination, as his very name becomes a sign of his willingness to live in apocalypse.

8

TOM MORE ONCE MORE

THE THANATOS SYNDROME

I   *The Second Coming* might easily have consummated Percy's career as a novelist. Writing the book exasperated him. "I'm bloody sick of making up stories," he admitted after its publication, and he spoke of turning away from fiction to write a sequel to *The Message in the Bottle*.[1] Over the next three years Percy completed the apocalyptic *Lost in the Cosmos*, which sometimes reads like a direly comic second coming to his first work of nonfiction. Whereas *The Message in the Bottle* recognized the need for revelation as a coming to consciousness that is celebrated in language, what Percy subtitled *The Last Self-Help Book* is a parodied advice manual for those living amid psychic and semiotic catastrophe. This respite from creating fiction suggests that *The Second Coming* had achieved some of the finality of its title. Percy himself considered the novel "a definite advance, a resolution of the ambiguity with which some of my other novels end." Likewise, William Rodney Allen notices "a sense of closure at the end of *The Second Coming*, a feeling of the rounding off of an imaginative world"; and Ted Spivey sees in Will's apocalypse "a kind of summing up of all of Percy's most important themes and ideas."[2]

Although Will's intimations of divine mystery through human love seem more certain and promising than the ends of Percy's previous novels, the last pages of *The Second Coming* mark no finale to his books of revelations. Rather, Percy began once more at what might have seemed an appropriate close. The religious novelist, claims Percy, just like "Thomas More and Saint Francis . . . is most cheerful with Brother Death in the neighborhood" (*MB* 109). Seven years after *The Second Coming*, the seventy-one-year-old Percy published the story of how Tom More redivivus diagnoses the universal death of *The Thanatos Syndrome* in down-home Louisiana. Just as *Love in the Ruins* looked beyond the perilous days of *The Last Gentleman* to the apocalypse in all of America, *The Thanatos Syndrome* portrays the latter days of the Century of the Love of Death, which the last gentleman redux saw most clearly embodied in his father.[3] In his second coming, as in his first, Tom More comes after Will Barrett, yet his return is no mere repetition of *Love in the Ruins* or *The Second Coming*. Choosing life, Tom achieves a modest form of the victory that earlier eluded him; he saves not America but one unhappy part of it in Percy's own Feliciana. However, Tom's defeat of death lacks the exuberance found in Will's embrace of life-giving sexual love. If *The Second Coming* portrays the triumph of eros over the thanatos that reigned in *Lancelot* and in the grim chivalry of the Barrett legacy, *The Thanatos Syndrome* places more of its wary hope in the loving-kindness of agape.

Although *Love in the Ruins* envisioned a crumbling and chaotic America, the fictional landscape of *The Thanatos Syndrome* makes the novel seem much less near the end of the world than was Tom More's earlier apocalypse. As John Edward Hardy has shown, the technology, economy, and psychology imagined in Percy's sequel seem almost contemporary.[4] No insidious vines crawl over the often highly gentrified architecture of the New South; no social or political violence threatens to keep the United States from surviving the very last years of the twentieth century. Yet the very lack of such futuristic signs actually indicates the lateness of the hour in a novel where a spiritual sickness attacks the basis for all semiotics. *The Thanatos Syndrome* is a medical mystery story in which a very unheroic physician must discover that despite all the ordinary and reassuring appearances, the eschaton may be caused by a plague so menacing that daily life becomes indistinguishable from living death.

Since Percy's apocalypticism at least seems more subdued to the everyday eye, Tom More is an appropriately inquisitive and tight-lipped detective-doctor rather than the mad scientist and madcap messiah of his first coming. He repeats the destiny that Kitty Vaught predicted for Will Barrett: the Exile and the Return. Percy's fondness for sequels dramatizes how incomplete and problematic is the end of any novel about spiritual vagrancy, for the comedowns and comebacks of wayfaring always imply a possible fictional continuation when all is still not well. Percy explains in "Notes for a Novel about the End of the World" that although the fiction of the past might leave Dodsworth in Capri or the Okies in California, the "contemporary novel deals with the sequelae. . . . Is all well with them or are they in deeper trouble than they were on Main Street and in the dust bowl?" (*MB* 103). Having just come back from prison for selling prescriptions that would be resold at a truck stop, Tom has already come to himself through the discipline of his captivity. Whereas his own psychic conflicts in *Love in the Ruins* reflected the violent contradictions afflicting the country, the later More seems from the very beginning of the novel sure and serene in an autumnal world of the dead and disembodied. He has been generally healed of his earlier selfishness and self-division, for he no longer suffers from the chronic angelism-bestialism that once turned a would-be saint into a devil's disciple. Lucy Lipscomb, Tom's distant cousin, even suggests that the good doctor may have deliberately committed a crime because he sought in prison a sane alternative to the crazy world outside its walls.

Tom's exile made possible his return to self. He has learned the humility and charity found in taking more time and paying more attention. Since Percy never makes clear how Tom lost the joyful but always tentative equipoise of the Christmas coda in *Love in the Ruins*, the imprisoned Dr. More rather incongruously seems as if he were still recovering from the much earlier July 4 debacle. Percy's once-feverish apocalyptist finds that confinement gave him, like John on Patmos, the space to see. He realized that he did not "have to be in a demonic hurry as I used to be," precisely what he had seemed to discover in the epilogue of *Love in the Ruins* but has inexplicably forgotten, and so his former breathless urgency is replaced by a calm and curious narrative voice (*TS* 67). If the first sentence of *Love in the Ruins* seemed to race against time, *The Thanatos Syndrome* starts with a much less impassioned report of a vigilant scientist recording his observations: "For some time now I have noticed that something strange is occurring in our region" (*TS* 3). The two-year term in prison limited his life to virtually nothing but protracted time and contracted space. Having spent his prison sentence behind a John Deere mowing the golf course at Fort Pelham air base, the landscape of everyday-ness in Percy's fiction, he could see the world that once rushed by him now distinctly enclosed, slowed down, and close up. The doctor found a cure for his vaulting ambitions in diagnosing certain discolored spots in the saint augustine grass as early signs of chinch bugs. "Instead of saving the world," he confesses as if still referring to his dream for the lapsometer, "I saved the eighteen holes at Fort Pelham and felt surprisingly good about it." The modest salvation defines the proper field for his own chastened life. Whereas he once "became grandiose, even Faustian" because he thought that he had to heal the entire country, his pride has been leveled by hours of daily mowing (*TS* 67). The exile regained the world by caring for a gardener's green.

Tom's new humility enabled him to listen to others in the penitentiary without asserting himself. He chatted with fellow criminals and overheard the arguments of captives polarized on every issue from religion to Barbara Walters. He concluded that all doctors should spend two years in jail because they would learn to treat all their patients with the camaraderie of inmates, "as fellow flawed humans" (*TS* 81). Tom even discovered the peculiar virtues of his own flaws. When he tried to end a fight between two contentious prisoners, he accidentally received the blows they aimed at each other. However, they immediately stopped feuding out of concern for their injured would-be reconciler. Tom realized that a "shrink accomplishes more these days by his fecklessness than by his lordliness in the great days of Freud" (*TS* 88). Now out of prison at the beginning of the novel, the once-megalomaniacal psychiatrist heals through his very ineffectiveness. Since he wonders whether a cure is even possible for his patients, the more mellow doctor listens to their frustrations and helps by performing small favors in the most unassuming of ways. "Life is fits and starts, mostly fits," he concludes. "Life doesn't have to stop with failure. Not only do you not have to jump in the creek," as did More's first American ancestor; instead, the formerly suicidal therapist reflects that "you can even take pleasure in the general fecklessness of life, as I do . . . I am a failed but not unhappy doctor" (*TS* 75). More finds good fortune even amid his fall. He enjoys not the stoic resignation of those pessimists in Percy's fiction who so often delight in doom but the pleasant tranquillity of a veteran who sees that the apparent end is not ultimate and so can savor the queer and quirky intermittency of life.

Tom's exile in prison has prepared him for the revelation that begins one week after his return. Because he appreciates the insignificant amid the unpredictable, the eye-catching oddness of human behavior, his diagnosis of the thanatos syndrome begins with just such a series of random, offhand observations. And throughout the novel Tom keeps experiencing these sudden small illuminations, what he variously calls "my wild idea, my piece of luck . . . part of my own nuttiness" (*TS* 8), something that "stirs in the back of my head" (*TS* 18), "a flash . . . a notion" (*TS* 22), a "discovery" (*TS* 88). Percy makes a familiar plot device of suspense novels serve his apocalyptic ends. The conventional moment of recognition in that genre, when the hero first intimates some enormous intrigue, becomes for the already alert Tom a coming into greater consciousness about his age's lack of consciousness. Tom's revelations bring no complete and immediate disclosure but only the inkling of awareness that, like Binx Bolling, he is "onto" a search. These epiphanies gradually lead him to discover the connections among apparently disconnected events: "It began with little things, certain small clinical changes which I observed. Little things can be important. Even more important is the ability—call it knack, hunch, providence, good luck, whatever—to know what you are looking for and to put two and two together" (*TS* 3). Rather than making a pioneering discovery like his lapsometer, More simply detects the pattern made by minor details as he pursues his own little way. Like Allie and Will, he is a coupler who joins one diminutive observation to another in Percy's world of hidden bondedness.

Tom's model for his investigation of the thanatos syndrome is a doctor who once diagnosed an outbreak of bubonic plague in New Orleans. This visionary physician was "one of those rare birds who sees things out of the corner of his eye, so to speak, and gets a hunch" (*TS* 3). After observing that several patients had such similar symptoms as fever and enlarged lymph nodes, he connected these signs with a chance remark overheard on a house call. Most doctors would have overlooked the black cook's complaint that the owner of the great Garden District house should not leave rat poison within the reach of his children; at best, the last of the gentlemanly practitioners might have shown affable condescension by departing "with a pleasantry to humor old what's-her-name" (*TS* 4). But Tom's exemplary physician was also a seer and a sayer. Because he noticed, he could name. He looked sidewise and listened with pricked ears, attended to seemingly irrelevant and unrelated data, honored the anonymous black servant as a person worthy of a name. When he questioned the cook, she showed him the dead rat that later inspired his diagnosis. While the doctor walked down St. Charles, "*click*, a connection was made": he suspected the Black Death (*TS* 4). Tom spends the entire novel hearing just such clicks of connections as he diagnoses a modern version of the medieval pestilence.

In his last novel Percy once again returns to his beginnings as a doctor to become, like his mentor Chekhov, "the literary clinician, the pathologist of the strange spiritual malady of the modern age."[5] The thanatos syndrome is the terminal stage of the physician-novelist's use of illness as metaphor. William Grey's tuberculosis, Binx's malaise, Will's psychic fallout sickness, and Tom's earlier angelism-bestialism have reached such a critical condition that they have become an apocalyptic plague. In Revelation (6–11, 16), thanatos seems to reign as the three cycles of disasters usher in Death under different forms: war, economic chaos, famine, martyrdom, and cosmic catastrophe. In the last series an angel pours a vial upon the earth that afflicts the followers of the beast with grievous sores. Medieval readers of the Apocalypse viewed this calamity as a prophecy of the Black Death, which killed about twenty million Europeans. Although modern historians in fact agree with the death toll cited by Jean Froissart, the fourteenth-century chronicler actually based his estimation of the plague's mortality rate on one-third of the world having perished just as Apocalypse apparently foretold (Rev. 8:7–12; 9:18). One witness in Sienna, where more than half the citizens died, mourned, "and nobody wept no matter what his loss because almost everyone expected death. . . . And people said and believed, 'This is the end of the world.'"[6] Science fiction writers have been echoing that cry since Mary Shelley's *The Last Man* (1826). In what W. Warren Wagar calls the "first purely secular novel of the world's end," Shelley imagined a plague that obliterates the population of the entire world except for one Englishman.[7] The lone Dr. More labors near a similar day of doom except that he does not combat the traditional ills of the genre. The psychiatrist, who also calls himself "an old-fashioned physician of the soul," sees the strange behavior of those around him as signs of a spiritual morbidity and then gradually learns to read those symptoms as the semiotics of the end (*TS* 16).

Tom receives his first clue about this apocalyptic plague shortly after he returns from prison. Mickey LaFaye's symptom is the lack of all her previous symptoms that signified a healthy discontent with her homelessness. Once this shy New Englander, who married a wealthy Creole tycoon, felt only terror before her new life in the New South. She trembled in her plantation-style home next to the sixth fairway because she faced the question that confronts all of Percy's searchers: "What to do with herself?" (*TS* 5). Mickey responded by doing nothing but hiding in her house and occasionally doing lifeless drawings of the Louisiana landscape. When Tom first saw her over four years ago, she was poised on his office couch like Andrew Wyeth's Christina—back to him, hip jutting out, arm lifted in the longing that Christina Olson's own crippled limb never manages in the picture of her world. Tom's case history of Mickey LaFaye turns the secluded painter into a portrait of a Percyan everywoman and everyman. Isolated as any castaway, she was not at ease in her own house because it was not properly her true home. Her distorted, extended body fleshed out her restless yearning for the very revelation that Tom himself has begun to seek.

Mickey heard the first tidings of that apocalypse in a recurrent dream that she retold at virtually every session with Tom. Although the vision haunted her sleep with signs of terror and promise that seemed unrelated to her anxious hours awake, it actually offered a visionary commentary on her spiri-

tual dissatisfaction and the comfortable amnesia of her everyday life. Longing to return to the haven of her grandmother's home in Vermont, Mickey
dreamed of smelling the winter apples stored in the farmhouse basement
and of glimpsing the green hills through the cellar's high, dusty windows.
Mickey's revelation in the dark called the housebound woman away from the
South's architectural restorations that throughout the novel substitute for
genuine renewal—her mock manor, Tom's quaint townhouse made from re-
furbished slave quarters, Van Dorn's plantation gaudily redesigned by Hollywood. The paradisal landscape of her dream summoned this Eve back to her
first and final home. Like Frost's dreaming picker who left his ladder pointing
to heaven, she saw a world of apples redolent of the long-desired Edenic har-
vest. Although Mickey always dreamed that she was alone in the cellar, she
felt that she was waiting for someone who would come and tell her a secret.
Tom wondered, "What was she, her visitor-self, trying to tell her solitary
cellar-bound self?" (TS 6). As she yearned for the news that could be heard
only in the self's deepest recesses, Mickey envisioned her own buried need
for revelation.

Percy understands such a psychic quest as part of a spiritual search. Tom
explains that he is a disciple of Freud because he championed the psyche, or
Seele, although More recognizes that his master spent his entire life denying the existence of the soul.[8] Tom received the deepest faith of his vocation
from Harry Stack Sullivan, who taught his disciples "a certain secret belief
which he himself could not account for": with the help of the analyst, each
patient could obtain what he or she needed, "the pearl of great price, the
treasure buried in a field . . . the patient's truest unique self" (TS 16–17).
Although Tom does not yet see beyond the psychic metaphors of Freud and
Sullivan to religious truths, the images locate the soul's true home in the
kingdom of heaven (Matt. 13:44–45). Mickey dreamed Sullivan's unexplain-
able conviction. Her expected messenger would enable her to obtain what
she needed, a return to that estranged part of herself whose absence caused
her peculiar terrors. So, Mickey visited Tom so that she might be visited.
Coming to themselves only by coming toward others, Percy's seekers always
find epiphany by way of advent.

Unlike those psychiatrists whom he derided as "brain engineers, neuro-
pharmacologists, chemists of the synapses," Tom did not believe in the medical model of personality that reduced all psychological ills to physiological imbalances (TS 13). Instead, he viewed Mickey's panic as a salutary
sign of a pilgrim's displacement. Tom's therapy followed the principles of

Sullivan's own "interpersonal" psychiatry, "a matter of two human beings going beyond labels and categories, even those like 'doctor' or 'patient,' and coming to affectionate, trusting terms with each other."⁹ More furthered Mickey's coming to consciousness by helping her to realize that her very terror might be a message to herself from herself. The self-confined artist improved enough to paint Louisiana bayous and egrets at first hand. However, her fitful restoration to the world was only part of a still greater coming when the sovereignty of Percy's wayfarers, pictured in the reference to Matthew's parables, would find its consummation in the kingdom of God. But when Mickey LaFaye returns to see Tom at the beginning of *The Thanatos Syndrome*, she is as inhuman and unnatural as her spritish name implies. She lacks all connections and contexts, as if instead of the promised coming to self she had gone away from herself, missed being Mickey, however inchoate and indeterminate she once was, and just become vacant and vapid. The symptoms of Tom's fey patient reveal the fatal illness of her soul. Her manners and sexuality, speech and memory, have become so hollowed because she no longer is quickened by her spiritual restlessness. She has lost her apocalyptic identity as one who watches and dreams. Devoid of all life, the cipher of a woman is no more than a kind of nonsign, an emptied self that signifies the death-in-life of the thanatos syndrome.

Tom's astute eye pieces together the stray evidence of Mickey's disintegration. She gives him the first sign of an age in which once again the psychic center does not hold. Since a patient's mannerisms are "as uniquely hers as her fingerprints," Tom first notices the change in Mickey by observing the "little things" to which he is so attuned (*TS* 5). His visionary sight detects that Mickey no longer carefully guards her looks but seems to gaze past him as if she had been diverted from herself and simply drifted away. Mickey's unfocused stare reminds Tom of women "who have given up on the mystery of themselves and taken somebody else's advice: Be bold, be assertive" (*TS* 7). Having lost her very soul, she is reduced to provocative posturing. The former recluse no longer rises with yearning like Wyeth's Christina but luxuriates on Tom's couch like Goya's fleshy *Naked Maja*, his supposed portrait of the duchess of Alba. All of her longing has become languor and lust. If Goya's nude stripped the human form of its traditionally idealized loveliness, Mickey's flagrant carnality borders on bestialism. The new mistress of the Bar-in-Circle Ranch straddles and swaggers like a horsewoman still in the mount. Because Mickey herself is a depleted sign, she can only use the most obscene sign language to demonstrate the sexual significance of her ranch's name. Gesturing like a schoolchild pleased with knowing a dirty joke, the salacious proprietress seems unconcerned that she sought to seduce a youthful groom at the Bar-in-Circle. Although Mickey claims that her stablehand "was coming on to me," Tom reports that the thirteen-year-old boy's parents charged "it was you coming on to him" (*TS* 8). The blowsy woman who once waited for the coming of a news bearer reveals her syndrome by nonchalantly dismissing her destruction of a prize horse and by inviting Tom to join the hot-blooded bucks of her ranch, "That stallion was a killer, Doc. Now. How about you? . . . you come on out by me" (*TS* 8). Mickey's former anxiety before the coming apocalypse in her own life has degenerated into apathy toward the creatures in her care and into bold sexual propositions that make her seem only a horse in heat.

Since Mickey is not humanly embodied, her words never become incarnate. When Tom casually asks his abstracted patient about what day it is or where St. Louis is, she responds with perfect equanimity, unsurprised that he should suddenly care to know. Her replies, always monosyllables and short phrases, are the unjoined responses of an incomplete self. Mickey speaks as if her absentminded words had no connection with her too-palpable flesh. Mickey's language does not arise from any personal context or from the desire for communion that Percy understands as the goal of speech; rather, she answers barely and bluntly but affirms neither her own bereft self nor the anonymous listener. Such speech virtually deprived of all significance is so impersonal that it might be spoken anywhere to anyone as if by a programmed machine. It is a computer language in this age of Pascal. Indeed, when Tom asks Mickey what will be the date of Easter next year, she automatically rolls her eyes to the top of her head "as if she were reading a printout" and gives him the answer (*TS* 9). He later checks, and Mickey is right.

Mickey's memory is as mechanical as the data bank of a computer because it stores and processes information but cannot attach any intimate significance to it. Since her consciousness has become nothing more than complicated brain circuitry, she can no longer remember her earlier presentiment of the apocalypse. The once-homesick woman again suffers from what Percy calls the "worst of all despairs"—imagining "one is at home when one is really homeless" (*MB* 144). When Tom asks Mickey about her dream, she responds with what sounds like a typical non sequitur, "Dream of Jeannie, Doc" (*TS* 9). Mickey once did dream of Jeannie, her real name, the sign of the true self whose coming she envisioned at night. But now that she has forgotten this apocalypse, "Jeannie" is simply Dr. Bob Comeaux's title for

256

his light-brown-haired love, who has been lulled into a reverie of lovely self-absorption.

| | Tom's initial interview with Mickey in the opening pages of *The Thanatos Syndrome* gives the apocalyptist his first glimpse of the approaching catastrophe. Unlike other Percyan seers, More is not startled into consciousness. He returns from prison keenly alert, and in an unaware society he simply becomes more aware. After noticing Mickey's strange behavior he begins to seek further signs and clues, for consciousness means not just seeing a single event but also detecting its significance in a network of implications. If the thanatos syndrome prevents its victims from joining words and flesh, self and others, Tom's healing quest is to make connections by joining one fact to another observation.

As the psychiatrist's research into this idiopathic disease turns into the typically Percyan search for the meaning of revelation, *The Thanatos Syndrome* merrily exploits all the plot devices of the thriller for its own apocalyptic end. The novel seems to take its inspiration from *Panic in the Streets* (1950), the film that Binx saw with Kate about the pursuit of criminals who may unknowingly be spreading the plague in New Orleans, as well as from the later *China Syndrome* (1980), a melodrama about the nearly disastrous effects of a nuclear meltdown.[10] Even more extensively than in *Love in the Ruins*, Percy uses the conventions of such mysteries—searches, concealment, suspense, chases, conspiracies, portents of doom—to dramatize the apocalyptist's progress toward the ultimate mystery. In Percy's equivalent to one of Graham Greene's entertainments, the plot secrets are the revelations that Tom needs to know—sometimes quite unwittingly—in order to confront not just America's eschaton but also his own. Yet unlike the story of Tom's earlier adventures near the end of the world, *The Thanatos Syndrome* stages a less ambiguous conflict between More and the powers of evil. In *Love in the Ruins* Tom actually unleashed the chaos through his Faustian lapsometer, but the older More is guilty of a less egotistical offense: he does not realize the demonic extent of the thanatos syndrome.

Like the hero of detective fiction, More sees with the eye turned outward rather than inward, and so the characteristic musings of the Percyan searcher—reflections on the moment, meditations on the past, ponderings over family history—are subordinated to the observation of facts, formation of conclusions, and confrontation with the enemy. Eschewing such introspection, this most impersonal of Percy's novels takes place not within the seer but before the social landscape. As Linda Whitney Hobson explains, it is "a 'public' work which posits that there is a definable good, a moral sense, which is perhaps askew but which the hero is working to fix." [11] Hence, action is more important than reaction, and the central metaphor of the title is more revealing than any individual victim of the disease. As if afflicted by the mysterious epidemic, most characters in the novel have lost their rightful mystery as humans and serve the plot as significant but not deeply affecting or intriguing humanoids. The plot of *The Thanatos Syndrome* proceeds with a greater singleness of purpose than the more varied and loosely structured episodes of *Love in the Ruins*, for it keeps its focus on the efforts of the relentlessly clinical Dr. More to discover the reason for the lifelessness of his sick world. However, Percy's medical investigator differs from such predecessors as the embittered Lancelot or the intolerant Will Barrett, who also tried to apply the scientific method to revelation and to announce their own apocalypses. Tom More, the failed psychiatrist, is Percy's most successful researcher because he does not arrogantly seek an unholy grail or sacred sign. He only wants to heal his patients. But if he is less spiritually perverted than Lancelot or Will, he is also less obviously religious. Since he claims that "I still don't know what to make of God, don't give Him, Her, It a second thought," he needs to learn that the ultimate discovery is a secret that he never expects, the sign of a divine bond (*TS* 81).

As Tom continues his search by observing his other patients, he notices that all seem as deadened as Mickey LaFaye. "What to make of these patients? What's in common? Nothing? Something? Enough for a syndrome?" Tom wonders as he tries to find a context for malaisians whose chief symptom is that they have lost all context (*TS* 84). In decoding these signs he takes his motto from Percy's own mentor in semiotics, Charles Sanders Peirce: "the most amazing thing about the universe is that apparently disconnected events are in fact not, that one can connect them" (*TS* 68). Tom searches for these baffling links by looking beyond his practice. He notices that the ironic civility of a black janitor has been ironed out into ordinary American niceness. He puzzles over the behavior of the doctors who oversee his parole, the amiable Bob Comeaux and his anxious longtime friend, Max Gottlieb. Tom glimpses the truth of Peirce's surprisingly interconnected cosmos when he discovers that his chief sign of catastrophe is his own wife, Ellen. The connection among all of those lost in the cosmos is their very disconnectedness.

Tom discovers that his love in the ruins with Ellen has turned into a love nearly ruined. She is no longer the moral center of his world but a reincarnation of earlier female extremes. Ellen has become at once as angelic as Tom's first wife but also as bestial as Moira or Lola. She has moved the Sears Best, the site of their Christmas morning celebration at the end of *Love in the Ruins*, out of their room and, like Doris, bought two iron beds, now in high fashion since the convents have closed. Ellen also shares Doris's love for all things English. Having converted from Presbyterianism to Anglicanism, she sneers at Roman Catholics as if they were foreign citizens. The Anglophile has even withdrawn their children from St. Michael's and enrolled them in Belle Ame, a private academy run after the English model.

Since Ellen distrusts the world of things that even a lapsed Catholic like her husband views as significant, she becomes a self without a center. Like Mickey LaFaye, Tom's wife seems to have a computer in her head, for she can calculate the probability of her opponents' playing a specific card at bridge. To become the most exalted of machines—the human-made creation whose artificial intelligence seems to surpass its creators'—is both the ultimate transcendence and the ultimate degradation. As a mechanical intellectual in an age of intellectual mechanics, Ellen is dead because she lives as pure flesh divorced from pure intelligence. John Van Dorn, world-class bridge champion and crusader for sexual liberation, takes advantage of this dichotomy when he invites Ellen to play mixed pairs with him. As he alternately exploits her mind and body, they become partners at bridge and in bed. Since bidding according to Van Dorn is "nothing more than a code for exchanging information" (*TS* 63), bridge becomes the supreme card game for abstracted intellects with minds like computers. And when Ellen is not processing information to win all the tricks of a deal, she becomes Van Dorn's adulterous playmate. The grand slams of the games intimate sexual scores. At matches, where middle-aged ladies often hire life masters as if they were gigolos, Ellen feels "like a dance-hall hostess. For open pairing you just stand there while they look you over" (*TS* 52). In *The Thanatos Syndrome* cards are eroticized, sex is a game, and both are played by debased codes and signals.

Tom begins to learn the conventions of the sport in bed. A slightly drunken Ellen stages her own invitational at which she takes the opening lead: when Tom comes to bed, he finds her on all fours. After he obligingly makes love to her, he hears his gamy partner murmur in her sleep disconnected phrases like "Schenken," "K.S.," "Roth-Steiner," and "Azalea." The bewildered Tom chooses the last, only to find that Ellen has swung round, "buckled and folded herself into me, her wiry head between my thighs" (*TS* 53). Tom later learns from Van Dorn that the names are all codes for exchanging information in bridge. Having lost the distinctively human ability to speak out of love, Ellen perverts orality into mechanical performance. In sex as in cards Tom's wife bids and does as she is bidden. But Tom has been mistaken about the pronunciation of her last muttered direction. The Azazel convention, Van Dorn explains, "means you're in a hell of a mess. It is a way of minimizing loss" (*TS* 61). Tom understands that a player can wave his partner off "by bidding hearts for one round, signaling to her: You go back to your suit and go down." His description makes Van Dorn suspect that Tom may even know more about the game than he reveals. "You know the jargon and you're even on to their harmless little double entendres. . . . You made one yourself—bidding hearts and going down" (*TS* 62). Amid the hellish mess and loss of their marriage, Ellen answers the cue in bed by expertly going down. The language of bridge is not so harmless. Mumbled and mispronounced at first, the Azazel convention articulates the fatal division when discourse has become so depersonalized that it degenerates into nothing but stimuli and responses. Ellen can only mouth esoteric terminology from bridge or erotic commands in bed. In an age of disconnection, the name of the game signifies no passageway to unity but a deadly sport where mind and body play out their disjunction.

The Azazel convention becomes the code word for the whole bedeviled world of the thanatos syndrome. By mistake bridge provides Tom with a metaphor for the malaise. Just as in *Love in the Ruins* Tom More saw malevolent principalities and powers reigning in the last days of America, in *The Thanatos Syndrome* he eventually learns that Azazel is the name of the demon that possesses victims of the current epidemic. More remembers that in Hebrew belief Azazel lived in the Syrian desert, "a particularly barren region where even God's life-giving force was in short supply" (*TS* 64). In Leviticus 16, the book of priestly commandments, Aaron was directed to obtain two goats, one to be sacrificed to Yahweh for sin, the other to be signed and sent into the desert, "a place of wantonness and freedom from God's commandments, as a gift for Azazel" (*TS* 64).[12] Moslems believe that Azazel is a desert jinn, a former angel who as a son of fire refused God's commands to worship Adam, a son of mere clay. Hence, he was expelled from heaven into the earthly hell of the Syrian desert, and his name was changed from Azazel to Eblis, which means "despair." The Islamic myth points to the same American inferno as the Jewish ritual: the desolate hopelessness that inevitably results from proudly transgressing the divine law. Milton understood such pandemonium. Tom More notes in his last sentence of chapter 1 that the author of *Paradise Lost* (1:1531–39) made Azazel "the standard-bearer of all the rebel angels" (*TS* 64).

Although Tom does not yet understand how the twentieth century has desecrated the ceremony for the Day of Atonement by its persistent social scapegoating, he suspects that Azazel names the evil genius of his age. The demon of the desert rules over the wasteland of the novel, whose tank farms and sullied waters depict the equally barren city of the spirit. Although the Louisiana landscape continually seems to disclose its inscape under Tom's eyes and in Percy's sensate prose, the buttery sunlight, glittering pines, and bejeweled sunfish that shine throughout More's quest only highlight by contrast the ugliness that pervades so much of Percy's befouled Feliciana. The end of the century shows the climactic effect of the covenant with death made at its beginning. Fascinated in *Love in the Ruins* by Stedmann's history of the Great War, Tom read a new study of the Battle of the Somme while in prison. Both Somme and Verdun, where two million youths were senselessly slaughtered, marked "the beginning of a new age, an age not yet named. . . . As Dr. Freud might have said, the age of thanatos had begun" (*TS* 86). Tom discovers that a fatal gravity drives his era to follow the graveward course charted in *Beyond the Pleasure Principle*, a series of "ever more complicated *detours* before reaching its aim of death."[13] The disease heralds the spiritual doom of the twentieth century, like the rider on a pale horse that John beholds in Revelation: "and his name that sat on him was Death, and Hell followed with him" (Rev. 6:8).

Living in the infernal realm of Azazel, Tom seeks throughout the novel to discover all the names for the death that devastates his now infelicitously named homeland. But although Percy's scientist considers whether the strange symptoms may point to a syndrome in the age of thanatos, it is significant in a novel about language that Percy as a writer of diagnostic fiction, never More as psychiatrist, actually calls the disease "the thanatos syndrome." The pronouncement shows how Percy is trying to fulfill the spiritual goal of his art defined in *Novel Writing in an Apocalyptic Time*: "before life can be affirmed for the novelist or his readers, death-in-life must be named."[14] Since the title of Percy's fiction is the diagnosis of the condition investigated by Dr. More, *The Thanatos Syndrome* is an extended act of naming the mortal illness of an age that perverts semiotics.

As the text of *The Thanatos Syndrome* expands the title into one of the work's major imaginative achievements, Percy portrays a spiritual disease with a complex and completely coherent pattern of symptoms. Since Percy is more interested in the sickness than in the sick, most of the characters seem like the analytical constructs of a perceptive clinician. But if *The Thanatos Syndrome* does not live as fiction through its felt portrayal of the nearly dead, it finds great vitality in its very name for the death-in-life. Out of seemingly discrete and disconnected signs, Percy creates a true syndrome, a metaphorical illness in which all the symptoms are not only united but also interrelated. The catastrophic illness has its origins in the angelism-bestialism that Tom diagnosed in his first coming. At the end of *Love in the Ruins* he almost foresaw his return when he looked forward to curing "the new plague, the modern Black Death, the current hermaphroditism of the spirit, namely: More's syndrome" (*TS* 383). The syndromes of these two novels seem even more alike when Tom notices that the present symptoms resemble the ones caused years before by the fallout of heavy sodium from an atomic reactor. The area of the brain affected is "not only the major speech center but, according to neurologists, the locus of self-consciousness, the 'I,' the utterer, the 'self'" (*TS* 22). The plague of death-in-life perverts the self's memory, sexuality, and speech, all of which express for Percy how humans may participate in but not be absorbed by the world. The thanatos syndrome violates this harmony so that the afflicted do not live in the first person but become, like the angels or beasts in *Love in the Ruins*, computers or chimps. Tom notes that such lost souls, driven by pure intelligence or instinct, either consider themselves above conscience and the law or simply do not care (*TS* 180). They are the twentieth-century followers of Azazel, whose lawless rebellion against God's life-giving commands has created hell on earth.

All of the novel's dead have fallen from the essential "locus of self-consciousness" (*TS* 22). They do not remember who they really are. No novel of Percy's looks back to the American past so frequently—through references to southern history and More's own ancestry, to the changing Louisiana landscape, to the literary tradition from Irving to Whitman—not out of idyllic nostalgia but from a desire to reconnect his unmindful world with the time that it prefers to forget. Yet if remembering often enables Percy's lost seekers to recollect themselves, Tom's age—patients all—lacks the normal memory that roots a wanderer in a temporal community and keeps the past from being annihilated by integrating it with the present. Mickey LaFaye has forgotten her dream of salvation, while Ellen seems to remember only for a moment the afternoons making love on the Sears Best. Instead of memories that become bonds with themselves and with others, these robots have a superhuman memory that creates no bridges, centers no self, locates no one. Ellen uses her brain circuitry like a fifth-generation computer so that she virtually knows what cards her opponents are holding in bridge. At Van Dorn's academy Tom watches young Ricky Comeaux play Concentration without even concentrating, for he simply matches the cards in suits and ranks as if recalling the information from a data bank. Lost in the cosmos, all of Tom's cases readily answer questions about the precise locations of American cities, yet they do not really live anywhere.

Tom discovers a saving counterpoint to the age's fatal amnesia when he later travels down Raccourci Chute in a pirogue with representatives of the Old and New South. Although Percy has always rejected any connection with the tradition of southern front-porch storytelling, his trio tell their own version of such shared and swapped oral traditions as an affirmation of how memory may provide a communion of the personalized past. Uncle Hugh Bob is a reservoir of local southern history and family legend, but during the first part of the trip he remains isolated from the freejack Vergil Bon because of his pride and ornery prejudices. When the old-timer recalls a yarn about the specter of a beached stern-wheeler, the future engineer dismisses the apparition as only the flotsam and jetsam of river folklore. Tom, always the reconciler, ends their quarreling by redirecting their attention to New Roads, a point on the river where they all have relatives. And the contentious pair come together, trading stories about the prosperity and misfortunes of those affected by the big oil strike in August 1977.

Having transcended the flesh to live outside such history and geography, the savants of *The Thanatos Syndrome* allow their marooned bodies to become mere brutes. Such cases of irrational violence as Mickey LaFaye's destruction of her horses or the slaying of thirty Florida coeds remind More of the behavior of rogue elephants. Although Tom had amusingly and affectionately grabbed Ellen from behind in *Love in the Ruins*, he discovers that the good-natured gesture has become typical of an entire age of bestialism. He is surprised when Donna S——, one of his patients, suddenly backs into him and clasps her hands at the back of his neck: "To describe her backward embrace, I can only use the word primatologists use, *presenting*. She was presenting rearward" (*TS* 20). Kev Kevin and Debbie Boudreaux leave More's office with "thanking noises" after they receive the necessary prescriptions to combat the sexual diseases spread by the matings at Beta House, which "sounds less like a couples' retreat than a chimp colony" (*TS* 84). At night Ellen appears in bed on all fours. The psychic fall in *The Thanatos Syndrome* turns "the descent of man" into another name for devolution.

The language of these less than human primates has likewise regressed. Their simple and fragmented sentences signify the loss of the self as utterer. Although Percy notes in *The Message in the Bottle* that Darwin heard language as separating humans from beasts (*MB* 16), these latter-day specimens of *Homo symbolificus* remand the species to its origins. Speaking without any personal involvement but merely as a reaction to a previous action, they resemble Washoe and Lana, the chimps scientists taught to communicate by pairs of signs: "Mickey like—Donna want—Touch me" (*TS* 85). Whereas most speakers would not answer such a pointless question as "Where is St. Louis?" because they have selves to which they must relate the inquiry, the chimplike humans in the late twentieth century respond to any request and then seek a pat of affection as reward for their performance. Although Tom More, student of nature and human nature, recognizes the difference between organism and mechanism, such primitive two-word sentences make the victims of the thanatos syndrome similar to computers that speak in their own system of binary communication. They do not particularly need to talk, and they answer absently as if reading some imaginary printout. Speakers who venture longer sentences make such persistent use of affectation, jargon, doubletalk, and bureaucratese that language dies on their lips. These living dead have fallen as humans for the same reason that Lewis Thomas explains computers will always fail to live up to their creators. There would have to be three billion of them with more rolling down the assembly line, all "wired together, intricately and delicately, as we are, communicating with each other, talking incessantly, listening. If they weren't *at* each other this way, all their waking hours, they wouldn't be anything like human, after all." [15] The automatons of *The Thanatos Syndrome* are not "at" each other in this hourly reciprocity, subtly receiving messages, making sense, and sharing. They simply fail to make connections.

Since language itself seems at an end in the last days of *The Thanatos Syndrome*, the novel's subhuman speakers cannot perform one of the essentially human activities for Percy: tell stories. As Patricia Lewis Poteat has argued, the very nature of a story embodies the tension between transcendence and immanence that Percy views as basic to humanity. Fiction requires both detachment from the events re-presented as well as sympathetic engagement in them.[16] But in *The Thanatos Syndrome* tales seem impossible, for their would-be tellers have become too abstracted from the incarnate world of the story or too assimilated into the plots of their own lives. Tom wonders how Mickey LaFaye could have possibly made it clear to Bob Comeaux that she shot her horses, "How did she tell you? In her present state I can't see her telling a story, relating an event" (*TS* 100). Comeaux's explanation that she must be questioned like a child assumes little difference between narrative creativity and Mickey's conditioned responses to interrogation. When Tom later asks Comeaux again about how the thanatos syndrome has affected language, the engineer of the disease is so incredulous that Tom must explain this archaic activity: language includes reading a book or writing a sentence. Comeaux blithely reassures Tom that children have gone beyond McGuffey Readers, themes on summer vacations, even comic books. "They're into graphic and binary communication—which after all is a lot more accurate than once upon a time there lived a wicked queen" (*TS* 197). Storytelling requires a self aware of a special predicament, one who can relate the narrative by joining a series of events that itself joins speaker and listener. Preferring factual precision over fictional truth about its own wickedness, the age acts out the supreme parable of endings: the story of Apocalypse. Because the inability to remember, embody, and tell stories portends the end of humanity as Percy knows it, the prognosis for the world suffering from this syndrome seems fatal.

Tom seems to discover the eros that overcomes thanatos in his distant cousin, Dr. Lucy Lipscomb. As a mistress of the erotics of information theory, she appears to offer him both love in and knowledge about the ruins. Since the epidemiologist has access to the data banks of virtually every federal health agency, she uses her computer to define the cause and extent of the malady that has converted humans into computers. In an age of disconnection, Lucy shares Tom's ability "to put two and two together" (*TS* 3). His kinswoman connects. By joining odd, miscellaneous facts she confirms Tom's suspicions that the patterns of strange behavior point to a widespread syndrome. Lucy also notices the link between these symptoms and the heavy-sodium intoxication that More studied years ago. And after creating graphics that plot Tom's patients and the distribution of all those in Feliciana who have elevated sodium levels, she makes a final revealing connection about the possible source of the contamination. The map of the thanatos syndrome conforms to a computer projection of homes whose water comes from the Ratliff number-one intake.

Lucy helps Tom to discover not just the public extent but also the private implications of the thanatos syndrome. Handing her partner at the computer a slip of paper, she touches his arm with the "tragic tingle of bad news, the sweet sorrow to come" (*TS* 156). Tom felt the same eschatological thrill while Lucy showed him the computer graphics, but now the prickling announces the disastrous state of his marriage. The slip records the positive results of a test for herpes IV antibodies that Ellen took six weeks ago when Tom was still in prison. Even as Tom learns about the possible ruin of Feliciana and his own wedded life, Lucy offers herself as his end-of-the-world love. Since Dr. Lipscomb blends science with sexuality, her very knowledge is enticing. "Come over here by me now," she says, inviting Tom to sit before the monitor with virtually the same seductive words that Mickey LaFaye used to summon him to her stable (*TS* 145). Throughout their research at the terminal she excitedly squeezes his arm, pulls up close, and yanks his sleeve. Always impressed with the sheer beauty of pure science, Percy uses Tom's incredible naïveté about computers to intensify the screen's and Lucy's loveliness. He gazes at the color-coded graphics and exclaims, "That's beautiful. . . . You're beautiful," while Lucy repeats the bywords of her life, "I know! I know!" (*TS* 155).

Ecstatic in her knowledge, the scientist grows even more attractive because of the allure of her science. Bodies become excited as well as minds at the computer terminal, and the intellectual quest of Tom and Lucy gradually builds to a sexual climax. Like the bidding at bridge, computers provide a system for exchanging coded information between partners. "What is a baud?" the novice More asks, with displaced bawdiness, the woman whose monitor responds to commands with such rapidity (*TS* 153). As he tingles under his collar, Tom feels "the heavy, secret, lidded, almost sexual excitement of the scientific hit—like the chemist Kekule looking for the benzene ring and dreaming of six snakes eating one another's tails—like: I've got you, benzene, I'm closing in on you" (*TS* 149).

Lucy feels equally aroused. She appropriately describes the computer projection of the thanatos syndrome as "a starry yin embracing a clear yang. It's telling us. It's practically shouting" (*TS* 156). The graphic reveals more than just the cause of the plague. The intertwined shapes repeat the logo of Kev and Debbie's bestial Beta House and picture clearly the love that Lucy has been making to Tom all evening by mechanical proxy. She admits to being on "intimate terms" with the mainframe (*TS* 147), and Tom seems to hear "her own circuits firing away like Hal thinking things over" (*TS* 153). Like the computer with a mind of its own in *2001: A Space Odyssey*, Lucy's machine "is sitting pleased, waiting to be patted," craving affirmation as do so many victims of the thanatos syndrome after they have performed their memory feats (*TS* 147). The mechanization of the person is complemented by the personalization of the machine. Sitting before the terminal with his computer-age love, Tom faces the very ruins that he sought to understand. The bewitching Lucy suffers from a less acute form of the syndrome that afflicts Tom's wife, for both women are experts at intellectual and erotic calculations. They process information with a keyboard and terminal, or with the memory of a data bank, while sending out sexual codes that are finally transacted in bed.

Later that evening Tom is seduced by Lucy's lovely gnosis. She offers the baffled doctor and cuckolded husband the scientific and carnal knowledge that he supposedly needs. When she visits his bedroom at Pantherburn, her coming seems to duplicate the sexual consummation in *The Second Coming*. First offering to cover him up, she proposes, "Better still, I'll warm you up" and covers More with her body much as Allie had formed the sun to Will's cold planet (*TS* 162). Tom feels her on top of him as "a sweet heavy incubus but not quite centered" and repeatedly emphasizes that she could be his focal point: "She needs centering. I move her a bit to center her. There is no not centering her. . . . The sweet heaviness and centeredness of her, I think, is no more or less than it should be" (*TS* 163). Yet the center here, unlike in *The Second Coming*, does not hold, for this appealing demon of the night embodies the very divisions in the age of Azazel.

Lucy's coming to Tom's bed is only one moment in a hallucinatory collage of fragmented dreams and imaginary memories that keep coming back to Tom throughout the night as images of his broken world. In the morning he realizes that all of the apparitions were only illusions except for Lucy, yet she never becomes the center of Tom's chaotic nighttime consciousness. His actual union with Lucy lacks the joyous communion of kissing Alice Pratt in his dream while panzer divisions, reminiscent of the Nazi horrors that Father Smith cannot forget, pass by. When he finally centers Lucy, he flatly reports that it is "no more or less than it should be" (*TS* 163). For More it may even be less rather than more. Several of his disconnected visions in this centerless night provide a disturbing psychic context for his corrupted love among the ruins. During an age when dreams are forgotten and anamnesis has become random access memory, Tom's very ability to remember his nocturnal fantasies suggests their significant connection with his waking world. Tom recalls a fellow inmate at Fort Pelham who called a dial-a-girl number that was answered in a quiet Alabama voice; Uncle Hugh Bob, who sounds like Ewell McBee in *The Second Coming* by telling More, "A little pussy never hurt anybody" (*TS* 165); and two of his patients who watch pornographic three-dimensional videos in their bedroom. In Tom's night with Lucy, the life-affirming meaning of Freud's eros degenerates into mere erotica.

As in *Love in the Ruins*, Tom again turns from despair at the catastrophe of his own marriage to desire. But unlike the caricatured ladies of his past, Lucy seems at first as if she might provide the love that could challenge the age's living death. She is more intelligent than the simpleminded Moira and a more genuine Scarlett O'Hara than Lola Rhoades. The chatelaine of Pantherburn presides over no Hollywood version of Tara but farms an estate cultivated by the Lipscombs for two hundred years. Although young enough to be More's daughter, she repeats Ellen's earlier role as mother, vowing to fatten Tom, scoffing at his outdated suit, even slicking his eyebrows with precisely the same gesture that his nurse once used. And whereas Allie earned her self-reliance throughout *The Second Coming*, the sure and stable Lucy possesses it from the beginning as if she could be the center for Tom. They turn to each other out of mutual need. Dr. More consults Dr. Lipscomb not simply as an epidemiologist but because she knows him as kindred and can perhaps validate his sanity in a strange and ill age. And Lucy needs Tom, her only relative besides the quack of an elderly uncle whose duck calls are driving her crazy. As the pair sip toddies on the gallery of Pantherburn at sunset, the bourbon warms Tom's heart with the gratifying intimacy of genuine conversation: "It is a pleasure telling her, talking easily, she listening" (*TS* 140). Since speech generally suffers from necrosis in the novel, during such a tête-a-tête Tom and Lucy seem to approach the love in language enjoyed by Allie and Will.

Despite such promise, Lucy never becomes the means for Tom to find love in the ruins. John Edward Hardy suggests that Dr. Lipscomb's obvious intelligence and overt sexuality may be too threatening to her kinsman.[17] The puzzled scientist and betrayed husband certainly tries hard enough to escape her formidable powers. Tom does not at first include Lucy in his plans to look at the Ratliff intake, and he consigns her to watching his children while he routs Van Dorn with the menfolk. But if Lucy seems to disappear from the last third of the novel, Tom also has a less egotistical reason to reject her. She is not really willing to oppose the doom. Later that night at Pantherburn, as Tom again drinks bourbon to forget his wife's adultery, he recalls his visits to the great house as a child. The making of toddies always signaled talk of the latest bad news about Roosevelt at Yalta, Truman at Potsdam, or Kennedy at Oxford, Mississippi. Yet amid the clink of silver spoon against crystal "there

268

in Psychiatry" that perhaps More's profession should take its direction from religion.[19] Although Tom is called to help Father Smith, the priest helps the psychiatrist see beyond Lucy's medical model into the mysteries of the thanatos syndrome. Freud viewed *Seele*, according to Bruno Bettelheim, as a psychological metaphor for "what is most valuable in man while he is alive . . . the seat both of the mind and of the passions,"[20] but Father Smith knows the soul in its spiritual origins. Like all of Percy's messengers, he hardly seems qualified to be a herald of the end. When Tom was confined at Fort Pelham, he used to visit his confessor from *Love in the Ruins* at Hope Haven, an asylum for alcoholic clergymen. Father Smith lacks the "perfect sobriety" which he confesses and Percy stipulates any credible news bearer must display (*MB* 149). Indeed, this part-time watchman for the forestry service seems almost insane. After Medicare allocated to the death-dealing Qualitarian Center the funds that once supported his hospice, the lunatic priest followed the example of his namesake and, like the fifth-century Saint Simeon who perched on a pillar for thirty-seven years, made his new home atop one of the hundred-foot fire towers. Father Simon even seems to suffer from many of the symptoms of the thanatos syndrome: forgetfulness, sentences out of context, distraction, and detachment. Yet all the familiar signs of the fatal affliction are transformed in the priest so that they become the marks of one intensely alive and loving amid the ruins. Although Father Smith may lose his thoughts, he beholds with a visionary eye the significance of his visit to Germany before World War II. His non sequiturs connect, but at a prophetic level that Tom cannot yet comprehend: his oracular utterances express his passionate concentration on the divine center.

Like Tom and Lucy, Father Smith is a researcher, but he understands the eschatological significance of his findings. Tom learns from the harried curate who only wants the old priest's return to St. Michael's parish that Father Smith has "discovered a mathematical proof of what God's will is, that is, what we must do in these dangerous times" (*TS* 111). But unlike Lancelot or Will Barrett, Percy's eremite never reduces theological mysteries to such intellectual demonstrations as this erring cleric may suggest. Father Smith has simply turned his avocation into an apocalyptic vocation. The lookout scans the sky for signals of smoke even as he holds vigil for the end of the world by searching for signs that will blaze out the Parousia. Like the fires at the end of *Love in the Ruins*, they portend destruction, but they may also burn with the news of the imminent theophany. Father Smith has not escaped into an apocalyptic delusion, for he uses the most mundane signs of his job to build a community before the advent of the saving doomsday. His labors themselves become for Tom a sign of how to live at the end as a watcher and worker. In spotting fires as in fishing for *sac au lait,* indeed for all consciousness in Percy's world, it is as Uncle Hugh Bob explains, carrying his aptly named Omega reel, "you got to have two" (*TS* 182).

After Father Smith derives one coordinate by sighting the smoke with his azimuth, he calls another tower for a second reading and then uses the techniques of triangulation to plot the exact point of the fire's origin. As he describes the process, he cannily directs Tom to perform each step and thereby initiates the psychiatrist into his ministry. Like Lucy elated before her computer maps, Father Smith "is pleased by the elegance of the tight intersected strings" that mark the fire's location on his less sophisticated chart (*TS* 120), but the stylite puts his science at the service of creating a semiotic community. He builds with his triangles a three-way delta before the omega caused by the loss of the human ability to use language, what Percy calls the delta factor. Just as Tom has been doing from the beginning, the sentinel pursues connections and intersections, yet by viewing his data according to the ultimate bond, the exegete provides the hermeneutics necessary to fathom the thanatos syndrome. In a world where all things have fallen and so fall apart, Percy's priest is the crossway that brings together sign and significance, word and meaning, seeker and fellow searcher, the near dead and the God of the living.

Speaking and listening from the tower that is the linguistic center of the novel, Father Smith detects the semiotic catastrophe of his dying century. Smoke definitely signifies fire, but words, which Tom considered his most important clue to the syndrome, no longer point to such unmistakable correspondences. "Can you name the one word sign," he challenges, "that has not been evacuated of meaning, that is, deprived by a depriver?" (*TS* 121). The preacher, who feels that he can no longer talk, hears the same disastrous emptiness that Tom sees in his patients and that Percy describes in *Lost in the Cosmos. Homo loquens* loses its humanity when it loses its eloquence. In the "first Edenic world of the sign-user," the world is known through the word, as when Helen Keller discovers water through *water.* Gradually, however, the sign is devalued either by custom or deliberate subversion until it no longer expresses the essence of the object. The "signified becomes encased in a simulacrum like a mummy in a mummy case. . . . The bird itself has disappeared into the sarcophagus of its sign" (*LC* 98, 104). Percy's funereal images reveal how the thanatos syndrome leaves only sounds and letters to entomb the once-vital meaning. Father Smith mysteriously refuses to speak not because he suffers from a stroke or from the linguistic impoverishment of the thanatos syndrome but because he seeks to make his quiet vigil the means to renewal. His windswept tower is a place cleared of the hollowed speech used so unconsciously by the novel's dead while they kill their victims with such murderous misnomers as "gereuthanasia" and "pedeuthanasia" or violate children under the pretense of playing "sardines" and "treat-a-treat." At Ground Zero the language of the tribe may be purified. In the space of silence the anchorite listens for a single sign that has not yet been "deprived by a depriver" (*TS* 121).

That sign achieves human significance in the Jews, for they make God's word present in history. Ever the ironic scientist, Father Smith plays mock analyst and makes Tom his patient so that the doctor might discover the cause and cure of the malaise. To prove his discovery about the meaning of the Jews, the priest invites Tom to respond to some free associations. Whereas Tom connects various stereotypes with the other verbal signs, *Jews* inspires him to think of actual people he has known. The name is not negated by being reduced to a token for standard responses; it lives as a personal word that finds embodiment in specific individuals. Father Smith views this proof of linguistic amplitude as pointing to the fullness of divine being: "That's the only sign of God which has not been evacuated by an evacuator. . . . The Jews—cannot—be—subsumed. . . . Since the Jews were the original chosen people of God, a tribe of people who are still here, they are a sign of God's presence which cannot be evacuated" (*TS* 123).

The Jews name the vital connection that seems lacking in the novel's lifeless world. As a tribe, they are united to each other by semiotic bonds; as a sign, they collectively form the intersection between humanity and divinity. The beloved people of God incarnate the word of the Lord before the world. Their continued existence points to God's perduring presence, for despite the thanatos syndrome the Jews cannot be nullified either in semantics or in history. Dwelling in speech and in time, they testify to what transcends any devaluation or destruction. Other words can be subsumed in their categories the way any pine tree can be included in the class of conifers, but the Jews, Father Smith argues, cannot simply be assimilated into some larger group like Caucasians or Semites. Since the word and the people are indivisible, the Jews cannot be generalized out of existence, although history has tried. Father Smith explains that "the Holocaust was a consequence of the sign which could not be evacuated" (*TS* 126). Suffering from the pervasive disjunction of the thanatos syndrome, the architects of the euphemistic Final Solution assumed that the eternal witnesses to the divine presence could be annihilated in number if not in name.

Just as Freud saw anti-Semitism as the violent result of the aggressive death instinct, Father Smith understands Hitler's attempted destruction of the Jews as the climax of the age of thanatos.[21] The Third Reich perverted Joachim of Flora's gnostic and trinitarian eschatology, as Eric Voegelin has shown, to create a Nazi apocalypse that found its consummation in the Holocaust.[22] Through such genocide the century of death rejected the spiritual kinship that Percy's seekers always discover with the Jews and allied itself with Sutter's denial "that my salvation comes from the Jews" (*LG* 307), Lancelot's neo-Nazism, and Ed Barrett's deadly German romanticism. Such anti-Semitism has devitalized the age by causing it to lose its human identity: its self-awareness as a community of wanderers, semiotic understanding of language, physical placement in the world, memory of revelatory history. Indeed, the twentieth century has replaced the Jewish sense of exile with mindless complacency; its fullness of speech with the emptiness of sounds; its incarnate existence with abstraction and slaughter; its salvation history with spiritual amnesia. The thanatos syndrome is another name for the truly mortal sin of the century: eliminating the inherent Jewishness that defines humanity.

Through the Holocaust, the century that loves death tried to deny its own identity as people who must be signs of the divine presence. Instead, the age followed the precedent of fourteenth-century Europeans suffering from the Black Death: it burned the Jews.[23] The Nazi crematories made God's chosen people into the scapegoat sent into the burning desert by the modern devotees of Azazel. Although Father Smith does not yet fully explain the connection between the cult of science and the desecration of the Jews, he implies that the hierophants in this twentieth-century idolatry are Tom's own kind: "You are a member of the first generation of doctors in the history of medicine to turn their backs on the oath of Hippocrates and kill millions of old useless people, unborn children, born malformed children, for the good of mankind—and to do so without a single murmur from one of you. Not a single letter of protest in the august *New England Journal of Medicine*" (*TS* 127). Father Smith reveals to Tom, who described himself as looking "somewhat Jewish" in *Love in the Ruins* (*LR* 123), the age's radical choice between life and death.

Tom does not wish to face such a dichotomy, for he belongs to the very humane group that Father Smith criticizes. Throughout the interview he feels entrapped as much by the sly priest's puzzling questions and nonsensical statements about language as by the trap door on which he keeps futilely pulling as he tries to escape. In the fire tower Tom faces a seriocomic "no exit" from confronting his infernal age that keeps making burnt offerings to Azazel. Feigning cordiality, dreaming of Lucy, looking at his watch as if more interested in a sign of the time than the signs of the times, he prefers not to listen to Father Smith and simply wants to dismiss him with an empty diagnosis: the priest is depressed. But just as Tom needs help to open the door, he needs Father Smith to complete his spiritual passage. He does not realize that this fire watcher sees even more clearly than the doctor himself the hope and despair of the age. The century renounces its salvation, which Father Smith traces to the Jews, through the kindest of killings. "Do you know where tenderness always leads?" the priest asks in a chilling conclusion to the interview. ". . . To the gas chamber. . . . Tenderness is the first disguise of the murderer" (*TS* 128).

Father Smith rejects such savage sentimentality for a selfless passion. He understands the vices of the century's virtues. The age is so nice that it eradicates whatever seems inhumane, so well-meaning that it extirpates whatever affronts its fastidious sensibilities. Like Val Vaught, the tough-hearted priest has run an outpost for the apocalypse, where his own ill will has been converted into a means for demonstrating love in the ruins to an age that knows only death. Father Smith can be so bitter that he later almost sounds like Lancelot when he confesses, "Love your fellow man, the Lord said. That's asking a lot. Frankly, I found my fellow man, with few exceptions, either victims or assholes. I did not exclude myself" (*TS* 243). The priest's extremism reveals that love is no mere effusion of idealized emotion but a costly and offensive burden. Such an outrage almost ought not to be. It is virtually unjustifiable; "victims" merit pity, "assholes" deserve only contempt, but none, not even oneself, is entitled to love, the greatest scandal of fellow feeling.

Father Smith's recoil from one of the central commandments of Judaism and Christianity makes love more radical by clearing away all pretenses to anything less than its extraordinary demands. Because he finds consolation in the God who "puts up with all types," Father Smith in spite of himself put up with all types of the terminally ill (*TS* 243). The hospitaler cared for those literally dying from a thanatos syndrome. Father Smith denies that he loved his patients. He only admits to having liked them and felt at home among them. The student of semiotics rightly shuns *love* because it seems deprived of its normal significance for patients in their final days when those called "their loved ones can't stand the sight of them, haven't a word to say to them, and they can't stand the sight of their loved ones" (*TS* 244). Father Smith did not love on such hollowed terms. Instead, he renewed the very meaning of the rejected name as if the end of the world at last made possible the experience of the word for those who were terminal. The frank priest liked the moribund for their honesty in a society where all were "dying too and spending their entire lives lying to themselves," because such integrity made the truly mortal speakers more alive than the apparently living victims of the thanatos syndrome (*TS* 244).

Father Smith's patients were at least more truthful than such fathers of lies as Comeaux, whose killing at the Qualitarian Center is called merciful, or Van Dorn, whose exploitation of children is labeled sexual liberation. Their misnomers represent the death of speech, for the word is divorced from the deed when benevolent progressivism becomes a name for such violence. But at the hospice, as at Allie's greenhouse, language was renewed by the single truth of love. And this linguistic apocalypse gave voice to a spiritual conversion. The priest recalls that one of his greatest accomplishments was occasionally enabling the living "to speak with truth and love to their dying father or mother" (*TS* 244). Talking at last without lying, the living assumed their rightful identity as the loved and loving only amid the ruins.

In the end, Father Smith's haven was sent only patients unwanted by the Qualitarian Center, those dying from AIDS (*TS* 244). Comeaux boasts that Project Blue Boy has reduced the cases of AIDS by 76 percent through simply reducing homosexual desire, but Father Smith's approach was more human, less "humane." He simply told the truth to his AIDS patients, stayed with them, and felt at home with them, only mentioning religion if asked. Amid this community based on honesty and the love that did not even use the name, Father Smith discovered the renewal of what opposed thanatos: agape. The priest is Percy's means for carrying *compassion* back to its wellhead in fellow suffering. Percy would define that word by its etymological origins just as does Flannery O'Connor, the source of Father Smith's comments on fatal tenderness: "the sense of being in travail with and for creation in its subjection to vanity. . . . this is a suffering with, but one which blunts no edges and makes no excuses."[24] Father Smith's era faces its doom because it prefers tenderheartedness over such courage in the root sense, the radical virtue of the heart.

Percy's use of the mystery plot allows Tom gradually to discover the truth

tive Catholicism. But the German belief unto death concealed a belief in death. This fatal faith was celebrated by the anthem "Fahnenlied" ("The flag and death," summarizes Father Smith), proclaimed as "Blut und Ehre" on German bayonets, worn as a Totenkopf insignia, and institutionalized in the concentration camps (*TS* 248). Father Smith's condemnation of the century's recurrent Nazism originates not in any abstracted moral arrogance but in sorrowful horror at what he once glimpsed in himself.

The Third Reich was a political version of the thanatos syndrome that is being dangerously repeated in the rationale for Project Blue Boy. As Tom explains to the priest, Comeaux believes "that every society has a right to protect itself against its enemies. That a society like an organism has a right to survive. Lucy agrees. So do I" (*TS* 234). Blue Boy would imitate Hitler's Germany by creating what Robert Jay Lifton has called a "biocracy," a purified American Volk.[27] From his watchtower Father Smith sees the dangerous implications of the nation's self-righteousness in the quarantine of AIDS patients and the extermination of the unborn, deformed, elderly, and dying. When society views itself only as a biological entity, it resorts to scapegoating as the supposedly sinless pervert the ritual for atonement to purge their enemies. No longer recognizing their own culpability, the sanctimonious cast the burden of their guilt onto the age's outcasts and deliver themselves not from but into evil. Azazel still receives his tribute. Father Smith turns his memories into a message for the inquiring Tom so that the scientist may realize how such faith in death has led in Nazi Germany as in fin de siècle America to the killing that is called compassion.

Smith's cousin Dr. Jäger was the most humane of executioners. His home in Tübingen that summer before the war was a salon for the most celebrated German and Austrian psychiatrists attending the Reich Commission for the Scientific Registration of Hereditary and Constitutional Disorders. In their enlightened debate on euthanasia, those doctors like Jäger who "took the more humane side" that mercy killing should be used only for patients useless to themselves opposed those physicians who favored its use for anyone useless to the state (*TS* 246). These sons of Goethe, like Will Barrett's equally romantic father, did not seem overtly evil, for they scoffed at the rabid pronouncements of Hitler and never mentioned the Jews. They were interesting, appealing, even apparently merciful as they argued for the extermination of the malformed and terminally ill. Yet as Frederic Wertham recognizes in *A Sign for Cain*, a "remarkable book" that Percy acknowledges as having inspired some of *The Thanatos Syndrome* (*TS* viii), the very terms used by these doctors deprived words of their significance. Their lies contributed to the hollowing of language that fills Father Smith with such despair, for by speaking of "help for the dying" or the "destruction of life devoid of value," they substituted the euphemisms of euthanasia for the rank actuality of their horror. Wertham explains that the mass exterminations of patients overseen by these physicians "were not mercy deaths but merciless murders." [28] The demons of thanatos do not even appear demonic. Azazel's triumph is that their very tenderness leads to the gas chambers.

Although the fictional extremes of *The Thanatos Syndrome* often dramatize the terminal illness of the century, Percy uses the most offhand and understated way to make the end of the priest's story so horrifying. He relegates the conclusion to a brief section called "Father Smith's Footnote," an appalling addendum that seems like an afterthought. Years later, when Simon Smith liberated Eglfing-Haar, he was shown the "special department" of the children's psychiatric ward, a stark and sunny room with a white-tiled table just large enough to hold a child. On the windowsill grew a luxuriant geranium. Like Lucy and Vergil after having discovered the outrages against children at Belle Ame, the nurse wished to speak of some unspeakable event but lacked the words that long ago had died with the children. So, she talked around it, telling Smith that five or six times a month a doctor, usually his kinsman Jäger, would take a child into the room and later return alone.[29] Father Smith still does not know whether the haunting smell whose memory evoked this vision of thanatos came from the geranium or from the Zyklon B often used to kill the children. The false love of the Century of the Love of Death makes murder most sweet.

Since Father Smith seeks to provoke horror in a century when most people can feel only interest, he crafts his narration to appeal first to Tom's sense of the interesting. The priest adds his footnote to his tale just as the impatient Tom is about to leave, so that as a storyteller he may eventually lead the scientist beyond mere intellectual inquiry to spiritual indignation. Father Smith recalls that neither he nor the nurse at Eglfing-Haar felt any horror at the time. "It was a matter of some interest. Soldiers are interested, not horrified. Only later was I horrified. We've got it wrong about horror. It doesn't come naturally but takes some effort" (*TS* 254). Tainted by the thanatos syndrome, they suffered from the same flatness of affect that the similarly deadened Lancelot described as characterizing a time when "curiosity and interest and boredom have replaced the so-called emotions we used to read about in novels or see registered on actors' faces. Even the horrors of the age translate into interest" (L 21). Tom responds as does the rest of the age, looking down "curiously" at his patient, "more interested in his story as a symptom of a possible brain disorder than in the actual events which he related" (TS 254). Yet this very interest, skillfully exploited by Father Smith, compels Tom to ask the priest about the fates of Jäger and his colleagues. He learns that many had killed themselves as a fitting testimonial to the age of death.

Father Smith dismisses his memory as just a tale or hallucination, but Tom suspects the irony in his crafty and glittering eyes. Like the stranger who will bring Mickey LaFaye some message from herself, the physician of the soul speaks as the double of Dr. More. Indeed, some of Tom's own dreams at Pantherburn were actually inspired by fragments of Father Smith's memories as if the two shared a communion of consciousness. The priest's story turns history into revelation and invites Tom to make the necessary effort to convert mere interest into outrage. Sufficiently disturbed, Tom asks Father Smith why he became a priest. If thrillers typically focus on the "naked choice of the most simplified and self-canceling alternatives" such as life or death, the clergyman's explanation of his vocation reduces all the mysteries of Percy's arabesque plot to their bare and uncompromising simplicity:[30]

> "What else?"
> "What else what?"
> "That's all."
> He shrugs, appearing to lose interest. "In the end one must choose—given the chance."
> "Choose what?"
> "Life or death. What else?" (TS 257)

Like Pynchon in The Crying of Lot 49, Percy uses the conventions of the thriller to dramatize a quest for revelation amid a semiotic babble, but whereas Oedipa Maas remains poised between paranoia and apocalypse, Tom must choose to act. The only alternative to such death in life is life in spite of death, the life of God that comes from love in the ruins. The priest's loss of interest slyly drives Tom beyond his purely clinical interest in the causes of this strange syndrome. Father Smith's casual ultimatum challenges Tom to his own Mutprobe.

Tom's test of courage comes the next morning. After having been arrested while trying to rescue Claude Bon from Belle Ame the night before, he hears the echo of Father Smith's options while he waits in a holding facility at

Angola. Tom prefers to avoid such choices because, unlike the ideologues at Fort Pelham or the eristic Bob Comeaux, he lacks a passionate center of belief. As a result of such listlessness rather than fervent conviction, Tom has been indirectly allied with the forces of thanatos from the beginning of the novel. Comeaux uses More's research into the age at which an infant becomes a person as justification for his own program in pedeuthanasia, and Van Dorn attributes much of the success of Blue Boy to More's earlier work in isotope brain pharmacology. The acedia that keeps Tom from decisively joining or opposing the pilot project also makes him "only a Catholic in the remotest sense of the word," a lapsed believer who neither completely accepts nor rejects the name of his family faith (*TS* 45–46).

Confinement at Angola reminds Tom of his prolonged delight in never making a decision, for he feels that "there is something to be said for having no choice in what one does" (*TS* 262). Yet when Bob Comeaux again tempts him to become a senior consultant for Project Blue Boy, Tom wonders what would happen if he refused. "That would be your choice. It would be out of our hands," Comeaux warns him (*TS* 265). Tom chooses life. After hearing Father Smith's confession about his fascination with German valor and his subsequent discovery of Nazi horror, Tom ends his own complicity as a scientist who tolerates the new brand of fascism. He escapes from prison, liberates Van Dorn's concentration camp–academy, and then proceeds to confound the current reich of social engineering.

Tom brings the end of the world at Belle Ame through the healing power of language. Although Hugh Bob has his gelding knife handy, Tom rejects the fit tool of the Old South to avenge sexual wrongdoing. He simply puts his professional word at the service of his newly discovered faith in life and speaks with the sovereignty of a Jewish apostle to the Gentiles. Father Smith earlier suggested such a messenger's persuasive power when he asked Tom, "Is it not the case, Doctor, that if a Jew speaks to a Gentile, speaks with authority, with sobriety, as a friend—*the Gentile—will—believe—him!*" (*TS* 125). Having chosen life, Tom uses his credibility as a doctor to convince others to participate in his seemingly senseless campaign against death. Repeatedly, the child abusers at Belle Ame as well as Tom's own allies, Vergil and Uncle Hugh Bob, ask about his inexplicable behavior or look at him askance, for he acts with the baffling certainty of a news bearer who is centered on his belief. He simply speaks to the Gentiles, and his audience of skeptics and pedophiles heeds his medical guarantees as if they were the gospel truth. When Coach, grazed by Hugh Bob's Woodsman, turns to the doctor for help, More reassures him. "You swear?" the panicky instructor asks; after Tom avers, "I swear," Coach believes him. "I'm going to be fine, Doctor, since you said I would" (*TS* 304, 305). Before Van Dorn gives himself a taste of his own unsavory medicine, he asks for Tom's word that the effect is reversible, and when Tom nods, "I have every reason to believe it is," the director of Belle Ame drains the glass without any hesitation (*TS* 307). Mrs. Cheney will not follow suit until she also gets Tom's pledge; when he promises, she obeys.

Tom harrows the hell of Belle Ame in a scene almost as wildly chaotic as his near triumph years ago in the Pit, but here he retains much greater control over the monkeyshines. Whereas Art Immelmann earlier caused the infernal anarchy by distributing the lapsometers, Tom creates the confusion as a means of restoring order. Since the thanatos syndrome threatens to reduce humans to beasts, the staff of Belle Ame after drinking the *elixir mortis* devolve into apes. Their antics prove to a disbelieving sheriff just how depraved these good folks really are as they turn the academy into an animal house. The monkey business helps to purify Tom's conquest of any pride, for the savior is himself a joke. Tom domesticates this planet of the apes by luring the primates into submission with candy bars until the sheriff can finally capture them. The circus tamer realizes the heroic impropriety of his improbable heroism. In *Love in the Ruins* the messianic More suffered from an allergic reaction to gin fizzes; amid his success in *The Thanatos Syndrome* he fights similar symptoms, which keep him duly unpretentious: "During the great crises of my life, I am thinking, I develop hay fever. There is a lack of style here—like John Wayne coming down with the sneezes during the great shoot-out in *Stagecoach*. Oh well" (*TS* 302).

Tom lacks the gestural perfection of the celebrated scene that Binx Bolling treasured as one of the most memorable moments of his life, yet the doctor can shrug off his deficient panache because he need not live in the screen world of consummate performance. Hence, when Percy later stages the novel's shoot-out, the finale never meets the grand expectations of Hollywood's "shoot-'em-up." When the Coach tries to escape, Tom gives a sign—here full of significance—and Hugh Bob reduces the bruiser to a quivering boy by blasting at the tip of his ear. Inspired by his own success, the uncle later fells the grave Mr. Brunette by a peppery shower of rubber pellets at his backside. Since Percy undercuts Tom's mastery through farce as well as through the assistance of Vergil and the uncle, the savior stays reasonably humble.

285

Having closed Van Dorn's model school, Tom wins another unspectacular victory by ending Comeaux's design for an ideal society. After he returns to prison, Tom More repeats his namesake's opposition to the secular usurpation of the spiritual realm. He threatens to inform the government about Comeaux's secret pilot project and the atrocities at Belle Ame unless those quarantined and sentenced to death at the Qualitarian Center are entrusted to Father Smith's defunct hospice. The maverick neither fights a John Wayne duel nor shoots it out in the tradition of Will Barrett's violent ancestors but once more relies on the power of a doctor's word. "Here's where movies and TV go wrong," he concludes. "You don't shoot X for what he did to Y, even though he deserves shooting. You allow X a way out so he can help Y" (*TS* 332). As the spirituals from the Angola work camp place Tom's triumph in its proper context, Tom again rejects the disappointing stardom that results from trying to live up to Hollywood's or the Old South's fatal ideals and accepts the less showy life of helping the doomed save each other. Instead of a gunfight Tom stages "mock warfare" by using Max to play the game of "tough cop and softy cop," a familiar strategy from group therapy (*TS* 333). When the stalwart Tom proposes that Father Smith care for all those destined for euthanasia, Comeaux detects the marksmanship of his words and angrily protests to the seemingly less staunch Max, "He's talking about shooting down the entire Qualitarian program in this area" (*TS* 334).

Tom's artful verbal sniping reverses the entire tradition of the movie gunfight and of gentlemanly manners by making words the most effective weapons against death in a century in which speech has been nullified. "Now here's what we ought to do," the news bearer casually proposes with the authority of his calling (*TS* 332). When Tom meets the defeated Comeaux at the end of the novel, the would-be Southerner claims, "The only difference between us is that you're the proper Southern gent who knows how to act and I'm the low-class Yankee who does all these bad things like killing innocent babies and messing with your Southern Way of Life by putting secret stuff in the water, right?" (*TS* 347). Although Comeaux cites his rival's style and good taste, the poseur from Long Island misses the soul of what finally makes Tom More, like Will Barrett, a last gentleman. Tom's victory depends not on cultural aesthetics but on the absurdity of a faith that opposes thanatos. More wins for the hospice all those consigned to death even though he suspects that the crazy Father Smith cannot properly care for himself. The doctor has learned from the priest's memories about Nazi Germany and from the Aryanism of modern America that "in the end the majority always gets in trouble, needs a scapegoat, and gets rid of an unsubsumable minority" (*TS* 352). Tom will no longer allow another sacrifice to Azazel.

V   Although Tom puts an end to the blissful thanatos of Blue Boy and saves many from the happy death of euthanasia, he never completely defeats the thanatos syndrome. The water contaminated with Na-24 is only one example of the fatal epidemic, not its real source. The entire century is sick unto death. Since the true cause of the illness is not physiological but spiritual, it cannot simply be purged by Tom's comic catastrophe. But if Tom's last judgment does not herald the death of death envisioned in Revelation 20:14, his indeterminate triumph does make possible the beginning of renovation out of the ruins. The highly episodic chapter 5 makes the novel take its time in coming to a close as it chronicles an age that is convalescing but not cured. Unlike television (constantly playing in the More household), which "has screwed up millions of people with their little rounded-off stories" (*TS* 75), Percy's deliberately ambivalent and unfinished end avoids such tidy denouements for a more truthful form of fiction. It evokes promise without fulfillment, longing without certainty, and faith without formal belief to create a sense of an ongoing apocalypse. This advent unfolds slowly and obliquely through Tom's ministry at the reopened hospice, the renewal of his marriage, and a sign of hope given by Father Smith. Working, loving, waiting, Tom More embraces the typically Percyan way of living at the end.

Like Will and Allie's building project at the end of *The Second Coming*, St. Margaret's hospice provides the center for a new communion. As Tom now helps Father Smith care for the victims of AIDS, the two simply talk to the patients, "we to them, they to us, and we to each other in front of them" (*TS* 363), sharing the intimacy of the word and the community of castaways. The dying even give the alcoholic priest and doctor advice about diet and drinking. Such therapy raises the basic Percyan situation of speaker and listener to the level of a mutually restorative art in which patients become akin to their physicians. "It seems to help them and us," Tom says, for the world of the thanatos syndrome gets well by discovering such healing reciprocity (*TS* 363).

The planners of Blue Boy never regain such well-being because they are too immersed in their own speech—Van Dorn in appearing on talk shows to promote his best-seller, Comeaux in talking like a Southerner about social engineering. But when the staff of Belle Ame are assigned to work at the hospice for five years, the once dead are resurrected by caring for those saved from death. Deprived of any opportunity to commit sexual violations, they are at last free to form more life-giving bonds with deformed infants, LAV-positive children, and the victims of Alzheimer's disease. Even Kev Kevin and Debbie Boudreaux, no longer joined in a pop psychology marriage, volunteer to help the elderly and AIDS patients. "All you have to do, I discover, is ask people," Tom reflects. "They do it because they're generous and, I think, a bit lonely" (*TS* 350). Tom's faith in the efficacy of the sovereign word finds its justification in his listeners' readiness to respond; he requests what they need to give and want to offer. Percy's local rendering of a new earth shows how an almost natural longing to love makes the dead once again able to live.

Tom searches for a similar renewal in the ruins of his marriage. Although a vacation to Disney World places the Mores among families as stunned as Tom's own, the novelty of living in a space-age mobile home brings its own re-creation for Percy's wayfarers who seem lost in the cosmos. The rotation delights Tom's rather dazed children and enables the withdrawn Ellen to recuperate. As husband and wife lie in the bed of the Bluebird, straight and stiff like the living dead, they still lack the good cheer of their Christmas celebration years ago, but Tom and Ellen are united by a more poignant passion: the sharing of mutual pain and frustration. When Ellen gently places her hand on Tom's thigh and utters, "I—good. . . . Soon—better" (*TS* 337), she begins to convert the binary language of computers into human speech through joining the tentative words to the tender deed.

Throughout the trip to Florida, in a motor home that resembles a spaceship, Tom and Ellen grope toward reestablishing their marriage, wandering hesitantly and haltingly toward each other. But although the trams, launches, and monorails of Disney World make it a diverting place for pilgrimage, this American utopia is too unreal, too far removed from Percy's temporal world of love and work. "Tomorrowland!—We don't even know what Todayland is!" Tom exclaims about Disney's vision of the new earth (*TS* 340). Percy's unfolding eschatology includes both tenses. *The Thanatos Syndrome* ends by looking to the future in hope, yet it never overlooks that daily land amid whose difficulties the promise is fitfully and partially revealed.

If Ellen gradually becomes as lusty and pragmatic as she was at the end of *Love in the Ruins*, Tom's apocalyptic marriage with her never achieves the same unity and intensity as Will's end-of-the-world romance with Allie. Having turned away from Lucy, much as he did from Lola and Moira years before, Tom again turns back to Ellen. As these mutually adulterous spouses rededicate themselves to each other, their love gains a grim and sober beauty, yet the marriage is always strained because More's wife never seems his equal in spiritual strength or vision. Nurse Oglethorpe offered herself as a sacrifice for Tom at the climax of *Love in the Ruins*; in *The Thanatos Syndrome* she does not help to defeat the devil but is herself delivered from Azazel. More's love for the wife he has saved seems more sexist and less sacred than the consummate passion of *The Second Coming*. No longer the entrepreneurial real estate agent, Ellen cooks hearty breakfasts for her man and responds to his invitation, "why not come over here by me? You're a very good-looking piece!" by sighing, smiling, and performing what Tom calls "a wife's duty" (*TS* 356). Although the chauvinism is lightened by considerable good humor, Tom's highly physical view of housewife Ellen reflects not just his old masculine bravado but also a fundamental religious difference between how husband and wife view the flesh.

Having joined a Pentecostal sect, Ellen has been baptized in the Holy Spirit and blessed with the gift to speak in tongues. "She is herself a little holy spirit hooked up to a lusty body," Tom realizes about his wife who is either carnal or spiritual. Allie overcame a similar disjunction in *The Second Coming*, but for Ellen "spirit has nothing to do with body. Each goes its own way. . . . What does the Holy Spirit need with things? Body does body things. Spirit does spirit things" (*TS* 353). Although Ellen is happy and thus Tom is content, her dualism keeps food from ever becoming eucharistic flesh, and her flesh from ever becoming consecrated by the Incarnation. And Tom seems inclined to view Ellen by her own dichotomy, to treat her as a "body" who "does body things" like making meals and making love, rather than to embrace her by his much less divisive faith. Hence their marriage lacks the same religious significance that it at least seemed to promise in *Love in the Ruins*, whose final scene showed how conjugal love may intimate the very meaning of Christmas. Percy's fiction has always stressed the need to discover the convergence of human and divine desire, yet in *The Thanatos Syndrome* these passions seem not unconnected but certainly farther apart. Alive in body or soul, Ellen has recovered from the terminal form of the thanatos syndrome. But she misses the grander sacramental union that makes Tom More a would-be Catholic in flesh and spirit despite his attempts to disassociate himself from the religion of his namesake.

Although Tom enjoys Ellen's love, he senses that spirit cannot be divorced from body. If Ellen "loves the Holy Spirit, says little about Jesus," Tom is attracted to the God born on Christmas, manifested on Epiphany, and intimately encountered through the very things that horrify Ellen—"bread, wine, oil, salt, water, body, blood, spit" (*TS* 353). Tom's wife reminds him of the literal-minded Nicodemus (John 3:1–21) as she objects, "How can a little baby be born again right after it has been born?" (*TS* 355). But his burgeoning Johannine faith understands that baptism, the sacramental opposite of the deathly river that flows through the novel from the sodium-contaminated water to the polluted Mississippi, brings paradoxical rebirth through the water that Ellen disdains and the Spirit sanctifies. When Tom rejects Ellen's invitation to attend a Pentecostal gathering where she will share her new-found Lord, his wife rightly suspects that Tom is still "a Roman" (*TS* 354). He has assisted Father Smith at Mass on June 22, the feast of Saint Thomas More, and on the fiftieth anniversary of the priest's ordination; and just as he did at the end of *Love in the Ruins*, he takes his children to Mass on Christmas. Helmut Jäger told young Simon Smith that Catholicism was part of the Jewish conspiracy. Having opposed the fascism of Comeaux and Van Dorn, Tom moves toward accepting the God worshipped in sign by Father Smith because such faith holds together word and flesh, spirit and thing, concepts fragmented by the thanatos syndrome. If the disease is the very unholy spirit of disjunction, its ultimate healing requires what forms for Percy a radical bond with reality: religious faith.

The Thanatos Syndrome ends by looking to agape even more than eros as the alternative to death. The Mass that Tom attends at the end of the novel to mark the reopening of the hospice is a remembrance of and a summons to such a divine kind of love. Since Tom still recalls the classic definition of a sacrament as a "sensible sign instituted by Christ to produce grace" (*TS* 125), the celebration of the Eucharist defies the devilish assault on semiotics. Father Smith appropriately begins by glorifying the name above all other names for Christians, "Jesus Christ is Lord!" and then further proclaims the linguistic center of his faith by adding, "Praise be to God! Blessed be his Holy Name!" (*TS* 358). Although the TV news team and the audience of religious and civic leaders expect a human interest story or community event, Father Smith refuses to let the rite, like language, be subsumed. Instead, he turns it into a liturgy for life in an age of death.

Still wearing his uniform from the fire tower, the ever-vigilant watchman startles the congregation by delivering a visionary exhortation about life near the end of the world. His sermon denounces the way that murder becomes acceptable when called by a different name. And it invites his audience of Qualitarians, abortionists, and euthanasists to reverse the victory of the Great Prince Satan, the Depriver of language, by no longer depriving of life the unborn, afflicted, and elderly. But then promising to tell the congregation one more detail of utmost importance, he falls silent, as if deprived of speech by the thanatos syndrome. Tom steps up to Father Smith after an uneasy pause, and putting aside Freud's "non-directive" therapy, simply tells the priest to continue. Each brings the other to God in a trick of grace that dramatizes how Percy's fond sign users may help to save each other. "You assist me," Father Smith commands in return, deprived of his regular acolyte. Seeing "no sign" of Milton Guidry, Tom kneels beside the priest "like an altar boy" and prays that he will go up to the altar of God who gives joy to his youth (*TS* 362, 363). In the void of the novel—no speech, no sign, no server—love alone steps forward to quicken Tom with his own juvenescence and to drive away the Great Depriver.

Tom's service at Mass becomes a sign of how he goes up to God, who is gradually coming to him. Throughout the last pages the Parousia is everywhere intimated and even seems to have begun, but it is not yet consummated. In such a tentative time More achieves a faith defined by hope and charity, not by formal belief, but that very lack of orthodoxy has an integrity and even necessity in the age of the Great Depriver. Although Tom continues to help Father Smith whenever he needs special assistance or Milton is ill, he refuses to serve as the priest's regular attendant. "It is easy to say no at the hospice, because honesty is valued above all," Tom explains, and since he is no longer sure about what he believes, daily participation in the Mass would be deceitful (*TS* 363). Despite his refusal, his frankness exerts a spiritual force in a novel where Comeaux and Van Dorn have deprived language of the truth through their equivocations and intrigue.

Father Smith readily understands the religious ambivalence behind such honesty. He knows that Tom lives at an hour when virtually everyone has been deprived of faith. Echoing Binx Bolling's explanation of his unbelief, the priest recognizes that any traditional proof "wouldn't make much difference. . . . It does not signify. It is boring to think of" (*TS* 364). Since such an argument has been deprived of its power in the age of the Great Depriver, Father Smith does not offer a rational demonstration that might appeal to a Kierkegaardian genius but not to Val Vaught in *The Last Gentleman* or to Tom More. Instead, he speaks like an apostle bringing good news, drawing Tom near to him as if he would confide a secret about the kind of faith needed by the scientist in fighting a spiritual sickness. His communion bespeaks the central religious vision of Percy's fiction: "I am a self with you under God" (*LC* 112). As always, Tom tries to escape the intimacy in which the word of the transcending God may be spoken, but the cunning prophet baits Tom by saying that he seeks his professional opinion about the Virgin Mary's alleged appearances to six children several years ago in Yugoslavia. In a time when all the signs seem hollowed out, he finds one detail of these apocalypses "highly significant—one of those unintentionally authentic touches which make a story credible" (*TS* 364).

What fascinates Father Smith is that the children at Medjugorge reported their visions with none of the usual Marian iconography—a woman crowned with stars, standing on a cloud and crushing a serpent. Instead, the mother of Jesus resembled an ordinary Jewish girl, an image whose very unconventionality may guarantee its truth. Mary becomes the apocalyptic woman for Percy's Century of the Love of Death. She is seen not as the traditional figure inspired by Revelation (12:1–4) but as the archetypal victim of the thanatos syndrome who speaks as the patroness of a possibly new age. Her message suits her manner, for unlike Our Lady of the Camellias in *Lancelot*, she calls a despairing last decade to live like the chosen people of God by placing faith in life. As an apostle, Father Smith brings her news to Tom because her charge, rather than any proofs, must define his eschatological faith: "Christians speak of the end time. Jews of the hopelessness of the mounting Arab terror. . . . But you must not lose hope, she told the children. Because if you keep hope and have a loving heart and do not secretly wish for the death of others, the Great Prince Satan will not succeed in destroying the world" (*TS* 365). Since the great apocalyptic battles are already being fought in everyday lives, only such confident expectation and loving-kindness can defeat the thanatos syndrome and usher in the holy spirit of a renewed earth.

Tom's work at St. Margaret's and his patient waiting for Ellen's recovery are signs of how his love already enables him to participate in the Second Coming heralded by Father Smith: "Perhaps the world will end in fire and the Lord will come—it is not for us to say. But it is for us to say . . . whether hope and faith will come back into the world" (*TS* 365). The priest's message virtually summarizes Percy's apocalyptic creed: it is never for his searchers to say when the Second Coming will occur, but it is their duty to say, to name, how they will live under God until that end arrives. Tom's decision for such a life of faith and love brings him a future of hope, whose promises he keeps hearing in the novel's final pages. Although Hudeen usually mumbles rather than talks, Tom's cook speaks clearly for once in a charismatic outburst at Thanksgiving that honors the holiest of signs, "I say bless God! . . . Bless his holy name!" Unlike Ellen, who prays a blessing in tongues, Hudeen's tongue clearly proclaims God's praises and assures Tom that he will be all right, "The good Lord will take care of you" (TS 356, 357). Father Smith confirms the hope for Tom's languishing career by hinting that the doctor's patients will come back and that he will add to the work of Freud and Jung.

Although such blessings open a graced future to Tom, he does not attain this well-favored time at once; he must realize it by individual decisions. Hence More again faces a dilemma on the anniversary of the reopening of the hospice as he sits vigil on the front porch of his office before calling Max. Once more he must decide—"I must tell him either/or" (TS 366)— and the existential alternatives are either death or life. On the feast day of Saint Simeon, he must choose between very profitable work with Max's elite clientele or succeeding Father Smith as the rather impoverished director of St. Margaret's. Max's offer would allow Tom to be comfortably at home in the world, but the hospice challenges him to turn his therapy into a form of ministry at the end of the world. Dr. More faces the crossroads of selfhood that Jerome Taylor sees as continually confronting Percy's heroes, one of the crucial moments when he must "choose to accept the catastrophe or ordeal that is laid upon him."[31] Tom never reports his decision. The open ending suggests that in the halfway world of Percy's apocalyptists every choice, no matter how final, is necessarily preliminary. Tom must decide and then decide again and again. Since the eschaton never completely ends, nor does the new world do more than begin, he lives in the process of always rejecting thanatos in favor of the radical compassion that leads to life.

Such decisions honor God's first and second coming, to which Percy continually looks at the end of the novel. When Tom enters his office from the porch, he listens to Mickey LaFaye's urgently whispered message on the answering machine, "I'm coming in—now" (TS 368). Ellen, once again his brisk and cheerful nurse, arrives first and tells him of a second coming. Father Smith has called him at home with a referral and would only give her a few hints about the identity of the new patient—royalty, a visit, gifts, and a Jewish connection—but Tom must meet this one to come tomorrow morning at eight. Ellen shrewdly supposes that Father Rinaldo Smith, well known in certain royal circles, will introduce Tom to the visiting queen of Spain, who comes from a noble Sephardic family and has a history of psychological problems. Since Ellen never appreciates the bond between things and spirit, she misreads the signs. Tom understands that the cryptic priest has actually asked him to serve Mass the next morning on the Feast of the Three Kings. Percy's last chapter portrays "no grand epiphanies," yet it awaits the feast of the Epiphany, the celebration of Christ's first coming to the entire world (*TS* 336). The liturgy of the holy day defines Tom's life. It recalls the visit of the Magi who came with gifts for the newborn Christ, and it celebrates God's ongoing manifestation in the world. Like the end of *Love in the Ruins*, the last pages of *The Thanatos Syndrome* use the Christmas season to hallow the daily revelations that anticipate the final Parousia. In Percy's Feliciana, humanity still comes to the deity who came into the world and is always coming.

On the eve of Epiphany, Mickey LaFaye, Tom's first sign of the thanatos syndrome, becomes his first patient to come back and the novel's final sign of the age to come. Tom pictures her coming to self as a portrait of becoming. No longer a lusty duchess of Alba, Mickey has almost regained the desolate loveliness of Wyeth's painting, once again ravaged by anxiety, drawn out in vigilant desire "but not yet too thin, not yet wholly Christina." Although she "blows" in "without a word," Mickey recovers enough of her humanity as *Homo loquens* to stammer her identity and to build that selfhood into a nearly complete sentence, "I—. . . I'm—. . . I'm having an—" (*TS* 370). After repeatedly affirming her efforts to talk, Tom finishes her thought, "You're having an attack," the listener sharing so deeply in her consciousness that he helps her to be a speaker. Even the return of her old trepidation is a sign of her coming into consciousness: "It's—It's not like anything I ever had before. Something is about to happen. I dread something, but I don't know what it is—." And Tom notices that her eyes seem to lose focus "as if she saw something, someone, behind me, far away but approaching" (*TS* 370–71). This distant Parousia is not just an intimidating psychic confrontation looming behind the healing efforts of her therapist; it is a fearful spiritual redetermination. Having recovered from the thanatos syndrome, this once-dead woman trembles before the imminent apocalypse when she will complete her coming to self and perhaps discover God's daily coming in others.

Mickey envisions both the awe and the hope that accompany all revelation through the now-recurring dream of the stranger whose coming she awaits in the cellar of her grandmother's farmhouse. Amid the profound intimacy of her soul, she senses that this visitor "is not someone to be terrified of, yet I am terrified. . . . I am trying to tell myself something. I mean a part of me I don't really know, yet the deepest part of me, is trying to—" (*TS* 371). Although Percy emphasizes in "The Message in the Bottle" that the news comes from afar, it is not so much an external and imposed truth as the proclamation of what the self already intuits but waits to be told. Mickey's need to know is matched by already knowing what she needs, so that revelation causes a natural coming of the self to the self. As the frightened patient tells of her nighttime apparition, Tom keeps replying "I see" until she suddenly falls silent, her eyes "searching mine as if I were the mirror of her very self" (*TS* 372). The playful equation of sight and selfhood makes it clear that Mickey comes to herself by coming to her visionary double in Tom. His ministry of the word provides the communion in which she can discover her own identity as both seer, speaker, and listener. When Percy's seekers meet, they always talk each other along the way of salvation, for speech itself is the most elementary of glad tidings. It draws his islanders out of their inexpressible selves, to others in conversation, and finally toward the God of all good news before whom they can say their names. Still awaiting the divine message that will consummate their own coming, both Tom and Mickey hear its first sounds in each other.

Ducking her head and touching the nape of her neck as she had done years ago, Mickey gives a sign of how far she has already come in rediscovering her essential well-being:

> "Well?" I say.
> She opens her mouth to speak.
> Well well well. (*TS* 372)

The whole novel seems to well up at the end of this resonant dialogue. Tom's final lines repeat Mickey's first ones in the opening pages and consummate the countless repetitions of the well-worn monosyllable throughout *The Thanatos Syndrome*. Heard as adjective, noun, adverb, and interjection, the single word is virtually the wellspring of Percy's fictional world. But if the book comes full circle in its narrative farewell, it then seems to continue after Tom's threefold conclusion. Percy's last novel ends in medias res so that the unwritten interview between patient and doctor can intimate the indefinite and ongoing process by which his wayfarers are always coming to themselves. As Mickey is poised to speak, Tom's literal benediction declares that in the beginning as in the end, and then even after the end, is the word for Percy, and it is triply good. Since the conclusions of his apocalypses can only be new beginnings, *The Thanatos Syndrome* looks ahead to a time when the sick will be healed and when all manner of things shall indeed be well. Tom ends as a benevolent listener to the word. Affirming and encouraging by wishing Mickey well, he performs the acts of love and hope that Father Smith enjoined for Tom's own spiritual welfare in these times before the end. On the eve of January 6, the narrative of Mickey's apocalyptic revelation brings news of the grander Epiphany still to come.

NOTES

Abbreviations used in the text:
GW   "The Gramercy Winner"
L   *Lancelot*
LC   *Lost in the Cosmos*
LG   *The Last Gentleman*
LR   *Love in the Ruins*
M   *The Moviegoer*
MB   *The Message in the Bottle*
SC   *The Second Coming*
TS   *The Thanatos Syndrome*

CHAPTER 1. Novels to Make All Things New

1 Lawson and Kramer, eds., *Conversations with Walker Percy*, p. 180.
2 May, *Towards a New Earth*, p. 39. For other helpful surveys of the apocalyptic tradition in American literature, see Lewis, *Trials of the Word*, pp. 184–235; Robinson, *American Apocalypses*; and Zamora, "The Myth of Apocalypse and the American Literary Imagination," in Lois Parkinson Zamora, ed., *The Apocalyptic Vision in America*, pp. 97–138.
3 Students of apocalyptic literature differ about the distinguishing traits of the genre. While Russell in *The Method and Nature of Jewish Apocalyptic* (pp. 264–71) and Mowinckel in *He That Cometh* (p. 271) view as central to apocalypse an eschatology that is dualistic, cosmic, and cataclysmic, Rowland emphasizes the revelation of divine mysteries as the chief characteristic and challenges the idea of a specifically apocalyptic form of eschatology in *The Open Heaven* (pp. 26–29). Percy's approach unites both emphases; for him, revelation is catastrophic. His writings seem to follow the apocalyptic rhythm noted by John May: judgment, disaster, and renewal (*Towards a New Earth*, p. 24).

4 Scott, "'New Heav'ns, New Earth'—The Landscape of Contemporary Apocalypse," p. 12.

5 Voegelin, *Order and History*, 1:2.

6 Lawson and Kramer, eds., *Conversations*, p. 124.

7 Wink, "Apocalypse in Our Time," p. 15.

8 Percy's eschatological understanding of revelation is similar to the view of Möltmann, in *Theology of Hope* (p. 66), who explains that revelation "discloses a self-understanding in authenticity, certainty and identity with oneself. The active event of revelation is itself the presence of the eschaton."

9 Kermode, *The Sense of an Ending*, p. 8.

10 Lawson and Kramer, eds., *Conversations*, p. 13. In *Writing the Apocalypse*, Zamora uses *Order and History* to understand *The Last Gentleman* (pp. 139–42). Brooks considers Voegelin and Percy as chroniclers of gnosticism ("Walker Percy and Modern Gnosticism," in Panthea Reid Broughton, ed., *The Art of Walker Percy*, pp. 260–72); and Lawson examines the influence of *The New Science of Politics* on *Lancelot* (*Following Percy*, pp. 196–209).

11 Voegelin, *Order and History*, 1:11, 139.

12 The fundamental differences between prophecy and apocalypse are discussed by Bergoffen, "The Apocalyptic Meaning of History," in Zamora, ed., *The Apocalyptic Vision in America*, pp. 11–36; Buber, *Pointing the Way*, pp. 192–207; Mowinckel, *He That Cometh*, pp. 125–54; Russell, *The Method and Nature of Jewish Apocalyptic*, pp. 264–71; and Schmithals, *The Apocalyptic Movement*, pp. 76–88.

13 Voegelin, *Order and History*, 2:162.

14 Ibid., 1:428–29; see also pp. 460–64.

15 Ibid., 1:453, 11; see also 4:325–26. In *Pointing the Way* Buber also criticizes apocalyptic theology for encouraging humanity to flee the responsibilities of history (p. 203).

16 See, for example, Eubanks, "Walker Percy: Eschatology and the Politics of Grace," in Jac Tharpe, ed., *Walker Percy: Art and Ethics*, pp. 121–36; and Fowler, "Answers and Ambiguity in Percy's *The Second Coming*," pp. 13–23.

17 For how Christianity modified traditional apocalypse, see Russell, *Apocalyptic: Ancient and Modern*, pp. 51–55; and Ellul, *Apocalypse*, pp. 29–31.

18 Russell, *Apocalyptic: Ancient and Modern*, p. 52.

19 Ellul, *Apocalypse*, pp. 65–124.

20 Abrams, *Natural Supernaturalism*, p. 48.

21 Caird, *A Commentary on the Revelation of St. John the Divine*, p. 294.

22 Bergoffen, "The Apocalyptic Meaning of History," in Zamora, ed., *The Apocalyptic Vision in America*, p. 28.

23 Ellul, *Apocalypse*, p. 161.

24 Ibid., p. 71.

25 The importance of catastrophe in bringing Percy's characters to selfhood has been recognized by Lewis J. Taylor in "Walker Percy and the Self," pp. 234–35, and in "Walker Percy's Knights of the Hidden Inwardness," pp. 130–32. Percy's interest in the value of disaster parallels Kierkegaard's belief in ordeal, a term that Percy frequently uses; see Lawson and Kramer, eds., *Conversations*, pp. 54, 81, 121, 219. Writing about the summer of 1864 with its "Götterdämmerung quality," Percy explains that "in the ordeal the man himself seemed to become more truly himself, revealing his character or the lack of it, than at any other time before or after" ("The American War," p. 656). Luschei discusses two types of ordeal in Percy's writing—shock and confronting death—in *The Sovereign Wayfarer* (pp. 41–45). In "The Eschatological Vision of Walker Percy," LeClair examines how Percy's characters confront personal and cultural eschatons (pp. 115–22). Zamora, in *Writing the Apocalypse*, emphasizes how disasters may bring renewal to the lives of Percy's isolated seers (pp. 125–27).

26 Percy, "The Failure and the Hope," p. 19.

27 Percy, "Stoicism in the South," p. 343.

28 Allen, *Walker Percy*, p. 6; Spivey, *The Writer as Shaman*, p. 116.

29 Samway, "An Interview with Walker Percy," p. 122.

30 Rafferty, "The Last Fiction Show," p. 91.

31 Wilder, "The Rhetoric of Ancient and Modern Apocalyptic," p. 451.

32 Zamora, *Writing the Apocalypse*, p. 14.

33 Robinson, *American Apocalypses*, p. 35.

34 Hardy, *The Fiction of Walker Percy*, p. 132.

35 Samway, "An Interview with Walker Percy," p. 122. In *Miracle Mile* (1989), writer-director Steve DeJarnatt filmed an apocalyptic melodrama similar to the romance imagined in Percy's scenario. When Anthony Edwards accidentally learns that a nuclear war will begin in sixty minutes, he spends the rest of the movie searching for Mare Winningham, his love of only a few hours, whom he met by chance at a museum exhibition.

36 Bultmann might have been describing the end of a novel by Percy when he explained in *Jesus Christ and Mythology*: "When, for example, I achieve through love a new self-understanding, what takes place is not an isolated psychological act of coming to consciousness; my whole situation is transformed. In understanding myself, I understand other people and at the same time the whole world takes on a new character. I see it, as we say, in a new light, and so it really is a new world" (p. 75).

37 Abrams, *Natural Supernaturalism*, pp. 335–47.

38 In *The Gift of the Other* Howland shows how Percy's lovers look to Marcel's

"Absolute Thou": "Loving communion between individuals depends for its investiture upon God who is Being in all its plenitude" (p. 15).

39 Kermode, *The Sense of an Ending*, p. 25.

40 Percy, *Novel Writing in an Apocalyptic Time*, pp. 5, 14–15.

41 Percy, "The State of the Novel," p. 360.

42 Lawson and Kramer, eds., *Conversations*, p. 41.

43 Frye, *The Great Code*, p. 136.

44 See Dowie, "Walker Percy: Sensualist-Thinker," pp. 52–65; and Stevenson, "Walker Percy: The Novelist as Poet," pp. 164–74. Tharpe surveys Percy's sensitivity to nature, especially clouds and storms (*Walker Percy*, pp. 37–40).

45 Bloom, Editor's Note and Introduction, in Harold Bloom, ed., *Walker Percy*, pp. vii–viii, 1–7.

46 For problems with Percy's chronology, see Hardy, *The Fiction of Walker Percy*, pp. 41–42, 225–32.

47 Lawson and Kramer, eds., *Conversations*, p. 100.

CHAPTER 2. From Autobiography to Apocalypse:
"The Gramercy Winner"

1 Percy, "From Facts to Fiction," p. 28.

2 Ibid.

3 Lawson and Kramer, eds., *Conversations*, p. 148; Percy, "From Facts to Fiction," p. 28; Coles, *Walker Percy*, p. 62.

4 Lawson, *Following Percy*, pp. 140–41, 226–36.

5 Percy, "From Facts to Fiction," p. 28.

6 Lawson and Kramer, eds., *Conversations*, pp. 273, 263, 152.

7 Lawson, "William Alexander Percy, Walker Percy, and the Apocalypse," pp. 397–99.

8 Percy, Introduction to *Lanterns on the Levee*, pp. xviii, xiii, xiv, xv.

9 Zamora, *Writing the Apocalypse*, p. 123. See pp. 120–24 for the similar sense of history shared by southern and Latin American writers.

10 Lawson and Kramer, eds., *Conversations*, p. 263.

11 See Percy, *Diagnosing the Modern Malaise*; Spivey, *The Writer as Shaman*.

12 Wood, *The Comedy of Redemption*, p. 145.

13 Lawson and Kramer, eds., *Conversations*, p. 89.

14 Baker, *The Percys of Mississippi*, p. 180.

15 Lawson and Kramer, eds., *Conversations*, p. 11; Coles, *Walker Percy*, p. 143.

16 Coles, *Walker Percy*, p. 65.

17 Foote, Shelby Foote Papers, letter to Walker Percy, April 6, 1978.

18 Coles, *Walker Percy*, p. 65; Robert Taylor, *Saranac*, p. 236.

19 Zamora, *Writing the Apocalypse*, p. 127.

20 Sontag, *Illness as Metaphor*, p. 26.

21 Mann, *The Magic Mountain*, p. 634.

22 Sontag, *Illness as Metaphor*, p. 12.

23 Percy, *Diagnosing the Modern Malaise*, p. 10.

24 Ibid., p. 4.

25 Percy, "From Facts to Fiction," pp. 28, 46.

26 Ibid., p. 28.

27 Ibid., p. 46.

CHAPTER 3. Last Picture Show: *The Moviegoer*

1 The reference to the Bomb is one of many in the novel that portend disaster; for others, see *The Moviegoer*, p. 8, 166, 190. Percy has called *Dr. Strangelove* "the great American movie." In New York in February 1977 he expressed his desire to see it again (Lawson and Kramer, eds., *Conversations*, p. 149). Percy briefly mentions *On the Beach* in *Lost in the Cosmos* (p. 202). For a discussion of prophetic and apocalyptic cinema, see Nelson, "The Apocalyptic Vision in American Popular Culture," in Lois Parkinson Zamora, ed., *The Apocalyptic Vision in America*, pp. 166–78.

2 In *The Book of Revelation* Perkins notes the cinematic quality of the Apocalypse (pp. 7–8).

3 Binx has enjoyed similar moments of revelation before and after being wounded in Korea (pp. 38, 42, 52), but he seems continually distracted from what could lead him on the search.

4 Percy, "Walter M. Miller, Jr.'s *A Canticle for Leibowitz*," p. 575.

5 Percy's working papers further reveal how the apocalypse looms in the imaginative background of the book. In an early sketch for the novel titled "Confessions of a Movie-Goer (from the Diary of the Last Romantic)," the narrator, a Will Barrett–like wanderer in the North, awaits catastrophe while waiting for a Henry Fonda Western to begin at Radio City Music Hall. He believes that only after such disaster can people speak to each other. Percy's apocalyptic moviegoer identifies with an eternally sad and solitary film star of his imagination, an idealized version of his own lonely self, because both need the liberty granted by the Last Days. Some vague and mysterious catastrophe will free them to buy a ticket, board a train, and then befriend a strange woman after they escape from the wreckage of the subway (Walker Percy Papers, Series I, *The Moviegoer*, item 2, pp. 17, 18).

6 Scott, "'New Heav'ns, New Earth'—The Landscape of Contemporary Apocalypse," p. 5.

7 Lawson and Kramer, eds., *Conversations*, p. 6.

8 Guardini, *The Lord*, p. 508.

9 See pp. 18, 19, 86, and 164 in *The Moviegoer* for Binx's awareness of mystery.

10 Percy, *Novel Writing in an Apocalyptic Time*, p. 13.

11 Sontag, *Against Interpretation*, pp. 209–25.

12 Frye, *Anatomy of Criticism*, p. 141.

13 Percy offers an existential interpretation of Westerns in "Decline of the Western," pp. 181–83. Nelson views the Western as an eschatological drama that became increasingly apocalyptic from the 1950s to the 1970s ("The Apocalyptic Vision in American Popular Culture," in Zamora, ed., *The Apocalyptic Vision in America*, pp. 166–72).

14 Lawson and Kramer, eds., *Conversations*, p. 140.

15 Greene, *The Lost Childhood*, pp. 173–76.

16 In *Lost in the Cosmos*, Percy might be describing Kate when he writes that the desire of the transcending self "to be informed in its nothingness—if only I can get out of this old place and into the right new place, I can become a new person—pins a quasi-religious hope on, of all things, travel" (p. 183).

17 Howland in *The Gift of the Other* offers a very attentive reading of how Binx and Kate grow toward Marcel's intersubjectivity (pp. 31–44).

18 de Rougemont, *Love in the Western World*, pp. 224–29.

19 Eliot, *Complete Poems*, p. 61.

20 Schmithals, *The Apocalyptic Movement*, p. 24.

21 Samway, "An Interview with Walker Percy," p. 122.

22 Lawson and Kramer, eds., *Conversations*, p. 305.

23 Percy comments on the novel's allusion to *The Brothers Karamazov* in Lawson and Kramer, eds., *Conversations*, p. 66.

24 Stressing the importance of this often-overlooked passage, Percy explains, "Binx doesn't joke. Like Alyosha he tells the truth. He wouldn't have said, 'Yeah' if he didn't mean it" (Binding, *Separate Country*, pp. 71–72). Culbertson finds that the understated reference to Lonnie's resurrection befits Percy's entire spirituality: "If the moment seems scarcely observable, its relative invisibility is consistent with Percy's theme: that in the search for significance, we must include the invisible moments of loving where grace is offered, the self is acknowledged, and everydayness is redeemed" (*The Poetics of Revelation*, p. 122).

CHAPTER 4. Percy's First Gentle Man: *The Last Gentleman*

1 "The Sustaining Stream," *Time*, p. 82. While working on an early draft of the novel, Percy wrote to himself that the action is overshadowed by a 100

megaton bomb (Walker Percy Papers, Series I, *The Last Gentleman*, item 1, p. 73).

2 Guardini, *The End of the Modern World*, p. 79. Zamora shows how Guardini's book casts its shadow over *The Last Gentleman* in *Writing the Apocalypse* (pp. 135–37).

3 Similarities between Percy's and Barth's protagonists have been extensively surveyed by Bradbury, "Absurd Insurrection," pp. 319–29.

4 Percy often refers to "The Second Coming" in his writing; see, for example, *Love in the Ruins*, p. 18; *The Message in the Bottle*, p. 14; and *Novel Writing in an Apocalyptic Time*, p. 11.

5 An earlier draft of *The Last Gentleman* reveals how doomed Will's high-minded life must have seemed to Percy in the tumultuous 1960s. It laments the death of John F. Kennedy, assassinated while Percy was writing the novel, by eulogizing him as a gentleman (Walker Percy Papers, Series I, *The Last Gentleman*, item 4, pp. 356–59). The social unrest of *The Last Gentleman* translates into fiction issues that Percy had long been exploring in his essays. In "Stoicism in the South" Percy contrasts Christian love, which grants civil rights to all because each person is sacred, with the stoic inheritance, which makes rights depend on aristocratic condescension toward those who behave with proper manners (pp. 342–44). In "The Fire This Time" he faults southern religion for perpetuating the cruelty it should have denounced (pp. 3–5).

6 Chaucer, *The Works of Geoffrey Chaucer*, p. 87.

7 Guardini, *The End of the Modern World*, p. 132.

8 Cady, *The Gentleman in America*, p. 211.

9 Rubin, "The Boll Weevil, the Iron Horse, and the End of the Line," p. 210.

10 Guardini, *The End of the Modern World*, pp. 92–114.

11 Although *Antichrist* is not used in the Book of Revelation, apocalyptic literature frequently envisions a supreme antagonist to God. Early sources for the tradition are Gog from the land of Magog in Ezekiel 38–39 and Antiochus in Daniel 7:8 and 11:40. The only New Testament allusions to the Antichrist occur in 1 John 2:18, 22; 4:3; and in 2 John 7. Variations of the figure appear in the beasts of Revelation 11 and 13 and in the Scarlet Woman of Revelation 17.

12 Hardy, in *The Fiction of Walker Percy*, appropriately regards Rita as a "secular salvationist" (pp. 69–73) whose humanistic gospel is also shared by Forney Aiken and Mort Prince (pp. 76–77).

13 Cady, in *The Gentleman in America* (pp. 10–16, 52–57), traces the tradition of the "fine" or Chesterfieldian gentleman that Sutter carries to its lewdest extremes. Val transforms the rather tame piety of the opposite school, the Christian gentleman, into the fiercest form of love.

14 Guardini, *The End of the Modern World*, p. 123.

15 Percy expresses his admiration for Dabbs and quotes from *Who Speaks for the South?* in "Random Thoughts on Southern Literature, Southern Politics, and the American Future," pp. 507–8. In "God and Honor in the Old South" Wyatt-Brown surveys how religious and cultural forces sometimes clashed yet often reinforced each other so that "neither honor nor evangelism wholly triumphed" (p. 295).

16 Percy, "The Failure and the Hope," p. 20.

17 Dabbs, *Who Speaks for the South?*, p. 115.

18 Ibid., p. 274.

19 Spivey, *The Writer as Shaman*, pp. 88–89.

20 Schwartz, in "Life and Death," suggests that the boy with whom Jamie hopes to live in New Mexico is a figure of Jesus. He considers the youth's plan to travel there after speaking with Val "the boldest, most daring stroke in the novel" (p. 124).

21 For a similarly skeptical view of the marriage between Will and Kitty, see Hardy, *The Fiction of Walker Percy*, pp. 72–74, 281–82, n. 6.

22 LeClair, "The Eschatological Vision of Walker Percy," p. 117.

23 Percy, "How to Be an American Novelist in Spite of Being Southern and Catholic," p. 14.

24 Vauthier, "Narrative Triangulation in *The Last Gentleman*," in Panthea Reid Broughton, ed., *The Art of Walker Percy*, p. 94.

CHAPTER 5. The Center Does Hold: *Love in the Ruins*

1 Foote, Shelby Foote Papers, letter to Walker Percy, December 12, 1960.

2 Ketterer, *New Worlds for Old*, pp. 15, 16, 123–24. In "Ambiguous Apocalypse: Transcendental Versions of the End" (in Eric S. Rabkin, Martin H. Greenberg, and Joseph D. Olander, eds., *The End of the World*, p. 56) Galbreath calls science fiction "the contemporary form of apocalyptic literature," for both speculative fiction and traditional apocalypses reveal "radical discontinuities in human and natural history" that may "entail cosmic transformation and renewal."

3 Percy, "Walter M. Miller, Jr.'s *A Canticle for Leibowitz*," p. 575. Percy again pays tribute to Miller's novel by freely borrowing the character of the Abbot for the last chapter of *Lost in the Cosmos*. The vines at the end of the world creep throughout Percy's writings. In the final sentence of "The Man on the Train," Percy alludes to a time when "the vines sprout in Madison Avenue and Radio City lies greening like an Incan temple in the jungle" (*MB* 100). Likewise, at the end of "Notes for a Novel about the End of the World," he

imagines as a sign of catastrophe "the sprouting of vines in the church pew" (*MB* 118).

4 Yeats, *Collected Poems*, p. 184.

5 Godshalk has very carefully worked out the novel's geography to demonstrate that Tom is at the imagined center of his world ("*Love in the Ruins*: Thomas More's Distorted Vision," in Panthea Reid Broughton, ed., *The Art of Walker Percy*, pp. 144–49). Gaston suggests that much of the mise-en-scène is inspired by Percy's own Covington, Louisiana ("The Revelation of Walker Percy," pp. 459–60, 468–70).

6 Lawson, *Following Percy*, pp. 153–56.

7 Schmithals, *The Apocalyptic Movement*, p. 35.

8 Webb, "*Love in the Ruins*: Percy's Metaphysical Thriller," pp. 55–66.

9 Harper, *The World of the Thriller*, p. 41. See pp. 46–55 for a discussion of the almost apocalyptic mood of the thriller.

10 America's racism also appears as a kind of original sin in "Notes for a Novel about the End of the World": "White Americans have sinned against the Negro from the beginning and continue to do so, initially with cruelty and presently with an indifference which may be even more destructive. . . . To the eschatological novelist it even begins to look as if this single failing may be the tragic flaw in the noblest of political organisms" (*MB* 117–18).

11 Frye, *The Great Code*, p. 166. Altizer, in "Imagination and Apocalypse," likewise envisions the apocalypse as an end to the dualism between subject and object (pp. 410–12).

12 Hardy, *The Fiction of Walker Percy*, p. 106. See also pp. 123–28 for a discussion of Tom's complicity in the evil that afflicts society and his family.

13 For a survey of the importance of angels and demons in apocalyptic literature, see Russell, *The Method and Nature of Jewish Apocalyptic*, pp. 235–62.

14 Lewis, *Trials of the Word*, pp. 210–12.

15 In a parody of Christ's words to the Samaritan woman at the well (John 4:14), Art says to Tom, "Drink this drink and you'll never want a drink" (*LR* 211).

16 Although Tom is confused about whether Art's surname is Immerman or Immelmann, he seems to decide that his visitor has the same name as the German ace in World War I, Immelmann (*LR* 166). Art is connected to the war that Tom considers a watershed in Western civilization because it demonstrated how easily technological abstraction could lead to slaughter.

17 Tuveson, *Millennium and Utopia*.

18 Bacon, *Francis Bacon: A Selection of His Works*, pp. 323–24. In a 1981 interview Percy said that he was writing a book called *Novum Organum*, which would explore the inability of science to examine "what it is to be a human being" (Lawson and Kramer, eds., *Conversations*, p. 221).

19 Reich, *The Greening of America*, pp. 305–43.

20 Guardini, *The Lord*, p. 508.

21 Browning, *Poetical Works, 1833–1864*, p. 557. For Birkin's comments on "Love among the Ruins," see Lawrence, *Women in Love*, pp. 112–13.

22 Lawrence, *Complete Poems*, 3:176.

23 Allen, *Walker Percy*, p. 91.

24 A poignant passage from one of Percy's drafts for the novel indicates how fully Samantha brought God's presence to Tom. More speculates that one's love for a child and one's agony before a child's suffering pierce the heart so unfailingly that they can only be understood as God's way of making contact with an otherwise unfeeling humanity (Walker Percy Papers, Series I, *Love in the Ruins*, item 4, p. 15).

25 Hawkins, *The Language of Grace*, p. 76.

26 Percy, "How to Succeed in Business Without Thinking about Money," p. 559.

27 Wood, *The Comedy of Redemption*, pp. 32–33.

28 Lewis, *Trials of the Word*, p. 184.

29 Plank, "The Lone Survivor," in Rabkin, Greenberg, and Olander, eds., *The End of the World*, p. 25.

30 Wagar, "The Rebellion of Nature," in Rabkin, Greenberg, and Olander, eds., *The End of the World*, p. 172.

31 Gunn, *The Interpretation of Otherness*, p. 205.

32 Spivey, *The Writer as Shaman*, p. 99.

33 Wink, "Apocalypse in Our Time," p. 18.

34 The connection between the eschaton and Incarnation is noted by Guardini, *The Lord*, p. 510.

CHAPTER 6. Rough Beast and Bethlehem: *Lancelot*

1 Frye, *The Great Code*, p. 138.

2 *Lancelot* uses most of the conventions of revenge tragedy as described by Hallett and Hallett in *The Revenger's Madness*, pp. 7–12.

3 See Hosea 2 for the prophecy of a return to the desert. The punishment was actually meant to bring a renewed relationship with God to fruition. Percy has written that like Hosea the novelist "finds himself stuck with the unpleasant assignment of pointing out to his fellow citizens that something is wrong" ("The State of the Novel," p. 363).

4 The ferocity of Lancelot's voice and Percy's justification for such a tone are studied by Brinkmeyer in "Percy's Bludgeon: Message and Narrative Strategy," in Jac Tharpe, ed., *Walker Percy*, pp. 80–90. In *Three Catholic Writers*, Brinkmeyer argues that the narrative assault is part of a shift in Percy's conception of his role as novelist (pp. 147–61).

5 Maclear quotes Belknap in "The Republic and the Millennium," p. 183. For the northern response to the Civil War, see Moorhead, *American Apocalypses*. For the southern theology of history, see Wilson, *Baptized in Blood*, pp. 63–66.

6 Simpson, "The Southern Aesthetic of Memory," p. 210.

7 Lancelot's distrust of *love* should be compared with Percy's comment that "the word has been polluted. Beware of people who go around talking about loving and caring" (*LC* 186–87). Likewise, he has suggested, "maybe there are times when an honest hatred serves us better than love corrupted by sentimentality, meretriciousness, sententiousness, cuteness" ("The State of the Novel," p. 359).

8 Rovit, "On the Contemporary Apocalyptic Imagination," p. 455.

9 Lawson, in " 'Spiritually in Los Angeles,' " examines how Raymond Chandler and film noir have inspired the sleuthing in *Lancelot*.

10 Johnson, in "*Lancelot*: Percy's Romance," locates the novel in the tradition of Hawthorne.

11 Julian of Norwich, *Showings*, p. 225.

12 By his very name Lance typifies what Percy describes as the demonic self in whom eros becomes violence (*LC* 175–92).

13 Lawson and Kramer, eds., *Conversations*, p. 140.

14 Percy, *Diagnosing the Modern Malaise*, p. 17.

15 Dale, "*Lancelot* and the Medieval Quests of Sir Lancelot and Dante," in Tharpe, ed., *Walker Percy*, pp. 105–6.

16 For Percy's use of Arthurian tradition, see ibid., pp. 99–106; and Coles, *Walker Percy*, pp. 212–34. John Desmond, in "Walker Percy and T. S. Eliot," shows how parallels between *Lancelot* and "Gerontion" point to a common concern with the dilemma of the self-conscious self in history.

17 Eliot, *Complete Poems*, p. 49.

18 Weston, *From Ritual to Romance*, pp. 12–21.

19 The apostle and the evangelist are associated in popular thought with the apocalyptist.

20 Percy has written that Percival's minimal use of language was "a chancy ploy—and a lot of people didn't get it" in a letter to Patricia M. Rogan, August 2, 1985 (in possession of the author).

21 The Creole women demonstrate what Percy has described as one of the great virtues of New Orleans: Saint Theresa's Little Way, "a talent for everyday life rather than the heroic deed" ("New Orleans Mon Amour," p. 88).

22 Lancelot's memory of Yeats's actual lines—"But Love has pitched his mansion in / The place of excrement" (*Collected Poems*, p. 255)—is tellingly incorrect. Lancelot's version echoes even more clearly John 1:14, in which "the Word was made flesh, and dwelt among us," or, more literally, "set up his tent" among us.

23 Andrewes, *Ninety-six Sermons*, 1:89.

24 Foote, Shelby Foote Papers, letter to Walker Percy, November 17, 1976.

CHAPTER 7. The Revelation of Romance: *The Second Coming*

1 Pascal, *Pensées*, p. 95.

2 Percy, *Novel Writing in an Apocalyptic Time*, pp. 8–9.

3 Kobre, in "The Consolations of Fiction," views all of Percy's fiction, but especially *The Second Coming*, as a dialogue with Faulkner (pp. 50–53).

4 Kennedy, "The Semiotics of Memory," pp. 103–25.

5 Mowinckel, *He That Cometh*, pp. 151–53.

6 Zamora, *Writing the Apocalypse*, p. 146.

7 Both Ewell and Will share a hollowing at the temple and a piggish nose. Allie also connects Will with the poacher who lives in a cove below the valley; after bathing Will, she thinks that he looks like a covite with a wad of chewing tobacco.

8 Howland, *The Gift of the Other*, p. 113.

9 Pascal, *Pensées*, p. 218.

10 Ibid., p. 190.

11 Percy has said that he is "happy about Allie. She's one of the few women characters I've been pleased with" (Lawson and Kramer, eds., *Conversations*, p. 229).

12 Will's chance meeting with Allie is an example of the rotation described in *The Message in the Bottle*: "When the Bomb falls and the commuter picks his way through the rubble of Fifth Avenue to Central Park, . . . everything depends upon his meeting *her* and meeting her accidentally" in the ruins (*MB* 90).

13 Allie describes herself when she imagines that the survivor of a plane crash must feel "as if he had crossed a time warp or gone through a mirror, no, not gone through, come back, yes, the only question being which way he went, from the sane side to the crazy side like Alice or back the other way" (*SC* 30).

14 Frye, *Anatomy of Criticism*, pp. 186–206. Sensing the spirit of romance, DeMott aptly compares the meeting of Will and Allie with that of Ferdinand and Miranda. He calls the novel an "enchantment" ("A Thinking Man's Kurt Vonnegut," pp. 82, 84).

15 Chase, *The American Novel and Its Tradition*, p. 19.

16 Laing, *The Politics of Experience*, p. 58.

17 Percy, "Naming and Being," p. 152.

18 Emerson, "Nature," 1:1052. J. Donald Crowley considers Percy's place in the American, and especially the Emersonian, literary tradition in "Walker Percy:

The Continuity of the Complex Fate," in J. Donald Crowley and Sue Mitchell Crowley, eds., *Critical Essays on Walker Percy*, pp. 259–285.

19 Roethke, *Collected Poems*, p. 35.

20 Lawrence, in *Apocalypse*, writes that we "*cannot bear* connection. That is our malady" (p. 125). For both Percy and Lawrence, apocalypse may occur through a healing rediscovery of connections.

21 Percy writes in *The Message in the Bottle* that "the coupling of subject and predicate is a special case of the more fundamental human capacity to couple any two things at all and through the mirror of the one see the other" (*MB* 308).

22 The similarities between *The Second Coming* and *The Man Who Died* have been discussed by Teunissen in "The Serial Collaboration of D. H. Lawrence and Walker Percy."

23 Jones, "Percy's *Parousia*," p. 54.

24 Rahner, *Encounters with Silence*, p. 87. For similarities between the visions of Percy and Rahner, see Samway, "A Rahnerian Backdrop to Percy's *The Second Coming*." Samway finds that the lovers' "consummation in the greenhouse has all the trappings right out of the Book of Daniel" (p. 141). Sue Mitchell Crowley views the glittering glass house as resembling the crystalline New Jerusalem ("Walker Percy's Wager," in Crowley and Crowley, eds., *Critical Essays on Walker Percy*, p. 238).

25 S. Crowley, ibid., pp. 235–36.

26 Wilder, "The Rhetoric of Ancient and Modern Apocalyptic," p. 446.

27 Pascal, *Pensées*, p. 95.

28 Percy, "The Left Hand of Sheed," p. 439. See also Lawson and Kramer, eds., *Conversations*, p. 79.

29 Guardini, *The Lord*, p. 530.

CHAPTER 8. Tom More Once More: *The Thanatos Syndrome*

1 Lawson and Kramer, eds., *Conversations*, pp. 186, 189, 215, 243.

2 Ibid., p. 184; Allen, *Walker Percy*, p. xii; Spivey, *The Writer as Shaman*, p. 33.

3 Even before Percy decided to focus on Will Barrett's return in *The Second Coming*, he thought of writing a science fiction novel in which only the narrator understood the strange catastrophe that had left its victims so disembodied (Walker Percy Papers, Series I, *The Second Coming*, item 1a(i), p. 5). Percy's notes for *The Thanatos Syndrome* indicate that he again considered a plot involving body snatchers (Samway, "Thoughts on the Genesis of Walker Percy's *The Thanatos Syndrome*," p. 39). Although he abandoned the idea inspired by Don Siegel's 1956 film, *Invasion of the Body Snatchers* provided Percy with an image for the disease that robs its victims of their very selves (*TS* 33).

4 Hardy, *The Fiction of Walker Percy*, pp. 228–29.

5 Percy, *Diagnosing the Modern Malaise*, p. 2.

6 Quoted in Tuchman, *A Distant Mirror*, pp. 94–95.

7 Wagar, "The Rebellion of Nature," in Rabkin, Greenberg, and Olander, eds., *The End of the World*, p. 162.

8 Bettelheim writes that Freud's "greatest concern was with man's innermost being, to which he most frequently referred through the use of a metaphor— man's soul. . . . It is the greatest shortcoming of the current English versions of his works that they give no hint of this." Instead, translators favor *mind* (*Freud and Man's Soul*, p. xi).

9 Coles, *Walker Percy*, p. 21.

10 In an interview while he was writing *The Thanatos Syndrome*, Percy informed Patrick Samway "that Dr. Thomas More has got himself in a great deal of trouble, that something is about to happen that is a lot worse than the physical meltdown in 'The China Syndrome'" (p. 123).

11 Hobson, *Understanding Walker Percy*, p. 150.

12 Although Tom views the outcast goat as an offering to Azazel, the animal also bore a symbolic role in a rite of atonement. Before it was expelled, Aaron placed on the goat's head the burden of Israel's sins (Lev. 16:20–22). Tom does not yet realize how his age continues a more heinous form of such victimization.

13 Freud, *Beyond the Pleasure Principle*, 18:39.

14 Percy, *Novel Writing in an Apocalyptic Time*, p. 18.

15 Thomas, *The Lives of a Cell*, p. 111.

16 Poteat, *Walker Percy and the Old Modern Age*, pp. 20–22.

17 Hardy, *The Fiction of Walker Percy*, pp. 238–39.

18 Desmond, "Disjunctions of Time," p. 64.

19 Percy, "The Coming Crisis in Psychiatry," p. 393.

20 Bettelheim, *Freud and Man's Soul*, p. 77.

21 Freud, *Civilization and Its Discontents*, p. 61.

22 Voegelin, *The New Science of Politics*, pp. 110–14. See Scullin-Esser, "Connecting the Self with What Is Outside the Self," for a discussion of the role of the Jews in the novel (pp. 70–76).

23 Tuchman, *A Distant Mirror*, pp. 109–16.

24 O'Connor, *Mystery and Manners*, pp. 165–66. Desmond discusses O'Connor's influence on *The Thanatos Syndrome* in "Walker Percy, Flannery O'Connor and the Holocaust."

25 Wertham, *A Sign for Cain*, pp. 158, 182. For Percy's debt to Wertham, see Johnson, "The Virgin and the Cooling Tower," p. 25.

26 As a watchman, Father Smith resembles many of O'Connor's vigilant prophets; see Giannone, *Flannery O'Connor and the Mystery of Love*, p. 149.

27 Lifton, *The Nazi Doctors*, p. 17.

28 Wertham, *A Sign for Cain*, p. 155.

29 Children were killed by gradual starvation but mostly by drugs given as medicine or mixed with food. Some were judged unfit to live because they had poorly formed ears, wet the bed, or seemed as if they could not be educated. At Eglfing-Haar, where Dr. Jäger worked, about three hundred children between ages six months and sixteen years, as well as about two thousand adult patients, were executed. In the window of the room where the young were murdered was a carefully tended geranium (Wertham, *A Sign for Cain*, pp. 180, 187).

30 Harper, *The World of the Thriller*, p. 51.

31 Jerome Taylor, *In Search of Self*, p. 97.

———. *The Lord.* Translated by Elinor Castendyk Briefs. Chicago: Henry Regnery Company, 1954.

Gunn, Giles. *The Interpretation of Otherness: Literature, Religion, and the American Imagination.* New York: Oxford University Press, 1979.

Hallett, Charles A., and Elaine S. Hallett. *The Revenger's Madness: A Study of Revenge Tragedy Motifs.* Lincoln: University of Nebraska Press, 1980.

Hardy, John Edward. *The Fiction of Walker Percy.* Urbana: University of Illinois Press, 1987.

Harper, Ralph. *The World of the Thriller.* Cleveland: Press of the Case Western Reserve University, 1969.

Hawkins, Peter S. *The Language of Grace: Flannery O'Connor, Walker Percy, Iris Murdoch.* Cambridge, Mass.: Cowley Publications, 1983.

Hobson, Linda Whitney. *Understanding Walker Percy.* Understanding Contemporary American Literature, Matthew J. Bruccoli, ed. Columbia: University of South Carolina Press, 1988.

The Holy Bible. King James Version, 1611. New York: American Bible Society, n.d.

Howland, Mary Deems. *The Gift of the Other: Gabriel Marcel's Concept of Intersubjectivity in Walker Percy's Novels.* Pittsburgh: Duquesne University Press, 1990.

Johnson, Mark. "*Lancelot*: Percy's Romance." *Southern Literary Journal* 15 (1983): 19–30.

———. "The Virgin and the Cooling Tower: Literature as Science in Percy's *The Thanatos Syndrome.*" *New Orleans Review* 16 (Winter 1989): 22–26.

Jones, Eric L. "Percy's *Parousia.*" *Southern Quarterly* 23 (Summer 1985): 48–56.

Julian of Norwich. *Showings.* Translated by Edmund Colledge and James Walsh. New York: Paulist Press, 1978.

Kennedy, J. Gerald. "The Semiotics of Memory: Suicide in *The Second Coming.*" *Delta* 13 (1981): 103–25.

Kermode, Frank. *The Sense of an Ending: Studies in the Theory of Fiction.* New York: Oxford University Press, 1967.

Ketterer, David. *New Worlds for Old: The Apocalyptic Imagination, Science Fiction, and American Literature.* Bloomington: Indiana University Press, 1974.

Kobre, Michael. "The Consolations of Fiction: Walker Percy's Dialogic Art." *New Orleans Review* 16 (Winter 1989): 45–53.

Laing, R. D. *The Politics of Experience.* New York: Ballantine Books, 1967.

Lawrence, D. H. *Apocalypse.* New York: Penguin Books, 1976.

———. *The Complete Poems of D. H. Lawrence.* Phoenix Edition. 3 vols. London: William Heinemann, 1957.

————. *Women in Love*. Edited and with an introduction and notes by
Charles L. Ross. New York: Penguin Books, 1982.

Lawson, Lewis A. *Following Percy: Essays on Walker Percy's Work*. Troy, N.Y.:
Whitston Publishing Company, 1988.

————. " 'Spiritually in Los Angeles': California Noir in *Lancelot*." *Southern
Review* 24 (1988): 744–64.

————. "William Alexander Percy, Walker Percy, and the Apocalypse." *Modern
Age* 24 (1980): 396–406.

Lawson, Lewis A., and Victor A. Kramer, eds. *Conversations with Walker Percy*.
Literary Conversations Series, Peggy Whitman Prenshaw, gen. ed. Jackson:
University Press of Mississippi, 1985.

LeClair, Thomas. "The Eschatological Vision of Walker Percy." *Renascence* 26
(1974): 115–22.

Lewis, R. W. B. *Trials of the Word: Essays in American Literature and the
Humanistic Tradition*. New Haven: Yale University Press, 1965.

Lifton, Robert Jay. *The Nazi Doctors: Medical Killing and the Psychology of
Genocide*. New York: Basic Books, 1986.

Luschei, Martin. *The Sovereign Wayfarer: Walker Percy's Diagnosis of the Malaise*.
Baton Rouge: Louisiana State University Press, 1972.

Maclear, J. F. "The Republic and the Millennium." In *The Religion of the
Republic*, edited by Elwyn A. Smith, pp. 183–216. Philadelphia: Fortress
Press, 1971.

Mann, Thomas. *The Magic Mountain*. Translated by H. T. Lowe-Porter. New
York: Vintage Books, 1969.

May, John R. *Towards a New Earth: Apocalypse in the American Novel*. Notre
Dame, Ind.: University of Notre Dame Press, 1972.

Möltmann, Jurgen. *Theology of Hope*. Translated by James W. Leitch. New York:
Harper and Row, 1967.

Moorhead, James H. *American Apocalypses: Yankee Protestants and the Civil War,
1860–1869*. New Haven: Yale University Press, 1978.

Mowinckel, Sigmund. *He That Cometh*. Translated by G. W. Anderson. New
York: Abingdon Press, 1954.

O'Connor, Flannery. *Mystery and Manners: Occasional Prose*. Selected and edited
by Sally and Robert Fitzgerald. New York: Farrar, Straus, and Giroux, 1969.

Pascal, Blaise. *Pensées and The Provincial Letters*. Translated by W. F. Trotter and
Thomas M. M'Crie. New York: Modern Library, 1941.

Perkins, Pheme. *The Book of Revelation*. Collegeville Bible Commentary.
Collegeville, Minn.: The Liturgical Press, 1983.

Poteat, Patricia Lewis. *Walker Percy and the Old Modern Age*. Baton Rouge:
Louisiana State University Press, 1985.

Rabkin, Eric S., Martin H. Greenberg, and Joseph D. Olander, eds. *The End of the World*. Carbondale: Southern Illinois University Press, 1983.

Rafferty, Terrence. "The Last Fiction Show." Review of *The Thanatos Syndrome*, by Walker Percy; and *Texasville*, by Larry McMurty. *New Yorker*, June 15, 1987, pp. 91–94.

Rahner, Karl. *Encounters with Silence*. Translated by James M. Demske. Westminster, Md.: Newman Press, 1960.

Reich, Charles A. *The Greening of America: How the Youth Revolution Is Trying to Make America Livable*. New York: Random House, 1970.

Robinson, Douglas. *American Apocalypses: The Image of the End of the World in American Literature*. Baltimore: Johns Hopkins University Press, 1985.

Roethke, Theodore. *The Collected Poems of Theodore Roethke*. Garden City, N.Y.: Anchor Press/Doubleday, 1975.

Rovit, Earl. "On the Contemporary Apocalyptic Imagination." *American Scholar* 37 (1968): 453–68.

Rowland, Christopher. *The Open Heaven: A Study of Apocalyptic in Judaism and Early Christianity*. London: SPCK, 1982.

Rubin, Louis D., Jr. "The Boll Weevil, the Iron Horse, and the End of the Line: Thoughts on the South." *Virginia Quarterly Review* 55 (1979): 193–221.

Russell, D. S. *Apocalyptic: Ancient and Modern*. Philadelphia: Fortress Press, 1978.

——— . *The Method and Nature of Jewish Apocalyptic*. Philadelphia: Westminster Press, 1964.

Samway, Patrick H. "An Interview with Walker Percy." *America*, February 15, 1986, pp. 121–23.

——— . "A Rahnerian Backdrop to Percy's *The Second Coming*." *Delta* 13 (1981): 127–44.

——— . "Thoughts on the Genesis of Walker Percy's *The Thanatos Syndrome*." *America*, July 15–22, 1989, pp. 37–39, 45.

Schmithals, Walter. *The Apocalyptic Movement: Introduction and Interpretation*. Translated by John E. Steely. New York: Abingdon Press, 1975.

Schwartz, Joseph. "Life and Death in *The Last Gentleman*." *Renascence* 40 (1988): 112–28.

Scott, Nathan A., Jr. " 'New Heav'ns, New Earth'—The Landscape of Contemporary Apocalypse." *Journal of Religion* 53 (1973): 1–35.

Scullin-Esser, Kathleen. "Connecting the Self with What Is Outside the Self in *The Thanatos Syndrome*." *Renascence* 40 (1988): 67–76.

Simpson, Lewis P. "The Southern Aesthetic of Memory." *Tulane Studies in English* 23 (1978): 207–27.

Sontag, Susan. *Against Interpretation*. New York: Farrar, Straus, and Giroux, 1966.

———. *Illness as Metaphor*. New York: Farrar, Straus, and Giroux, 1977.

Spivey, Ted R. *The Writer as Shaman: The Pilgrimages of Conrad Aiken and Walker Percy*. Macon, Ga.: Mercer University Press, 1986.

Stevenson, John W. "Walker Percy: The Novelist as Poet." *Southern Review* 17 (1981): 164–74.

"The Sustaining Stream." *Time*, February 1, 1963, pp. 82–84.

Sweet, J. P. M. *Revelation*. Westminster Pelican Commentaries. Philadelphia: Westminster Press, 1979.

Taylor, Jerome. *In Search of Self: Life, Death & Walker Percy*. Cambridge, Mass.: Cowley Publications, 1986.

Taylor, Lewis J[erome]., Jr. "Walker Percy and the Self." *Commonweal*, May 10, 1974, pp. 233–36.

———. "Walker Percy's Knights of the Hidden Inwardness." *Anglican Theological Review* 56 (1974): 125–51.

Taylor, Robert. *Saranac: America's Magic Mountain*. Boston: Houghton Mifflin Company, 1986.

Teunissen, John J. "The Serial Collaboration of D. H. Lawrence and Walker Percy." *Southern Humanities Review* 21 (1987): 101–15.

Tharpe, Jac. *Walker Percy*. Boston: Twayne, 1983.

———, ed. *Walker Percy: Art and Ethics*. Jackson: University Press of Mississippi, 1980.

Thomas, Lewis. *The Lives of a Cell: Notes of a Biology Watcher*. New York: Viking Press, 1974.

Tuchman, Barbara W. *A Distant Mirror: The Calamitous 14th Century*. New York: Alfred A. Knopf, 1984.

Tuveson, Ernest Lee. *Millennium and Utopia: A Study in the Background of the Idea of Progress*. Berkeley: University of California Press, 1949.

Voegelin, Eric. *The New Science of Politics: An Introduction*. Phoenix Books. Chicago: University of Chicago Press, 1966.

———. *Order and History*. 4 vols. Baton Rouge: Louisiana State University Press, 1956–74.

Webb, Max. "*Love in the Ruins*: Percy's Metaphysical Thriller." *Delta* 13 (1981): 55–66.

Wertham, Frederic. *A Sign for Cain: An Exploration of Human Violence*. New York: Macmillan Company, 1966.

Weston, Jessie L. *From Ritual to Romance*. Doubleday Anchor Books Edition. Garden City, N.Y.: Doubleday and Company (by arrangement with Cambridge University Press), 1957.

Wilder, Amos. "The Rhetoric of Ancient and Modern Apocalyptic." *Interpretation* 25 (1971): 436–53.